本书由大连外国语大学“科研基础建设年”经费资助

特此致谢

隐匿之真

卡莱尔真理观批评研究

王威 著

中国社会科学出版社

图书在版编目(CIP)数据

隐匿之真：卡莱尔真理观批评研究／王威著．—北京：中国社会科学出版社，2022.4

ISBN 978-7-5203-9877-0

Ⅰ.①隐… Ⅱ.①王… Ⅲ.①卡莱尔(Carlyle,Thomas 1795-1881)—真理观—思想评论 Ⅳ.①B023.3

中国版本图书馆CIP数据核字(2022)第041082号

出 版 人 赵剑英
责任编辑 张 林
特约编辑 宗彦辉
责任校对 冯英爽
责任印制 戴 宽

出 版 中国社会科学出版社
社 址 北京鼓楼西大街甲158号
邮 编 100720
网 址 http://www.csspw.cn
发 行 部 010-84083685
门 市 部 010-84029450
经 销 新华书店及其他书店

印刷装订 北京君升印刷有限公司
版 次 2022年4月第1版
印 次 2022年4月第1次印刷

开 本 710×1000 1/16
印 张 18.25
插 页 2
字 数 292千字
定 价 99.00元

前　言

本书在我的博士学位论文《卡莱尔真理观研究》（北京大学，2015）基础之上几经修改扩充而成。原论文停笔时已经达到十五万字，后去其三一，留其三二，最终构成学位论文。本次成书主要对所去部分重新修改、填补并润色，使之可以融入原论文。这样就算了结了一桩多年以来的心愿。毕竟，敝帚自珍。当年毕业之际，为达到学位论文的要求，不得不对文稿进行大幅度的删减。所删部分几乎全部是兴趣所在而实力难以实现的内容。毕业后可谓卧薪尝胆，阅读了大量有关所删部分的一手文献和研究材料。目前虽然不能说已经完全把握了所有涉猎内容，但是与当年毕业时相比，已然实现了质的飞跃。如今将这部分重新整理出来并纳入全书，欣喜至极。

原学位论文大概于2011年最终确定选题。将卡莱尔确定为研究对象，一方面来源于我本人的研究兴趣，另一方面则考虑到与硕士研究话题之间的关联。我的硕士毕业论文主要聚焦于狄更斯《荒凉山庄》中的表象与本质之间的关系［参见附录（二）］。考虑到这一作品中的批评结构从卡莱尔所受到的影响，我最终决定，将卡莱尔的思想作为博士修业期间的研究话题。2011—2012年，我收集并阅读了大量卡莱尔的原著，包括小说、评论、书信和日记等。2012—2013年在哥伦比亚大学（美国纽约）访学期间，我有幸借阅以及收集到大量有关卡莱尔思想研究的文献。这些文献的阅读极大地丰富了我的视野，也让我对之前所读的一手文献形成了深入的认识。在此基础之上，我的博士论文选题最终确定为卡莱尔真理观研究。因当时未能在本体论和认识论等哲学话题上形成有效的理解，故批评研究未能实现。

根据我所收集和阅读的文献，卡莱尔思想研究可以分为加尔文主义思想、德国思想以及历史和社会思想等内容。这一线索在几部比较重要的传记作品中可以更为明确地表现出来。弗劳德（James Anthony Froude）将卡莱尔的思想发展史大概分为前后两期。前一时期对应于加尔文主义思想和德国思想之间的交融期，后一时期对应于历史和社会思想的应用和践行期。基于这一认识，他的传记作品以卡莱尔定居伦敦分为上下两部。同一线索见于凯普仑（Fred Kaplan）。他的作品虽然没有分为上下两部，但是在叙事内容中可以明显地判断出前后两期之间的区别。即使像海福尔（Simon Heffer）的作品，虽然以卡莱尔的道德思想发展史为线索，但是发展动机在前后两期的不同依然清晰地体现出来。基于以上判断，卡莱尔思想发展史作为一个整体被确定为我的研究话题。但是，随着研究的深入，我逐渐发现，早期思想之中的德国因素不是可以在短期之内实现把握的对象。最终，我决定，将研究重点放在后期的思想发展，而仅在“导论”部分对前期进行简要的介绍。

几部文献对于我研究卡莱尔的历史和社会思想具有重要的意义。奈夫（Eremy Neff）的《卡莱尔和穆勒》是一部将卡莱尔的历史和社会思想综合在一起进行解读的研究。其中不但包括功利主义作为社会批评对象、英雄崇拜的绝对性以及社会预言的历史依据等内容，甚至还有德国思想因素对卡莱尔后期思想的影响的讨论。与奈夫相似，坎佩尔（Ian Campbell）同样以后期思想为主要解读对象。但是，与奈夫不同，加尔文主义思想被认为是后期思想的基础。罗森堡（Philip Rosenberg）的作品同样聚焦于卡莱尔的社会思想，并对他的工作伦理观进行比较详细、深入的探讨。有关卡莱尔历史思想的研究文献在数量上比较多。杨戈（Louise Merwin Young）、韦勒克（René Wellek）、塞恩（Hill Shine）和罗森堡（John D. Rosenberg）等的作品在不同程度上给我以启发，让我实现洞见。

除以上作品之外，还有一部分以作品解读为主要内容的研究令我受惠。这些作品或以卡莱尔的生平为线索，既对作品的历史评价进行再现，也不失有关现代解读的讨论。勒·凯内（A. L. Le Quesne）的作品虽然篇幅不大，但是在许多主要作品的解读中不乏洞见之笔。同样，卡佳明（Louis Cazamian）的《卡莱尔》是一部法国卡莱尔研究的经典之作。因为视角的不同，作品往往可以提示一些英语评论忽视的细节。《旧衣新裁》可谓卡莱尔作品中最为重要的一部。这部处于卡莱尔前后两期转型的作品，得到了丁尼生（G. B. Tennyson）、迪布尔（Jerry A. Dibble）和李德（Walter L. Reed）等的关注和研究。相关文献的阅读让我明确了该作品在叙事手法、主题呈现和思想背景等方面的研究思路。

原学位论文主要分六部分对卡莱尔的思想发展史进行呈现和研究。除“导论”部分简要涉及前期思想外，主体部分五章均从一个方面以后期思想为主要研究对象。英雄崇拜、历史观、文学观、社会批评和工作伦理等分别对应于一章。此次修改，“导论”部分得到了大幅的扩充。卡莱尔早期思想发展史的概貌，是本书“导论”部分中的主要内容。卡莱尔的生平经历，是这一部分的主要线索，主要涉及加尔文主义思想、启蒙教育、德国思想研究、信仰恢复以及思想转变等。其中，德国思想研究是主要的研究对象。

卡莱尔德国思想因素研究是一个具有悠久研究传统的研究领域，涉及英、法、德和意大利等众多欧洲语言。在英语世界，相关研究在20世纪初便开始发展。沃恩（C. E. Vaughan）的研究文章《卡莱尔和他的德国大师》（“Carlyle and his German Masters”）可谓这一领域的开山之作。作品主要研究了卡莱尔与歌德和费希特之间的思想关联。瑞（Frederick William Roe）的《托马斯·卡莱尔作为文学批评家》（*Thomas Carlyle as a Critic of Literature*）和约翰逊（William Savage Johnson）的《托马斯·卡莱尔——文学学徒期研究》（*Thomas Carlyle：A Study of his Literary Apprenticeship，1814 – 1831*）虽然不是专门的研究作品，但是依然辟有专门章节对此话题进行解读。奈夫（Emery Neff）紧承这一批评传统。在《卡莱尔和穆勒》以及《卡莱尔》（*Carlyle*）中，卡莱尔的德国思想得到了一定程度上的解读，甚至在被作为一条思想脉络，用于他后期社会思想的解读。雷曼（B. H. Lehman）的《卡莱尔的英雄理论》（*Carlyle's Theory of the Hero：Its Sources，Development，History，and Influence on Carlyle's Works*）在这一领域颇具代表性。作品主要研究了英雄崇拜理论的德国思想资源，触及了德国思想资源对于卡莱尔思想的解释力。塞恩（Hill Shine）在这一领域也有建树。他的《卡莱尔与德国哲学问题》（“Carlyle and the German Philosophy Problem during the year 1826 – 1827”）主要探讨了卡莱尔德国思想研究的文本和研究方法。韦勒克也是这一领域的研究专家。《卡莱尔与德国浪漫主义》（“Carlyle and German Romanticism”）首次将卡莱尔与德国浪漫派之间的思想关系纳入视角，可谓开山之作。《康德在英格兰》（*Immanuel Kant in England*：*1793 – 1838*）以康德思想在英国的传播史为研究对象。其中，卡莱尔的康德思想研究是主要内容之一。穆尔海（John H. Muirhead）的《安格鲁 – 撒克逊哲学中的柏拉图主义传统》（*The Platonic Tradition in Anglo – Saxon Philosophy*：*Studies in the History of Idealism in England and America*）将卡莱尔的德国思想研究纳入英国的超验主义哲学传统。这一研究立场的贡献在于明确了卡莱尔德国思想研究所在的思想传统，建立起与其他思想事件之间的关联。第二次世界大战前，这一领域里的扛鼎之作是哈罗德（Charles Frederick Harrold）的《卡莱尔和德国思想》（*Carlyle and German Thought*：*1819 – 1834*）。作品对卡莱尔的德国思想资源进行了全面的解读，基本触及了所有主要话题。然而，作品的缺陷在于过分聚焦于技术性问题。这样的研究虽然可以厘清卡莱尔与德国思想之间的偏差，但是难以展示他思想的特征。此外，哈罗德还有《卡莱尔的康德研究》（“Carlyle's Interpretation of Kant”）和《卡莱尔和诺瓦利斯》（“Carlyle and Novalis”）等两篇论文。这些作品从不同侧面丰富了相关研究。

第二次世界大战后，相关研究持续发展。司米德（J. W. Smeed）的文章《托马斯·卡莱尔与让·保罗·里希特》（“Thomas Carlyle and Jean Paul Richter”）主要以里希特对卡莱尔文风上的影响为研究对象。丁尼生（G. B. Tennyson）的名作《所谓新裁的旧衣》（*Sartor Called Resartus*：*The Genesis*，*Structure*，*and Style of Thomas Carlyle's First Major Work*）可与哈罗德的作品媲美。作品详细解读了各种德国思想因素的发展脉络，并着重研究了它们在《旧衣新裁》中的交会状况。塞恩的文章《卡莱尔的早期作品与赫尔德的〈观念〉》（“Carlyle's Early Writings and Herder's *Ideen*：The Concept of History”）继韦勒克之后，再次将卡莱尔与赫尔德之间的思想关联作为研究对象。继哈罗德之后，依科勒（A. Abbott Ikeler）探讨了卡莱尔的加尔文主义思想与德国思想因素之间的关系。《清教秉性与超验信仰》（*Puritan Temper and Transcendental Faith*：*Carlyle's Literary Vision*）聚焦于两个异质的思想传统在卡莱尔精神发展史中的相互作用。与丁尼生一样，迪布尔（Jerry A. Dibble）同样将卡莱尔的德国思想研究作为一个整体进行研究。《皮提亚的醉酒之歌》（*The Pythia's Drunken Song：Thomas Carlyle's and the Style Problem in German Idealist Philosophy*）虽然以文体为主要研究对象，但是涉及卡莱尔德国思想研究的背景、方法和内容等。紧随司米德、维恩（J. P. Vijn）的《卡莱尔与让·保罗》（*Carlyle and Jean Paul：Their Spiritual Optic*）探讨了卡莱尔与里希特之间在文风上的借鉴关系。私语（*Rede*）被认为是卡莱尔最为重要的借鉴内容。维妲（Elisabeth M. Vida）的《浪漫主义亲和力》（*Romantic Affinities：German Authors and Carlyle：A Study in the History of Ideas*）延续了韦勒克的研究思路。卡莱尔与德国浪漫派之间的思想关系得到了更加深入的探讨。

在法语世界，对卡莱尔德国思想因素的关注更早。泰纳（Hippolyte Taine）在19世纪60年代便开始关注相关话题。《英国唯心论》（*L'Idéalisme anglaise：Étude sur Carlyle*）多次触及卡莱尔的德国思想因素。作品因出版年代过早，故不能就德国思想对卡莱尔的影响作出更加深入的判断。然而，这部作品在许多方面可谓相关研究的开山之作。巴泰勒米（Edmond Barthèlemy）是最早为卡莱尔专门立传的法语作家。《托马斯·卡莱尔传》（*Thomas Carlyle：Essai Biographique et Critique*）虽然不是专门的研究作品，但是依然辟有专章就有关问题展开讨论。博思（Camille Bos）的《卡莱尔的康德主义》（“Le Kantisme de Carlyle”）是最早聚焦于卡莱尔康德思想研究的作品。因篇幅所限，作品未能就有关问题展开说明。不过，多数相关话题均被提及。在这一领域，杨德尔（F. F. Yandell）的《托马斯·卡莱尔》（*Thomas Carlyle：Sa Métaphysique，sa moral，sa conception religieuse*）是最早的比较全面的研究文献。特别是作品的第一章，主要聚焦于卡莱尔的形而上学思想。在此，德国思想因素的影响得到了一定程度的发掘。卡佳明（Louis Cazamian）是这一领域的专家。他的《卡莱尔》（*Carlyle*）以大篇幅探讨卡莱尔的德国思想因素，并以之为线索，作为后期思想的解释脉络。同一研究思路一直贯穿到他与勒谷依（E. Legouis）合编的《英国文学史》（*Histoire de la Littérature Anglaise*）。其中，介绍卡莱尔的章节以“哲学的唯心派”（“L'Idéalisme Philosophique：Carlyle”）为题。这颇能说明他的研究立场。嘉瑞（Jean – Marie

Carré）主要以歌德在英国的传播史为研究对象。在《歌德在英格兰》（*Gœthe en Angleterre*）中，几乎一半的篇幅被用以说明卡莱尔与歌德之间的思想关联。巴氏（Victor Basch）的《卡莱尔》（*Carlyle：L'Homme et l'Œuvre*）是另外一部比较重要的卡莱尔法语传记。其中，德国思想因素依然是比较重要的研究对象。

除英、法语世界之外，德语世界最为关注卡莱尔的德国思想因素。考虑到德国是思想输出国，这一点很好理解。在费希尔（Thomas A. Fischer）的《托马斯·卡莱尔》（*Thomas Carlyle：Eine Geschichte seines Lebens*）和亨塞尔（Paul Hensel）的《托马斯·卡莱尔》（*Thomas Carlyle*）两部较为早期的传记作品中，卡莱尔的德国思想研究经历得到了整理和再现。福吕格尔（Ewald Flügel）的《托马斯·卡莱尔的宗教和道德发展及其世界观》（*Thomas Carlyles religiöse und sittlche Entwicklung und Weltanschauung*）和舒尔策－盖威尔尼茨（Gerhart von Schulze－Gaevernitz）的《托马斯·卡莱尔的世界和宗教观》（*Thomas Carlyles Welt－und Gesellschaftsanschauung*）均以相当可观的篇幅对卡莱尔的德国思想因素进行解读，并以之作为线索对他有关社会、宗教、道德和自然等所形成的观点进行解析。狄尔泰（Wilhelm Dilthey）的《托马斯·卡莱尔》（"Thomas Carlyle"）和费尔（Bernhard Fehr）的《卡莱尔〈旧衣新裁〉中的德国唯心论》（"Der Deutsche Idealismus in Carlyles *Sartor Resartus*"）等两篇文章均以《旧衣新裁》中的德国思想因素为研究对象，主要涉及卡莱尔与康德和费希特之间的思想借鉴关系。施特罗利（Wilhelm Streuli）的《托马斯·卡莱尔作为德国文学和德国思想的引介人》（*Thomas Carlyle als Vermittler deutscher Litteratur und deutschen Geistes*）和克莱格（Heinrich Kraeger）的《卡莱尔的德国语言和文学研究》（"Carlyles Stellung zur Deutschen Sprache und Litteratur"）等两部作品在最大限度上实现了综合。卡莱尔德国思想因素研究的基本框架、方法和内容确立下来。此外，德语研究还涉及卡莱尔与个别德国作家之间的思想关联。顾席勒（Frohwalt Küchler）的文章《卡莱尔与席勒》（"Carlyle und Schiller"）聚焦于卡莱尔与席勒之间的思想关联。鲍姆加顿（Otto Baumgarten）的《卡莱尔与歌德》（*Carlyle und Goethe*）则以卡莱尔与歌德之间的思想关联为研究对象。

最后，意大利语世界在这一领域也有一定的建树。罗伯托（Diego de Roberto）的传记作品《托马斯·卡莱尔》（*Tommaso Carlyle*）中有较大的篇幅介绍他的德国思想研究，并在一定程度上涉及德国思想因素的作用。费尔米（Laura Fermi）的《托马斯·卡莱尔》（*Thomas Carlyle*）将卡莱尔的德国思想研究作为他思想发展史上具有革命性的事件，并以之对他的后期思想进行解释。

以上作品便是我在毕业之后主要的阅读书目。随着阅读的深入与扩大，我渐渐意识到，卡莱尔的德国思想研究其实并不是一个单一的思想事件，而是一个思想潮流的表现和特例。除他之外，柯尔律治（Samuel Coleridge）、德昆西（Thomas De Quincey）、哈兹利特（William Hazlitt）和罗宾逊（Henry Crabb Robinson）等均在不同程度上进行了德国思想研究，从中获得资源，从而构建起自己独具特色的思想体系。在这一时期，英国表现出对德国从狂飙运动到浪漫派文学的极大兴趣。这正是英国浪漫主义文学蓬勃发展的时期。可见，卡莱尔的德国思想研究有强烈的浪漫主义背景。他思想的前后两期，简单而言是浪漫主义和现实主义之间的分期。这也是我目前为止最大的理论框架。为理解卡莱尔思想的浪漫主义背景，我主要阅读了韦勒克、亚布拉姆斯（M. H. Abrams）以及洛夫乔伊（Arthur Lovejoy）的相关作品。然而，我关于这一部分内容所进行的研究与思考无法与我的博士论文实现有效的接轨。毕竟，在卡莱尔思想的前后两期之间存在较大的分裂。我的博士论文主要聚焦于卡莱尔的后期思想，而我目前的研究集中于前期。这样，我仅仅对当年所删部分进行重新加工润色，使之与毕业论文构成整体，而没有将毕业以来的所有思考纳入本书。

与原论文相比，本书的导论部分得到了最大限度的扩充。导论以卡莱尔的生平为线索，对他德国思想研究的原因、过程和效果进行再现和诠释。在本书中，真理观作为独立的内容而单独成章。后四章分别从英雄崇拜、历史、社会和工作观等方面对之进行诠释。其中，第二章（英雄崇拜）不但在结构上得到了一定的调整，而且对英雄崇拜思想的发展进行呈现。第三章（历史观）基本以原论文内容为主，但是增加了介绍部分，主要是有关卡莱尔历史认识的发展过程。最后两章因为我关注点的改变，未有太大的改动。

本书的完成有赖于多方面因素，在此不再一一赘述。我的博士论文当年被题献给我心爱的女儿。如今四年的光阴匆匆度过。女儿如朵花儿，茁壮成长。然而，我年迈的奶奶却在书稿完成之际身患重病，与世长辞。我本想一仍其旧，依然将本书题献给女儿。不过妻子提议，本书最应该献给我的奶奶。奶奶与女儿之间竟然是八十年的距离。从论文到成书，从女儿到奶奶，这之间是我满腔的不舍与爱意。

目　录

导　论

托马斯·卡莱尔（Thomas Carlyle，1795—1881）是英国浪漫主义中后期和维多利亚前中期重要的文学家和思想家。他的重要性甚至被同时代的法国思想界注意。蒙泰古（M. É. Montégut）把他看作“我们时代最为杰出的人物之一”。[①] 易祖烈（J. B. J. Izoulet – Loubatières）视他为“当代英格兰思想界的英雄”。[②] 他被舍瑞（Edmond Scherer）比作维多利亚时期的苏格拉底，“即使不是一位哲学家，至少是一个思想的助产士”。[③] 杨德尔（F. F. Yandell）指出，“在维多利亚时代的英国作家之中，卡莱尔占据显耀的地位”，因为他“对同时代人的精神产生了巨大的影响”。[④] 泰纳（H. Taine）如此描绘，“当你问英国人——如果他们尚未超过四十岁——他们当中谁人依然在进行思考，他们马上会说出卡莱尔的名字［……］他们带着别样的情怀阅读［卡莱尔的二十卷作品］，每天清晨都会推翻前一天的判断”。[⑤] 在巅峰时期，卡莱尔作为“切尔西的圣贤”的形象深入人心，[⑥] 是一个文化群体的中心和灵魂。

1795 年 12 月 4 日，卡莱尔诞生于苏格兰西南部的乡村埃克尔费亨（Ecclefechan），是一位泥瓦匠（James Carlyle）的长子。1809 年进入爱丁堡大

---

① “Thomas Carlyle,” p. 278.

② Carlyle, *Les Héros et l'Héroïque*, Intro., p. 7.

③ “Thomas Carlyle,” p. 68.

④ *Thomas Carlyle*, Intro., p. 5.

⑤ *L'Idéalisme Anglais*, p. 3.

⑥ “The Sage of Chelsea,” Tennyson, *A Carlyle Reader*, Intro. p. 8. Chelsea is the street in which Carlyle's permanent residence in London since 1834 is found.

学学习文科。1814 年毕业，未获得学位。毕生后以教学、演说和写作为职业。1834 年春移居伦敦，写作并发表主要作品。1865 年当选为爱丁堡大学名誉校长，次年就职。1874 年接受普鲁士颁发的荣誉勋章。1881 年 2 月 5 日去世。遵其生前意愿，葬于故乡埃克尔费亨乡村教堂墓地。

卡莱尔一生著书立说，著作等身。从 1820 年开始为《爱丁堡百科全书》（*The Edinburgh Encyclopædia*）撰写“蒙田”等词条开始，① 至 1875 年完成《挪威早期帝王史》，② 作品超过 30 部，涉及文学、文化、社会、历史和时政

---

① From 1820 to 1823, Carlyle contributes a series of articles, 17 in total, to *The Edinburgh Encyclopedia* (ed. David Brewster, pub. William Blackwood, Vol. 18, 1808 – 1830), in most of the cases, for the sake of making a living out of writing. Carlyle's contributions are, alphabetically, "Montaigne" (*The Edinburgh Encyclopaedia*, Philadelphia: Joseph and Edward Parker, Vol. XIII, pp. 718A – 719A), "Montagu" (719A – 721B), "Montesquieu" (721B – 724B), "Montfaucon" (724B – 725B), "Montucla" (730B – 731B), "Dr. John Moor" (731B – 732B), "Sir John Moor" (732B – 733B), "Necker" (Vol. XIV, pp. 447B – 451A), "Nelson" (451A – 455B), "The Netherlands" (459B – 471A), "Newfoundland" (473A – 477B), "Norfolk" (494A – 497B), "Northamptonshire" (498B – 500A), "Norhtumberland" (505A – 507B), "Mungo Park" (Vol. XV, pp. 380A – 383B), "William Pitt, Earl of Chatham" (689A – 692B), and "William Pitt, the Younger" (692B – 696B). All the above articles are, after Carlyle's death, reassembled into one volume and published (cf. *Montaigne and Other Essays Chiefly Biographical*, London: James Gowans & Son, & Philadelphia: J. B. Lippincott Co., 1897, with a foreword by S. R. Crockett).

In a letter to Robert Mitchell (27th Nov. 1818), one of his frequent correspondents in the earlier stage of his literary career, Carlyle first mentions the name of Brewster and expresses the wish to make his acquaintance (Let.[1], I, 189 – 190). The formal introduction to, and then a subsequent though brief conversation with, Brewster is mentioned in a letter to his mother (17th Dec. 1818), Margaret Aitken Carlyle, which, however, fails to result in his employment as one contributor to the encyclopedia (201). It is only "late in 1819 or early in 1820" that the desired employment is realized (Shepherd, *Memoirs*, Vol. I, p. 31). His first contribution, "The Life of Montesquieu," to the encyclopedia, together with the plan for further cooperation, is mentioned in a letter to his brother, Alexander (1st Mar. 1820, L. – B., 36).

The release of his financial embarrassment is, on the whole, Carlyle's motif in the acceptance of Brewster's offer. He, with other occasional literary contributions, is able to earn "two pounds a week," an amount on which he contrive[s] to live without trenching on his capital (Froude, *First Forty Years*, Vol. I, p. 49). His first experience in literary apprenticeship is, in the main, unsatisfactory and bitter (Let.[1], I, 289, 322).

Those articles, as referable from the titles of the entries, are mainly biographical and geographical, descriptive and expository. Though Carlyle's original thinking is scarcely retractable in them, a better source for the study of Carlyle's stylistic development in the earliest stage is, except his early letters, hardly available elsewhere.

② *Early Kings of Norway* is a series of papers first published in installments in *Fraser's Magazine* (New Series, Vol. XI) in the first three months of 1875 (Ch. I – VII, pp. 1 – 26; Ch. VIII – X, pp. 135 – 155; Ch. XI–XVI, pp. 273 – 288) and then in a volume together with "The Portrait of John Knox" (pp. 407 – 439). This volume, *Early Kings of Norway: Also an Essay on the Portrait of John Knox* (London: Chapman and Hall, 1875), is the last literary production of Carlyle's when he is alive. He, after the decease of his wife, Jane Welsh Carlyle, is mainly occupied with the edition of Jane's and his own biographical documents.

等众多领域，体裁包括小说、评论、传记和散文等多种样式，可谓琳琅满目。其中，虚构类作品是《旧衣新裁》。① 演说集有《论历史上的英雄、英雄崇拜和英雄业绩》以及《文学史演说集》。② 散文集为《批评杂文集》。③ 时政评论集包括《过去和现在》（*Past and Present*，1843）和《晚近文集》（*Latter – Day Pamphlet*，1850）等。传记作品为《席勒传》④ 和《约翰·斯特林传》（*The Life of John Sterling*，1851）等两部。翻译作品两部，为《威廉·迈斯特的求学和漫游时代》和《德国故事集》。⑤ 历史作品三部，为《法国大革命》（*The*

---

① *Sartor Resartus* is composed between 1830 and 1831. It is first published serially in *Fraser's Magazine* (Vol. Ⅶ, 1833, pp. 581 – 592, 669 – 684; Vol. Ⅸ, 1834, pp. 177 – 195, 301 – 313, 443 – 455, 664 – 674; Vol. Ⅹ, 1834, 77 – 87, 182 – 193) and in a volume in America in 1835 (Boston: James Munroe and Co., with a preface by Ralph Waldo Emerson) and in England in 1838 (*Sartor Resartus*: *The Life and Opinions of Herr Teufelsdröckh*, London: Saunders and Otley).

② Carlyle has given, in total, four public lectures during the years 1837 – 1840. Those lectures are, chronologically, "German Literature" (1837) in 6 lectures, "History of Literature, or, the Successive Periods of European Culture" (1838) in 12 lectures, "The Revolutions of Modern Europe" (1839) in 6 lectures, and "Heroes and Hero – Worship" (1840) in 6 lectures. Only the second and fourth lectures are preserved and published (*Lectures on the History of Literature*, ed. J. Reay Greene, New York: Charles Scribner's Sons, 1892, with all the 9th lecture amiss but the title "Voltaire—The French—Scepticism—From Rabelais to Rousseau"; *On Heroes*, *Hero – Worship*, *and the Heroic in History*, London: Chapman and Hall, 1840).

③ Carlyle's *Critical and Miscellaneous Essays* is a collection of his contributions to various reviews, journals and magazines since 1827. Though they are published in America in a book form either wholly or partially, it is only in 1839 that the first collection is published in England (4 Vols., London: James Fraser).

④ *Schiller's Life and Writings* is first published serially in *London Magazine* in the years 1823 – 1824 [Part I. His Youth (1759 – 1784), Vol. Ⅷ, pp. 381 – 400; Part Ⅱ. From his Settlement at Manheim to his Settlement at Jena (1783 – 1790), Vol. Ⅸ, pp. 37 – 59; Part Ⅲ. From his Settlement at Jena to his Death (1790 – 1805), Vol. Ⅹ, pp. 16 – 25, 149 – 162, 259 – 269]. It is then considerably expanded and enlarged, and published in a volume (*Life of Friedrich Schiller*, *Comprehending an Examination of his Works*, London: Taylor and Hessey, 1825). For a detailed discussion of the expansion and enlargement made to the book, cf. Max Batt, "Carlyle's Life of Schiller," *Modern Philology*, 1. 3 (1904), pp. 391 – 392.

⑤ *Wilhelm Meister's Apprenticeship and Travels* (2 Vols., Edinburgh: Oliver & Boyd, & London: G. & W. B. Whittaker, 1824) is a translation of Wolfgang von Goethe's *Wilhelm Meisters Lehrjahre* (1795 – 1796) and *Wilhelm Meisters Wanderjahre* (1st ed. 1821, 2nd ed. 1829). As Carlyle's translation is proceeding, Goethe has made no substantial expansion and enlargement to the *Wanderjahre*, and still nothing is known about the existence of *Wilhelm Meisters theatralische Sendung* (ca. 1776, pub. 1911). It, thus, results in that, in Carlyle's version of translation, *Apprenticeship* is tremendously larger than *Travels*. For a discussion of Carlyle's translation, cf. Susanne Howe, "Carlyle and Wilhelm Meister," *Wilhelm Meister and his English Kinsmen*: *Apprentices to Life*, Columbia University Studies in English and Comparative Literature, New York: Columbia Univ. Pr., 1930, pp. 82 – 125.

German Romance: *Translations from the German with Biographical and Critical Notices* (2 Vols., 1827) is a collection of tales and stories in translation by five German romantics, Musæus, Fouqué, Tieck, Hoffmann and Richter.

French Revolution, 1837)、《克伦威尔书信及演说集》(*Cromwell's Letters and Speeches*, 1845)和《腓德烈大帝传》(*Frederick the Great*, 1858 – 1865)。

除以上作品外，在他去世之后，还有多部未刊行的作品经整理得以出版。最初得到整理出版的作品是回忆录。① 此后，卡莱尔的笔记问世。② 书信作品的出版最为壮观，基本持续了一个世纪。③ 此外，散论集、文学史和历史片段等作品陆续被整理出版。①这些作品的出版极大地丰富了卡莱尔研究的文本资源，为解读他的生平和思想提供了许多珍贵的线索。

---

① The first published version is *Reminiscences* (ed. James Anthony Froude, New York: Happer & Brothers, 1881). It is believed, however, to be inaccurate in some of the details. Then, seven years later, a second version, *Reminiscences* (ed. Charles Eliot Norton, 2 Vols., London: Macmillan, 1887) follows in publication. This reminiscence is composed of six parts, "James Carlyle," "Edward Irving," "Lord Jeffrey," "Jane Welsh Carlyle," "Southey," and "Wordsworth," with the last two in appendix.

Besides, two other reminiscences are also published (*Reminiscences of my Irish Journey in* 1849, London: Sampson, Low, Marston, Searle, & Rivington, 1882; *Two Reminiscences of Thomas Carlyle*, ed. John Clubbe, Durham, N. C.: Duke Univ. Pr., 1974).

② See *Two Note Books of Thomas Carlyle* (ed. Charles Eliot Norton, New York: The Grolier Club, 1898), spanning from 23rd Mr. 1822 to 16th May 1832, a period of crucial importance in Carlyle's intellectual development, replete with valuable clues and insights into the details of his thoughts and doctrines.

③ The first collection of Carlyle's letters is *Early Letters* (ed. Charles Eliot Norton, 2 Vols., London: Macmillan, 1886). In the same pattern follows *Letters* (ed. Charles Eliot Norton, 2 Vols., London: Macmillan, 1888). Of the same series comes finally *New Letters* (ed. Alexander Carlyle, 2 Vols., London & New York: John Lane, 1904). These six volumes covers the span in time from 1814, in which the earliest of Carlyle's letters is preserved, to 1879, just two years before his death. Various themes are discussed, and an insight into Carlyle's intellectual growth is obtainable, in them.

Carlyle's letters to a specific correspondent are also published in collections. The first to come out of this type is *Correspondence between Goethe and Carlyle* (ed. Charles Eliot Norton, London: Macmillan, 1887). Carlyle's letters to Ense, another German correspondent, is also published, in German (*Briefe Thomas Carlyles an Darnhagen von Ense aus dem Jahren* 1837 – 1857, ed. Richard Preuß, Berlin: Gebrüder Paetel, 1892). Also available are the letters exchanged between him and Emerson (*The Correspondence of Thomas Carlyle and Ralph Waldo Emerson*, 2 Vols., Boston & New York: Houghton, Mifflin and Co., 1899; *The Correspondence of Emerson and Carlyle*, ed. Joseph Slater, New York & London: Columbia Univ. Pr., 1964). To add to this list is *Letters of Thomas Carlyle to John Stuart Mill, John Sterling and Robert Browning* (ed. Alexander Carlyle, London: T. Fisher Unwin, 1923). To complete this list are *Letters of Thomas Carlyle to William Graham* (ed. John Graham, Princeton: Princeton Univ. Pr., 1950) and *The Correspondence of Thomas Carlyle and John Ruskin* (ed. George Allan Cate, Stanford, California: Stanford Univ. Pr., 1982). This group of works, in each case, cover a relatively shorter span and, usually sheds light upon a certain stage in Carlyle's development as a thinker.

Publication of letters in the family circle is made available by *Letters of Thomas Carlyle to his Youngest Sister* (ed. Charles Townsend Copeland, Boston & New York: Houghton, Mifflin & Co., 1899) and *The Letters of Thomas Carlyle to his Brother Alexander* (ed. Edwin W. Marrs, Cambridge, Mass.: The Belknap Pr. of Harvard Univ. Pr., 1968). These two works serve as a mirror to the tender side of Carlyle the brother.

在西方世界，卡莱尔的作品得到了大量的翻译。法国最先开始翻译他的作品。早在1829年，《时代的标记》（“Signs of the Times,” 1829）一文便被圣西门学派（the Saint – Simonians）关注，译为法文发表。①19世纪30—70年代，法

Letters between him and his wife from courtship to marriage are accessible by two works, *The Love Letters of Thomas Carlyle and Jane Welsh* (ed. Alexander Carlyle, London: John Lane, & New York: John Lane Co., 1909) and *Letters to his Wife* (ed. T. Bliss, London: Gollancz, 1953). These are gateway to Carlyle's interior life and emotional experiences.

References to Jane Welsh Carlyle's letters are made possible by the following three works, *Early Letters of Jane Welsh Carlyle* (ed. David G. Ritchie, London: Swan Sonnenschein & Co., 1889), *Letters and Memorials of Jane Welsh Carlyle* (ed. James Anthony Froude, 2 Vols., New York: Charles Scribner's Sons, 1894), and *New Letters & Memorials of Jane Welsh Carlyle* (ed. Alexander Carlyle, London & New York: John Lane, 1903). These are valuable supplements to a thorough and profound understanding of Carlyle's thoughts.

The most ambitious endeavor in the field is *The Collected Letters of Thomas and Jane Welsh Carlyle* (ed. Charles Richard Sanders, 44 Vols., Durham, N. C.: Duke Univ. Pr., 1970 –; also available at “The Carlyle Letters Online: A Victorian Cultural Reference,” http://carlyleletters.dukeupress.edu/clo/browse_date), covering almost everything that has been preserved of the letters both to and from the two Carlyles, spanning from 1812 to 1881. It is indispensable to any study of Carlyle, either biographical or intellectual, literal or moral.

④ See *The Rescued Essays of Thomas Carlyle* (ed. Percy Newberry, London: Leadenhall Pr., & New York: Charles Scribner's Sons, 1892), *Carlyle's Unfinished History of German Literature* (ed. Hill Shine, Lexington: Univ. of Kentucky Pr., 1951), *Historical Sketches of Notable Persons and Evens in the Reigns of James I. and Charles I.* (ed. Alexander Carlyle, London: Chapman and Hall, 1902), and the “Guises” [Rodger L. Tarr, “ ‘The Guises’: Thomas Carlyle's Lost Renaissance History,” *Victorian Studies*, 25.1 (1981), pp. 7 – 80].

① For the interactions, and the contacts, between Carlyle and the Saint – Simonians, cf. K. J. Fielding, “Carlyle and the Saint – Simonians (1830 – 1830): New Considerations,” *Carlyle and his Contemporaries: Essays in Honor of Charles Richard Sanders*, ed. John Clubbe, Durham, N. C.: Duke Univ. Pr., 1976, pp. 35 – 59; Ella M. Murphy, “Carlyle and the Saint – Simonians,” *Studies in Philology*, 33.1 (1936), pp. 93 – 118; Emery Neff, *Carlyle and Mill: An Introduction to Victorian Thought*, 2nd ed. Revised, New York: Columbia Univ. Pr., 1926, esp. pp. 208 – 221; Richard Pankhurst, *The Saint Simonians, Mill and Carlyle: A Preface to Modern Thought*, London: Sidgwick & Jackson, 1957; Hill Shine, *Carlyle and the Saint – Simonians: The Concept of Historical Periodicity*, Baltimore: Johns Hopkins Press, 1941.

For the documents, especially the letters, exchanged between Carlyle and Gustave d'Eichthal, the leader of Saint – Simonianism at the time, cf. G. d'Eichthal, Thomas Carlyle & Eugène d' Eichthal, “Carlyle et le Saint – Simonisme: Lettres à Gustave d'Eichthal,” *Revue Historique*, 82.2 (1903), pp. 292 – 306; David Brooks Cofer, *Saint – Simonism in the Radicalism of Thomas Carlyle*, College Station, Texas: English Publishing Company, 1931.

After the publication of “Signs of the Times” [*Edinburgh Review*, Vol. XCLX (1829), pp. 439 – 459], it is taken notice of by the Saint – Simonians for the similarities in it to their own doctrines, especially to their conception of history as a kind of periodic development. The French translation, “Caractère de notre Époque” [*Revue Britannique*, Vol. XXV (1829), pp. 5 – 29], then issued. It is, however, an incomplete translation, with the part from the beginning to “whereby our own relation to it [...] may also become clearer” (Wks., XXVII, 56 – 59) untranslated.

国学界多有评论而鲜有翻译。[①] 从80年代后期开始至20世纪前20年，法国迎来了卡莱尔作品法译的高峰。[②] 此后，卡莱尔作品的法译虽然陆续有精品

Carlyle mentions his interactions with the Saint – Simonians in various sources. The reception of "a strange letter from some Saint – Simoniens at Paris, grounded on [his] little *Signs of the Times*" is first mentioned (Nt. B., 158). He, then, asks for Goethe's opinion upon his relation to the Saint – Simonians, only to be advised "von der Société St. Simonienne [...] Sich fern zu halten," "from the St. Simonian Society [to] hold [himself] aloof" (Goethe to Carlyle, 17th Oct. 1830; C. – G., 225, 226). In spite of Goethe's admonition, a translation has been done by him of "Saint – Simon's *Nouveau Christianisme*, a heterodox Pamphlet" (to Dr. Carlyle, 19th Dec. 1830; Let. 2, Ⅰ, 243). He even has an interview with "a Brother of Gustave's the French Saint Simonian," and conceives a generally fair impression of him as "a very intelligent youth" and "a general seeker after Light" (15th Oct. 1831; L. – B., 280). At the end of the year, Gustave d'Eichthal, head of the Saint – Simonianism, presents himself to the Carlyles. Jane, his wife, tells, in a letter to Jean Carlyle (N. D. Dec. 1831), of the pleasure "when a card bearing the name of Gustave d'Eichthal was sent up the other day" (Froude, *First Forty Years*, Vol. Ⅱ, pp. 181 – 182).

The relation of Carlyle to the Saint – Simonians is hardly classifiable as a matter of the influence of a master upon a disciple. Carlyle, in general, is too intellectually independent to be placed under indebtedness to the French proto – socialists.

① The only French translation of Carlyle's major works, during this period, is *The French Revolution* (*Histoire de la Révolution Française*, trans. Élias Regnault, Odysse Barot & Jules Roches, 3 Vols., Paris: Germer Baillière, 1865 – 1867).

For a thorough and detailed study of French criticism of Carlyle of the 30s – 60s, cf. Alan Carey Taylor, *Carlyle: Sa Première Fortune Littéraire en France (1825 – 1865)*, Bibliothèque de la Revue de Littérature Comparée, Vol. 61, Paris: Librairie Ancienne Honoré Champion, 1929, esp. pp. 29 – 108, 121 – 157.

② The first of Carlyle's major works to be translated into French, since the 80s, is *Heroes and Hero – Worship* (*Les Héros, le Culte des Héros et l'Héroïque dans l'Histoire*, trans. J. B. J. Izoulet – Loubatières, Paris: Armand Colin, 1888). In the first ten years of the twentieth century, *Past and Present* (*Cathédrales d'Autrefois et Usines d'Aujourdhui: Passé et Présent*, trans. Camille Bos, Paris: Revue Blanche, 1901), *Sartor Resartus* (*Sartor Resartus: Vie et Opinions de Herr Teufelsdröchk*, trans. Edmond Barthèlemy, Paris: Mercure, 1904), *Latter – Day Pamphlets* (*Pamphlets du Dernier jour*, trans. Edmond Barthèlemy, Paris: Mercure, 1906), and *Critical and Miscellaneous Essays* (*Essais Choisis de Critique et de Morale*, trans. Edmond Barthèlemy, Paris: Mercure, 1907; *Nouveaux Essais Choisis de Critique et de Moral*, trans. Edmond Barthèlemy, Paris: Mercure, 1909) follow subsequently in translation. There is an anthology of Carlyle's major works in French translation (*Pages Choisies des Grands Écrivains: Carlyle*, trans).

Émile Masson, (Paris: Armond Colin, 1905). Two collections of Carlyle's letters are also translated, *Early Letters* (*Carlyle Intime: Lettres de Thomas Carlyle à sa Mère*, trans. Elsie et Émile Masson, Paris: Mercure, 1907) and *Love Letters* (*Carlyle Intime: Lettres d'Amour de Jane et Thomas Carlyle*, trans. Elsie et Émile Masson, Paris: Mercure, 1910).

During the 20s in the twentieth century, the rest of Carlyle's major works, mainly letters, are translated into French. At the beginning of the 20s, *Correspondence between Goethe and Carlyle* (*Carlyle et Goethe: Correspondance* 1824 – 1834, trans. Georges Knopff, Paris: Librairie Française, 1921) comes to finish the list of Carlyle's works in French translation. *Cromwell's Letters and Speeches* (*Olivier Cromwell, sa Correspondance, ses*

问世，[①] 但是在数量和规模上均无法与前一黄金时期相提并论。这些法译作品基本涵盖了卡莱尔所有的主要著作，为法语世界卡莱尔研究奠定了坚实的文本基础。

在法语之外，德语是卡莱尔作品另一个比较重要的译入语。第一部德译作品仅比法译晚一年出版。[②] 20 世纪之前，有两部比较重要且有影响力的德译文集问世。[③] 此外，一些主要作品也被译为德文。[④] 甚至传记作品也有德译问

Discours, trans. Edmond Barthèlemy, 3 Vols., Paris: Mercure, 1910 – 1914), *The Correspondence of Thomas Carlyle and Ralph Waldo Emerson* (*Carlyle et Emerson*: *Correspondance* 1834 – 1872, trans. E. – L. Lepointe, Paris: Armand Colin, 1912), and *Reminiscences* (*Carlyle intime*: *Jane Welsh Carlyle*, trans. Elsie et Émile Masson, Paris: Mercure, 1913) are accessible in the French language.

So far, all the major works, either fiction or biography, essays or letters, except the voluminous *Frederick the Great*, are available to the French readers.

① After the 20s, available are new editions of *Sartor Resartus* (*Sartor Resartus*: *La philosophie du Vêtement*, trans. Louis Cazamian, Paris: Aubier – Montaigne, 1973; *Sartor Resartus*: *En Trois Livres*, trans. Maxime Berrée, Paris: Corti, 2008), and *Heroes and Hero – Worship* (*Les Héros*, trans. François Rosso, Paris: Maisonneuve et Larose, 1998). Also available are translation of "Count Cagliostro" (*Le Comte Cagliostro*, trans. Georges – A. Garnier, Fribourg, Suisse: Egloff, 1945), "The Diamond Necklace" (*Le Collier de la Reine*, trans. Georges – A. Garnier, Porrentruy, Suisse: Portes de France, 1946; *Le Collier de la Reine*, trans. Paul Choleau, Toulouse: Ombres, 1999), "Occasional Discourse on the Negro Question" (*Discours de Circonstance sur la Question Noire*, *Suivi de la Réponse de John Stuart Mill*, trans. Thierry Gillybœuf, Paris: Mille et une Nuits, 2010), and *The Early kings of Norway* (*Les Premiers Rois de Norvège*, trans. Thierry Gillybœuf, Paris: Félin, 2013).

② The first of Carlyle's works to be translated into German is *Life of Friedrich Schiller* (*Das Leben Schillers*, Frankfurt am Main: Heinrich Wilmans, 1830). Though no information of the translator is given, it is specially noted that the translation is "eingeleitet durch Goethe."

③ See *Ausgewählte Schriften* [trans. A. Kretzschmar, 6 Vols. Leipig: Otto Wigand, 1855 – 1856: Vol. 1, "Goethes Portrait," "Goethes Tod," "Goethes Werke," "Schiller," "Graf Cagliostro," & "Das Diamantenhalsband"; Vol. 2, "Voltaire," "Diderot," "Novalis," & "Charakteristiken"; Vol. 3, "Jean Paul Friedrich Richter" (2 parts), "Boswells Lebensgeschichte Johnsons," "Sir Walter Scott," & "Über Geschichte" (2 parts); Vol. 4, "Dr. Francia," "Mirabeau," "Burns," & "Deutsche Dramenschmiede"; Vol. 5, *Sartor Resartus*; Vol. 6, *Einst und Jetzt*], and *Socialpolitische Schriften* (trans. E. Pfannkucke, ed. P. Hensel, 3 Vols. Göttingen: Dandenhoed und Ruprecht, 1895 – 1899: Vol. 1, "Der Chartismus," "Die Negerfrage," & "Den Niagara hinunter—und dann"; Vol. 2, "Charakteristik unserer Zeit," & *Flugschriften aus erster Stunde*; Vol. 3, *Einst und Jetzt*). Obviously, a great portion of Carlyle's works are translated in these two selected works.

④Before the twentieth century, a lecture in *Heroes and Hero – Worship* is translated into German (*Doctor Martin Luther*: *Eine Stimme aus England*, Wiesbaden: Commission der Friedrich'schen Verlagsbuchhandlung in Siegen und Wiesbaden, 1843). Then follows the translation of *The French Revolution* (*Die Französische Revolution*, trans. P. Feddersen, 3 Vols., Leipzig: Brockhaus und Avenarius, 1844). During the 50s – 60s, the translation of the voluminous *Frederick the Great* is done (*Geschichte Friedrichs* Ⅱ: *Von Preußen genannt*

世。[①]20世纪之后，卡莱尔作品的德译进一步完善，部分填补了之前留有的空白。[②]90年代以来，德译的卡莱尔作品依然有精品陆续问世。[③]在所有作品中，《英雄与英雄崇拜》的德译作品数量最多。[④]与法译相比，德译更为全面，基本覆盖了卡莱尔作品的所有方面。

在其他欧洲语言之中，卡莱尔的作品也得到了比较普遍的翻译。以《旧衣新裁》为例，除德、法之外，还有荷兰语、波兰语、瑞典语、西班牙语、

Friedrich der Grosse, trans. J. Neuberg, 6 Vols., Berlin: Königlichen Geheimen, 1858 – 1869). In the 70s, there is a translation (*Der Jesuitismus*: *Ein Pamphlet*, trans. Adolph Holtermann, Braunschweick: Häring und Co., 1871). The 80s witnesses the publication of *Sartor Resartus* (trans. Thomas A. Fischer, Leipig: Otto Wigand, 1882) and *Goethes und Carlyles Briefwecksel* (Berlin: Wilhelm Hertz, 1887). Finally, in the 90s, another collection of Carlyle's letters is translated into German (*Briefe Thomas Carlyles an Darnhagen von Ense aus den Jahren* 1837 – 1857, trans. Richard Preuß, Berlin: Gebrüder Paetel, 1892). Besides, an anthology of his works is also available in German translation (*Beiträge zum Evangelium der Arbeit*: *Aus Schriften Thomas Carlyles*, *trans. J. Neuberg*, *Berlin*: *G. Reimer*, 1851).

So, even in the nineteenth century, almost all the major works of Carlyle in translation are available to the German readers.

① See James Anthony Froude, *Das Leben Thomas Carlyles*, trans. Thomas A. Fischer, 2 Vols., Gotha: Friedrich Andreas Perthes, 1887.

② Before the World War Ⅱ, *Reminiscences* (*Lebenserinnerungen* trans. Paul Jäger. 2 Vols., Göttingen: Verlag Vandenhoeck & Ruprecht, 1901) and "The Diamond Necklace" (*Das Diamantenhalsband*, München: Musarion, 1920) are newly produced in translation. A new translation of *The French Revolution* [*Die grosse Revolution*, trans. Adalbert Luntowski, Berlin: Verlag Neues Leben (Wilhelm Borngräber), 1911)] and *Correspondence between Goethe and Carlyle* (*Goethes Briefwechsel mit Thomas Carlyle*, ed. Georg Hecht, Dachau: Einhorn, 1913) is produced. Two selected works are also available (*Vermischte Aufsätze*, Göttingen: Verlag Vandenhoeck & Ruprecht, 1910; *Heldentum und Macht*: *Schriften für die Gegenwart*, ed. Michael Freund, Leipzig: Alfred Kröner, 1935).

③ Since the 90s, *Sartor Resartus* (*Sartor Resartus*: *Leben und Meinungen des Herrn Teufelsdröckh*, trans. Peter Staengle, Zürich: Manesse, 1991) and *Heroes and Hero – Worship* (*Über das Heroische in der Geschichte*, trans. Egon Friedell, St. Gallen: Sabon, 2001) are still receiving new translations. Besides, an anthology is also available (*Arbeiten und Nicht verzweifeln*: Auszüge, ed. & trans. Karl Robert, Düsseldorf & Leipzig: Langewiesche Verlag, 1990).

④ See *Über Helden*, *Heldenverehrung und das Heldentümliche in der Geschichte* (trans. Friedrich Bremer, Leipzig: Wigand, 1895), *Über Helden*, *Heldenverehrung und das Heldentümliche in der Geschichte*: 6 *Vorträge*, Bibliothek der Gesamt – Literatur des In – und Auslanders (Halle: Hendel, 1898), *Thomas Carlyle Über Helden*, *Heldenverehrung und das Heldentümliche in der Geschichte* (trans. E. Pfannkuche, Leipzig: Reclam, 1900), *Heldenverehrung und das Heldenthümliche in der Geschichte*: *Sechs Vorlesungen* (trans. J. Neuberg, 4th ed. Berlin: Decker, 1901), *Über Helden*, *Heldenverehrung und das Heldentümliche in der Geschichte* (trans. Walter von Molo, Berlin: R. v. Decker, 1917).

意大利语、匈牙利语和丹麦语等译文问世。① 在所有这些欧洲语言之中，卡莱尔作品的意大利语译文在数量上占比较突出的地位。② 所有这些译文的存在说明，卡莱尔不仅是一位英伦作家，更具有欧洲声誉。伴随着译文的传播，他的思想融入欧陆文化。

在东方世界，日本最早开始译介卡莱尔的作品。卡莱尔去世前后（1881），他的作品流传到日本。③ 至明治二十年（1887），他的思想已经得到了比较广泛而深入的接受。④ 20 世纪前后，卡莱尔的作品已有日译流传。⑤ 20 世纪 40—80 年代，日译陆续有作品问世。⑥ 特别是 60 年代出版的《卡莱尔选集》极为系统，⑦ 基本涵盖了所有主要作品。

与日本相比，中国对卡莱尔思想的接受相对滞后。虽然梁启超、辜鸿铭以及梅光迪等对他的思想有所介绍，⑧ 但并未产生明显的影响。与此相对应，

---

① For the translations in other European languages, see Carlyle, *Sartor Resartus*, ed. Charles Frederick Harrold, Intro., p. lxiv.

② Besides *Sartor Resartus*, other Italian translations of Carlyle's works are *Dante e Shakespeare* (trans. Cino Chiarini, Firenze: G. C. Sansoni, 1896), *Gli Eroi* (trans. Maria Pezzè Pascolato, Firenze: Barbèra, 1897), and *La Rivoluzione Francese* (trans. Ernestina Ciccotti - d'Errico, Vol. I, Roma: Luigi Mongini, 1906).

③ 段怀清、若杉邦子：《日本和中国对西方英雄主义的接受》，第 2 页。

④ 段怀清、若杉邦子：《日本和中国对西方英雄主义的接受》，第 3 页。

⑤ 以时间为序，《英雄和英雄崇拜》（『英雄論』，土井晚翠译，東京：春陽堂，1898）、《旧衣新裁》（『鬼臭先生衣裳哲學』，土井晚翠译，東京：大日本圖書株式會社，1909）、《批评杂文集》（『カーライル論集』，高橋五郎译，東京：武井万二，1912）和《法国大革命史》（『仏国革命史』，高橋五郎译，2 卷，東京：共同印刷株式會社，1917）等作品先后有日译问世。

⑥ 参见『過去と現在』（岩波文庫，石田憲次、石田英二译，東京：岩波書店，1941）、『衣服哲学』（岩波文庫，石田憲次译，東京：岩波書店，1946）、『英雄崇拜論』（岩波文庫，老田三郎译，東京：岩波書店，1949）、『ゲーテ＝カーライル往復書簡』（岩波文庫，山崎八郎译，東京：岩波書店，1951）、『衣服哲学』（谷崎隆昭译，京都：山口書店，1983）和『追想 ジェーン・ウェルシ・カーライル』（多田貞三译，京都：山口書店，1986）。

⑦ 参见『カーライル選集』（6 卷，東京：日本教文社，1962 - 1963：卷 1，「衣服の哲学」，宇山直亮译；卷 2，「英雄と英雄崇拝」，入江勇起男译；卷 3，「過去と現在」，上田和夫译；卷 4，「妻と友へ」，入江勇起男译；卷 5，「文学と人生」，高村新一译；卷 6，「歴史の生命」，宇山直亮译）。

⑧ 有关梁启超对卡莱尔思想的介绍，参见段怀清、若杉邦子《日本和中国对西方英雄主义的接受》，第 5—6 页。有关辜鸿铭，参见第 6—8 页。此外，有关辜鸿铭还可参见乔修峰，《维多利亚时代文人思想的回响：辜鸿铭的焦虑》，《巴别塔下：维多利亚时代文人的词语焦虑与道德重构》，中国社会学科出版社 2017 年版，第 225—255 页，特别参见第 231—236 页。

梁启超在《文野三界之别》、《英雄与时势》、《善变之豪杰》、《豪杰之公脑》、《无名之英雄》、《过渡时代论》（《饮冰室合集》文集六）和《南海康先生传》等作品中论及卡莱尔的思想。

卡莱尔作品的汉译在数量上明显不足，不能满足思想研究的需要。民国时期及以前，仅《英雄和英雄崇拜》一书有汉译。[①] 参见《英雄与英雄崇拜》,曾虚白译，商务印书馆 1932 年版。新中国成立后（1949），如周祖达所言，卡莱尔“是被批判的唯心主义英雄史观的代表人物”,[②] 卡莱尔：《论历史上的英雄、英雄崇拜和英雄业绩》，译序，第 1 页。故著作很少得到翻译出版。80 年代末以来，卡莱尔的著作才陆续得到了一定程度的汉译。[③] 相比于欧陆和日本，卡莱尔作品的汉译有明显的突破空间。

在英国 19 世纪思想发展史上，卡莱尔占有一席之地。他“作为最伟大的预见家，处于维多利亚时代思想生活的核心”。[④] 虽然他的声誉几经沉浮，但是在生前，特别是 19 世纪三四十年代，对他的评价以褒奖为主。[⑤] 众多思想界和文学界的有识之士对他的重要性持肯定观点。马森（David Masson）把他看

辜鸿铭主要在《中国人的精神》中论及卡莱尔的思想（*The Spirit of the Chinese People*, Beijing: Foreign Language Teaching and Research Pr., 1998, esp. pp. 33 - 340）。

梅光迪对卡莱尔思想的介绍可参见《卡莱尔与中国》一文（《梅光迪文存》，中华梅氏文化研究会编，华中师范大学出版社 2011 年版，第 228—236 页）。此外，《近世欧美文学趋势讲义》（第 92—118 页，特别参见“卡莱尔”，第 114—116 页）、《文学概论》（第 119—126 页，特别参见第 124 页）和《现今西洋人文主义》（第 156—160 页，特别参见第 158 页）等作品对卡莱尔亦有所论及。最后，梅光迪有写作计划，并将卡莱尔纳入“欧洲题材”名下（第 258 页）。

① 参见《英雄与英雄崇拜》,曾虚白译，商务印书馆 1932 年版。

② 卡莱尔：《论历史上的英雄、英雄崇拜和英雄业绩》，译序，第 1 页。

③ 参见《英雄和英雄崇拜：卡莱尔讲演集》（张峰、吕霞译，生活·读书·新知三联书店 1988 年版）、《英雄与英雄崇拜》（何欣译，辽宁教育出版社 1998 年版）、《论历史》（刘鑫译，载《历史理论与史学理论》，何兆武编，商务印书馆 1999 年版，第 230—242 页）、《英雄与英雄崇拜》（刘鑫节译，同上，第 243—250 页）、《拼凑的裁缝》（马秋武等译，广西师范大学出版社 2004 年版）、《文学史演讲集》（姜智芹译，广西师范大学出版社 2005 年版）、《卡莱尔、艾默生通信集》（李静滢译，广西师范大学出版社 2008 年版）、《论历史上的英雄、英雄崇拜和英雄业绩》（周祖达译，商务印书馆 2010 年版）、《文明的忧思》（郭彩凤译，金城出版社 2011 年版）和《法国大革命：一部历史》（刘毅译，2 卷，吉林出版集团股份有限公司 2017 年版）。很明显，除《英雄和英雄崇拜》有多个译本之外，其他作品只有一个汉译。而且，以上翻译作品在质量上存在较大的差距，个别译本甚至在细节上存在严重的错误，很难满足研究之需。

④ Hunt, “Carlyle and Coketown,” p. 59.

⑤ 方志强根据丁尼生（G. B. Tennyson, “Carlyle Today”）的意见，将卡莱尔的声誉变迁总结为三个阶段：受欢迎阶段（1830—1840）、倒退阶段（1881—1930）和学术批评阶段（1930— ）。总体而言，这是一个以下降为主要趋势的发展过程，他的声誉并没有恢复到第一阶段的高度（《平民的先知》，第 3 页；关于整个发展过程参见第 3—17 页）。

作英国思想转变的先导，“在近期的不列颠哲学历史中省略对他的认识，就是在《哈姆雷特》这一剧作中省略哈姆雷特的父亲”。①戴维（Samuel Davey）视他为“一位稀有的天才”，因为他“将影响涉及这个时代一些领先的头脑，比如穆勒、罗斯金、廷戴尔、艾默生、狄更斯等”。②阿诺德（Matthew Arnold）将卡莱尔的影响比喻为倾听“强劲的声音”，“清新而合理，带着真实的、荡气回肠的雄辩抵达心灵”。③勃朗特（Charlotte Brontë）坦言随着时间的推移“越发敬重卡莱尔”，“对真理的热爱，对内在卓越、对思想和道德价值的诚实辨认和无畏守护”，④这些品质令她倾倒。艾略特（George Eliot）对卡莱尔的影响作出肯定的说明，“这个时代所有高等或活跃的头脑都被卡莱尔的作品影响过；最近十或十二年以来所写的英语作品都因为他而发生了改变”。⑤甚至与他意见相左的人也同样受到影响，“虽然一些人最不赞同他的意见，但是《旧衣新裁》的阅读恰恰构成他们精神历史的新纪元”。⑥这样的影响被形象地类比为攀登高峰，“你被一条向上通往阿尔卑斯山顶峰的路激励着，却因在顶峰看到了神圣之物而变得平静，充满敬畏之情”。⑦

卡莱尔崇高的声誉建立在他对工业社会准确的判断和把握基础之上。实现社会的良性发展，可谓他的责任所在。如马志尼（Giuseppe Mazzini）所说，“卡莱尔有意识担负起寻找治理社会弊病的责任，并且从未停止过尽责”。⑧他所在的维多利亚时代经历了巨大的变动。这一变动主要表现在社会制度方面，总体趋势是英国“正在快速地失去中世纪特征”。⑨这一变动进一步被视为新与旧，或者传统与现代之间的转变。“以往的封建和农业秩序，被民主和工业社会取代”。⑩卡莱尔很早便有留意，并进行了一定的观察。大学修业期

---

① *Recent British Philosophy*, p. 236.

② *Darwins, Carlyle, and Dickens*, pp. 47 – 48. Besides, for Carlyle's influences upon Dickens, especially *Bleak House*, see appendix Ⅰ.

③ *Discourses in America*, pp. 142 – 143.

④ *Letters*, Vol. Ⅱ, p. 202.

⑤ Quoted in Seigel, ed., *The Critical Heritage*, Intro., p. 3.

⑥ Quoted in Seigel, ed., *The Critical Heritage*, Intro., p. 3.

⑦ Quoted in Seigel, ed., *The Critical Heritage*, Intro., p. 409.

⑧ “Genio e Tendenze di Tomaso Carlyle,” p. 222.

⑨ Neff, *Carlyle and Mill*, p. 61.

⑩ Houghton, *The Victorian Frame of Mind*, p. 4.

间，他便开始留意时事的发展。“拿破仑的倒台”、“法国大革命”以及“战争结束后苏格兰的遭遇”等，是他观察和思考的主要对象。① 19 世纪 20 年代前后，他在书信中多次提到贫穷问题。② 这一时期，他深信“英格兰和苏格兰社会的根基出现了严重的危机”，“人民状况问题”是他经常谈论的话题。③ 他甚至在笔记（Feb. 1829）中记录道，“我最想做的事情就是了解英格兰，了解我们这个岛国社会生活的本质”（Nt. B.，132）。1830 年前后，《时代的标记》和《特征》两篇重要的社会批评文章发表。④《时代的标记》可谓卡莱尔“对当代社会思想的第一个主要贡献”，堪称“英国社会批评传统中的一个重要成分”。⑤《特征》标志着他已经成为“具备一定实力的社会评论家”。⑥ 总体而言，两篇文章都是“对当代思想直接、公开的抨击”。⑦ 通过这两部作品，“卡莱尔 *in propria persona*［本人］发展为社会批评家和文化先知”。⑧

---

① Froude, *First Forty Years*, Vol. Ⅰ, p. 29.

② Around the 1820s, the prevalence of poverty among the masses, especially among the working classes, is mentioned several times in his letters. In a letter to John Carlyle (11th Nov. 1819), "much poverty" is found to exist "among the lowest orders," a "crisis" that "seems anxiously anticipated by all" (Let. 1, Ⅰ, 245). In another latter to the same addressee (26th Jan. 1820), "the common people" are described to be "in great distress," a distress that "is less felt here [i. e. in Edinburgh] than in manufacturing districts" (271). "The use of arms for the purpose of suppressing the imaginary revolts of the lower orders" by the ruling classes, "the substantial burghers and other idle loyalists," only draws "a bitter smile" from Carlyle "at the selfishness and stupidity of men" (271 - 272).

In 1822, his father, James, then a farmer, draws to his mind the deteriorating condition of agriculture in England. It is a period in which "times are very bad for farmers" (from James Carlyle; Ⅱ, 19). It is so impressive with him that it is kept in Carlyle's memory for years. In *Reminiscences*, he remembers that James says to him "that the lot of a poor man was growing worse and worse; that the world could not and would not last as it was; but mighty change, of which none saw the end, were on the way" (Rem. 1, Ⅰ, 48). Carlyle sympathizes with James by deploring at "such a fate as sometimes overtakes the improvident or unfortunate cultivator of the soil in our days" (22nd Feb. 1822; L. - B., 106). He, immersed in the Lockean and Humean doctrines as he is at that time, looks to legislative reformation as the solution to the problem, asserting that "something permanently beneficial to the farming interests must be effected soon by the Legislature: the state of the Country imperiously requires it" (to James Carlyle, 5th Feb. 1822; Let. 1, Ⅱ, 45).

③ Froude, op. cit., Vol. Ⅰ, p. 52.

④ See "Characteristics," *Edinburgh Review*, Vol. LⅣ (1831), pp. 351 - 383.

⑤ 威廉斯：《文化与社会》，第 107 页。

⑥ Campbell, *Thomas Carlyle*, p. 177.

⑦ Roe, *The Social Philosophy of Carlyle and Ruskin*, p. 61.

⑧ Carlyle, *Sartor Resartus*, Oxford World's Classics, Intro., p. xvii.

1830—1831 年创作《旧衣新裁》期间，他的一些主要社会思想已经形成，并写入作品。① 1831—1832 年的伦敦之行给了他直接观察社会现状的机会，社会危机可谓触目惊心。② 在拜访期间（Aug. 1833），艾默生（Ralph Waldo Emerson）对他的社会意识留有深刻的印象。"［卡莱尔］总会返回到英国的贫困、拥挤的国家以及公众人物对本应完成的任务的放弃"等话题。③

迁居伦敦（May 1834）后，卡莱尔对社会状况的观察、分析与评论开始常态化。《法国大革命》既是一部历史作品，同时也是一个社会预言。"革命所造成的恐惧"对于卡莱尔而言"是一种惩罚，专门降临在与神圣天意相背离的社会之上，在这样的社会里，神意的存在遭到了否定，所有先前作为神圣天意超然存在的象征已经变成了明显的虚假的陈设，特别是这个社会的统治阶级已经忘记了它被赋予的神圣职责，其中最主要的是他们被授予的统治权，他们记得的只是自身的特权和享乐"。④ 很明显，卡莱尔在法国大革命和英国现状之间发现了关联，并将前者看作后者的警示。在《宪章运动》（"Chartism，" 1839）中，"英格兰现状问题"被首次提出（Wks.，XXIX，118）。该作品可谓"在卡莱尔的全部著作中，是一部最优秀的关于社会批评的著作"。⑤《过去和现在》是卡莱尔社会批评的巅峰之作。这部著作"是卡莱尔所有关于社会问题的著作中内容最丰富、影响最大的一本，而且，因为公众的注意力正集中于那些社会问题，此书的出版适逢其时"。⑥ 作品被时论评价为"清新的兴奋剂，甜于美酒"。⑦ 艾默生称之为"一位强大的、有成就

---

① For the social doctrines in *Sartor Resartus*, cf. Carlyle, Sar., Intro., pp. xlvii – li.

② In a letter to his mother（10th Nov. 1831），Carlyle depicts the conditions in London as ominous："There is no doubt but these are threatening times, full of risk and distress：a country agitated with political discontent, with economical embarrassment；the lower orders, strained by want；exasperated by disappointment, all ready for any kind of change, whether by revolt or otherwise；nowhere any Wisdom, any Faithfulness to give them counsel；and now while the dark Winter is setting in, a pestilential malady arrived on our coasts, to carry off doubtless many into the land of Silence!"（Let. 2, Ⅰ, 360）.

③ Shepherd, *Memoirs*, Vol. Ⅰ, p. 125.

④ Le Quesne, *Carlyle*, p. 41. 译文参考段忠桥译本（《卡莱尔》，外国著名思想家译丛，中国社会科学出版社 1987 年版），个别地方为行文方便，略有改动，不一一注明。下同。

⑤ Le Quesne, *Carlyle*, p. 48.

⑥ Le Quesne, *Carlyle*, p. 67.

⑦ Seigel, ed., op. cit., p. 213.

的思想家的作品，最近几年以来他便以带有透视力的目光观察英格兰可怖的状况”。① 即使对作品持批评和否定态度的人也不得不承认，“总体而言这是一部神奇的作品；每句话都充满思想，每一部分都完美相互联系”。②《黑人问题偶论》（*Occasional Discourse on the Negro Question*，1849）毁誉参半。作品在被看作“对全部虚假人道主义者的辛辣讽刺”的同时，也被认为“在思想和倾向上不言而喻地邪恶，会激起每一个心思健全读者的惊讶和反感”。③《晚近文集》备受争议，是卡莱尔的声望由极盛而衰的转折。

卡莱尔的社会批评，并不是完全客观的社会研究。相反，他的许多社会观点带有强烈的主观色彩，以他带有鲜明个体性的个人经历为基础。这一点，在《旧衣新裁》中即可得到体现。狄奥根尼（Diogenes Teufelsdröckh）便将自己的信仰危机归因于时代特征。“我们的时代是非信仰的时代”（Sar.，112），在此环境下，个人信仰问题成为时代问题的一个个体化表现，个人与时代之间建立起关联。这一点也为丁尼生（G. B. Tennyson）认同。“虽然卡莱尔的处理方式在当时的英语世界具有独特性，但是这一［宗教信仰危机］经验居于19世纪对世界回应的中心地位。”④ 同样，他对功利主义（utilitarianism）的批评和反抗，以人的二元构成为基础。“卡莱尔在功利主义问题上的立场在很大程度上可以归结为他将人看作由两个不可协调的方面构成：一方面是内在的，可以辨认永恒、幻象和心灵；另一方面是表层的、肤浅的，导向自爱和‘算数性质的理解’。”⑤ 具有明显个体性的对人的构成的理解，在此与社会原则构成对立。最后，在他对社会机械论（social mechanism）的理解中，个体经验同样扮演着重要的角色。“他社会批评的关键要素之一便是他看到‘机械’的内在和外在含义，理解科技变化的情感效果。”⑥ 在卡莱尔思想中存在的个体经验普遍化的倾向，是他的作品在维多利亚时代得到接受和敬重的根源。“与我们对卡莱尔的作品所形成的认识相一致，最令我们愉悦的，便

① Seigel, ed., op. cit., p. 219.
② Seigel, ed., op. cit., p. 227.
③ Seigel, ed., op. cit., pp. 310, 311.
④ *Sartor Called Resartus*, p. 303.
⑤ Welch, “Thomas Carlyle on Utilitarianism,” p. 380.
⑥ Sussman, “Transcendentalism and the Machine,” p. 35.

是这些在特征上完全是个体性的作品，令读者处于自省的状态。"① 这一倾向并非为卡莱尔独有。穆勒（John Stuart Mill）的《自传》（*Autobiography*）和纽曼（John Newman）的《自辩》（*Apologia pro Vita sua*）在很大程度上可以与《旧衣新裁》相媲美。这些作品都"建立在认为个体经验是理解社会问题以及人与宇宙关系的关键这一认识之上"。② 个体经验的普遍化既是卡莱尔社会批评的特征，也是时代趋势，两者交融在一起，成就了卡莱尔一代"时代精神的代言人"的身份和地位。③

理解卡莱尔的思想，有必要理解他的个人经历。在成为"实事的跟进评论者"之前，④ 他经历了剧烈的思想转变。这一转变可以以正题（thesis）、反题（antithesis）和合题（synthesis）概而括之。正题是他从小所接受的加尔文主义思想（Calvinism），这一根基性的思想在启蒙主义教育反题的冲击下瓦解，两者最后通过德国思想的纳入而实现合题。综合后的思想是他日后进行社会观察、分析、研究和批评的背景和底色，决定了他社会思想的所有基本内容。理解卡莱尔的精神发展史，有必要从最初的正题开始。

一 加尔文主义思想

卡莱尔从小便生活在具有浓郁加尔文主义色彩的家庭氛围里。同"许多苏格兰人一样"，他们"家庭里的加尔文主义氛围"非常"强烈"、十分"严苛"。⑤ 父亲詹姆士（James Carlyle）是一个虔诚的加尔文教信徒。据卡莱尔回忆，在所有同辈亲属之间，只有他"具有明确的宗教情感"（Rem.[1]，Ⅰ，33）。这种宗教情感的获得是他"全部机能共识"的结果（14），可谓自然天成。他有"每天给自己或者家人阅读《圣经》"的习惯，并知晓一定数量的加尔文教经典。⑥ 宗教是詹姆士看待世界、进行价值判断的基础。他"所有的

① Seigel，ed.，op. cit.，p. 213.

② Dibble，*The Pythia's Drunken Song*，p. 71.

③ Tillotson，"Carlyle，" p. 57.

④ Tillotson，"Carlyle，" p. 55.

⑤ Schapiro，"Thomas Carlyle，Prophet of Fascism，" p. 97.

⑥ Kaplan，*Thomas Carlyle*，pp. 21，21 – 22.

观点”，几乎全部“深入地根植于加尔文教之中”。[①] 卡莱尔对此有深刻的认识。“宗教是我父亲的原则：他虽粗野、未经开化，但是宗教让他‘在所有方面成为一个人’。”（15）在宗教方面，卡莱尔深受父亲影响。詹姆士所树立的“榜样”，对托马斯而言是“最早的”，而且是“最为重要的”。[②] 母亲玛格丽特（Margaret Aitken Carlyle）同样怀有强烈的加尔文主义宗教情怀。在卡莱尔的回忆中，她是“一位血统最为高贵的女性；一位虔诚、公正和明智的女性”（42）。与父亲相比，“母亲的影响几乎同样深远”。[③] 作为“一位加尔文主义者”，玛格丽特相信“汤姆的命运已经永久地确定下来”。[④] 这一具有浓郁加尔文主义色彩的命定论思想，在卡莱尔的作品之中也有表现。卡莱尔从小便沉浸在这种家庭氛围之中。他的加尔文主义思想，便在这样的家庭氛围里形成。这一经历甚至被移嫁给狄奥根尼。他从小所接受的“教育”同样是“宗教性的”（Sar.，99）。

对上帝存在的无条件接受，位居卡莱尔加尔文主义思想的核心。在所有主要作品里，对上帝存在的伸张是一条贯穿的主题。在《旧衣新裁》中，上帝被认为存在于自然和人。“自然”是“上帝活着的、可见的衣服”（55），而“人自身不过是上帝的象征而已”（220）。在《法国大革命》中，革命产生的根源在于对上帝存在的无视。“他们在自己头上看不到上帝，或者除了通过天文望远镜外，他们也不屑仰视。”（Rev.，32）[⑤] 在《英雄和英雄崇拜》中，穆罕默德（Mahomet）成为卡莱尔加尔文主义信条的代言人。“上帝创造了大地，［……］上帝创造了你们，‘用一小块泥土塑造了你们’。”（H. & H.，68）。[⑥] 在《过去和现在》中，上帝被看作事实。“［上帝的信息］是事实，以奇迹般的雷霆之音再一次从世界的中心传递出来；对于少数的倾听者

---

① Heffer, *Moral Desperado*, p. 28.

② Campbell, op. cit., p. 173.

③ Heffer, op. cit., p. 28.

④ Garnett, *Life of Thomas Carlyle*, p. 12.

⑤ 本书所有《法国大革命》的引文参考刘毅译本（吉林出版集团股份有限公司 2017 年版），个别地方为行文方便，略有改动，不一一注明。下同。

⑥ 本书所有《英雄与英雄崇拜》的引文参考周祖达译本（商务印书馆 2010 年版），个别地方为行文方便，略有改动，不一一注明。下同。

而言，这声音清晰、不可否认、严厉且有益。”（P. & P.，34）同样的主题也出现在《晚近文集》之中。“如果我们‘违背上帝而行罪’，非常明显‘上帝的审判’就会降临。”（Wks.，XX，298）

在卡莱尔的加尔文主义思想之中，信仰被置于至高无上的地位。这一点被转化为对虔敬（sincerity）的强调。他“从未停止过重复，虔敬可以贯穿人所有层面的活动”。[①] 作为上帝意志的代言人，英雄的核心品质表现在虔敬之上。“在我看来，虔敬是伟人和他的一切言行的根基。”（H. & H.，45）“应该说，虔敬，即一种深沉的、崇高而纯粹的虔敬，是各种不同英雄人物的首要特征。”（Ibid.）诗人的卓越也表现在虔敬之上。“彭斯的卓越便是［……］他的虔敬，这种对真理不可辩驳的追求。”（Wks.，XXVI，267）“歌德作为一位诗人和思想家的个性”，便“以虔敬为真正的根基，表现出虔敬的特征”（249）。同样，工业社会问题的解决也依靠虔敬。中世纪的社会以虔敬为规范方式。“有必要看到，对于［参孙修道院院长］而言，有关首先需要完成的任务的虔敬性洞见引导他们走向了成功之路，假以时日他们也的确实现了成功。”（P. & P.，243）与之相应，工业社会只有以虔敬为规范方式，所有的社会危机才可以解决。

卡莱尔的加尔文主义思想以对幸福的否定为主要特征。“浪漫主义关于具有创造性的想象的观点”，在一定程度上存在于卡莱尔的“加尔文主义诠释”之中。[②] 据此人被视为上帝的象征，目的并非在于幸福的实现。“在人之中，有一个比对幸福的热爱更高等的存在；人没有幸福同样可行，反而会因此而得到保佑。”（Sar.，192）狄奥根尼甚至将此看作思想转变和信仰恢复的表现。“不要热爱快乐，而要热爱上帝。这就是永恒的肯定，其中所有的矛盾全部化解。”（Ibid.）在极端情况下，对幸福的追求甚至被降低到最低水平。断念（renunciation）是卡莱尔加尔文主义思想的极端形式。所谓断念即“将回报的夙愿降低至无”（191），即不将幸福作为目的。断念被视为人生的起点。

① Yandell，op. cit.，p. 20.

② Anger，“Carlyle，” p. 82.

“只有通过断念（*Entsagen*），[1] 真正意义上的人生才可谓开始。”（Ibid.）断念的存在，使得卡莱尔的加尔文主义获得强烈的“廊下派思想”（Stoicism）特征，也使之“教条性弱化”。[2] 在卡莱尔的加尔文主义思想中，断念还存在道德化的倾向。“自我的湮没”可谓“最为首要的道德条款”（186）。其实现与否，直接关系到有关世界本质的洞见可否获得。只有在断念在自我湮没的情况下，“心灵的眼睛才不是封闭的，心灵的双手才不是被束缚的”（Ibid.）。家庭环境，对这一思想的形成具有一定的塑造意义。“虽然笑声偶尔可以在卡莱尔一家之中听到，但是愉悦无人知晓，快乐是一种罪，幸福是极力避免的状态。”[3] 这种具有禁欲特征的家庭氛围融入了卡莱尔的加尔文主义思想。

卡莱尔的加尔文主义思想最终落实为行动。在此，宗教信仰获得道德表现。如卡佳明（Louis Cazamian）所言，卡莱尔的“宗教意志以行动为终结；是行动神圣而有效的保证”。[4] 行动被进一步转化为对责任的强调。在致妹妹的信中，卡莱尔认为“你如何表现是无限重要的事情：即使你有一个王国，或者二十个王国，与此相比都无足轻重，这便是你需要按照上帝的命令行事，你需要履行对上帝和所有人的责任”（23rd Jan. 1832；L.－S.，44）。可见，信仰便是履行责任，而行动则是履行责任的表现。在《旧衣新裁》中，狄奥根尼最终将信仰转化为行动。“当此时还是今天的时候工作吧；如果黑夜来临，我们便无工可做了。”（197）在这段道德劝诫之中，信仰是劳动的来源，而劳动是信仰的检验。在《过去和现在》中，行动甚至与信仰直接等同：

Laborare est Orare（P. & P.，205）[5]

这里所谓的“Laborare”并非简单的劳动，而是“将不可见之物表现出

---

① “*Entsagen*”是德语，含义为“断念”（to renounce）。
② Harrold，“The Nature of Carlyle's Calvinism，”pp. 477－478.
③ Hanson，*Necessary Evil*，p. 21.
④ *Carlyle*，pp. 16－17.
⑤ 拉丁语，含义为“劳动即是崇拜”（to work is to worship）。

来”的过程（Ibid.）。在这种具有强烈宗教意义的行动里，“不可见的力量［即上帝］会垂怜这样的人；他为不可见之物工作，在不可见之物的恩典下工作”（Ibid.）。在卡莱尔的现实经历中，詹姆士的事迹为他产生上述思想树立了榜样。父亲的宗教情感便直接转化为行动的动力。他亲手所建的房屋不但是卡莱尔的出生地，① 更被视为“人自由意志福音的文本”（Rem.[1]，I，3）。在詹姆士的身边，卡莱尔从小便耳濡目染“工作（无论是物质性的还是精神性的）是我们唯一需要做的事情；所有的原则和榜样都教给我们要好好完成工作”（44）。这种建立在家庭生活经历基础上的工作福音，得到了普遍的接受。“对于［卡莱尔］的同时代人，工作福音极具吸引力。”② 卡莱尔作为一代先知和智者的身份，在很大程度上依赖于他对劳动和责任所持有的观点。

加尔文主义思想对于理解卡莱尔的社会观具有重要的参照意义。总体而言，卡莱尔对社会的思考主要聚焦于权利的合理性问题。“放任主义（*Laissez-faire*）、竞争和供求关系”等作为社会的规范方式（P. & P.，189），在他看来并不合理。非常明显，社会权利的合理性并未被认为仅仅建立在经济基础之上。虽然卡莱尔从未明确表达，但是此处蕴含的意义十分明显，社会在结构和复杂性方面是高于经济的总体。任何建立在以局部代替整体基础之上的权利，在合理性上都面临着挑战。与工业社会权利结构不同，卡莱尔将社会权利的来源视为神意，即上帝的法则。“这个宇宙有其法则。如果我们以法行事，则法则的制定者与我们为善；若否，则不善。”（30）这样，只有可以解读神意的有识之士才可以成为社会权利的行使人。这便是卡莱尔所谓的英雄，他们是“灿烂夺目的光源，能使接近者受益与愉悦，其闪烁的光芒照亮了世界的黑暗。它不仅像盏明灯，更像上帝赐予的日月光辉；如我所说，这是一种体现天赋创见、豪迈刚毅和英勇崇高品德的永不熄灭的光源；——在其光辉的照耀下，人人都会感到受惠无穷”（H. & H.，1-2）。在此意义上，只有英雄崇拜才被视为合理的社会规范方式。“英雄崇拜［……］是人类所有社会

① Froude，op. cit.，Vol. Ⅰ，p. 2.

② Campbell，op. cit.，p. 178.

事务的灵魂。”（P. & P. ，39）社会的管制，即英雄崇拜的良性开展。非常遗憾，英雄崇拜也不过是局部而已。以英雄崇拜替代放任主义和供求关系等经济手段，不过是一局部替代另一局部。卡莱尔社会观的局限，在此得到一定的体现。他提出的替代方案，在结构上与他否定的对象如出一辙。

以上便是卡莱尔加尔文主义思想的概貌。这一思想来源于他早年的成长经历，是生活过程和家庭氛围综合在一起共同产生的效果。特别是父亲的言行和榜样，对于卡莱尔加尔文主义思想的形成具有重要的促进意义。对上帝存在的非理性接受，位居这一思想的核心。一个不可见的上帝潜在于万事万物，构成信仰的主要内容。对此信仰的反复重申贯穿卡莱尔几乎所有的主要作品，是解读他的思想一条重要的线索和脉络。对信仰地位的强化，发展为对虔敬的强调。作为一项具有本质意义的主要属性，虔敬被赋予给英雄、诗人以及其他社会权利的行使人。在卡莱尔的加尔文主义思想里，人与上帝被置于表现与被表现的象征性关系之中。作为神意的工具和手段，人的目的并不在于幸福。在极端情况下，具有强烈廊下派思想特征的断念被视为人的最终目的。卡莱尔的加尔文主义思想最终指向行动，终结于人的劳动或者工作。在终结阶段，信仰与道德融为一体。道德实践成为判断宗教信仰的基础和依据。对于卡莱尔社会观，特别是对于他英雄崇拜为主要内容的社会理想的理解，加尔文主义思想是不容或缺的要素。社会权利的合理性，主要来源于这个加尔文教的上帝。只有少数的选民，才可以成为上帝意志的代言人以及社会权利的拥有者。在此，政教合而为一。这与现代社会的主要特征之一背道而驰。在此意义上，卡莱尔的建立在加尔文主义思想基础之上的社会观具有明显的反现代性。

总体而言，卡莱尔的加尔文主义思想具有明显的非理性特征。对信仰和虔敬的强调、对幸福的否定和断念等因素的存在以及宗教信仰和道德实践的转化等内容，均是这一特征的表现。强烈的非理性特征，是卡莱尔加尔文主义思想危机产生的隐患和根源。在他接受启蒙教育的过程中，宗教信仰危机爆发而来。

二 启蒙教育

卡莱尔于1809年进入爱丁堡大学求学。此前，他接受过一定的基础教育，甚至在数学和语言学习等方面表现出一定的天赋。① 通过大学教育获得一份神职，是他的家庭，特别是他的母亲的一份夙愿。“还在很早的时候，母亲的雄心便是卡莱尔注定在教会从业。”② 然而，他在大学期间接受的教育并不

---

① In his preschool ages, Carlyle is taught to do arithmetic by his father, and to do reading by his mother (Heffer, *Moral Desperado*, p. 29). It is "in [his] fifth year," as he remembers, that "his teaching [him, i. e. Carlyle] Arithmetical things: especially how to divide" begins (Carlyle, Rem.[1], Ⅰ, 45). His first school experience comes only locally and he distinguishes himself as a competent learner in mathematics and classical languages. He is reported by "the schoolmaster in Ecclefechan" to have "a good account of his progress in 'figures'," and by "the minister" to be proliferate in "his Latin" (Froude, *First Forty Years*, Vol. Ⅰ, p. 11). He is then (1801), on account of the inferiority of the local village school in reputation (Kaplan, *Thomas Carlyle*, p. 23), sent, by his parents, to a "Tom Donaldson's School at Ecclefechan," who, obviously a student "from Edinburgh College" though only for "one session probably" and "a severely correct young man," is "always merry & kind to [Carlyle]" while "harsh & to the ill – deserving severe" (Carlyle, Rem.[3], 29 – 30). The next year, he enters Hoddam School. He, there, on the basis of the judgment given by Sandy Beattie of him as "complete in English," is considered as in great need of "go [ing] into Latin" in order not to "waste [his] time" (30). As "the poor Schoolmaster [does] not himself know Latin," Carlyle, in consequence, "[gets] altogether swamped and bewildered under him" (Ibid.). After that, some help is sought, at first, from a reverent Mr. Johnstone, "the venerablest & most venerated Clerical Person [he has] ever seen," and, then, from his son, when "home from College" (Ibid.). Though Latin is taught by the younger Johnstone "in a careless but intelligent manner," Carlyle, "once pulled afloat again," still " [makes] rapid & sure way" (Ibid.).

The next important stage in his pre – university education is the entrance into Annan Grammar School. His experiences there is partially integrated, as "historical," into "the account of the first launch of Teufelsdröckh into the Hinterschlag Gymnasium" (Froude, *First Forty Years*, Vol. Ⅰ, p. 11). He remembers to be " [taken] dawn to Annan Academy on the Whitsunday morning, 1806," he "trotting at [his father's] side," in the same way as Teufelsdröchk does (Rem.[1], Ⅰ, 46). As it is the first time that he takes leave of his parents, left to " [be] among strangers, harshly, at best indifferently, disposed towards [him]," orphanage and loneliness is the main characteristic in his first impression at the school (Sar., 103). The education at Annan is said by Carlyle as "limited, and of its kind only moderately good" (Froude, Ibid., Vol. Ⅰ, p. 13). It is composed of "Latin and French," which Carlyle " [gets] to read with fluency," "some geometry," "algebra," "arithmetic," "vague outlines of geography," and the elemental knowledge of "Greek" in the form of only "alphabet" (Ibid.). Carlyle's performance at Annan as a student is outstanding and "the reports from the Annan masters [are] all favourable" (Ibid., p. 16). It is then decided as necessary for him to continue his education at Edinburgh University. November 1809, he, entrusted by his parents to "the charge of a carter" and "another university – bound boy," to walk, only with "a two – volume Bible" given as a present from his mother "to keep him company," to the destination, feeling lonely all the way there (Kaplan, Ibid., p. 28).

The above, in summary, is the outline of Carlyle's education before the entrance into university.

② Cazamian, op. cit., p. 19.

十分正规。如他自己所言，“他从大学所学甚少”。[①] 在古典语言学习方面，他的表现比较平庸。拉丁语课程主讲教师甚至未能将他与另外一位同姓学生区分开来。[②] 据本人回忆，他在这一领域仅限于阅读大量的古代经典文献。[③] 在哲学学习方面，他虽然建树甚少，但是大学期间的某些见闻和经历极有可能对他日后的阅读选择产生了深刻的影响。特别是苏格兰启蒙运动的代表人物斯图尔特（Dugald Stewart）此前曾经在此校进行过专题讲座，虽然他“在卡莱尔入学前两年离开”，[④] 但是对于理解后者有关英国经验主义哲学传统书籍以及法国启蒙作家的代表作品阅读兴趣的形成具有一定的参考价值。[⑤] 在所有科目当中，卡莱尔在数学方面的表现最为优异。“只有在数学上，他才取得了真正的进步”。[⑥]

大学求学期间，卡莱尔并未将大量优势时间投入神学研究之中。“在神学之外，他的阅读种类十分多样，但是总体上是文学性质的”。[⑦] 他所读的文学类书目主要包括库克（James Cook）的《游记》（*Voyages*）、拜伦（Lord Byron）的《叙事诗》（*Narrative*）、莎士比亚的剧作、《天方夜谭》（*Arabian*

---

① Froude, op. cit., Vol. Ⅰ, p. 20.

② Froude, op. cit., Vol. Ⅰ, p. 20.

③ During the university years, in the field of classical studies, Carlyle, as he remembers, "[learns] to read [Homer] in the original with difficulty, after Wolf's broad flash of light thrown into it; Æschyius and Sophocles mainly in translations. Tacitus and Virgil [becomes] really interesting to [him]; Homer and Æschyius above all; Horace egoistical, leichtfertig, in sad face [he] never [cares] for; Cicero, after long and various trials, always [proves] a windy person and a weariness to [him], extinguished altogether by Middleton's excellent though misjudging life of him" (Froude, *First Forty Years*, Vol. Ⅰ, p. 20).

Carlyle's competency in classical languages is, on the whole, common and mediocre. He, before the entrance into Edinburgh University, "[has] been so [...] grounded in Latin at Annan School," and "to the end of his life, at all events, he" is classifiable as "a fair Latinist" (Masson, *Edinburgh Sketches & Memories*, p. 230). He, in terms of Greek, however, never [... makes] any pretence, either during the school years or in later life (Ibid.).

④ Froude, op. cit., Vol. Ⅰ, p. 20.

⑤ Cazamian holds a much more optimistic opinion of Carlyle's presence in Stewart's lectures and, in accordance, of the latter's influences upon the former. "Il [i. e. Carlyle] peut entendre les dernières leçons de Dugald Stewart, dont les coeurs attiraient d'Écosse et d'Angleterre un nombreux public" (*Carlyle*, p. 20). His view upon the role of Stewart in drawing Carlyle to the Enlightenment literature, however, is, at best, doubtful. "Ce n'est pas de lui," according to him, "que Carlyle devait recevoir l'illumination et l'initiation philosophiques; il parla, plus tard, de l'école écossaise avec respect, sans le moindre enthousiasme" (Ibid.).

⑥ Froude, op. cit., Vol. Ⅰ, p. 21.

⑦ Cazamian, op. cit., p. 20.

Nights)、勒萨热（Alain-René Lesage）的《吉尔·布拉斯》（*Gil Blas*）以及艾迪逊（Joseph Addison）和斯蒂尔（Richard Steele）主编的《旁观者》（*Spectator*）。[①] 此外，他还阅读了一定数量的历史作品，包括罗伯特逊（William Robertson）的《苏格兰历史》（*History of Scotland*）、吉朋（Edward Gibbon）的《罗马帝国衰亡史》（*Decline and Fall of the Roman Empire*）和休姆（David Hume）的《英国史》（*The History of England*）等。[②] 虽然这些书目并未与启蒙思想直接相关，但是卡莱尔的阅读选择所表现出来的变化在其中可以得到明显的体现。特别是吉朋和休姆的历史作品，[③] 是此后他阅读启蒙作品的先导。在阅读中，卡莱尔培养起独立思考的习惯。据弗劳德（James Anthony Froude）所述，卡莱尔本人曾经透露，"只有在孤独之中，他的思想才会以合适的形式呈现出来"。[④] 这种习惯的养成一方面固然与卡莱尔本人孤僻的性格相关，[⑤] 另一方面在一定程度上也是他思想转向的表现。大量启蒙思想的摄入使他意识到，"在知识界有一些思想潮流与他父母的信仰不可调和"。[⑥]

1814 年，卡莱尔从爱丁堡大学毕业。毕业之后，他一方面以教书为业，

---

① Masson, *Edinburgh Sketches & Memories*, p. 231.

② Masson, *Edinburgh Sketches & Memories*, p. 231.

③ Froude even adds "Hume's Essays" to Carlyle's reading list during his university years (*First Forty Years*, Vol. Ⅰ, p. 29.

④ Froude, op. cit., Vol. Ⅰ, p. 21.

⑤ A great variety of sources mention loneliness, shyness, seriousness and exclusiveness as the peculiarities in Carlyle's character. Before he enters school, Carlyle is noted as "a shy thoughtful boy, shrinking generally from rough companions" (Froude, *First Forty Years*, Vol. Ⅰ, p. 11). As a child, "son caractère se montrait déjà fier, méditatif, solitaire; d'une gravité au-dessus de son âge, il se mêlait rarement aux jeux de ses camarades" (Cazamian, *Carlyle*, p. 19). He is even exaggerated to "[have] never learned to smile, to laugh freely, to open his mind, to display his many good qualities" (Hanson, *Necessary Evil*, p. 21). Secluded in a sense, he "[makes] no friends, and [begins] to take a savage pleasure in his isolation" (Ibid.). The character of James, his father, plays an important role in the formation of his own. "Ainsi le dédain paternel serait devenu, à un degré plus haut, le fameux Silence du fils; cette foideur hautaine du premier pour les menues paroles et les menus faits charriés en myriades par la vie courante, pour les innombrables verbosités et activités inconscientes où s'éparpille et se perd l'immense trésor sombre et rayonnant de la Conscience, — aurait tourné chez le second, sa sensibilité propre et ses études particulières aidant, en faculté métaphysique et stoïque: car la pensée de Carlyle paraît parfois singuilièrement dure, par excès de sensibilité, comme le caractère du père était escarpé et triste par excès de conscience" (Barthèlemy, *Thomas Carlyle*, p. 13). Loneliness in character, in the main, is the cause of Carlyle's seclusion from the crowd.

⑥ Shine, *Carlyle's Fusion of Poetry, History, and Religion by 1834*, p. 3.

虽然“他从未喜欢过教书”；另一方面继续保持他的阅读习惯，“将自己与书籍锁在一起”。① 1814—1819 年是卡莱尔启蒙思想作品阅读的高峰时期。这一期间，从文学性作品到思想性的转变可以在他的阅读选择之中反映出来。②

---

① Froude, op. cit., Vol. Ⅰ, p. 27.

② In the year 1814, Carlyle gives a list of his readings: fiction, Jane Porter's *Thaddeus of Warsaw* (Let.[1], Ⅰ, 7), *Scottish Chiefs* (18), *Waverley* (18, 19); history, Bossuet's *History of Mathematics* (6); poetry, John Leyden's *Scene of Infancy* (7-8), Byron's *Poems* (18), Scott's *Poems* (Ibid.), William Wilkie's *Leonidas*, the *Epigoniad* (Ibid.), Cauclor's *Poems* (Ibid.); drama, Shakespeare (10, 18); translation, John Hoole's Tasso (18), Sotheby's version of Wieland's *Oberon* (Ibid.). Obviously, fiction, poetry and literary translations occupy a dominant proportion.

In the year 1815, his reading list is as follows: philosophy, Cicero, *De Officiis* (33), *De Finibus* (33N), Dugald Stewart's *Elements of the Philosophy of the Human Mind* (39), David Hume's *Essays* (41), works upon the Epicurean, Stoic, Platonist and Sceptic (42), Sir Benjamin Thompson, Count Rumford's *Essays* (51), Berkeley's *Principle of Knowledge* (Ibid.), Dugald Stewart's *Essays* (Ibid.); poetry, Voltaire's *La Pucelle d'Orléans* (34); science, Simpson's *Fluxion* (51); review and journal, *Quarterly Review* (39), *Edinburgh Review* (46-47); miscellany, Lord Chesterfield's *Letters* (33-34), Mackenzie's *Travels* (51), Humboldt's *New Spain* (Ibid.). The rise in philosophical readings is the most notable in this year, which, safely, may serve as the mark of transition in Carlyle's choice of books.

In the year 1816, the same tendency is still detectable in Carlyle's readings: science, Bossuet's *History of Mathematics* (64), Wood's *Optics* (64), Cunn's *Euclid* (64), Newton's *Philosophiæ Naturalis Principia Mathematica* (64, 65, 73), Leslie's *Trigonometry* (71-72), Delambre's *Abrégé d'Astronomie* (73), Wood's *Optics* (73), John Keill's *Introductio ad Veram Physicam* (74); philosophy, Lucan's *Pharsalia* (64), Flaccus's *Poemata* (71), Xenophon's *Anabasis* (72), Stewart's *History of Philosophy* (81-82); theology, François Fénelon's *Dialogues des Morts* (64); poetry, Scott's *Waterloo* (65); fiction, Scott's *Guy Mannering* (Ibid.); biography, Thomas Mortimer's *The British Plutarch* (69); poetry, Crabbe's *Poems* (73); review and journal, Addison's *Spectator* (69); miscellany, Chesterfield's *Letters* (69-70), John Hamilton Moore's *Practical Navigator* (71), *Encyclopædia Britannica* (74); translation, Pope's version of Homer (72). Carlyle's readings, it is discoverable, are increasingly becoming philosophical and scientific.

In the year 1817, Carlyle's readings are: philosophy, Stewart's *Philosophy of the Human Mind* (88, 127), Adam Smith's *Wealth of Nations* (101), Pascal's *Lettres Provinciales* (101-102), Madame de Staël's *De l'Allemagne* (119), Flaccus's *Poemata* (125), Francis Bacon's *Essays* (127); Science, Bailly's *Historie d'Astronomie* (102-103, 106), Wallace's *Fluxions* (119, 126); fiction, Scott's *Tales of my Landlord* (89), Matthew Lewis' *Monk* (121); travel, Von Buch's *Travels in Norway and Lapland* (102), Coxe's *Travels* (133); history, Hume's *Hisotry of England* (Ibid.), Edward Gibbon's *Declien and Fall of the Roman Empire* (Ibid.); review and journal, *Scotsman* (91), *Edinburgh Review* (101, 109), *Quarterly Review* (101, 119), *Scotsman* (110), *Literary and Statistical Magazine* (119), *Constable's Magazine* (121), *Blackwood's Magazine* (121, 133), *Edinburgh Magazine* (134). Besides, he mentions the name of David Hume, Toby Smollett and La Rochefoucault without giving the titles of their works that he has read (127-128,

卡莱尔特别提到在好友欧文（Edward Irving）处的阅读经历，印象极为深刻。“欧文的图书馆对于［他］来说用处很大：吉朋、休姆等，［他］一定全部通读了。”（Rem.[1]，Ⅱ，28）特别是吉朋的作品，他“以每天一本的速度读完”（Ibid.）。启蒙性质作品的阅读数量不可谓不大。

启蒙思想的大量摄入彻底地动摇了卡莱尔的宗教信仰，加尔文主义思想的根基开始动摇。早在爱丁堡大学求学期间，卡莱尔的信仰危机便已经开始显露。1810 年夏，他对上帝的存在产生怀疑。“万能的上帝真否降临人间，在店铺里制作独轮手推车”，① 这一问题便是卡莱尔信仰危机的初始表现。非常明显，他开始以不同的角度看待上帝的存在问题。母亲对他的信仰问题忧心忡忡。“她在晚间几个小时都无法入睡，在痛苦中祈祷并痛哭。”② 此后，信仰危机进一步升级。卡莱尔最终决定，不再以神职为业。1818 年，这一决定被

133）. This year witnesses the, if not sudden, then at least conspicuous, appearance of Carlyle's interest in periodicals. It is in the same vein, and shows consanguinity, with his increasing intellectual attachment to the Enlightenment.

These are Carlyle's readings in 1818: philosophy, Hume's *Essays* (146), Chaucer's *Astrolaby* (152), Stewart's *Preliminary Dissertation* (159); science, Leslie's *Conics* (150), Lagrange's *Mécanique Analytique* (Ibid.); history, Hume's *History of England* (142), Gibbon's *Decline and Fall of the Roman Empire* (142 – 143), Watson's *History of the two Philips* (187); fiction, Godwin's *Mandevelle* (146N), Scott's *Rob Roy* (146), Thomas Moore's *Lalla Rookh* (153), Maria Edgeworth's *Harrington and Ormond* (187); poetry, Byron's *Childe Harold* (153); travel, Saussure's *Voyages dans les Alpes* (190); biography, Roscoe's *Life of Lorenzo de' Medici* (193); miscellany, Hazlitt's "Fine Art" and "Standard Novels" (147), *Encyclopædia Britannica* (Ibid.); review and journal, *Edinburgh Review* (147, 153, 155). Besides, he mentions the names of Pascal, Montaigne (162), Epictetus (165), and Frances Dixon (190). For this year, the proportion of the philosophical and literary studies seems to be kept in balance.

Carlyle's readings in the year 1819 are as follows: philosophy, Madame de Staël's *Considerations sur quelques Événements de la Révolution* (213), Bailly's *Mémoires d'un Témoin de la Révolution* (Ibid.); science, Lesage's *Traité de Physique Mécanique* (239); history, Hume's *History of England* (224); travel, Saussure's *Voyages dans les Alpes* (213), Bernardin de Saint – Pierre's *Indian Cottage* (224), Faujas de.

Saint – Fond's *Voyage en Angleterre, en Écosse et aux Iles Hébrides* (239); geography, Bristed's *America and her Resources* (233), Morgan's *France* (239); biography, Jean – Jacques Rousseau's *Confessions* (234); fiction, Scott's *Guy Mannering* (224); poetry, Klopstock's *Messias* (233); review and journal, *Edinburgh Review* (244). Beside, he mentions the names of Sismondi (213), Tasso (238). From the above chronological progress of Carlyle's choices in his readings, so far, books of the philosophical, scientific, historical and geographical themes have occupied a larger proportion in Carlyle's reading choices than those of the fictional, dramatic and poetic ones. Philosophies, histories, sciences, geographies and travels are gradually commanding a prominence in Carlyle's reading list in the years 1814 – 1819.

① Allingham, *A Diary*, p. 253.

② Allingham, *A Diary*, p. 253.

最终确认。“此时，卡莱尔已经放弃了将‘神职’作为未来可能职业的想法。”① 在通信中，未来职业规划的变化也被提到。他对好友（28th Jul. 1818；to Thomas Murray）坦言，“出于多种原因，我已经放弃了有关教堂的打算”（Let. [1]，Ⅰ，165）。他甚至认为“自己不适合神学研究”（27th Nov. 1818；to Robert Mitchell；194）。

信仰危机对卡莱尔的身体健康产生了严重的影响。1818—1821 年，他患上严重的胃肠病。② 1818 年，他提到服药。“几天以来［他］的健康欠佳”，但是药物并未“有减轻病情的趋势”（188 - 189）。至 1821 年，他的健康状况恶化到极点。他在信中（10th Feb. 1821；to John A. Carlyle）提到，“至上周一以来我的病情非常非常严重——事实上，我一天都没有好过”（320）。这一顽症“最为折磨人的形式”被描述为“一只老鼠在他的胃里啃食”。③ 惨状之烈，可见一斑。

理解卡莱尔信仰危机产生的逻辑过程，对于理解危机的性质和后来的解决办法具有重要意义。怀疑（doubt），是卡莱尔信仰危机产生的直接根源。怀疑作为一种视角，彻底地改变了他对上帝存在所怀有的信念。如弗劳德所言，“卡莱尔与他的母亲对宗教进行着同样多的思考，但是他的思维形式与她的并不一样”。④ 如果玛格丽特以信仰（faith）为视角，托马斯则以怀疑观之。在此视角下，卡莱尔意识到“所有的事情并非与教给他去思考的形式一模一样”。⑤ 怀疑最终导致信仰的失效。处于“永恒的否定”之中的狄奥根尼“完全丧失了宗教情怀”，“怀疑黯淡成为无信仰”（Sar.，159）。同样的经历也发生在莱恩弗莱德（Wotton Reinfred）的身上。“能看到的只有怀疑，这惨淡的怀疑，像魅影一样升起，让善的和神圣之物破碎、消失；甚至有些时候，将最为神圣的存在从他眼前遮蔽起来。”（Wds.，32）非常明显，怀疑是信仰失效的逻辑前提。

---

① Froude, op. cit., Vol. Ⅰ, p. 43.

② 关于卡莱尔胃肠病的讨论，参见方志强《炼狱与新生——卡莱尔的病（1814—1823）与雷丝路事件》，《新史学》2006 年第 17 卷第 3 期，第 61—119 页。

③ Froude, op. cit., Vol. Ⅰ, p. 47.

④ Froude, op. cit., Vol. Ⅰ, p. 51.

⑤ Froude, op. cit., Vol. Ⅰ, p. 51.

卡莱尔的怀疑有其内在的运作机制。强烈的实证精神（positivism），表现在卡莱尔式的怀疑之中。实证精神对确定性（certainty）提出了严格的要求。这一点主要来源于卡莱尔大学期间在数学学习方面获得的启发。在他的理解中，数学知识是一种“结论无可争议、每一步都可以带着信心落脚的知识”。① 在一段时间里几何甚至被看作“所有科学之中最为高贵的一门”，值得“将最好的时间和最佳的状态投入其中”。② 与在几何证明中结论有必要建立在确定的前提下一样，卡莱尔要求宗教信仰同样需要以确定的前提为基础。特别是关于上帝存在的信仰，有必要在确定性方面得到证明之后才可以获得合理性。否则，他“拒绝所有的可能性，并拒绝承认任何假设，除非假设可以被直接的、不可反驳的证据支持”（5th Jul. 1817；to Robert Mitchell；Let.[1]，Ⅰ，108）。然而，上帝的存在无法通过感官（senses）察觉。③

① Froude, op. cit., Vol., p. 21.

② Froude, op. cit., Vol., p. 21.

③ In the empirical tradition of the British philosophy, senses, or rather sensible knowledge, are, in general, taken as the certain, and the only certain, knowledge, the ground upon and from which other knowledge, mainly deductive, is to be derived. Such an epistemological view is best represented by John Locke and David Hume, two of the most notable British empiricists. Sensible knowledge is taken by Locke, in *Human Understanding*, as *principia prima*. It is asserted that "*the certainty of things* existing in *rerum natura*, when we have *the testimony of our senses* for it, is not only as great as our frame can attain to, but as our condition needs" (*Human Understanding*, p. 560; B. Ⅳ, Ch. xi, §8; Locke's italicization). It is the same with Hume in *Human Nature*, though in a much more complicated manner. "The objects of knowledge and certainty," *in principio*, are reduced to and as four kinds of relations, those of "*resemblance*, *contrariety*, *degrees in quality*, and *proportions in quantity or number*" (*Human Nature*, p. 118; B. Ⅰ, Par. ⅲ, §1). Those four relations are next integrated into the domain of cause and effect, on the ground that they imply either of the two qualities, "*contiguity* and *succession*," which, in turn, are actually the "[essence of] causes and effects" (p. 124; §2). "All our arguments concerning causes and effects" are, *in ultima*, assumed to "consist both of an impression of the memory or senses" (p. 132; §5). It is clear, so far, that senses are taken as the justification of the validity of certain knowledge.

Carlyle's loss of the Calvinist faith, it is clear, is attributed by him to the acceptance of the British empiricist point of view. "Locke" is presented by Carlyle as the one to "[have] paved the way for banishing religion from the world" (Wks., XXVI, 215). His attacks upon British empiricism, especially upon the Lockean and Humean positions is clear, decisive and violent in "State of German Literature" (1827). British empiricism is placed, in the work, in diametrical polarity against the German transcendental idealism. "The Kantists" are said to be "in direct contradiction to Locke and all his followers, both of the French and English or Scottish school," and to "[commence] from within, and proceeds outwards; instead of commencing from without, and, with various precautions and hesitations, endeavouring to proceeds inwards" (79). Here, Carlyle is, obviously,

特别是上帝的存在与物质世界之间，有着难以逾越的鸿沟。所以他意识到，"基督教自身不过建立在可能性的基础之上；当然这些可能非常强烈，不过依然是可能而已"（Ibid.）。狄奥根尼在绝望中悲叹，"我的封住的眼睛虽然带着不可言说的向往，但是哪里都看不见他［即上帝］"（Sar.，162）。卡莱尔同样"并没有在物质世界之中找到精神上帝存在的足够证据"。[①] 上帝存在物质证明的缺失，是信仰危机的最终根源。

非常明显，卡莱尔式的怀疑的运作机制是一个将物质（M）置于逻辑起点，以可感知性（S）作为检验原则的演绎过程。在这一演绎过程中，物质或者物质性的存在被看作第一原则（P），是确定性的来源。任何不能通过感官被确定为是物质性的事物，即任何不具备可感知性的事物，均被认为不具有确定性。在此意义上，上帝的存在（G）因为不是物质性的，所以非常明显不能被感官感知，由此成为怀疑（D）的对象。如上所述，上帝的存在是卡莱尔加尔文主义思想的根基。对上帝存在的质疑，必会导致整个信仰（F）体系的崩溃。若以负号（"－"）表示否定，则卡莱尔信仰危机产生的整个逻辑形式如下：

$$\{[(M\to P)\to S]\to D\}\to -G\to -F$$

显然，（M→P），即将物质作为 *principia prima*，是整个演绎过程的基础。卡莱尔信仰危机解决的根本办法，在微观上在于逻辑起点的重置。此外，以上逻辑形式还表明，信仰被置于一个逻辑推理的结论环节。这明显是一个以逻辑的手段实现宗教的目的的办法。据此，将信仰从逻辑之中脱离出来，是卡莱尔信仰危机在宏观上的方法。事实上，微观和宏观方法均得到了卡莱尔的应用。他的精神发展史进入下一阶段。

---

challenging the Lockean identification of the senses, the outward in his words, as the *principia prima* of knowledge. The attack upon Humean empiricism is carried in the same track. "The Germans," once again, are said to "take up the matter [i. e. our evidence for an external independent existence of Matter] differently," and it is likely that they "would assail Hume, not in his outworks, but in the centre of his citadel" (81). The Humean premise, "his first principle, that Sense is the only inlet of Knowledge, that Experience is the primary ground of Belief," (Ibid.) is completely denied. Here, as in case of the attack upon Locke, the German idealists serve as a mouthpiece to repeat Carlyle's own opinions.

① Shine, op. cit., p. 8.

三 德国思想研究

卡莱尔进行德国思想研究的目的在于宗教信仰的恢复。“毫无疑问，卡莱尔在生命中的这段时间里接触德国文学，就像他接触法国和意大利文学一样，他的目的在于精神需求的满足。”①

他一方面将德国思想看作法国思想的反题而对之进行研究。早在1822年，这一对比结构便在《论〈浮士德〉》（“*Faustus*：From the German of Goethe”）这一最早的德国研究作品中得到表现。靡非斯特（Mephistopheles）被认为是“一个绝对的‘否定者’”（“Fst.，”326）。否定同样是法国思想的主要特征。“在许多方面，靡非斯特类似于某些上个世纪的法国哲人”（Ibid.）。两者被看作否定者的根源在于，他们“都有智性机能的完美，却完全没有德性机能；都有极端的想象性的礼仪和尖锐的思想，以及贫瘠的自私和带有鄙视性质的冷漠”（Ibid.）。可见，以智性凌驾于德性之上是卡莱尔否定法国思想的根源。这一认识贯穿至卡莱尔的晚年。“我将德国远远置于任何其他古代的或者现代的民族才智和个性之上；特别高高置于任何可以叫作法国的事物之上。”（15th Jul. 1874；C. – R.，204）法国人被认为“充满自欺”，虽然“在所有方面都是纯粹德国的”，但是“并不是德国中最优秀的”（205）。可见，卡莱尔研究德国思想的目的之一在于抵消法国启蒙思想的影响。

另一方面，德国思想被认为是英国思想的反题。德国思想主要被置于与洛克和修姆为代表的英国经验主义哲学传统的对立之中。这一立场在《德国文学现状》（“State of German Literature，”1827）之中的表现最为明显。康德哲学的主要特征被认为在于“与每一个所知的［哲学体系］相区别；主要与现在在不列颠所教授的，以及曾经所教授的形而上学哲学不同”（Wks.，XXVI，79）。康德哲学甚至被认为“到目前为止从未［在英国］存在”（Ibid.）。可见，德国思想与英国思想在最大限度上构成反题。在英国哲学传统中，洛克哲学与德国哲学构成反题。一方面，在认识结构上，康德哲学与洛克不同。“康德主义者”所接受的认识方式与“洛克以及他的追随者，无论

① Ikeler，*Puritan Temper and Transcendental Faith*，p. 72.

是法英学派，还是苏格兰学派”，均“完全相反”（Ibid.）。另一方面，在第一原则问题上，两类哲学存在分歧。关于“必要的真”，洛克认为“存在于某些被修正的经验以及感官证据”（80）。康德哲学则认为感官不是第一原则。另外，休姆哲学与德国哲学构成反题。这一分歧首先表现在物质的独立性问题之上。根据休姆，“物质的外在、独立的存在”毋庸置疑（Ibid.）。德国哲学否定物质的独立存在。分歧还表现在感官与知识之间的关系之上。“［德国人］否认［休姆］的第一原则，否认感官是知识的唯一来源，否认经验是信仰的首要基础。”（81）综上可见，德国哲学被卡莱尔看作是英国哲学的反题。

卡莱尔最早接触德国思想的可能来源主要有二。其一是斯图尔特的《形而上学、伦理和政治哲学进步论》（*Dissertation on the Progress of Metaphysical*, *Ethical*, *and Political Philosophy*）。根据哈罗德（Charles Frederick Harrold）的观点，这一作品“对卡莱尔产生的帮助要比他意识到的大许多”。① 1816—1818 年，卡莱尔比较集中地阅读了《进步论》。② 特别是 1818 年，他在通信中（26th Jun.；to James Johnstone）提到，《进步论》“已经是第二次阅读了”（Let.[1]，Ⅰ，159）。该作品中有一定篇幅涉及德国哲学，并特别将莱布尼茨（Leibniz）的哲学思想与洛克（John Locke）相对立，以及将康德（Kant）哲学作为德国哲学最新的发展趋势进行介绍。③ 这一立场影响了卡莱尔对德国思想，特别是对康德哲学的解读。“阅读斯图尔特，极有可能为卡莱尔理解康德做出一定的准备。”④ 此外，卡莱尔还阅读过斯图尔特的《人类意识哲学原

① *Carlyle and German Thought*, p. 33. My discussion of Stewart's influence upon Carlyle's study of German thought, here, in this part, is largely indebted to Harrold's work quoted here and Jessop's *Carlyle and Scottish Thought.*

② In a letter to Robert Mitchell (3rd Aug. 1816), Carlyle mentions that he "［has］ lately read Stewart's *History of Philosophy* in the Supplement to the *Encyclopœdia Britannica*" (Let.[1], 81－82). He is, obviously, trying to understand the work. He tells his correspondent that he "［does］ not recollect of ever having bestowed as much attention with so little effort upon any author as upon Professor Stewart" (82). *Dissertation* is first published as prefix to *Encyclopœdia Britannica* (1815) under the title *History*, and then assimilated to Stewart's *Works*, vol. Ⅰ (ed. William Hamilton, Edinburgh: Thomas Constable, 1854). What Carlyle is reading in 1816, clearly, is the original version.

③ See, in *Dissertation*, Par. Ⅱ, Sect. 1. Historical and Critical Review of the Philosophical Works of Locke and Leibniz, Sect. 2. Continuation of the Review of Locke and Leibniz, and Sect. 7. Kant, and other Metaphysicians in the New German School.

④ Jessop, *Carlyle and Scottish Thought*, p. 126.

理》（*Elements of the Philosophy of the Human Mind*）和《散论集》（*Essays*）等作品，甚至还在期刊作品中关注他与赖依德（Thomas Reid）之间的争论，并可以做出较为准确恰当的评价。① 但是，这些作品对他的德国思想研究所产生的影响相对不大。

其二是斯塔尔夫人（Madame de Staël）的名作《论德国》（*De l'Allemagne*）。卡莱尔最早于1817年提到阅读这部作品（25th Sep.; to James Johnstone; 119）。1820年，他产生翻译斯塔尔夫人传记的想法。"我也有翻译一本法语书的（渺茫的）希望——这便是斯塔尔夫人的生平［即索绪尔（Necker de Saussure）的《斯塔尔夫人性格及作品简介》（*Notice sur le Caractère et les Écrits de Mme. de Staël*）］"（L. – B., 41）。在1821年与简（Jane Welsh）开始通信以后，他多次提到斯塔尔夫人，并将《论德国》作为必读书目推荐给她。② 卡莱尔对德国思想产生的兴趣，在很大程度上来源于《论德国》的阅读。1869年《边界信使》（*Grenzboten*）中的一篇评论便将《论德国》看作卡莱尔研究兴趣的导火线。"正是这本书，激发了他熟知德国文学经典的浓厚兴趣。"③ 诺顿（Charles Eliot Norton）认为，"［卡莱尔］对［德国诗人和文学家］的兴趣由［斯塔尔夫人论德国的名作］引起"。④《论德

---

① Jessop, *Carlyle and Scottish Thought*, pp. 34 – 35.

② Madame de Staël is a constant topic in the correspondence between Carlyle and Jane Welsh in the years 1821 – 1823. Even in the very first letter (4th Jun. 1821) ever addressed to her, Carlyle recommends works of "De Staël" for Jane's "improvement" and "employment," which, it is believed, "will amply fill up the summer, and very profitably also" (L. – J., I, 2). Madame de Staël is, as far as *De l'Allemagne* is concerned, presented as "misty and inconsistent here and there," but she "has none of that sprightliness, that bland and sparkling wit, which so gracefully adorns the higher qualities of a young lady [Carlyle] once met [s] with: but if a brilliant imagination, a magnificent intellect, a noble heart, can yield [to Jane] delight, then here is for [Jane]" (3 – 4). Jane, on her side, reads not only *De l'Allemagne*, but also *Delphine*, a romance of de Staël (42). As for the latter work, she "cannot for [her] life help liking it better than any novel of six volumes [she] ever [reads]" (43). And she shows her liking to De Staël by "[declaring] the idea of having Madame de Staël for an acquaintance in the world of spirits makes [her] half wish to die" (Ibid.). When Jane becomes fairly familiar with De Staël's works, Carlyle proposes to Jane to make a composition on the topic of her, actually, an "essay on Madame de Staël" (51). By the middle of 1821, De Staël has already become a "favourite" between them (67). In 1823, Carlyle resumes the proposal of composition by suggesting to Jane to give a consideration to "a Life and Criticism on Madame de Staël" (159).

③ Quoted in Jaeck, *Madame de Staël and the Spread of German Literature*, pp. 216 – 217.

④ Carlyle, C. – G., Intro., p. viii.

国》分四部分分别对德国的生活习惯、文学和艺术、哲学和道德以及宗教和狂热进行介绍。特别是书中第三部分，有相当多的篇幅介绍德国哲学。① 虽然卡莱尔对这一部分的总体评价不高，认为“第三部分特别具有神秘的倾向；一些时候甚至会十分荒唐”（L. -J.，Ⅰ，6），但是他本人的德国思想研究受惠颇多。“席勒与歌德的剧作”以及“多数德国作品”，卡莱尔“部分地在《论德国》的指导下”进行研究。② 甚至据他人回忆，“第一本令他产生了解德语愿望的作品［也］正是斯塔尔夫人的《论德国》”。③ 此外，卡莱尔还阅读过《关于革命某些事件的思考》（*Considération sur quelques Événement de la Révolution*，15th Feb. 1819；to Robert Mitchell；Let.[1]，I，213）和《论激情对于个体和民族幸福的影响》（*Influence des Passions sur le Bonhuer des Individus et des Nations*，13th Feb. 1822；to Jane Welsh；L. -J.，Ⅰ，27）等作品。

卡莱尔于 1819 年开始学习德语。他的德语学习方式比较特别，具有强烈的互助性。他“从一位罗伯特·贾丁（Robert Jardine）那里获得些许的德语知识”，再作为回报，将“些许的法语知识传递”给对方（15th Feb. 1819；to Robert Mitchell；Let.[1]，Ⅰ，209）。最初，他学习德语的目的并不在于文学和思想。如他所说，“［他］依然记得，正是出于以原语阅读维尔纳（Abraham G. Werner）矿物学原则作品的意愿，［他］才开始研习德语”（C. -G.，156 -157）。初期，作为语言学习的补充，他阅读了科茨布（August Kotzebue）的剧作和埃亨霍尔茨（Johann W. Archenholz）的《七年战争史》（*Seven Years' War*）等作品。④ 1820 年，他大量阅读德国文学作品，可谓“与席勒、歌德和其他作家终日为伴”。⑤ 学习德语时，他十分刻苦。“他读过了所有的在

---

① The third part in *De l'Allemagne* is entitled "La Philosophie et la Morale." Of twenty - one chapters in this part, chapters one to eleven, more than a half, are devoted to the discussion of "la philosophie." Among those eleven chapters, chapter five to seven, three in total, are devoted to the introduction of German philosophy before and after Kant, and, thus, may shed lights upon the peculiarities in Carlyle's study of German thoughts.

② Harrold, op. cit., p. 40.

③ Adrian, "Dean Stanley's Report of Conversation with Carlyle," p. 73.

④ Jaeck, op. cit., p. 217. Carlyle mentions his reading of Kotzebue's play in a letter to Alexander Carlyle (29th Mar. 1819). "A stupid play of Kotzebue" is being read (L. -B., 28). Obviously, it is not an impressive reading.

⑤ Wilson, *Carlyle*, Vol. Ⅰ, p. 201.

大学图书馆以及书店里可以获得的书籍”。① 1821 年，他已经具备稳固的阅读能力，甚至可以帮助简的相关学习（16th Jul.；L. -J.，I，8）。在阅读力的支持下，卡莱尔开始了漫长的德国思想研究经历。德国思想对于他全新思想体系的形成具有至关重要的作用。“卡莱尔的思想”可谓“受惠于德国思想家颇深”。②席勒（Friedrich Schiller）是第一位受卡莱尔关注的德语作家。③早期生活经历上的相似，极有可能是兴趣的来源。④

---

① Fischer，*Thomas Carlyle*，p. 22.

② Carlyle，op. cit.，Oxford World's Classics，Intro.，p. XV.

③ The first set of works in German that Carlyle procures in the year 1820 is Schiller's，through the help of a Mr. Swann（Jaeck，*Madame de Staël and the Spread of German Literature*，p. 217）. Some time later，he borrows Goethe's books from the library of the University of Edinburgh（217 - 218）. He，in the beginning，shows preference to Schiller's rather than Goethe's works，"more attracted by Schiller than by Goethe，as Schiller [seems] to him to possess in the highest degree all good qualities"（218）. It is，thus，Schiller，instead of Goethe，that is the first German author that draws Carlyle's attention at first.

④ A great number of similarities between Schiller and Carlyle's living experiences are traceable in the *The Life of Friedrich Schiller*. It is especially their earlier living experiences，in particular，that are glaringly similar and，in some of the cases，even capable of substitution with each other. Schiller's early education seems to be as difficult as that of Carlyle. Both of them are "favoured by the dispositions，" but，unfortunately，"obstructed by the outward circumstances of [their] parents"（Wks，XXV，3）. Both mothers command absolute confidence from the sons. "[Their] kindness and tenderness of heart [endear themselves] to [the sons]"（4）. Both fathers leave an ineradicable religious impressions upon the filial memories. "[Their] religion" is remembered to "[mingle] itself with every motive and action of [their] life"（5）. Schiller，in his childhood，is，in almost every sense，an observant Diogenes Teufelsdröckh，by showing "a certain earnestness of temper，a frank integrity，an appetite for things grand or moving，[...] discernible across all the caprices of his boyhood"（Ibid.）. The surgeon's son in Würtemberg and the mason's boy in Ecclefechan are，in the same stage in their path to maturity，encouraged，one mainly by the father while the other by the mother，to conceive "the idea of consecrating [themselves] to the clerical profession"（6），only to be disillusioned by the fact that "the project [hovers] before [them] at a great distance，and the path to its fulfillment [offers them] but little entertainment"（7）. Thus，it follows，in consequence，that "[their] studies [do] not seize [their] attention firmly；[they follow] them from a sense of duty，not of pleasure"（Ibid.）.

Neither is Schiller contented with his life in *Karls - schule*，nor Diogenes satisfied with his university years. "The Stuttgart system of education [...] formed on principle，not of cherishing and correcting nature，but of rooting it out，and supplying its place with something better，" together with "the process of teaching and living [...] conducted with the stiff formality of military drill"（9），is as despicable to Schiller as the "Rational University"（Sar.，112）is to Diogenes. The constrained conditions effect both young men's characters. "The misery [they endure] in this severe and lonely mode of existence" are believed to have "strengthened or produced in [them] a habit of constraint and shyness，which [cling] to [their] character through life"（Wks.，XXV，10）. To make a change，both try "the study of Law"（Ibid.）but neither succeeds. Schiller takes it to be "the representative of all these evils，" and "[has] never felt any predilection"（Ibid.）for it.

早在1821年，《三十年战争史》（*Geschichte des Dreißigjährigen Kriegs*）的部分章节便翻译完成，并有出版计划（2nd Jan.；L. – B.，56）。同年，他还读过《华伦斯坦》（*Wallenstein*；18th Mar.；to Robert Mitchell；Let.[1]，Ⅰ，332）。在简的德语学习计划里，席勒的作品被推荐（28th Jun.；L. – J.，Ⅰ，6）。推荐的根源在于作品之"美"（14）。1822年，《威廉·退尔》（*Wilhelm Tell*）的阅读完成（25th Jul.；to John A. Carlyle；Let.[1]，Ⅱ，103）。同年底，他向简推荐了大量席勒的剧作，包括《退尔》、《墨西拿的新娘》（*Die Braut von Messina*）、《华伦斯坦》和《唐·卡洛斯》（*Don Karlos*）等（25th Dec.；L. – J.，Ⅱ，131 – 132）。1823年，卡莱尔致力于《席勒传》的写作。①总体而言，卡莱尔未能有效理解席勒的美学思想。②他对席勒思想的接受有很大的保留。不过，几乎在席勒作品开始研读的同时"他［便］从席勒转向歌德，而歌德为他开启一个全新的世界"。③

歌德（Wolfgang Goethe）是卡莱尔最为主要的思想来源之一。④卡莱尔最早于1820年接触歌德的作品。1821年，他开始阅读《浮士德》。⑤1822年，他

Carlyle considers it as "a shapeless mass of absurdity and chicane," and has to "［renounce］" it for better (18th Mar. 1820; to Robert Mitchell; Let.[1], Ⅰ, 281). When the study of law is abandoned, both turn to literature as the object of pursuit. It is only through, and after, hardships and sufferings that literary fame is finally achieved. "The hard circumstances of ［their］ fortune ［have］ prevented the natural development of ［their］ mind; ［their］ faculties ［have］ been cramped and misdirected; but they ［have］ gathered strength by oppositionand the habit of self – dependence which it ［encourages］" (Wks., XVV, 13). The publication of *Robbers* is parallel to that of *The French Revolution*. When literary laurel is crowned, their separate paths diverge, one to academic research in university, the other to prophetic career at Chelsea. The Jena scholar and the Chelsea sage take root in similar soil and bloom in different flowers.

① See Froude, op. cit., Vol. Ⅰ, pp. 157 – 161.

② For Carlyle depreciation of Schiller's aesthetics, cf. Dale, *The Victorian Critic and the Idea of History*, pp. 21 – 22; Frohwalt Küchler, "Carlyle und Schiller," *Anglia* 26 (1903), pp. 1 – 93, 393 – 446; Shine, *Carlyle's Fusion of Poetry, History, and Religion by* 1834, esp. pp. 18 – 19; Tom Lloyd, " 'High Air Castles': Carlyle's Reactions to Schiller's Aesthetics," *Victorians Institute Journal* 12 (1984), pp. 91 – 104; "Madame Roland and Schiller's Aesthetics: *Carlyle's The French Revolution*," *Prose Studies* 9 (1986), pp. 39 – 53.

③ Baumgarten, *Carlyle und Goethe*, p. 36.

④ Wilson, op. cit., Vol. Ⅰ, p. 201.

⑤ It is mentioned in the first letter addressed by Carlyle to Goethe (24th Jun. 1824) that "four years ago, ［... he］ read ［s］ ［Goethe's］ *Faust* among the mountains of ［his］ native Scotland" (C. – G., 2). It, thus, becomes clear that it is in 1821, four years before 1824, that *Faust* is first being perused by him.

的第一份重要评论作品《论〈浮士德〉》发表。① 1823 年春，《威廉·迈斯特》系列作品的翻译计划被制订，夏季正式开始实施。② 在致简的通信中，他提到相关计划（11th May； Ⅰ，216）。1822—1823 年，在卡莱尔的启发下，《浮士德》成为简的主要阅读书目。③ 1824 年，卡莱尔首次致信歌德，随信附有《迈斯特》的译文（24th Jun.； C. –G.，1）。歌德的回信被看作"来自仙境的消息"（20th Dec.； L. –J.，Ⅱ，60）。④ 1828 年，卡莱尔写有《歌德的海伦娜》（"Goethe's Helena，" 1828）和《歌德》（"Goethe，" 1828）等两部关于歌德的评论作品。他们之间的通信关系一直持续到歌德逝世（22nd

---

① Carlyle mentions the composition of "*Faustus*: from the German of Goethe" (*New Edinburgh Review*, Vol. Ⅱ, pp. 316 – 344) in a letter to his brother Alexander [12th (?) Jan.]. After a return from Kirkcaldy, he "[sets] to a criticism on *Faust*" (L. – B., p. 103). A few months later, he is able, and proud, to "enclose the critique on *Faust*" to be sent to his family in eager expectation of it (7th Apr.; Let.[1], Ⅱ, 55).

On the other side, Carlyle's criticism upon *Faust* is also a topic in the correspondences between him and Jane in the year 1822. Jane mentions her interest in Carlyle's composition of the criticism (29th Dec. 1821 / 2nd Jan. 1822). She asks him to "send [one copy] to [her]" "when [he has] finished [his] review of *Faustus*" (L. – J., Ⅰ, 16). Carlyle finishes the criticism in the beginning of the year 1822. He tells to Jane that "[he] finish [es] *Faust* on Saturday; and [has] not yet courage to read it over" (14th Jan.; 17). The criticism, when finished, seems to offer little satisfaction to him. He "cannot without indignation behold the paltry rag," "so ambitious, so bombastic, so jejune" (Ibid.). He expresses his reluctance to comply to Jane's requirement, considering it as "so very insufficient a performance to [her] perusal" (Ibid.). He, nevertheless, sends one to Jane, to make "Women [...] have their way," even if it is considered as "very wrong in [her] to disturb the repose of *Faust*" (109 – 110).

② Kaplan, op. cit., pp. 84, 85.

③ Jane expresses her wish to "read *Faust* when [she has] finished *Wallenstein*" (6th Dec. 1822; L. – J., Ⅰ, 116). Carlyle, in accordance, promises to "send [her] *Faust* whenever [she has] finished [*Wallenstein*]," though in fear that "[she] will not like it so well as [she expects]," taking it as "a hard effort, one which few in [her] circumstances would be capable of making" (16th Dec.; 121). Jane, however, is "too late by a day in asking for *Faust*," and has still to wait (25th Dec.; 131). By the time when she is actually in the process of reading it, however, she seems to encounter some difficulties in making a clear understanding. Carlyle, soon, tells her "not [to] plague [herself] any more about *Faust*" (8th Jan. 1823; 142). As no more, since then, is mentioned of Jane's reading of *Faust*, it seems safe to conclude that Jane's acquaintance with Goethe's best known work is, at best, slight and incomplete.

④ Goethe's first reply to Carlyle is also mentioned by Jane. "The most pleasurable thing which has befallen [her]" is to "[receive] *two* packages from England in the same night," among which there is "a letter from Goethe" (18th Jan. 1825; to Miss Stodart; *Early Letters*, p. 100). She keeps telling that "Goethe's [reply] [is] written to Carlyle himself," and "it is highly complimentary; and coming from the man that he honours, almost to idolatry, must have gratified him beyond measure" (101).

Mar. 1832）。直到此时，两位文人尚未谋面。① 歌德的逝世被卡莱尔“看作不但是一个政治事件，也是一个文学事件”（Nt. B.，259）。“这个杰出的人物”“开创了德国在全欧洲知名的文学时代”，这一时代“与他而去”，几乎就是“他的个人历史”（260）。卡莱尔致歌德最后一封书信“永远也不会抵达终点，那个伟大的好友已不在人世”（Ibid.）。在至德国友人（Wohlgeboren Eckermann）书信（27th Jul. 1832）中，他坦露真情。“任何属于他的东西现在于我都变得加倍珍贵；我认为他辉煌的存在没有结束、不可结束，而仅仅从我们物质性的视野里消失而已，却像白天的火柱和夜里的云柱一样引导着我，让周围的一切神圣起来。”② 1832 年，《歌德的肖像》（“Goethe's Portrait”）、《歌德之死》（“Death of Goethe”）和《歌德的著作》（“Goethe's Works”）三篇文章发表。眷眷之意，跃然纸上；拳拳之情，溢于言表。

卡莱尔从文学向哲学转向的关键，是《席勒传》的写作。他意识到“康德哲学对于诗人思想形成产生的影响”的重要性，③ 并开始有意识地阅读先验唯心论相关著作。然而，这一过程并不顺利，经历也不愉快。康德是卡莱尔最早接触的德国哲学家。早在 1820 年，他便在通信（18th Mar.；to Robert Mitchell）中提到康德。“柏拉图（Plato）令毕达哥拉斯（Pythagoras）的盛名黯淡，卡德沃斯（Ralph Cudworth）和康德令柏拉图的盛名黯淡。”（Let.[1]，Ⅰ，283）非常明显，剑桥柏拉图学派是卡莱尔此时理解康德哲学的主要视角，这也是一个外部视角。1821 年，他的康德研究毫无进展。“至于康德、谢林（Frieclrich Schelling）、费希特（J. G. Fichte）以及其他伟人，[他] 承认自己根本一无所知。”（18th Mar.；333）1823 年，康德哲学的总体特征被描述为“无限地巨大”、“包裹在乌云和黑暗之中”以及“仅以类型和象征得到展现”

---

① It is only in 1852, in his first voyage to Germany (1851–1852), that Carlyle pays, finally, a belated visit to Goethe's house. In a letter to Jane (20th Sep.), he tells her that "Goethe's house, which [is] opened by favour, [keeps him] occupied in a strange mood for two hours or more" (L.–W., 295). He, then, gives a tolerably detailed description of the house and even finds there "the last book [he] ever sen [ds] Goethe — Taylor's — *Survey of German Poetry*" (Ibid.). Jane expresses her wish to "have seen G [oe] the's [...] house with [him] (*Letters and Memorials*, Vol. Ⅰ, p. 436). Such a visit "look [s] to [her] quite tempting" even if "the travel" may prove "rather disagreeable than otherwise" (Ibid.).

② Flügel, "Carlyle und Eckermann," p. 9.

③ Muirhead, *The Platonic Tradition in Anglo–Saxon Philosophy*, p. 132.

（Nt. B. ，41）。这类描述暴露了他对康德哲学的无知。在此情况下他发出感叹，“我希望我完全了解康德哲学”（46）。直到 1826 年，他才首次阅读康德的著作。“［他］行进至《纯粹理性批判》（*Kritik der reinen Vernunft*）的第 150 页”，却发现“康德深奥难懂”，也许“司各特（Walter Scott）的小说更加合适”（27th Sep. ；L. –J. ，Ⅱ，324）。① 以上便是卡莱尔对康德著作的阅读情况。这种程度的文献把握严重影响了卡莱尔对康德哲学的解读。未完成的《德国文学史》仅有一处提到康德。他被看作“德国人可以以自己的语言、以自己的基础研究哲学”的代表，堪比“形而上学领域里的亚当（Adam）”（Ger. ，32）。40 年代，在为文学青年解答疑惑的回信（28th Aug. 1841；to Espinasse）中，康德哲学被认为是“德国哲学复杂内容之中最为珍贵，也是唯一最为珍贵的事物”。② 显然，两处评价仅涉及身份定位，而非思想和学说。在晚年（1871—1872），卡莱尔依然偶尔与友人谈论康德的时空观。③ 但是所有这些评价均在不同程度上暴露了他对康德哲学的误解和错读。事实上，从技术层面考虑，卡莱尔的康德研究并不成功。“经过这种方式的解释，康德哲学并不能对［卡莱尔］典型的英国思想产生影响。”④ 他始终未能体验到康德哲学的内在魅力。“虽然在思想上受惠于这位伟大的德国哲学家，但是卡莱尔依然无法将康德体系看作‘真理的终结’。”⑤ 不过，卡莱尔依然将一些康德思想因素纳入自己的思想体系，实现了信仰恢复的目的。

费希特是另外一个卡莱尔重点解读的德国哲学家。1821 年，费希特被首次提及（18th Mar. ；to Robert Mitchell；Let. 1，Ⅰ，333）。1823 年的笔记中记录有他对费希特形成的总体印象。“一位形而上学的无神论者”作为费希特的描述（Nt. B. ，46），可谓偏执至极。直到 1827 年，他才正

① As to the extent to which Carlyle's familiarity with Kant's *Vernunt* goes, his related accounts contradict each other. In an entry in his notebook after the date 16th Jan. 1827, it is recorded that "［he has］only read 100 pages of［Kant's］works"（Nt. B. , 113）, 50 pages shorter than that recorded in the letter. No matter which data is more correspondent to the fact, it is safe to draw the conclusion that his familiarity with *Vernunt* is, at best, limited and insufficient.

② Espinasse, *Literary Recollections and Sketches*, p. 59.

③ Allingham, op. cit. , pp. 203 – 204.

④ Fermi, *Thomas Carlyle*, p. 9.

⑤ Hensel, *Thomas Carlyle*, p. 43.

式开始阅读费希特的作品。“［他］一直在阅读霍恩（Franz Horn）、费希特和谢林”，但是阅读效果并不理想，“固定的观点尚未形成”（27th Aug.；to Dr. Carlyle；Let.[2]，Ⅰ，72）。“费希特的超验唯心论”学说（Nt. B.，112），是努力解读的对象。特别是“客体的取消”和“从我之中演绎出非我”两点（Ibid.），对理解造成了严重的障碍。康德和费希特思想之间的关系，被特别留意。“费希特认为他的体系是从康德的体系之中演绎出来的，但是康德激烈地予以反驳。”（Ibid.）据他后来回忆（28th Aug. 1841；to Espinasse），《论学者的地位》（*Über das Wesen des Gelehrten*）是“他在［德国哲学领域］里读到”的最有影响力的作品，“在他的记忆里光芒超越了其他作品”。① 与康德相比，卡莱尔对费希特著作的熟悉程度同样堪忧。对原始材料的生疏，影响了解读的质量。《德国文学史》中有一处提及费希特。他的学说被用于解答“文学”和“印刷对话”之间的区别（Ger.，12）。很明显，文学理解是卡莱尔解读费希特的主要视角。1840年，费希特在通信（8th Oct.；to Thomas Ballantyne）中被提到。他被看作“坚定的自由主义者”，虽然“声势浩大”，但是“从者甚少”（Let.[3]，Ⅰ，216－217）。显然，费希特此时已经成为卡莱尔理解时事的标签。《德国文学现状》发表大概20年后，对费希特的评价也发生了重大转变。这个昔日“冷静、伟岸和坚韧的，挺拔而引人注目的精神”（Wks.，XXVI，77），最终沦为“感觉迟钝的家伙”。②

此外，卡莱尔对其他德国作家的思想也有涉猎。其中，里希特（Jean Paul Richter）深刻地影响了他的写作风格。③ 特别是《旧衣新裁》，里希特可

---

① Espinasse, op. cit., p. 59

② Espinasse, op. cit., p. 220.

③ Carlyle's first interest in Jean Paul Richter is aroused by De Quincey. "Perhaps it [is] little De Quincey's reported admiration of Jean Paul," as it is remembered, that "first put [s] [him] upon trying to be orthodox and admire [Richter]" (Froude, *First Forty Years*, Vol. Ⅰ, p. 323). As early as the first quarter of the year 1824, "Jean Paul" is designed "to [be included]" in "this Book of 'German Novelists'," and Carlyle is looking for the copies of "Jean Paul's *Leben Quintins* (sic.) *Fixlein and Reise des Feldprediger* (sic.) *Schmelzle nach Flätz*" (14th Mar.; Pitollet, "Lettres Inédites," pp. 300, 301). In the next year, Carlyle

谓“提供了主要的参考样式”，甚至“在此后依然影响卡莱尔的写作风格”。①作品中的“编辑”，一方面“既是材料收集者，又是解释人”，另一方面“是故事与读者之间的中介”，在这一设置中“让·保罗的特征可以得到辨认”。②“私语”（*Rede*）作为一种写作手法贯穿卡莱尔的中后期写作，令他关于“个体或者普遍问题的讨论”表现出里希特的影响。③甚至在思想结构上，卡莱尔被认为“与让·保罗高度相似，而与费希特、康德或者甚至是歌德并非如通常所认为的那样相近”。④在里希特之外，施莱格尔兄弟（August & Friedrich

---

proposes to give "three or four volumes of Translations from the German intended as Specimens of their chief novel writers," and Richter is one of his "chief dependence [s]" (29th Apr.; Carré, "Quelques Lettres Inédites," pp. 40, 41). By this time, he "[has] looked into [Richter's] Herbst – Bluminen (sic.), his *Flegeljahre* and [is] now reading his *Fibel*" (Ibid.). At the end of the year, it is planned, if not decided, that some of Richter's works are to be assimilated into *German Romance*, as part of "the second [volume of the book]" (4th Nov.; L. – J., Ⅱ, 188). In 1826, the inclusion of Richter in "the Book of 'German Novelists'" is reaffirmed, and, this time, he "[sends] for *Schmelzle's Reise* and also for the *Leben Quintus Fixlein*," and has "the *Picnic* and *Déjeûner dansant zu Kuhschnappel* of Richter" in his possession for perusal (25th Apr.; Carré, "Quelques Lettres Inédites," pp. 43, 44). Also, at about this time, Carlyle shows an intense interest in the life of Richter, most likely to the end of the composition of a biography in his translations. He is, accordingly, informed of "two *höchst interessante* Lives [i. e. Döring's *Vie de Jean – Paul* and *Leben und Charakteristiken*] of Jean – Paul [...] in the press" while "no life whatever of him has yet come out of it" (44). At the end of the year, however, one "copy of Dœring's *Jean Paul*" is being perused by him though it is "too late for assisting [his] *printed* critical labours" (4th Dec.; Pitollet, "Lettres Inédites," p. 206). Richter as "a subject of such attraction" makes welcome "any account of him however meagre," and "Otto's *Life of Richter*" is becoming the object of Carlyle's expectation (Ibid.). When *German Romance* is finally published in 1827, two copies are specially sent, one to Henry Crabb Robinson, the other to N. H. Julius, for their separate helps and supports.

Carlyle's Translation of Jean Paul Richter is, however, on the whole, blemished by mistakes made by misunderstanding and misinterpretation. "Carlyles Übersetzung [ist] so verschroben und undurchsichtig, daβ es nicht mehr möglich ist festzustellen, ob er Jean Pauls Ausdruck richtig verstanden hat oder nicht," to quote Smeed's opinion ("Carlyles Jean – Paul – Übersetzen," p. 264).

① Smeed, "Thomas Carlyle and Jean Paul Richter," p. 252.

② Vida, *Romantic Affinities*, p. 47.

③ Vijn, *Carlyle and Jean Paul*, p. 90.

④ Wellek, "Carlyle and German Romanticism," p. 77. The same position is maintained in *Immanuel Kant in England*. It is hinted that "Carlyle stands rather with Jacobi and Jean Paul, who [is] his faithful disciple, than with the German Idealists" (201).

Schlegel）也产生了一定的影响。[①] 这一影响主要表现在卡莱尔对“人与无限之间的关系”的强调之上，这也是施莱格尔兄弟的主题之一。[②] 此外，卡莱尔不但在“德国题材的作品”中借鉴了“弗·施莱格尔的批评原则”，而且“将之贯穿到英国诗人的评价之中”。[③] 然而，卡莱尔对施莱格尔兄弟思想的解读存在问题。总体而言，他将自己的思想赋予施莱格尔兄弟，

---

① As early as 1823, when he is devoted to the composition of *Life of Schiller*, Carlyle is also thinking about "Schlegel's great solution to the mystery of life" (Nt. B., 42). He seems to disagree with the Schlegels' admission that "nature gives people dim intimation of true beauty and just principles in Art," by holding the opposite view that "*the bildende Künstler* and the *richtende* ought to investigate the true foundations of these obscure intimations and set them fast on the basis of reason" (Ibid.). In *Life of Schiller*, Carlyle continues to attack Au. Schlegel's depreciation of Schiller's *Kabale und Liebe* (Wks., XXV, 36). The next year, in the preface to *Wilhelm Meister*, he quotes, and approves of, Au. Schlgel's judgment of the novel (XXⅢ, 7). In 1827, Carlyle's quotation from the two Schlegels increases. August's belief of the "probable influence" of "the Critical Philosophy" upon "the moral culture of Europe," "on a line with the Reformation" (XXⅥ, 77), is mentioned in "State of German Literature." Next, Friedrich's verdict of "British Philosophy, since the time of Hume," as "nothing more than a 'laborious and unsuccessful striving to build dike after dike in front of our Churches and Judgment-halls, and so turn back from them deluge of Scepticism'" (80), is, if not warmly applauded, at least merrily accepted. Finally, August's review of Ludwig Tieck's *Peter Leberrechts Volksmährchen* in the *Jena Litteraturzeitung* is considered as a brilliant one, in and by which "its author [has], for the first time, [been] brought under the eye of the world as a man of rich endowments, and in the fair way for turning them to proper account" (XXI, 258-259). Besides, in the same year, Carlyle inquires his brother, John Carlyle, who is then travelling in Germany, of his meeting with the Schlegels. "Schlegel" is taken, curiously, as like "a 'puppy'" (25th Oct.; Let. ^{2}, Ⅰ, 92). Some days later, Carlyle talks about John's chance to "[have] talked one hour with Schlegel" (19th Nov.; to James Johnstone; 104). In "The Life of Heyne" (1828), the two Schlegels are referred to as "the most ingenious and popular commentator" of "classical study" (Wks., XXⅥ, 351, 350). This is Carlyle's nearest approach to an understanding of the Schlegels as classical philologists. This year, Carlyle is still concerned with "F[r]. Schlegel's Philosophy of Life" (Nt. B., 129). In "Characteristics" (1831), Fr. Schlegel is mentioned, in all, four times. His conversion to "Catholicism" (XXⅧ, 31), his "*Lectures* delivered at Dresden" (33), considered as "the apotheosis of Spiritualism" (34), and his complaint of "the fruitlessness, the tumult and transiency of German as of all Metaphysics" (41), reveal Carlyle's ignorance, and his use, of Friedrich's doctrines. In 1832, Carlyle seems to miss, on purpose, a visit from, and a meeting with, Au. Schlegel. An entry in his notebook reads that "Schlegel is here: I left my card; and hope not, care not, to see the old fool" (Nt. B., 258). The unoffended August still considers him as "[the only] living Englishman [...] who could do [justice to Goethe] as it ought to be done" (6th Apr.; from Hayward; Wilson, *Carlyle*, Vol. Ⅱ, p. 284). Since then, no important mention is made of the Schlegels by Carlyle. My discussion of the relations of Carlyle to the two Schlegels, here above, is largely indebted to Wellek's "Carlyle and German Romanticism," esp. pp. 51-54. Besides, cf. Vida, *Romantic Affinities*, pp. 9-23.

② Vida, op. cit., p. 12.

③ Vida, op. cit., p. 19.

使之成为自己观点的代言人。如韦勒克所说，“卡莱尔好似并不理解施莱格尔［兄弟］的观点，而将他喜爱的而且以自己的方式理解的唯心论归结为他［们］的”。① 最后，诺瓦利斯（Novalis）也是卡莱尔比较重视的德国作家。②“在德国浪漫派之中，诺瓦利斯最为吸引卡莱尔。③”他对诺瓦利斯作品的阅读比较满意，认为虽然“奇怪、神秘、深不可测”，但是“里面满是可以产生严肃思考的内容”（Nt. B.，135）。诺瓦利斯也因此被看作“机械论的反对者、深刻的人、现代最完美的具有精神视野的人”（140）。相比于其他德国浪漫派，“诺瓦利斯更加吸引卡莱尔”。④ 虽然“道德意志、*Vernunft*［理性］、幻想、直觉、历史以及神性在人之上的启示”等观点只能被局部地接受，⑤ 但是卡莱尔主要“通过诺瓦利斯将费希特的哲学更为具体地解释为对物质本质性的否定”。⑥ 诺瓦利斯可谓他与费希特思想之间的中介。

以上便是卡莱尔德国思想研究的概貌。在所有德国作家之中，他主要将歌德的思想看作自己信仰危机解决的关键。⑦ 特别是歌德可以“将理解和信仰

---

① Wellek, “Carlyle and German Romanticism,” p. 53.

② At the end of the year 1828, Carlyle has conceived the plan to “write one [article] on *Novalis*” (26th Dec.; to Dr. Carlyle; Let. 2, Ⅰ, 178). In the first quarter of the next year, he is busy with the preparation for the article in question, “another [Essay] on *Novalis*,” “to appear in *Fraser's Review*, about the first of April” (5th Mar.; 190). Around that time, he has “read *Novalis Schriften* for the second time” and “[written] a review of them” (Nt. B., 135). The publication of the article is recorded in his notebook (140). After that, Novalis' conception of “religion” as “a social thing” seems to be appreciable to him (149). There is also a theme of religious sustenance of society in *Sartor*. The remark that “without such Vestures and sacred Tissues Society has not existed, and will not exist” (Sar., 215) is not very distantly similar to that of Novalis as a motif. Next, he quotes Novalis' saying that “there is but one Temple in the Universe [...] and that is the body of man” (Nt. B., 166). The human body as a temple is a regular theme in Carlyle's works. The same saying is repeated and quoted in *Sartor* (B. Ⅲ, Ch. ⅵ; Sar., 239) and in “Goethe's Works” (Wks., XXⅦ, 390).

③ Wellek, “Thomas Carlyle,” p. 96.

④ Wellek, “Carlyle and German Romanticism,” p. 56.

⑤ Harrold, “Carlyle and Novalis,” p. 48.

⑥ Harrold, *Carlyle and German Thought*, p. 101.

⑦ Goethe as the key to Carlyle's conversion, however, is only gradually established. As early as 1820, “Goethe with all his fellow singers, tho' they might console a disembodied spirit, with some lunar gleams of happiness — are very insufficient for a man of flesh and blood” (L. – G., 10). As William Graham observes, it is almost “heresy indeed,” in particular, “from Carlyle about Goethe” (7). It is clear that the Goethean contribution to the Carlylean conversion is still in the air around this time. When and how Carlyle begins to realize the importance of Goethe in the approach to his spiritual conversion, at best, is only a guesswork for the scarcity, and sometime even rarity, of textual evidences.

综合在一起”,[①] 对于卡莱尔而言格外具有启发意义。“［他］当时感觉，而且依然感觉在［皈依］问题上有赖于歌德；［歌德］是第一位现代人，在［他］之前便以自己的方式走过了陡峭崎岖的道路。”（Rem.[1]，Ⅱ，180）在致歌德的第一封通信中，卡莱尔视他为“一位父亲”，“可以完全理解、可以完美展现［卡莱尔］内心的痛苦和挣扎”（C. －G.，2）。即使在晚年（1877），歌德依然被看作“平静和满足”的来源，“将［他］从［怀疑］之中解救；交给［他］基督教的本质不变，永远为真”。[②] 然而，即使这样，卡莱尔信仰问题解决的逻辑过程远为复杂。

歌德的泛神论（pantheism）是卡莱尔信仰恢复的直接来源。如前所述，卡莱尔信仰危机产生的根源在于上帝存在物质证明的缺失。因此，在物质世界之中获得上帝存在的证明是信仰恢复的初步。歌德的泛神论直接启发了卡莱尔全新的自然观，并集中表现在《旧衣新裁》之中。如卡佳明所说，“［卡莱尔］关于世界的一般理论满是德国影响”。[③] 在世界观、自然观方面，“［歌德］的一般哲学是《旧衣新裁》形而上学的主要来源之一”，特别是“［歌德］的泛神论［……］更具诗性、想象性和色彩；可以更好地表达作为自然的象征论，即自然是神圣理念的外衣”。[④] 歌德可谓不但“协助卡莱尔想象出［唯心泛神论（panthéisme idéaliste）］”，而且“为他提供了［这一思想］的表达，即形式”。[⑤] 依靠歌德的泛神论，“在感官世界和精神世界之间，在我们有确定‘知识’的可见世界和我们‘只能隐约猜测’的不可见世界之间的联系”可以被保持。[⑥] 在《旧衣新裁》中，自然被直接“命名为上帝”，是“上帝活着的衣服”，“［上帝］通过［自然］进行言说”（Sar.，188）。在这一视角下，“宇宙不是死寂的和属魔的，不是一间满是幽灵的停尸房；却是属灵的，是我圣父的”（Ibid.）。在这个“以星空作为穹顶的上帝之城”之中，“每一颗星”、“每一片草叶”以及“每一个活着的灵魂”都“闪耀着一个在

---

① Rosenberg, *The Seventh Hero*, p. 7.

② Allingham, op. cit., p. 253.

③ “L’Idéalisme Philosophique,” p. 1071.

④ Cazamian, *Carlyle*, p. 49.

⑤ Carré, *Gœthe en Angleterre*, p. 167.

⑥ Vaughan, “Carlyle and his German Masters,” pp. 182 – 183.

场的上帝的光辉”（264）。带有强烈歌德式泛神论的自然观让狄奥根尼“首次正视一直以来令他窒息的心结”，让他“立即打开［心结］”，最终“获得自由”（189）。在直观上，卡莱尔已经实现了上帝存在物质证明的实现。不过，自然作为神性的表现这一思想还有更为深层的逻辑基础。

康德的时空唯心性（spatio－temporal ideality）学说，是卡莱尔泛神论合理性的来源。这一学说甚至是“卡莱尔哲学体系的根基”。[①] 卡莱尔在《诺瓦利斯》（“Novalis，”1829）一文中表现出对康德的“哥白尼革命”的某些了解。“思维的机能，即所谓的理解，同样表现出任意性和偶然性。”（Wks.，XXⅦ，25）以康德的术语言之，不是客观决定主观，而是主观投射出客观。“根据康德，思维的过程不是由外到内，而是由内向外。”[②] 卡莱尔对康德学说的正确理解也仅仅停留于此。根据这一基本认识，时间和空间不是客观的存在，而是主观的认识形式。“时间和空间本身不是外在的，而是内在的实体：两者毫无外在的存在，在意识之外既没有时间也没有空间；两者不过是人精神存在的形式，不过是人的思维赖以运作的法则而已。”（25－26）在此解读中，卡莱尔关注的重点在于“空间和时间的唯心性”，而不是“两者在认识论意义上表现在认识过程之中的形式性本质”。[③] 这是对康德学说立场的背离。而且很明显，卡莱尔在时空的形式性（formality）之外加入了精神性（spirituality）。时空的精神性被卡莱尔用于上帝存在物质证明的实现。“空间和时间如此神秘地与我们的思维不可分割，不过是思维的外在物质依附；观察者如果可以升华到神性的无限和永恒，便可以识破两者。”（Sar.，55）“时间和空间不是事物，而是形式；不是外在于我们的存在，而是意识的形式；是不可见的事物将自身表现给我们有限的感官的形式。”（Wds.，136）显然，时间和空间在此被看作超越的对象。只有超越时空，上帝的存在才可以在物质世界之中发现。有基于此，康德的“唯心论”才会被卡莱尔“简单地看作是精神与物质之间的对立”，“唯心论”由此也成为“唯物论”的对立。[④] 同

① Streuli，*Thomas Carlyle als Vermittler deutscher Litteratur und deutschen Geistes*，p. 119.

② Dilthey，“Thomas Carlyle，” p. 267.

③ Harrold，“Carlyle's Interpretation of Kant，” p. 352.

④ Bos，“Le Kantisme de Carlyle，” p. 38.

样在此基础之上，康德才会被看作是“精神性单子的［发现者］和［命名人］”（Ger.，32）。无论卡莱尔是否认识到“［康德］的时空唯心性学说被误读为其他含义”，[①] 也无论是否意识到形式性与精神性之间的断裂，康德学说依然将带有理性色彩的逻辑基础赋予他非理性的宗教信仰。然而，他的信仰并不是一个单纯的自然有神论（natural theism）问题。上帝存在的物质证明，仅仅是信仰恢复的最外层要求。实现人的行动，才是最终的目的。

在最终目的实现的过程中，人作为神性的载体具有至关重要的作用。歌德的泛神论被进一步发挥为所谓的“衣服哲学”（the Philosophy of Clothes）。在内容上，衣服哲学基本重复了卡莱尔从泛神论之中借鉴的所有主要内容。不过，与之相比，衣服哲学主要将人的维度纳入视野。这一点，明显地表现在主要人物狄奥根尼的姓名设计之上。这一奇怪的姓名的含义是，人的起源（-genes）是神性的（Dio-），却处于魔鬼（Teufel-）的包围（-dröckh）中。[②] 非常明显，这是泛神论在人维度上的应用。《旧衣新裁》中甚至有言，“把一个人叫作狄奥根尼·妥伊福尔斯德洛克，此人将开启衣服哲学”（Sar.，88）。可见，衣服哲学的要义是人的神性问题。在衣服哲学中，人与衣服之间的穿戴关系被类比为人的精神组成与物质组成之间的内外关系。在内，人是“某些被表现的、被成像的永恒意识之中的理念”；在外，人是“一个声音、一个运动、一个表象”（53）。精神和物质之间的这种内外之别，是衣服哲学有效性的基础。在此基础上，人被看作上帝的象征。“人自身不过是上帝的象征而已”（220）。人性与神性之间表现在人之上的融合是卡莱尔对人提出道德要求，进而将信仰问题转化为行动问题的关键。

人性与神性的融合不仅是泛神论的结果，其中更有费希特学说的要素。在卡莱尔所接受的所有费希特的学说之中，“被选择的个体作为上帝授意的处于不变的神圣理念与变化的感官世界之间的中介这一思想”最具意义。[③] 特别

---

① Wellek, *Immanuel Kant in England*, p. 188.

② For the dual meanings of the name Diogenes Teufelsdröckh, cf. Harrold's discussion in Sar., Intro., pp. xl-xlii.

③ Shine, "Carlyle and the German Philosophy Problem," pp. 818-819.

是《论学者的地位》等作品，是卡莱尔的“英雄［理论］的主要来源”。[①] 其中，费希特关于“民族‘英雄’作为历史的创造者”这一观点“对卡莱尔的影响最为深刻”。[②] 在《德国文学现状》中，“文人”被看作“神圣理念指定的解释人；几乎可以说，是一个永恒的教士，一代又一代作为上帝永恒智慧的传播者和代表而站在众人之前，以文字和行动进行表现”（Wks.，XXVI，58）。这一思想在《英雄与英雄崇拜》中被进一步发挥为文人英雄崇拜。在一个“神圣理念对于众人而言不再可以辨认”的世界里，文人就像以赛亚（Isaiah）一样，“被特别遣送到人间，主要是为他自己、也是为别人指明这种神圣理念”（H. & H.，156）。这样的“文人学者是永恒的教士，他们一代又一代向所有的人们宣传上帝依然存在于他们的生命之中”，他们是“人间的光明”和“世人的教士”，“引导人们在艰难的人生征途中不要浪费光阴”（157）。可见，人的神性在此被转化为英雄，而且特别是文人英雄的认识对象。至此，无论是通过歌德的泛神论，还是通过费希特的“文人”学说，人性与神性得到了最终的融合。从此，卡莱尔的信仰恢复开始转向道德要求。

卡莱尔的道德学说有两个主要的来源。其一，是康德对幸福论（Eudaemonism）的反对。[③] 如韦勒克所言，在所有借鉴学说之中，“卡莱尔对康德的道德学说的把握更为准确”。[④] 与康德一样，卡莱尔反对将幸福作为人的最终目的。“幸福可以是一个目标，但绝不应该成为我们存在的目的。”（Wds.，1）他甚至在某种程度上触及了行为法则的普遍性问题。道德不是“苦工的交易”，而是“美德的神圣法则”（100）。这样，“道德的根基被置于偶然之外，置于批评之上”。[⑤] 然而，卡莱尔对康德道德学说的理解总体上停留在对幸福作为目的的反对之上。其二，也是更为主要的来源，是歌德的“断念”思想。“在道德问题上”，卡莱尔可谓“歌德的学生”。[⑥] 他们怀有相同的基本主张，

---

① Lehman, *Carlyle's Theory of the Hero*, p. 113.

② Cole, *Socialist Thought*, p. 225.

③ My discussion of Carlyle absorption of the Kantian opposition to, and criticism of, Eudaemonism is largely indebted to Wellek's discussion in *Immanuel Kant in England*, esp., pp. 188 – 189.

④ Wellek, op. cit., p. 188.

⑤ Cazamian, op. cit., p. 43.

⑥ Cazamian, op. cit., p. 48.

都认为“人的目的在于劳动，劳动的意义大于纯粹的享乐”。① 人的神性是这一主张的依据。在卡莱尔的世界观里，上帝是最为高等的存在。“上帝是伟大的；其他所有的一切均是渺小的”（5th Apr. 1842；to J. G. Lockhart；Let. 3，Ⅰ，263）。在此意义上，人的目的不在于人性，而在于神性的实现。于是，人便通过劳动成为上帝意志实现的工具。卡莱尔将这一思想看作来源于歌德。“合上你的拜伦；打开你的歌德”（Sar.，192），即为此意。但是，“歌德的*Entsagung*［断念］只有在一个美学背景之中才可以得到理解”，而且其中绝无“道德和社会意义上的严苛特征”。② 与施莱格尔兄弟的情况相似，卡莱尔主要将自己的道德思想赋予歌德，让他成为自己主张的代言人。两方面来源综合在一起，最终使得卡莱尔的信仰发展到道德实践领域。

除人的神性之外，信仰向道德实践的发展还有另外一个思想来源。虽然物质世界是上帝的表现形式，但是这种表现与被表现关系有一个新陈代谢的过程。“时间给象征添加了好多神性，在同一过程中也最终毁灭了象征，甚至抹杀其中的神性；就像所有物质的衣服一样，象征最终变得陈旧。”（224）象征的时间性决定了道德实践的连续性。狄奥根尼“当此时还是今天的时候工作”的理念（197），便是这一普遍生成思想的延续。卡莱尔式的“普遍生成的思想”固然与他对“时间之谜”的思考相关，③ 但主要受费希特的“文人”学说影响。文人对神圣理念的解读，表现出明显的历史性特征。“每一个时代根据其本性法则的要求，与其他时代均不一样”，因此“对神圣理念要求一个不同的表现”（Wks.，XXVI，58）。文人的解释方法是“特别的”，符合“特别的时代的要求”（Ibid.）。历史意识的背后，是普遍流变的思想。卡莱尔的道德实践，最终转化为文人的历史使命。

如果以上是卡莱尔信仰恢复的本体论基础，他在认识论方面还有最后的逻辑任务需要完成。虽然自然与人都是上帝的物质表现，作为神性的象征而存在，但是“象征之中既有隐匿又有启示”（Sar.，219）。而且，“象征的神

① Stawell，“Goethe's Influence on Carlyle. Ⅱ，” p. 269.

② Ashton，“Carlyle's Apprenticeship，” p. 16.

③ Carré，op. cit.，p. 167.

奇功能"主要在于"隐匿"（Ibid.）。在此，理性（reason）被看作是可以透视物质外表而最终抵达精神内核的认识机能。"理性［……］具有更高等的本性"，"通过更加精微的方式运作"，而且作用于"更加高等的对象"（Wks.，XXVI，82）。"理性可以分辨真理本身，分辨这绝对的、原始的真"（Ibid.）。在所谓的"纯粹理性之眼"的注视下，人才意识到其内在是"一个灵魂、一个精神和神性的表现"，其外在是"一层肉体的（或者感官的）衣服"，再在其外是"一个有着蔚蓝的、满是星星点缀的空间，以及有着漫长的千年的宇宙"，其中有着"在场的上帝"（Sar.，65，66）。在对理性认识功能肯定的背后，隐藏着对启蒙教育的深刻反思与否定。狄奥根尼毫不讳言，正是因为接受了启蒙教育，"所有的一切立即沦为空虚的辩论；善者以无能的怀疑论告终；恶者则在自欺中崩溃（*crepiren*），所有的精神内容全部死寂"（112）。理性最终使得行动成为可能。"创造的开端是光"，理性使得"眼睛具有视觉"（197）。至此，卡莱尔的信仰恢复获得认识论上的根基。

以上便是卡莱尔信仰恢复的概貌。在宏观上他主要依靠歌德的泛神论创造了一个自然对上帝普遍进行表现的世界，从而获得了上帝存在的物质表现。他进一步依赖费希特的"文人"学说，将人看作上帝的表现形式，使得神性和人性交融并统一于人，为从信仰转向道德实践做好准备。在微观上康德的时空唯心性学说使得卡莱尔将时间和空间，这两个物质世界最为基本的存在方式看作精神存在成为可能，从而让他重新组建的精神信仰获得了相对具有理性特征的基础。另外，在认识论方面，卡莱尔赋予理性以具有高度透视性的认识能力，使之成为认识具有泛神论色彩的世界的认识手段。最后，信仰被转化为道德实践，人的持续不断的劳动便是信仰恢复的表现。

四 信仰恢复

卡莱尔的信仰恢复不但是一个逻辑过程，也是一段人生经历。如弗劳德所说，《旧衣新裁》虽然"不能完全当作一个传记方面的权威文本"，但是"在主要线索上可以采信"。[①] 处于信仰危机之中的狄奥根尼宛若置身"一片

① Froude，op. cit.，Vol. Ⅰ，p. 21.

惨淡的荒漠”，其中“只能听见野兽的号叫，只能听见绝望的、愤恨的人的长嘶；白天没有云柱，夜里没有火柱指引朝圣者的方向”（161）。这一描写用于卡莱尔本人，也格外合适。在一段相当长的时间里，失去信仰的卡莱尔也曾迷失了方向。狄奥根尼的转机出现在“地狱的圣托马斯大街”（Rue Saint - Thomas de l'Enfer）之上（166）。① 在此，一个全新的思路“像一条火焰的泉水一样穿越了［他］全部的灵魂”（167）。同样，“永恒的否定（*das ewige Nein*）在［他］的存在、在［他的］自我的深处发出轰鸣；就在此时［他］全部的自我站立起来”（Ibid.）。这一时刻就是“［他］精神的新生”（168）。据卡莱尔后来回忆，狄奥根尼在圣托马斯大街的遭遇与他本人于1821年在雷丝路（Leith Walk）上的经历如出一辙。② 虽然“《旧衣新裁》中这些内容均不是事实”，均是“具有象征性的神话”，但是“地狱的圣托马斯大街的事件”的确“在雷丝路上真实地发生在［他］的身上”（Rem.[3]，49）。这一时期正是卡莱尔已经具备德语的阅读能力，开始大规模阅读文学和哲学文献的时期。德国思想研究在他信仰恢复过程之中所起的作用，可见一斑。

理解卡莱尔宗教信仰的性质，对于理解他的思想构成，特别是对于理解加尔文主义思想、启蒙思想和德国思想综合到一起之后的体系具有至关重要的意义和作用。总体而言，卡莱尔的宗教经历不同于奥古斯丁（Augustine）和圣保罗（Saint Paul）。前后信仰体系之间的裂隙和分裂，在他的宗教经验之中无处可寻。他的信仰危机并没有表现为一个旧有体系的完全崩溃，一个全

① For the reality in the existence of la Rue Saint - Thomas de l'Enfer, cf. Conway's witness, "This walk in Paris must not be supposed allegorical. Carlyle told me that it actually stood in his life as it is written in his book. He had not heard the story of how this Rue de l'Enfer came by its name until I encountered it while writing my 'Demonology.' In the time of Saint Louis, it was a road supposed to be haunted by a fearful green monster, the Diable Vauvert, a dragon - man, who twisted the necks of all he met. It would appear to have been a phantasm got up by a murderous band of money coiners, who occupied the ancient Château Vauvert. The Carthusian monks having offered to exorcise the devils if Saint Louis would give them the château, that was done. The Diable Vauvert left his trail only in the name of the street, now called Rocherau - Enfer. Near - by is the convert Saint Michael. But the only real dragon - slayer from the time of Saint Louis until now who has passed that way was the young Scotchman [i. e. Thomas Carlyle in the person of Diogenes Teufelsdröckh] who there lay low the phantasm of Fear with the poised spear of a free mind" (*Thomas Carlyle*, p. 45).

② 关于雷丝路事件发生的具体时间，学界一般有1821年和1822年两个选择。本书采信方志强的研究成果，认为该事件发生于1821年。《炼狱与新生》以“卡莱尔的骇伯症”（hypochondria）为线索，对整个事件进行详细的考证研究，详见第90—104页。

新的信仰体系取而代之。相反，加尔文主义宗教观在他的精神发展史之中一脉贯穿。这一点集中地表现在上帝的存在所遭受的威胁之上。信仰危机产生的根源在于上帝存在物质证明的缺失，而远远不是上帝存在本身沦为怀疑的对象。虽然“地上没有路标”，令卡莱尔“完全迷惑了”，但是他“感谢上帝”，因为“天上依然有星星在闪耀”（L. – M.，38）。绝望之中的狄奥根尼坦言，“即使生活在一个没有上帝的世界里，［他］依然没有被完全剥夺，失去上帝之光；［……］在［他］的心中，上帝是在场的，他那书写在天堂里的法则清晰可见、神圣无比”（Sar.，162）。非常明显，即使在至深的怀疑和否定之中，狄奥根尼未对上帝的存在失去信仰。

卡莱尔虽然从来没有从正面试图证明上帝的存在，事实上他甚至声称反对以逻辑的方式对上帝的存在进行证明，① 但是关于这一问题的逻辑思考过程

① The denunciation of logic as the means to the demonstration of the existence of God is a constant theme in Carlyle's works between the year 1829 and the completion of *Sartor*. In “State of German Literature,” “endeavouring, by logical argument, to prove the existence of God,” is taken as analogous to “taking out a candle to look for the sun” (Wks., XXVI, 81). The more one tries to “gaze steadily into [the] candle – light,” the more “the sun himself may be invisible” (Ibid.). Actually, the demonstration of the divine existence is considered as beyond the scope of logic. “To discern the [truth]” that “God exists” is attributed to “the province of Reason” (83). The existence of God is not to be proved “by logic and argument,” the “domain” of which “lies in that higher region whither logic and argument cannot reach; in that holier region, where Poetry, and Virtue and Divinity abide, in whose presence Understanding wavers and recoils, dazzled into utter darkness” (Ibid.). In “Voltaire” (1829), social disorder culminating in the French Revolution is seen as the outcome of the fact that “things human and things divine alike” are “cited without misgivings before the same boastful tribunal of so – called Reason, which means here a merely argumentative Logic” (416). It is the same with the position of Diogenes. He, too, depreciates the “Logic – mill” of the “foolish Wordmonger and Motive – grinder” only as a vain attempt to “[have] an earthly mechanism for the Godlike itself” (Sar., 160). In a word, it is fruitless to prove logically the existence of God.

Carlyle's denunciation of logic as the means to the demonstration of divine existence is closely connected with his decision of the inferiority of logic to reason. Logic is inferior to reason in terms of stability. Logic is said to “vary in every age” while reason “last [s] forever, and [is] the same in all forms of manhood” (Nt. B., 83 – 84). It is on ground of the difference in stability that it is concluded that “the decisions of Reason (*Vernunft*) are superior to those of Understanding (*Verstand*)” (83). Besides, Carlyle seems to conceive another approach to a theory of the inferiority of logic to reason. “Understanding is to Reason as the talent of a Beaver (which can build houses, and uses its tail for a trowel) to the genius of a Prophet and Poet” (142). Obviously, understanding to reason is talent to genius. The assimilation of the relation between understanding and reason to that between talent and genius may be suggested to him by Coleridge. Carlyle, personally, is not ignorant of Coleridge's doctrines. He remembers to be “taught [...] by Coleridge” (Rem.[1], II, 41) and, even,

可以得到一定程度的再现。线索来源于他对上帝的称谓。在他的中后期作品之中，上帝的主要称谓之一便是大写的“制作者”（Maker）。[①]这一称谓固然相符于《旧约·创世记》中“起初，神创造天地”（1：1）所表达的思想，但是在逻辑上，这是因果关系（cause – effect）或因果性（causality）生效的标志。借用罗素（Bertrand Russell）的相关论述，因果关系可以定义为“某一事件 A 造成某一事件 B，由此可以引申出，只要有事件 B，一个更早的事件 A 就可以得到发现，两者之间的关系为——（1）只要 A 发生，其后有事件 B；（2）在此顺序之中，先有 A 而后有 B 具有其必然性，而不仅仅是 de facto［事实］”。[②]可见，因果性主要规定了原因（C）和结果（E）之间的必然性关系。而且，这一关系是一个双向的过程。一方面，由原因必然可以推论出结果，即

$$C \rightarrow E \quad (\text{I})$$

另一方面，与之相应，由结果同样必然可以推论出原因，即

$$E \rightarrow C \quad (\text{II})$$

卡莱尔的逻辑论证过程是（Ⅱ）。从自然到人，从社会到历史，万事万物在他看来不过是上帝存在的效果而已。万事万物作为创造的效果（the made），必然意味着创造的主体（the maker）的存在。这样，万事万物的存在成为上帝存在的证明。事实上，卡莱尔寻找上帝存在物质证明的思路也与这一逻辑线

---

considers him as “a marvellous sage and man”（111）. Though his private meeting with Coleridge can hardly be taken as a pleasure, it is about “‘reason’ versus ‘understanding’,” in particular, that he tries to engage him into a talk（130）. In *Table Talk*, understanding and reason are discussed in the light of talent and genius. “Talent, lying in the understanding, is often inherited; genius, being the action of reason and imagination, rarely or never”（21st May 1830; *Complete Works*, Vol. Ⅵ, p. 319）. The parallel between those two conceptions are easily discernible. Carlyle, on his side, fails, however, to pursue his conception to any significant profundity in later works. The Coleridgean concept comes to him at a too late time, when his attention is gradually drawn to social crisis, for him to be interested in the discrimination of those Romantic terms.

① Diogenes takes the lead in referring to the God by the appellation of “the Maker.” He ridicules the scientists by questioning whether “the Maker take them into His counsel” at the moment of creation (Sar., 256). In the series of lectures, *Heroes and Hero – Worship*, the God is referred to as the “Maker” to whom “［Mahomet's］last words are a prayer”（Her., 71）, “the Make of［that little bird, ... the stars and deep Heaven of Worlds］”（141）, and, more briefly, “the great Maker of the Universe”（163）. In *Past and Present*, the appellation of the God as “the Maker” increases in a geometrical ratio. It would occupy pages to present them all.

② “Psychological and Physical Causal Laws,” p. 287.

索相符合。

以上的因果论证进一步建立在类比（analogy）基础之上。借用亚里士多德（Aristotle）在《诗学》（*De Poetica*）中的相关论证，类比是隐喻（metaphor）的一种（$1457^{b}10$），由类比可以推论出，“当 β 对 α 的关系等于 δ 对 γ 的关系时，δ 可以代替 β，或 β 可以代替 δ”（$1457^{b}20$）。[①] 若以逻辑符号表述，则

$$(\beta:\alpha=\delta:\gamma)\rightarrow(\delta:\alpha=\beta:\gamma);\ (\delta:\alpha=\beta:\gamma)\rightarrow(\beta:\alpha=\delta:\gamma)$$

同样，在卡莱尔的理解中，上帝（G）与万事万物（U）之间的关系便是创造者（C^{+}）与造物（C^{-}）之间的关系。即

$$G:U=C^{+}:C^{-}$$

非常明显，上帝相对于万事万物便是创造者相对于造物。由此，上帝被置于创造者的地位。上帝作为万事万物的创造者最终得以确定。这便是“制作者”等相关类似称谓的逻辑基础和来源。

然而，卡莱尔式的类比的运用存在深刻的问题。首先，类比在范畴（category）方面的合理性未被留意。如上所述，上帝与万事万物之间的关系被直接看作创造者与造物之间的关系（$G:U=C^{+}:C^{-}$）。非常明显，此处两个不同范畴内的关系被看作等值。如果创造者与造物之前的关系是已知（known）范畴，那么上帝与万事万物之间的关系则是未知（unknown）范畴。这是两个在性质上完全相异的范畴。这两个范畴之间的等值，其实是从已知领域到未知领域的过渡，也是一个将未知领域完全纳入已知领域的过程。上帝与万事万物之间的关系是一个全新的现象，需要全新的知识才可以实现理解。类比的解决手法不过是以旧有的知识直接应用于全新的现象的解释。这是旧有知识的再次利用，而不是全新知识的首次产生。

其次，本体论（ontological）和认识论（epistemological）证明被混为一谈。即使以上不同范畴之间转换的合理性不受质疑，此处的证明也将认识论的结论直接误认为对本体论同样有效。以上类比证明只是认识论证明，只能

① 此处引文参见陈中梅译文（商务印书馆 1996 年版，第 150 页）。为行文方便，引用时略有改动。

获得有关上帝存在的知识（knowledge，G_1），而不能获得上帝存在的实体（entity，G_2）。若以逻辑符号表述，则

$$[(G: U = C^{+} : C^{-}) \rightarrow G_1] \rightarrow -G_2$$

但是在卡莱尔最有可能采取的证明之中，认识论所得到的结论被直接推广到本体论，即

$$[(G: U = C^{+} : C^{-}) \rightarrow G_1] \rightarrow G_2$$

非常明显，有关上帝存在的知识被误认为是上帝存在的实体。这是一个非常典型的将知识直接看作存在的思维过程。然而，就像从“龙”（the dragon）的知识不能推导出“龙”的存在，同样有关“上帝”的知识不能推导出“上帝”的存在。上帝存在的本体论证明，对于卡莱尔也同样是一个不可逾越的困境。

最后，类比只是一个修辞手段（rhetoric），而不是求知方法（means to knowledge）。在卡莱尔最有可能的逻辑论证之中，修辞手段被当作求知方法，类比被看作实现上帝存在知识的手段。作为修辞，类比和隐喻的运用固然赋予了卡莱尔的语言以生动的表意效果。他“有意识地赞美别人隐喻的使用”，而且“他自己也有意识地实现类似的生动表达风格”。① 不过，隐喻和类比的运用还有超越修辞的作用。上帝存在物质证明的实现便通过修辞获得。“卡莱尔的隐喻几乎永远实现一个功能：它们将死的物质事实转变为活的精神真理”，在此意义上修辞“不是美学感受的表达，而更是宗教信仰的伸张”。② 作为一种手段，卡莱尔的修辞的目的在于“协助证明一个更加内在的现实的存在”。③ 然而，这种以求知为目的的修辞必将以失败为结果。如罗素所说，“类比性质的论证”根本无法“实现完全的确定性”。④ 类比论证只能实现旧有知识的条理化和系统化，但是无法实现全新知识的产生和发现。就像苏格拉底（Socrates）的辩证法（dialectics），只能实现像正义、虔敬、义务以及理念等旧知识的整理，而不能实现诸如细胞、万有引力、血液循环以及元素周

① Deaton, “Thomas Carlyle's Use of Metaphor,” p. 314.

② Reed, “The Pattern of Conversion in *Sartor Resartus*,” p. 416.

③ Ralli, *Guide to Carlyle*, Vol. Ⅰ, p. 144.

④ “The Validity of Inference,” p. 158.

期表等全新知识的产生一样，卡莱尔的修辞并非一个求知方法。

在以上分析中，卡莱尔宗教信仰的性质表现出来。他的信仰在品质上最为明显的表现，是非知识性的。在他的思想之中，信仰（F）与知识（K）是完全对立的，即

$$F \rightarrow -K;\ K \rightarrow -F$$

上帝的存在是卡莱尔信仰的核心。一个全在的、全知的和全能的上帝深入他生活的所有细节，可谓他“赖以生存的不可见的太阳”。[①] 这个从小便生活在具有浓郁加尔文主义色彩的家庭氛围里的苏格兰清教徒，“属于那类没有上帝就无法生存的人”。[②] 然而，所有的知识无论经过怎样的努力，均无法证明上帝的存在。无论卡莱尔是否在现实中考虑到以上证明过程以及其中所存在的问题，他的信仰没有任何办法可以在知识领域获得稳固的基础。而且，随着知识的积累和深化，宗教信仰根基上的缺陷只能更加不容置疑地暴露出来。就这样，信仰与知识形成尖锐的对立。

信仰的性质，决定了信仰恢复的手段。如果卡莱尔式的信仰在品质上表现为非知识性，那么信仰恢复的手段便是改变信仰的品质，使之成为知识性的，即

$$F \rightarrow K;\ K \rightarrow F$$

信仰和知识之间的调和集中地表现为“心”（heart）与“脑”（head）之间的调和之上。从《让·保罗·弗里德里希·里希特》（“Jean Paul Friedrich Richter”, 1827）到《旧衣新裁》，心脑统一是一个贯穿的主题。在论证里希特的幽默感时，卡莱尔指出“真正的幽默并非仅仅来源于脑，而更来源于心”（Wks.，XXVI，17）。在讨论彭斯（Robert Burns）的生存环境时，他指出“那一时期的爱丁堡知识界大体主要因为脑的清晰，而不是因为心的温暖而知名”（301）。在此，心脑分裂是批评的对象。在《伏尔泰》（“Voltaire,” 1829）中，表现在这位法国最为杰出的启蒙哲人身上的“心在没有脑的指导下行动，或者违抗脑的指导而行动”，被看作一个“矛盾”（436）。同样的线

---

① Willey, “Thomas Carlyle,” p. 113.

② Moore, “*Sartor Resartus* and the Problem of Carlyle's ‘Conversion’,” p. 669.

索一直贯穿到狄奥根尼对科学所持有的观点。如果“没有心的影子”，而仅仅依靠“科学的脑”，“科学”就不可能被“运行”（Sar.，68）。心与脑的统一，便是信仰与知识的调和。“宗教通过真理表现出来”，[①] 这是卡莱尔信仰恢复的手段。可见，卡莱尔式的信仰恢复不是信仰的重新建立，而是信仰与知识的握手言和。

信仰与知识的调和只是意志（volition），而不是逻辑（logic）的效果。如上所述，卡莱尔式的信仰完全不可能通过知识而得到实证（verification）。事实上，知识所得到的唯一结果是上帝存在的伪证（falsification）。信仰与知识之间调和的实现，只能以逻辑上的严谨和连贯的牺牲为代价。如泰纳（H. Taine）所言，卡莱尔“不懂得逻辑推理，而只会描描画画”。[②] 斯宾塞（Herbert Spencer）甚至认为逻辑的缺陷是他的本性。“无论在思想上还是在道德上，卡莱尔的本性表现为连贯性的缺乏。”[③] 在逻辑性的欠缺方面，他与卢梭（Jean – Jacques Rousseau）非常相似。“基本在［与卢梭］一样的精神状态下，卡莱尔先生放弃了逻辑”，甚至还在此基础之上“习惯性地将理性的规范置于意志情感性的要求之下”。[④] 与金斯利（Charles Kingsley）一样，卡莱尔可谓是“一位演说家”，而远远不是“一位推论者”，他“从来没有在最为严格的意义上进行过逻辑推理”。[⑤] 逻辑性的缺失，可谓卡莱尔信仰的主要特征之一。在此意义上，弗劳德将他看作“一位没有神学的加尔文主义者”可谓恰到好处。[⑥] 以意志取代知识在维多利亚时代还具有一定的普遍性。“他们在智力确定和情感安慰上所失去的，他们从单纯的意志力量中获得补偿。”[⑦] 卡莱尔与时代的关联在此得到一定的表现。

信仰与知识的调和作为意志的效果，更为直接地表现在上帝存在的证明之上。总体而言，上帝的存在不是证明的结论，而仅仅是意志的结果。上帝

---

① Roberto, *Tommaso Carlyle*, p. 15.

② *L'Idéalisme Anglaise*, p. 9.

③ Spencer, *An Autobiography*, Vol. Ⅰ, p. 383.

④ Morley, “Carlyle,” p. 148.

⑤ Greg, “Kingsley and Carlyle,” p. 126.

⑥ Froude, op. cit., Vol. Ⅱ, p. 2.

⑦ Altick, *Victorian People and Ideas*, p. 237.

的存在如果不能通过知识证明，那么便无须证明，而且不证自明。这已经超越了信仰，而进入意志领域。卡莱尔可以说“并没有尝试对上帝的存在进行证明，或者对一个可能的上帝进行推理，而是承认上帝存在，认为其不证自明，并且是其他所有真理的基础和本质”。[①] 就这样，上帝所受到的威胁被直接抵消，信仰通过意志的协助被置于知识之上。“当上帝受到威胁之时，危机或者大量的危机就会产生，此时无论是否逻辑前后一致，他终极的目的就是抵消上帝所受到的威胁。”[②] 这一点集中地体现在他对第一原则（*principia prima*）所进行的思考之上。在弥尔顿（John Milton）作品的研读中，他发现“其中的推理方式有些奇怪”，因为弥尔顿“根本不依赖任何第一原则”，而是“旁征博引”，“运用所有［相关材料］协助他［的论证］”（Nt. B.，4）。弥尔顿的论证效果使得卡莱尔产生怀疑，“我们的‘第一原则’［是否］比他的更加牢靠”（Ibid.）。他进一步意识到逻辑证明的相对性（relativity），即非绝对性。“我们逻辑推理的百分之九十都是人为性的过程，并非依赖于事物真实的本质，而仅仅依赖于我们特别的审视事物的角度。”（Ibid.）这是康德的“哥白尼革命”的完美应用。由此，卡莱尔对知识本身开始思考：

真理 *immer* WIRD *nie* IST（Ibid.）[③]

知识是一个永远处于生成的过程，而不是一个既定的状态。此处颇有赫拉克利特（Heraclitus）的万事万物皆为流变的思想的风味，也颇有帕默尼德（Parmenides）的生成的普遍性的意味。关于生成思想，卡莱尔的来源不是古希腊，而最有可能是被他几经曲解的施莱格尔兄弟的浪漫主义理论。与柯勒律治（Samuel Taylor Coleridge）的“天分”（talent）与“天才”（genius）的区分一样，生成思想未能在卡莱尔的思维中获得更加深入的逻辑推进。最终，知识所指向的目的被意志实现。这是对知识的放

① Davey, *Darwin*, *Carlyle*, *and Dicken*, pp. 84 – 85.

② Moore, op. cit., p. 669.

③ 此处为德文，直译为“真理永远成为，从不是”。意译为“真理永远是一个生成的过程，而不是一个既定的状态”。

弃，也是对知识的背叛。①

知识被意志取代，集中地表现在卡莱尔的德国思想研究之中。“卡莱尔在德国唯心论方面，特别是在康德哲学方面所表现出来的兴趣［……］主要不在于认识论的研究，而在于道德和信仰体系的重建。”② 一方面，他并不适合逻辑思考，在形而上学方面所具备的能力非常有限。对于德国思想研究，他并不具有“一个适合进行形而上学思辨的头脑”。③ 因此，他的德国思想研究存在严重的问题。他虽然涉猎了众多德国思想，但是每一次他都是“从某一哲学家那里借来一个形而上学词汇，再通过一个浪漫诗人和神秘主义者的头脑进行考虑，最终应用这一词汇以阐释他早期清教训练的某一信仰，从而获得概念的基础”。④ 研究目的腐蚀了研究质量。另一方面，也是更为主要的一方面，德国思想被严重地道德化。作为一个持之以恒的趋势，卡莱尔不断地在他的德国思想研究之

---

① My conclusion, here, is largely inspired by Russell's summarization of the Platonic Socrates as a philosopher. Socrates is depicted as "dishonest and sophistical in argument, and in his private thinking he uses intellect to prove conclusions that are to him agreeable, rather than in a disinterested search for knowledge. ... His courage in the face of death would have been more remarkable if he had not believed that he was going to enjoy eternal bliss in the company of the gods. Unlike some of his predecessors, he was not scientific in his thinking, but was determined to probe the universe agreeable to his ethical standards. This is treachery to truth, and the worst of philosophic sins. As a man, we may believe him admitted to the communion of saints; but as a philosopher he needs a long residence in a scientific purgatory" (*History of Western Philosophy*, pp. 140 – 141). The Russellian denunciation of the Platonic Socrates is largely shared by Popper. He, too, conceives Plato as a betrayer of the Socratic doctrines. "One of the fundamental tenets of Socrates," according to Popper, is "his moral intellectualism" (*The Open Society and its Enemies*, Vol. Ⅰ, p. 135). It consists in, on the one hand, "his identification of goodness and wisdom, his theory that nobody acts against his better knowledge, and that lack of knowledge is responsible for all moral mistakes," and, on the other hand, "in his theory that moral excellence can be taught, and that it does not require any particular moral faculties, apart from the universal human intelligence" (136). It is clear that Carlyle is more akin in doctrine to Plato than Socrates. Though he is similar to Socrates in identifying morality with knowledge, the Carlylean morality is rather authoritarian than intellectual. It leaves no room for the assertion of intelligence. Moral perfectibility is close and exclusive for Carlyle while open and inclusive for Socrates. Like the Platonic Socrates, Carlyle, too, is argumentatively sophisticated in the sense that knowledge is pursued, not for the sake of knowledge itself, but to the advantage of his moral propensities. In the above light, Carlyle is capable of being accused of intellectual dishonesty. He, too, is unscientific in his thinking, and, in some cases, even to the extent of disregarding factual evidences and logical coherence. His probe into the German thoughts is only a reaffirmation of his predetermined Calvinist faith. He is guilty of treachery to truth, the worst of philosophic sins. The Victorian age adores him as a sage but, as a philosopher, he is in great need of a scientific purification.

② Flügel, *Thomas Carlyles religiöse und sittliche Entwicklung und Weltanschauung*, p. 166.

③ Stawell, "Goethe's Influence on Carlyle. Ⅰ," p. 182.

④ Harrold, "Carlyle and Novalis," pp. 57 – 58.

中“将一个哲学学说转化成一项道德条款”。[①] 这一点鲜明地体现在他对超验唯心论一派哲学家的介绍之上。康德的哲学体系被说成是一个“道德的崇高体系、更加纯粹的神学［以及］从中推演出的有关人的本质的高妙视角”（Wks.，XXVI，78）。费希特被比作“堕落人群之中的老加图（Cato the Elder）；可以成为廊下派的导师，在学园的树丛中谈论美与德”（77）。就这样，超验唯心论传统中的两位哲人被当作道德说教家介绍给英国读者。

至此，卡莱尔的终极目的最终表现出来。不是求知（to know），而是致行（to do），才是他的归宿。如迪布尔（J. A. Dibble）所说，他“的兴趣不在于知识本身的追求，而在于知识的改造世界的力量”。[②] 狄奥根尼更为直接地表达了这一思想。“如果一位从天而降的神圣使者，或者墙上的神奇文字令人信服地向我宣称，这就是你需要做的，我都会像我经常认为的那样无所犹豫，即使是投入地狱的火焰。”（Sar.，162）而且，这是一种没有知识作为指导的行动。他将“基督教”仅仅理解为“服从上帝”，无条件地赞美上帝“是伟大的”“是善的”是唯一的“命运安排”（L. －M.，95）。非常明显，这与阿诺德笔下的希伯来精神（Hebraism）相差无几。“希伯来精神中最重要的是行为和服从”，这与将“如实看清事物之本相”作为“最为重视的理念”的“希腊精神”（Hellenism）相去甚远。[③] 与阿诺德不同，卡莱尔未能意识到希腊精神的珍贵，甚至未能意识到希腊精神与希伯来精神之间的平衡的意义。他固执己见，偏执一端；视局部为全体，认个性作普遍。玛格丽特的泪水没有白白流下，卡莱尔最终回归了他最初的精神家园。他无论曾经遨游在多么宽广的思想领域里，最终都没有离开过埃克尔费亨那狭小的格局。就好像坍塌的恒星，抛洒出外围物质之后，仅仅留下浓缩的内核。

卡莱尔的精神信仰恢复，是一场不折不扣的闹剧（farce）。其中的荒唐，在尼采（Friedrich Nietzsche）的笔下，或者锤子下被评估出来。一个漫游的不合时宜者如是说，“卡莱尔，一个大言不惭和趾高气扬的家伙，一个不得已

① Fehr，“Der Deutsche Idealismus in Carlyles *Sartor Resartus*，” p. 97.

② Op. cit.，p. 73.

③ *Culture and Anarchy*，p. 97. 本处引文参见韩敏中译文（《文化与无政府状态》，生活·读书·新知三联书店2008年版，第99页）。为行文方便，引用时略有改动。

的雄辩家。不断地受到对一种强大信仰之渴望和对此又无能的感觉的骚扰（——在这点上是个典型的浪漫派作家!）对一种强大信仰的渴望不是一种强大信仰的证明，而是相反。一个人有了信仰，就可以允许自己享受怀疑的美好和奢华：他对此就足够安全，足够坚定，足够受约束。卡莱尔对具有强大信仰的人强烈地（*fortissimo*）表明他的敬仰，对不太幼稚的人表明自己的愤怒，由此来麻痹自己内心的某些东西：他需要喧闹。一种面对自己的持续和狂热的不诚实——这是他的特性（*proprium*），因此他是，依然是饶有趣味的"。① 尼采一语中的。坚定的信仰可以容纳激烈的怀疑，信仰的伸张反而是信仰薄弱的表现。在此视角下，卡莱尔精神信仰恢复的荒诞暴露无遗。他以本来不能实现信仰目的的知识作为手段，去恢复一个在根基上本来就没有瓦解的信仰。然而，卡莱尔的魅力在于他对此不但全然不觉，而且还带着认真、带着虔敬、带着尊严投入其中。他说服了自己，也说服了维多利亚时代。在此意义上，一个时代的精神面貌可以通过一个个体得到表现。

无论尼采评估中的合理性是否可以为卡莱尔发觉，他都成功地度过了人生当中最为险恶的时期。至 1825 年，他的身体状况早已恢复，精神状态也比较理想，除前途依然堪忧之外，一切皆好。他在笔记中这样写道，"这一年我发现我已经征服了我所有的怀疑，痛苦的怀疑以及同我所在时代那肮脏、邪恶、扼杀灵魂的淤泥神灵的可怕挣扎；我实现了逃脱，好像从冥府中逃脱一样，其中还有地狱火河和冥河藻泽；我实现了精神的自由，走进了永恒的蓝天——那里有天堂的保佑，我在精神上得到了永生"（Rem.[1]，Ⅱ，179）。他对德国思想的研究热情并未因为目的的实现而直接告终。在《旧衣新裁》完成之前，他的主要关注点依然在于美学、浪漫派文学理论以及超验唯心论等德国话题。1832 年可以看作"卡莱尔'德国时期'，这一他与德国文学接触最为密切时期"的终结。② 此后，他的关注点开始偏移，工业社会成为他全新

---

① Nietzsche, *Twilight of the Idols*, pp. 54 – 55. It needs to acknowledged, here, in concern with this quotation, that my attention to Nietzsche's evaluation of Carlyle is drawn by Kerry McSweeney and Peter Sabor in their edition of *Sartor* (Oxford World's Classics, Intro., p. xxviii). Instead of fragmentary, a full quotation is given here, in my book. The Chinese translation is from Wei Maoping's（卫茂平）version of *Götzen – Dämmerung* (Shanghai: East China Normal Univ. Pr., 2007, pp. 127 – 128)。

② Küchler, "Carlyle und Schiller," p. 426.

关注的对象。

五 思想转向

《旧衣新裁》完成之后，这位“英国的第一批日耳曼学者”开始投身时代问题的解决。[1] 卡莱尔的社会批评并不是简单地对现实社会现象的观察、分析、批评和研究。这种纯粹的政治经济学的研究方法，为这位苏格兰的“博学之人”和“万物之学者”所不齿。[2] 如果套用高尔斯华绥（John Galsworthy）的《福尔赛世家》（*The Forsyte Saga*）中篇名，卡莱尔可谓一位“有要义的人”（man of message）。就像他笔下的英雄，他的消息直接来源于上帝的启发，构成他本人信仰的内容，经受过德国思想的验证，最终被投射到维多利亚社会。可见，加尔文主义思想、启蒙教育以及德国思想综合在一起所形成的思想体系是卡莱尔后期思考的思想来源。这一复杂的思想体系以对真理内容的诠释为核心，被集中地转化成为英雄崇拜理论，表现在社会、历史和道德等方面。这便是卡莱尔的真理观，也是本书的研究对象。

以真理为核心的论述作为一条线索贯穿卡莱尔中后期所有的主要作品。作为“卡莱尔最为出色的作品”，[3]《旧衣新裁》是解读真理观的主要作品之一。其中，真理的构建表现在“对于功利主义的恐惧，社会的宗教基础，皈依的过程［……］，天职的重要性，断念相对于幸福寻求的优越性，劳动、责任和敬畏的道德要求，英雄的必要性，当代英国划分为贫富两极的社会图景”等诸多方面。[4] 在反对“其年代的主流道德哲学，即功利主义”的基础之上，真理的主要内容被确定为“责任、劳动、行动和奉献”。[5]《法国大革命》，这部被穆勒看作既是“史”又是“诗”，而且两者“合而为一”的作品是同一主题的延续。[6] 在延续基础之上，作品将历史维度纳入思考，是一次“历史反

① Carré, “Un Inédit de Fichte,” p. 22.

② Masson, *Carlyle Personally and in his Writings*, p. 63.

③ Carlyle, *Sartor Resartus: Oder Leben und Meinungen*, Vor., p. iii.

④ Carlyle, *Sartor Resartus*, *Oxford World's Classics*, Intro., p. vii.

⑤ Vitoux, “Carlyle et le Culte du Héros,” pp. 19 – 20.

⑥ *Early Essays*, p. 271.

思的严肃尝试”。[①]“法国大革命对于现时代的意义，就像索多玛（Sodom）和蛾摩拉（Gomorrah）相对于古代以色列一样”。[②] 作为历史真理的解读人，卡莱尔向世人宣告，法国大革命“不是历史，而是对英格兰的警告，发生在法国的事情‘可以发生在这里’”。[③] 最后，《过去和现在》将真理在最大范围内应用于社会。在“过去的有序和现在的无序的对比”中，真理的内容得到表现，“当今社会要素的研究可以避免潜在的混乱，这是社会构建的根基”。[④]《过去和现在》涉及英雄崇拜、历史、社会和道德等诸多领域，在一定程度上是卡莱尔真理观所有内容的综合。

然而，卡莱尔真理观的解读实非易事。虽然是“最为关注时代的作家”，虽然“他所有的思想、所有的作品均与现时代存在关联”，[⑤] 但是在他对时代思考的背后是艰深而复杂的思想体系。如福斯特（Joseph Forster）所说，“卡莱尔从来不停留在任何问题的表面；这就是肤浅之徒不喜欢他的原因。他的办法是渗透到深处，渗透到他所谓的根源”。[⑥] 事实上，洞见力也是卡莱尔本人的追求目的。只有表现出“深入事物内核的洞见力”的作品，才会被他称为“在思想上是纯粹的”作品。[⑦] 然而，并不是所有人，甚至包括享有更多资源和更多角度的后辈，都可以像他那样“看到一条根脉与另外一条之间的联系”。[⑧] 在如此具有洞见力的作品里，卡莱尔进一步将“个性与共性融合在一起。一方面没有一行字不是作者个体在场的表现，另一方面他所处理的每一个人或者每一本书都是一面共同生活或者文学的镜子”。[⑨] 个性与共性的交融最终实现了极强的包容力。“在他特别的思想组成之中有许多看似具有多样性的因素，这些因素如果没有使他成为一个具有原创性的作者，至少给了他

---

① Vitoux, op. cit., p. 22.
② Levin, *The Condition of England Question*, p. 41.
③ LaValley, *Carlyle and the Idea of the Modern*, p. 184.
④ Vitoux, op. cit., p. 20.
⑤ Montégut, “Thomas Carlyle et John Sterling,” p. 134.
⑥ Forster, *Four Great Teachers*, p. 66.
⑦ 15th Jul. 1840; Faulkner, “Carlyle's Letters to Charles Redwood,” p. 145.
⑧ 15th Jul. 1840; Faulkner, “Carlyle's Letters to Charles Redwood,” p. 145.
⑨ Ralli, op. cit., Vol. Ⅰ, p. 109.

一个鲜明的个性，使他从其他人区分开来。”① 多样的思想所表现出来的交融性，是卡莱尔思想体系的主要特征之一，也是难点所在。“思考的时候他是一元论者，行动和感觉的时候是多元论者、摩尼教徒。”② 思维方法上的不确定性进一步给他的思想解读设置了障碍。

与思想的复杂相对应的，是文体的多样性。③ 泰纳在卡莱尔生前对此便有察觉。“卡莱尔的二十卷作品”在文体上极其多样，其中包括“评论、历史、小册、幻想、哲学”等各类体裁，这是“建议不要阅读”的根源所在。④ 众多文体混杂在一起固然极大地加强了作品的表现力，但是在很大程度上对解读，有时甚至是理解造成了困扰。特别是《旧衣新裁》，在文体上极其多样。“评论家们甚至在《旧衣新裁》发表之前便开始就文体问题提出疑问。”⑤ 甚至卡莱尔本人对作品的设计也经历了从“超验小说”到“诗性历史”的巨大转变。⑥《法国大革命》在文体上同样存在不确定性的问题。该作品“既不是历史也不是小说，既不是悲剧也不是喜剧，而是自成一体”。⑦ “无论在形式还是在节奏方面”，《法国大革命》“与标准的历史写作之间存在着显著的差

① Davey, op. cit., p. 45.

② Carré, *Gœthe en Angleterre*, p. 175.

③ The heterogeneity in the genres of the Carlylean texts is, most probably, derived from his study in the Romantic literary theories of the Schlegels, especially, of Fr. Schlegel. In "*Athenäums*" – *Fragmente*, "die romantische Poesie" is defined as able "Poesie und Prosa, Genialität und Kritik, Kunstpoesie und Naturpoesie bald [zu] mischen, bald [zu] verschmelzen, die Poesie lebendig und gesellig, und das Leben und die Gesellschaft poetisch [zu] machen, den Witz [zu] poetisieren, und die Formen der Kunst mit gediegnem Bildungsstoff jeder Art an [zu] füllen und [zu] sättigen, und durch die Schwingungen des Humors [zu] beseelen" (No. 116; *Kritische und theoretische Schriften*, p. 90). Obviously, the Schlegelian Romantic poetry is heterogeneously comprehensive, inclusive of all the major literary genres. It does not stop here. The Romantic poetry, further, "umfaβt alles, was nur poetisch ist, vom gröβten wieder mehr Systme in sich enthaltenden Systeme der Kunst, bis zu dem Seufzer, dem Kuβ, den das dichtende Kind aushaucht in kunstlosen Gesang" (Ibid.). It, even, embraces all the human emotions in their purest essence. The above description is characteristic of a great variety of Carlyle's works, and, in particualr, of *Sartor*. For Carlyle's readings of, and acquaintances with, the Schlegels' works, see the section above.

④ Op. cit., p. 3. Cf., also Masson's description of the heterogeneity in the genres of the Carlylean texts as "des essais critiques, des biographies, des livres d'histoire, des pamphlets politiques, un roman philosophique" (Carlyle, *Pages Choisies*, Intro., p. vii).

⑤ Helmling, *The Esoteric Comedies of Carlyle, Newman, and Yeats*, p. 42.

⑥ Bossche, *Carlyle and the Search for Authority*, p. 55.

⑦ Desaulniers, *Carlyle and the Economics of Terror*, p. 9.

异”。[①] “将卡莱尔评价为一位历史学家的标准”，由此成为“卡莱尔研究中的一个核心问题”。[②] 文体问题带来相应的翻译问题。《法国大革命》的法译者虽然并不认同，但依然指出“甚至以他们自己的母语理解都有困难的英国人声明，卡莱尔是不可译的”。[③] 不过，不同语种诸多译本的存在似乎说明，挑战越大，魅力越大。

最后，艰深的思想和多样的文体几乎必然导向语言的晦涩。卡莱尔的语言风格具有强烈的德语特征。“在英国人的风格里，卡莱尔反映了德语古典文学和哲学的基本风格。”[④] 他的思想可谓“通过复杂、奇怪、有时甚至可怕的语言表现出来”，以致英语“并不能满足他狂放思想的特殊内容”，[⑤] 甚至“与他的背景相比”，“他的文风［也］显得格外不同寻常”。[⑥] 同时代的一份评论甚至极尽讽刺、挖苦之能事，认为他的语言“古怪而荒唐，极其含混、矛盾”，这样的作家只能写出“世人当中最为杂乱无章的英文［作品］”。[⑦] 卡莱尔似乎“不满足于简单的表达方式；他每一步都要运用修辞；他赋予思想以形体；他有触摸形体的需求”。[⑧] 如此特别的文风使得卡莱尔“在英语中独树一帜。有时极其口语化并满是精巧的隐喻；联系词被清除掉以获得效果；词语在句子中好像因为意外而被取代，却总可以获得力量加强和表达紧迫的效果；词形失去通常的功能，进入新的、奇异的节奏。［……］新词和合成词、像托福尔斯德洛克这样奇怪的诨名，奇异的隐喻出现在一个段落之中，有时竟出现在一句话之中：整体上有一种既辞藻绚丽、滑稽、隐晦又充满活力的幽默”。[⑨] 同样，语言的独特也是思想艰深的表现。“同具有高度个体性的文风联系在一起的，是包罗万象的思考力。”[⑩] 甚至如果不研究“在如此特

---

① Cumming, *A Disimprisoned Epic*, p. 52.

② Ben－Israel, “Carlyle and French Revolution,” p. 127.

③ Carlyle, *Histoire de la Révolution Française*, Vol. Ⅰ, Not., p. xxii.

④ Kraeger, “Carlyles Stellung zur deutschen Sprache und Literatur,” p. 241.

⑤ Davey, op. cit., p. 45.

⑥ Levin, op. cit., p. 35.

⑦ Seigel, ed. op. cit., p. 217.

⑧ Taine, op. cit., p. 9.

⑨ Symons, *Thomas Carlyle*, p. 132.

⑩ Ralli, op. cit., Vol. Ⅰ, p. 109.

别的精神状态下产生的如此特别的文风”，便只能“误解［卡莱尔］作品的价值”。[①] 可谓人如其文，文如其人。

本书分五章对卡莱尔的真理观进行解读。第一章介绍真理的内容，分析真理的性质。第二章分析真理观在英雄崇拜中的表现。第三章至第五章分别研究真理观在历史、社会和道德等领域中的表现和应用。

① Carlyle, *Pages Choisies*, Intro., pp. vii – viii.

第一章　真理观

追求真理，是维多利亚时代早期（1830—1845）的主要趋势之一。虽然“不会全心投入其中”，但是“对于伟大的维多利亚人来说，真理是一件至关重要的事情”。① 一方面，维多利亚时代的真理具有强烈的道德性。“善即真，真即善”，这可谓“一个十足的维多利亚观念，而且根深蒂固”。② 这样的真理在很大程度上不是“知识”，而是“个性的真理”，即在道德行为上“避免所有形式的虚情假意”。③ 另一方面，真理具有物质性。他们关于真理的认识与时代所取得的物质进步以及物质所带来的恐慌具有紧密的关联。维多利亚时代因为对“物质主义是唯一的真理”这一观念“开始产生惧怕”，甚至“以哥特教堂的形式建造火车站”。④ 无论他们是否意识到道德性和物质性之间在可互换性（interconvertibility）方面存在的问题，道德被认作表现真理的主要手段。对真理的探求，在很大程度上被转化为探求态度的真诚（sincerity）。

总体而言，维多利亚时代所追求的真理是一个单层结构的知识体系。所谓单层结构的真理，是对现实的直接表现。这一点鲜明地表现在现实主义（realism）文学之上。虽然表现手法上彼此不同，但是英国

---

① Wingfield - Stratford, *The Victorian Tragedy*, p. 288.

② Levine, *Realism, Ethics and Secularism*, Pref., p. ⅵ.

③ Houghton, op. cit., p. 426.

④ Wilson, *The Victorians*, p. 322.

“19 世纪现实主义作家典型地宣称他们的兴趣在于传达‘真理’”。[①] 追求真理是作家的天职。“真理可谓［现实主义作家］共同怀有的理想和责任”。[②] 追求真理也是作品的主要内容。“维多利亚时代的作家和评论家关于现实主义小说怀有某些共同的认识：现实主义小说的天职在于再现‘真实’生活的‘真理’。”[③] 作为一位“现实主义者”，狄更斯“不会在真理问题上敷衍了事”，认为真理即是“产生在他身上的印象（impression）”，而他的任务便是“以真诚传递印象”。[④] 甚至像卡瓦娜（Julia Kavanagh）这样的无名作家也沾染了时代思想氛围，认为她的无名之作《瑞秋·格蕾》（*Rachel Gray*）是一部“建立在事实基础之上的故事”，并在序言中写道，“真理是本作的主要价值，作者仅仅声称［……］尽她全力传达真理”。[⑤] 可见，真理作为现实的直接反映是维多利亚单层结构真理观的主要表现。

对真理的探寻，也是卡莱尔持之以恒的追求。如同《少年维特之烦恼》（*Die Leiden des jungen Werther*）中的主人公一样，“对绝对标准、对客观价值的渴望”是“［卡莱尔］所有努力的根源”。[⑥] 狄奥根尼在人生的低谷时期也曾表达过类似的愿望。虽然“对真理的探寻给［他］带来莫名的痛苦”，但是“［他］依然热爱真理”，甚至仰天呼唤，希望得到“真理［……］而不是谎言”（Sar.，161）。卡莱尔还化用《尼各马可伦理学》（*Nicomachean Ethics*）中的名

① Levine, “Victorian Realism,” p. 85.

② Matz, *Satire in an Age of Realism*, p. 25.

③ Moran, *Victorian Literature and Culture*, p. 80.

④ Gissing, *Charles Dickens*, p. 73.

⑤ P. v.

⑥ Stawell, op. cit., p. 179.

句（$1096^{a}11-15$），①

Amicus Plato, sed magis amica veritas.（Sar.，14）

“妥伊福尔斯德洛克是我们的朋友，真理是我们的神灵”（Ibid.），可谓他在《旧衣新裁》中的真理宣言。对真理的追求，贯穿卡莱尔毕生的事业。“甚至直到《晚近文集》，长期支持卡莱尔的是他有关谎言和假象的揭穿可以启示实在的世界是神圣之物的象征的信仰。”②

卡莱尔所谓的真理，不过是加尔文主义思想、启蒙教育以及德国思想等综合到一起之后所形成的思想体系。其中，融入有众多德国因素的加尔文主义思想是真理的核心。“对真的敬畏和信仰，对假的深刻的痛恨，对世界中上帝永恒不变的法则、对履行义务的神圣责任以及对人类生活的尊严和神圣性的信仰”，所有这些便是“他带着热情称颂”的对象，③ 在很大程度上也是卡莱尔式的真理的梗概。总体而言，他以信仰替代了知识。对真理的探寻，也就是对信仰的伸张。他所揭示的真理具有极强的宗教性。上帝不但存在，而且具有有效的约束力，无论对于人还是社会。这便是“有要义的人”的“要义”所在。

与维多利亚早期的主流观念相比，卡莱尔的真理观在结构上表现出明显

---

① It is a Latin phrase and means in English, literally, “Plato is friend, but more friend is truth,” and, in paraphrase, “Plato is my friend, but truth is a better one.” This maxim is usually attributed to Aristotle as a paraphrase from *Nicomachean Ethics* at 1096a11 – 15, “we had perhaps better consider the universal good and discuss thoroughly what is meant by it, although such an inquiry is made an uphill one by the fact that the Forms have been introduced by friends of our own” (*The Basic Works*, p. 939). Carlyle's source, according to Harrold (Sar., 14N), is, most likely, derived from *Tristram Shandy*, humorously adapted by Sterne in Vol. I, Ch. xxi. Harrold also gives another hint for the origin of the source. Some of the last words of Socrates before his death is “παρεσκευασμένος δή, ἔφη,ὦ Σιμμία τε καὶ Κέβης, οὑτωσὶ ἔρχομαι ἐπὶ τὸν λόγον· ὑμεῖς μέντοι, ἂν ἐμοὶ πείθησθε, σμικρὸν φροντίσαντες Σωκράτους, τῆς δὲ ἀληθείας πολὺ μᾶλλον, ἐὰν μέν τι ὑμῖν δοκῶ ἀληθὲς λέγειν, συνομολογήσατε, εἰ δὲ μή, παντὶ λόγῳ ἀντιτείνετε, εὐλαβούμενοι ὅπως μὴ ἐγὼ ὑπὸ προθυμίας ἅμα ἐμαυτόν τε καὶ ὑμᾶς ἐξαπατήσας, ὥσπερ μέλιττα τὸ κέντρον ἐγκαταλιπὼν οἰχήσομαι” [So, thus prepared, Simmias and Cebes, I proceed to the argument. But as for you, if you do as I tell you and think little of Socrates, but much more of the truth, and if you think I'm telling the truth agree with me, but if not, resist with every argument you've got, while taking care that I do not deceive both myself and you in my enthusiasm, and won't get away like a bee leaving its sting behind] (*Phaedo* 91b – c). On considering Carlyle's familiarity with classics and his acquaintance with modern fictions, it is safe to conclude that his source is rather Sternean than either Platonic or Aristotelian.

② Peckham, “Frederick the Great,” p. 203.

③ Davey, op. cit., p. 48.

的特征。他的真理观不再是一个单一结构，取而代之的是一个理想（the ideal）与现实（the actual）处于具有高度张力性结构之中的知识体系。一方面，理想与现实构成两极对比。在他的笔下，理想与现实之间的差别宛若天堂与地狱。另一方面，理想与现实之间存在转化的可能。只要真理被认识，人间天堂不再只是愿望。卡莱尔式的真理不再是对现实的简单描绘。相反，真理所展示的是一个理想世界。这个理想世界被首先当作样本（model），是卡莱尔观察现实世界的主要视角。在此视角下，他仅仅有选择性地留意了那些与理想完全相左的现实。这一理想被进一步看作法则（law），是现实世界的应然状态。现实世界是对应然状态的背离，有必要符合法则的要求。可见，实然真理和应然真理共同统一于卡莱尔的真理观。理解实然真理和应然真理的各自内容和彼此关系，对于理解卡莱尔的真理观具有重要意义。如果将维多利亚中后期真理观所发生的变化纳入思考，卡莱尔的真理观可谓处于新旧之间，是一种思想转折的样本。在此意义上，认识他的真理观对于认识维多利亚有关真理的认识所发生的变化同样具有启发和借鉴价值。

本章主要分两部分对卡莱尔的真理观进行解读。其一为实然性的真理，其二为应然性的真理。

第一节 实然的真理

卡莱尔式的真理在性质上首先表现为，真理是实然性的（descriptive）。实然的真理，是对事实（fact）所形成的理论（theory）。真理作为一种理论，或者是对有关事实的判断与归类，或者是分析与解释。在实然的真理中，事实居于基础地位。同样，在卡莱尔式的真理观中，事实作为核心而存在。与维特根斯坦（Ludwig Wittgenstein）在《逻辑哲学论》（*Tractatus Logico－Philosophicus*）中的学说十分相似，[①] 世界（the world）同样被理解为“事实的总和”，虽然卡莱尔对“［世界作为］事物（things）的总和”（§1.1）也持有肯定的观点。在这样的结构里，世界被事实规定（§1.11，1.12），而且

① 本书所有《逻辑哲学论》的引文均引自贺绍甲的译本（商务印书馆1996年版），引用时给出章节号（§n），不注明页码。

分解为事实（§1.2）。对世界的认识，即是对事实的认识。这一点在卡莱尔的作品主要表现为事实与自然之间的等值。“统治阶级”在统治上的“有所作为”，是“自然和事实”的要求（P. & P.，178）。在给皮尔（Robert Peel）的建议中，行动有必要建立在对“事实和自然本身”的“艰苦、忠实的调查”基础之上（Wks.，XX，97）。可见，自然即是事实。认识世界，即是认识自然。

卡莱尔式的事实在性质上表现为，事实是精神性的（spiritual）。事实的精神性主要来源于物质（matter）与精神（spirit）之间的关系。两者之间的关系是，“物质［……］是精神，是精神的表现”（Sar.，66–67）。两项对于卡莱尔而言最为重要的结论可以从中推演得到。首先，作为精神的表现的物质不具有实在性（reality）。这样的物质不是本质（essence），而仅是表象（appearance）而已。在不具备本质性（essentiality）这一意义上，物质是非实在的（unreal）。“物质只有作为精神的表现才是存在的，其目的在于表现某些理念，赋予其以形体。”（72）很明显，物质因被取消了本质性而不具有实在性。事实上，卡莱尔解读德国超验唯心论的主要目的之一便是取消物质的实在性。在“形而上学的超验体系”之中，“物质的古老的敌对性终结了，物质本身被消灭了”，因而“自然起源和存在的问题被极大地简化了”（Wks.，XXVI,26）。这样的研究卓有成效。至1830年，他在笔记中写道，“我想我已经解决了物实论（Materialism）：物质在我看来不再古老，不再确定，不再如精神一样可感”（Nt. B.，151）。全部德国哲学的研究所得，几乎唯一用于一个先入为主的思想的证明和辩护。

其次，精神性（spirituality）是整个世界的基本属性。如果精神和物质这两个二元要素可以看作全部世界的基本构成，那么两者之间的关系，特别是其一向另一的转化具有至关重要的意义。在物质被看作精神，或者在物质被纳入精神的范畴之后，万事万物的基本构成由二转一。这样，万事万物在本质上无一例外，均表现为精神。在此意义上，精神性成为基本属性。卡莱尔虽然未在作品中对以上逻辑推理过程进行展现，但是相应的结论被他应用到人、社会和历史等对象的认识之上。人是“一个灵魂、一个精神”（Sar.，65）。社会是“一个精神性原则”“一个理念”的“表现”（Wks.，XXⅧ，

13－14）。历史，尤其是“世界历史”，是“理念是如何实现，又是如何巧妙地游走于混乱无序的现实之外”的展示（Rev.，10）。[①] 可见，精神性作为万事万物的本质被卡莱尔推广到所有事物的认识之上。作为世界的基本属性，精神性被进一步赋予生成性（inventivity）。处于“冷漠中心”的狄奥根尼经思考后发觉，只有“灵实论”（Spiritualism）才是“具有生成性的”（inventive），才是“所有的一切”（Sar.，180）。然而，作为一条线索和一个话题，灵实论生成性的论述在卡莱尔的作品中未见后续的展开。

卡莱尔式的实然性的真理的主要内容在以上分析之中表现出来。如果真理是对事实所形成的理论，是对事实进行判断与归类、分析与解释，那么卡莱尔的真理便是将事实看作精神性的，即将精神性视为事实的主要属性。这一理论若以《旧衣新裁》之中的术语冠之，则为“自然超自然论”（natural supernaturalism）。顾名思义，这是一个将自然看作具有超自然属性（supernaturalness）的理论，即这是一个将超自然性作为一个整体属性赋予自然的理论。自然的超自然性的论证，主要通过康德的时空唯心性学说实现。只要“承认时间和空间仅仅是一种思维的形式”，只要承认两者具有“不相匹配的实在性”，那么“上帝最为耀眼的光辉”便不会被时间和空间的“假象”隐匿下去（262）。可见，时间和空间不过是精神性的上帝的存在方式，并对上帝进行表现。这样，时间和空间具有超自然的属性。非常明显，自然超自然论的最终目的在于证明上帝的存在。在此，康德的时空唯心性学说对于卡莱尔的意义变得清晰起来。“康德将《圣经》和柏拉图的语言翻译为现代语言”，并使得卡莱尔“相信这些信仰在现代世界依然是可能的”。[②]

综上可见，实然的真理所描述的世界是一个不可见的上帝潜在于万事万物的世界。这样的真理观可以称为有神内在论（theist immanentism），或者内在有神论（immanentist theism）。在这样的世界里，“事实与真理同义，或者，［……］事实是永恒在时间之中的表现”。[③] 认识事实，即是认识潜在于自然

① 引文参见刘毅译本（吉林出版集团股份有限公司2017年版，第11页）。为行文方便，引用时略有改动。下同。

② Johnson，*Thomas Carlyle*，p. 24.

③ Roe，*Thomas Carlyle as a Critic of Literature*，p. 27.

之中的上帝。上帝普遍存在于万事万物之中，这便是卡莱尔实然的真理的主要内容。“如果有一个真理卡莱尔更愿意强化，那么这就是一个人化的、全能的神灵的存在，他号召人和国家对其进行崇拜，只要他们怀有这样的信仰，他们才在智慧真正的意义上是明智的。”① 知识与信仰在此等同起来。

然而，无论是有神内在论，还是内在有神论，以之为主要内容的真理存在深刻的问题。这样的真理所呈现的事实内容，这样的真理所意味的关于事实的认识，不但与普通经验和科学发现相互背离，而且无法得到实证。非常明显，卡莱尔对事实进行了严重的篡改。为理解这一点，有必要引用波普尔（Karl Popper）的相关论述。“事实是某种语言和实在的共同产物那样的东西；它们是由描述性陈述严格确定的实在”。② 事实既不是对象（things），也不是过程（processes）。事实之中融入有主体（subject）关于客体（object）的所进行的选取、排列、组合和综合等主体性的（subjective）而非客体性的（objective）因素。在此意义上，事实可以类比为摘录（abstraction）。“［事实］有如从一本书里摘录出来，这种摘录使用的语言不同于原书的语言，不仅由原书决定。而且几乎同样程度上也由选择原则、其他摘要方法和新语言的处理手段所决定。”③ 同样，卡莱尔的真理所描述的事实也是语言（language）和实在（reality）共同作用的产物，并由描述性陈述（descriptive statement）最终确定下来。他的陈述也是一个类似于摘录的过程。严格来说，他仅仅选取了自己的认识结构允许他认识的内容，这也是他最愿意认识的内容。如果他对康德的“哥白尼革命”有更加深刻的思考、有更加广泛的应用，那么他将不难发现，自己不过将个人信仰（Fth.）投射到了外部事实（Fct.），使得信仰成为了事实，即

$$\text{Fth.} = \text{Fct.}$$

事实上，卡莱尔对语言问题也产生过一定的思考。语言和实在之间的关

① Davey, op. cit., p. 84.

② *Conjectures and Refutations*, p. 290. The Chinese translation is from Fu Jizhong（傅季重）, Ji Shuli（纪树立）, Zhou Changzhong（周昌忠）, and Jiang Yiwei（蒋弋为）'s version（Shanghai: Shanghai Translation Publishing House, 1986, p. 306）。

③ *Conjectures and Refutations*, p. 290.

联（correspondence），是他思考的焦点。信仰恢复之前的狄奥根尼需要一种“将人的灵魂之中最为神圣的部分所发生的事情描述给感官性的眼睛”的手段，需要一种“将不可言说之物言说给世俗时代的语言”（185）。语言的隐喻性（figurativity，metaphoricity），是他的思考方向。“除了与感官对象相关，所有的语言都是或者曾经是隐喻性的。”（Nt. B.，141－142）这是他第一次意识到“隐喻异常巨大的影响”，并有相见恨晚之憾，“只是最近［他］才明白这个道理”（142）。他甚至萌发写作计划，想完成一部以“《论隐喻》”为名的作品（Ibid.）。考虑到他形而上学方面的思辨能力，以及考虑到隐喻在他语言观方面所起的作用，这部作品十分值得期待。作品虽然未付笔端，但是在《旧衣新裁》中可以看出其中的梗概。“语言被叫作思想的衣服”，是“思想的肉体衣服和身体”（Sar.，73）。非常明显，这是“衣服哲学”在语言理解方面的应用。语言成为思想的衣服，主要是“想象（imagination）编织”的结果（Ibid.）。在此，“隐喻”被看作“［想象］的材料”（Ibid.），是想象实现编织所凭借的手段。最终，语言这层思想的肉体衣服一方面由“原始因素”成就其“骨骼”，另一方面由“隐喻”成就其“肌肉、筋骨和活着的外皮”（Ibid.）。可见，语言的隐喻性暗示出语言与实在之间的张力性结构（tension）。如果沿着这一思路继续向下思考，卡莱尔极有可能会发现事实的主体性（subjectivity），会发现真理的人格性（anthropomorphicity）等问题。然而，他前进的方向出现了偏差。有些隐喻“是瘦弱的、满是灰尘的、瘦长的，肌肉本身看起来是骨化的”，而有些隐喻“在健康的光泽和具有生命力的成长趋势中发出光彩”（Ibid.）。于是，语言的隐喻性问题被转化为理想修辞风格的确定问题。于是，卡莱尔成就了一代修辞大师的地位，却失却了成为哲学家的机会。

卡莱尔式的实然的真理所描述的带有有神内在论或者内在有神论特征的事实，是他观察外在世界的思想背景。在这一视角下，他看到了一个与之完全不同的世界结构。这是一个让狄奥根尼幻灭的生存环境，其中“整个世界被卖给了无信仰”，“神灵古老的庙宇长久以来饱经风雨，最终坍塌”（161）。在这个世界里，卡莱尔所珍重的事实被无视。在“准则不断旋转的混沌里，我们已经不知不觉地失去了对事实的关注”（P. & P.，177）。“［人们］已经从事实的宇宙之中转过头来；与幻象的宇宙朝夕相伴。”（Wks.，XX，206）在这一背景下，实然性的真理所描述的事实（F_1）变得容易理解。非常明显，这是一个描述事实与现实（actual）事实（F_2）完全对立的结构，即

$$F_1 \rightarrow -F_2; \quad F_2 \rightarrow -F_1$$

描述事实与现实事实对应于两个完全不一样的情况。一方面是一个精神性的潜在于万事万物的上帝被普遍信仰的世界，另一方面是一个无人认为上帝存在，也无人信仰上帝的世界。两个事实在上帝存在问题上产生了严重的分歧。非常明显，这是信仰与时代之间的分歧。

至此，卡莱尔真理观中的实然真理的内容一目了然。在本质上，所谓的实然的真理并不是对现实的再现，相反却是对理想的描写。其中，描述事实与现实事实不相匹配，与理想内容却完全一致。实然的真理描绘了一个具有明显有神内在论或者内在有神论特征的事实，这是卡莱尔信仰世界的主要内容。可见，在实然真理中卡莱尔主要将理想事实与现实事实对立起来。这一对立结构，也是卡莱尔观察外部世界的视角。在此视角下，他只能看到一个理想与现实完全对立、信仰与时代完全相左的世界结构。为实现对立的消除，他的真理观发展到应然的真理。

第二节　应然的真理

描述事实与现实事实之间的对立，是卡莱尔的真理观从实然真理发展到应然真理的关键。如果“实然陈述的真值，由事实条件决定”，那么“应然陈述也许同实然陈述联系在一起，导致至少一条命令”。[①] 与实然判断相比，应然判断的目的在于“规定行动、告诉自己或者他人做此或者做彼”，所凭借的手段可以是“直接命令”或者“价值判断”。[②]《傲慢与偏见》的开场白可供一例。“饶有家资而又尚未婚配的男子一定需要一位内贤，这是一个举世公认的真理。”[③] 非常明显，这与卡莱尔实然的真理非常不同。如果后者描述了一

① Kenny, *A New History of Western Philosophy*, p. 940.

② Kenny, *A New History of Western Philosophy*, p. 940.

③ Austen, *Pride and Prejudice*, p. 3; Vol. Ⅰ, Ch. ⅰ.

个事实，那么前者则规定了一种行动。在行动的规定中，同样存在对事实的描述。男子只有在“饶有家资而又尚未婚配”的情况下，才会产生娶妻置室的行动。可见，行动规定（A）以事实描述（F）为前提，即：

If F，then A

卡莱尔的真理在性质上进一步表现为，真理是应然性的（prescriptive）。与奥斯丁（Jane Austen）的名篇名句相比，卡莱尔的应然性的真理同样规定了一种行动。这便是对法则（law）的遵从（obedience）。于是，在实然的真理中对上帝存在的描述，在应然的真理中变成了对法则遵从的伸张。“这个宇宙有其法则”（P. & P.，30），可谓言简意赅，直接道明卡莱尔在这一问题上的立场。“造物主的法则无论是在西奈的雷霆里宣告，还是以其他方式宣告给听觉或者想象，都是上帝的法则”，在级别上“超越一切”，在时间上“永恒长存”，“要求所有人的绝对服从”（227）。无形的法则甚至被赋予种类各样的形体。非常明显，应然性的真理没有描述一个事实，而是做出一种规定。在规定中，知识（K）让位给法则（L）。探求知识就是遵从法则，即

K = L

求知与遵法合流于卡莱尔的论述。“通过所有神圣的探求和思考，[他] 要尝试发现 [宇宙的法则或者上帝的法则]”，他希望“在人类手段所允许的范围内尽力靠近 [其中之一]”，这样，“所有的人将通过 [他] 看到 [其中之一]”（Wks.，XX，78）。非常明显，知识即是法则，求知便是遵法。

卡莱尔应然的真理有两项主要的内容。其一是遵从。遵从被规定为具有必然性（necessity）。必然性当然没有被生硬地直接赋予，而是经历了一定的论证。遵从的必然性一方面来源于人的本性。“自然如此精巧地做出规定，无论人需要遵从的对象为何，他都不得不遵从。”（Sar.，251）来源于本性的遵从甚至无论等级。“即使是在最微弱神圣之物的启示面前，人都需要表示敬意”，因为“一种真正的宗教忠诚深植于 [人] 的内心”（Ibid.）。另一方面，遵从的必然性来源于人的社会性。“无论多么微小，人都有必要遵从高等级的存在。”（P. & P.，241）这是人作为社会存在的要求。“正是根源于这一必然性，[人] 才是一个社会存在；否则，人便只是群居动物而已。”（Ibid.）两方面综合在一起可见，遵从的必然性来源人的本性和社会性的要求。

其二，是法则。一方面，与遵从的必然性相应，法则具有不可抗性（irresistibility）。法则的不可抗性集中表现在其效力（effect）之上。法者必效。“无论［他人］相信与否”，对于卡莱尔而言，“这个宇宙的永恒法则”的生效是“绝对确定的”（Wks.，XX，77）。法则在效力上的不可抗性特别表现在违法的后果之上。违法必罚。“自然的法则”虽然“声音微小”，但是“发自［人］内心的深处”，而且如果被“忽视”，则必将产生“可怕的惩罚”（P. & P.，145）。甚至“没有一个人可以不对自身造成伤害而远离真理；一百万个人不会；两千七百万人也不会”（Ibid.）。违法与遵法可以导致不同的结果。“遵法”是“与人的生命本身同样神圣的责任”（187）。只有遵法，“自然才会与［人］为伍，［人］才可以劳动，享受高贵的奖励”；否则，“自然就会与［人］为敌；［人］就不能在自然的帝国里劳动”（Ibid.）。顺之则昌，逆之则败。遵法与否决定了人类事务的兴衰成败。“如果我们按照法则发展，法则的制作者就会与我们为善；否则不善。”（30）卡莱尔特别强调背离法则的可怕后果。背离法则必将以失败为终。特别是在国家事务上，“国会如果不顾天堂的法则，就会在许多问题之上处于 *reductio ad absurdum*［归为谬误］之中”（85）。法则的不可抗性还表现为法则的重新伸张。法者必伸。违法只能是暂时的，因为“不断的叛乱、争斗、怨恨、孤立和诅咒将接踵而至，直到所有的人发觉所得到的［……］不是成功，而是成功的缺失”（Ibid.）。最终，法则将被遵从。

卡莱尔的正义（justice）观在以上过程之中表现出来。法之遵从，则为正义；法之背离，则为不义。在正义的论述中，卡莱尔将法则的遵从转化为上帝意志（will）的实现。“我们每天都祈祷的天堂之王国已经到来；上帝的意志在地球上实现了，就像在天堂之中一样”，这“便是神圣的正义的闪耀”（25）。可见，遵法即是尽意。据此，法则的不可抗性被转化为正义实现的必然性。“事实的法则是，正义一定而且将要被实现。”（19）以上过程所展示的正义观具有鲜明的特征。卡莱尔关于正义的认识与《游叙弗伦》（*Euthyphro*）中的苏格拉底非常不同。他并未定义正义的概念，分析其中的逻辑关联,[①] 而是直接规定正义的内容，强调正义的生效。非常明显，这是一个以道德规定取代知识获得的过程。知识是苏格拉底的手段，而道德是卡莱尔的方法。

另一方面，法则具有极强的约束力。首先，人的道德实践为之约束。法则被形象地看作一位法官。“正是在这间终极法庭之内，事实的普遍灵魂和真理履行着法官的职责。”（15）所有一切的人类道德实践，都是裁决的对象。“今天所有的原因都涌向那里，速度惊人，而且越来越快，只为判定。”（Ibid.）最终的结果或者是“肯定”，或者是“修定”，甚至或者是“有代价的重定”（Ibid.）。可见，人的道德实践并不是自由的，而是受到法则的约束。另外，人的社会实践也为之约束。同样，社会实践也不是自由的，而是受约束的。“英格兰一定要符合活生生的永恒法则，否则英格兰就会死去。”（Wks.，XX，134）人的道德和社会实践均受到约束，法则的不可抗性由之可见。

法则是卡莱尔式的应然真理的主要内容。非常明显，在两项主要内容之中，遵从的必然性以法则的不可抗性为基础和前提。只有法则不可违抗，遵从才必不可缺。这样，法则是遵从的基础。理解法则，即是理解应然的真理。卡莱尔所谓的法则不是某一具体领域内的法则。“这些‘自由主义’‘供求关系’‘金钱关系’等对于社会中的人而言过去、现在以及将来都不是一个可行的组合原则。”（38）他所理解的法则与上帝具有紧密的联系。法则是“上帝之法”（165），是“万能的上帝让他的宇宙运行的法则”（38）。在此意义上，“这个宇宙［……］是根据法则创造的”（227），遵法即是遵守事物的内在规则。可见，卡莱尔通过将法则与上帝之法等同，使得他所谓的法则披上了一层神圣的外衣。神性的存在使得法则获得了至高的权威。在此情况下，只有“真实的法则被认作人类的规则”，只有“人类紧密地遵从这一法则”（Wks.，XX，4），才可以实现良性的发展。

法则的内容规定了世界的应然状态。在应然状态下，上帝是万事万物的

① For Socrates' analysis of justice, see *Euthyphro* 11e7 - 12d4, 12e6 - 9, 13d5 - 14e7, 14e10 - 15b6.

法则，规定所有的一切。“在世界旋涡的中心，现在就像在最为古老的时期一样，上帝存在着并言说着”，这个作为“世界的正义的伟大灵魂”是万事万物的规定者（P. & P.，14）。在人的层面上亦然。对于人而言，“在高贵的人的内心深处这一点都十分清楚，就像一个不可见的正义的上帝创造了人一样，上帝的正义，也只有上帝的正义最终才会在所有的分歧、竞争和争夺之中实现，即使这是不可见的”（191－192）。非常明显，将这种应然状态作为法则，在很大程度上便是将现实置于上帝法则的控制之下。

应然的真理对应于一个法则失效，或者法则不再发挥管制作用的现实。维多利亚时代被卡莱尔称为“无神的世纪”（168）。在这样的时代里，“宗教、基督教教堂、道德责任；人还有一个灵魂的事实；在人的生命之中还有永恒的真理或者正义，——所有这些都在人的视野之外”（Ibid.）。人已经忘记了上帝法则的约束力。卡莱尔发出疑问，“你知道那法庭吗；你在那里处理过任何法律事务吗？［……］你从来没有提交过纠正、收回、免责或者抗辩等申请？［……］你仅仅通过微弱的传统听说过，这法庭是过去的事物或者曾经存在的事物？”（16）非常明显，现实世界与应然的真理所规定的状态完全背离。

在以上分析中，卡莱尔应然真理的主要内容变得清晰起来。在本质上，应然的真理规定了现实世界的应然状态。现实世界处于上帝的法则失效而且不再发挥管制作用的状态之下。非常明显，这与卡莱尔的信仰理想完全相反。他就此规定了一个上帝的法则作为万事万物规范的应然状态，看作现实世界的转化对象。为实现转化，他对法则的不可抗性和约束力进行了大量的设计。最终，人的绝对服从从中推演而来。在以上过程之中分明可见，卡莱尔的终极目的在于实现现实世界向自己的信仰理想的转化。

至此，卡莱尔真理观中的实然真理和应然真理之间的关系昭然若揭。实然的真理所描述的对象与应然的真理所规定的内容其实是同一个对象。这便是卡莱尔信仰的内容，即他的理想世界。在他对真理的探寻中，理想世界首先作为实然事实被描绘，再作为应然事实被规定。这一过程与博耐特夫人（Mrs. Bennet）对未婚男子婚配前景所形成的判断别无二致。他们都将个人理想误认为现实，又在此基础之上规定现实符合自己的理想。毫无疑问，这样的真理不是知识，而更是意愿（wish）。卡莱尔没有博耐特夫人的运气。简和伊丽莎白（Jane & Elisabeth Bennet）的婚嫁成就了这个“神经脆弱”的女人母亲生涯之中的华彩乐章，而维多利亚社会始终未能符合“切尔西的圣贤”的心意。卡莱尔漫长的生命超越了他盛名的期限。妻子去世之后，他无心问学。时代辜负了他的美意。意之愈笃，伤之弥切。

综上可见，在卡莱尔的真理观中，真理表现出一种明显的双层结构。这种双层结构首先在实然的真理中表现为理想与现实之间的对立。实然的真理并不是对现实的简单再现，而是以卡莱尔的宗教理想为视角，主要选取了与之完全对立的现实作为对比对象。这种双层结构进一步在应然的真理中表现为现实的既定状态与应然状态之间的对立。现实的既定状态并不是一个稳定的结构，而是存在向应然状态发展的必要性。由此可见，理想与现实交织在卡莱尔的真理观之中，形成了一种复杂的张力性结构。

这种由理想和现实交织在一起所形成的具有高度张力性的真理观，与维多利亚早期的相关认识具有本质的区别。早期现实主义作家将现实再现作为最高目的的观念，在卡莱尔的笔下增添有理想的描写和应然状态的转化等两个全新的维度。他虽然没有认识到语言的相对性、事实的主体性以及真理的人格性等更加深刻的认识论问题，但是他的真理观依然是一种认识在复杂性上的发展，对于理解真理以及认识真理在维多利亚中后期的发展具有重要的借鉴意义。

第二章　英雄崇拜

卡莱尔的英雄崇拜理论在他的思想体系之中占据着极其重要的地位。英雄崇拜理论可谓“既是他观察的结果，也是他研究的原则”。[①] 虽然这一理论的主要载体《英雄和英雄崇拜》不过是一部只有六讲的系列演说集，但是其中的许多内容从他的早期思想发展而来，甚至贯穿到中后期几乎所有主要的作品之中。作为一个线索性的主题，“在卡莱尔以后全部作品中，英雄崇拜这种思想日益突出，最后成为他的主导思想”。[②] 特别是“歌德、彭斯、约翰逊、半虚构类人物妥伊福尔斯德洛克——所有这些人物以及诸如参孙院长和克伦威尔等晚期主要人物”均可谓“充实了在《英雄和英雄崇拜》中发展的理论”。[③] 作为一个理论，英雄崇拜融入有卡莱尔的众多思想要素。“他的［英雄崇拜］理论将众多通过大量的阅读而获得的［思想］因素融合为一个整体。”[④] 在很大程度上，英雄崇拜理论是卡莱尔思想的综合。理解英雄崇拜理论对于理解他的思想体系具有重要的意义。

《英雄和英雄崇拜》来源于同名系列演说。“英雄和英雄崇拜”并不是一个孤立的作品，而是 1837—1840 年一系列演说中的最后一部，也是最为重要、最为精彩的一部。前三个系列演说分别是“德国文学”（“German Litera-

① Gazeau, *L'Impérialisme Anglais*, p. 55.

② Le Quesne, *Carlyle*, p. 64. The Chinese translation is from Duan Zhongqiao（段忠桥）'s verison（Beijing: China Social Sciences Pr., 1987, pp. 122 – 123）。

③ Spivey, “Carlyle and the Logic – Choppers,” pp. 63 – 64.

④ Lehman, op. cit., p. 39.

ture,” 1837）、“文学史”（“History of Literature,” 1838）以及“当代欧洲革命”（“The Revolutions of Modern Europe,” 1839）等。除“文学史”系列演说被保留下来之外，其余两部均未能得到记录。“德国文学”系列演说基本来源于未完成的《德国文学史》。加之德国文学是卡莱尔长期以来关注的话题，这样系列演说的主要内容基本可以通过相关作品得到一定的复原。“当代欧洲革命”系列演说同样未能得到记录。不过，演说的梗概在当时的报刊上均有报道。① 这样，这部系列演说同样可以得到一定程度的复原。这四部演说在话题上存在一定的相关性。理解前三部系列演说对于理解《英雄和英雄崇拜》具有一定的意义。

卡莱尔进行演说的主要目的在于解决收入问题。《法国大革命》的出版未能有效地改善卡莱尔一家的收入情况。如他对艾默生所说，“必要的刺刀抵在我的背上，我被迫走进演说厅，被迫处于那种状态，被人命令或者说话，或者死亡”（16th Mar. 1838；C. – E.，182）。卡莱尔本人对于演说怀有比较复杂的情感。一方面，他认为演说具有一定的严肃性。演说被他叫作“预言与表演的混合”。② 另一方面，他对自己的演说才能有一定的认识。“演说（或者我应该把它叫作说话）是一个一直以来我便有所渴望的对象：如果我被投入其中，我好想真地可以在这样的元素中遨游：事实上，演说可以发展我所具备的一些品质，这些品质剧烈地需要发展。”（3rd Feb. 1835；117）甚至在“德国文学”系列演说开始之前，他说道，“［演说］是一个长久以来［他］所需要的事物，长久以来有意尝试的事物”（5th Mar. 1837；L. – B.，418）。虽然卡莱尔对于演说有所期待，但是演说于他而言还是颇有压力。在卡莱尔夫人的描述中，演说简直就是“殉道”。③

“英雄和英雄崇拜”系列演说于 1840 年 5 月 5—22 日完成。其中，第二讲“先知英雄”被认为是最好的。第二讲“被众人叫作是［他］所做的最好的［演说］，甚至过分地好”（12th May 1840；495）。第三讲“诗人英雄”虽

---

① See Shepherd, *Memoirs*, Vol. Ⅰ, pp. 197 – 214.

② Froude, *Life in London*, Vol. Ⅰ, p. 117.

③ *New Letters and Memorials*, Vol. Ⅰ, p. 79.

然“仅以普通方式完成，但是与［他］所愿一样，十分顺利”（494）。总体而言，“英雄和英雄崇拜”是他最为成功的系列演说。关于他的演说，有一份现场记录如此评论，“他手臂和身体的肢体活动并不多；但是他的眼神和表情里有某些东西暗示出意图的虔敬，暗示出对主题的强烈兴趣”。① 甚至在卡莱尔“最为热烈、最具活力的时刻”，“他最内在的灵魂”都表现在“他的脸上”。②“英雄和英雄崇拜”系列演说获得巨大成功。就在此时，卡莱尔决定不再进行演说活动。“［他］有时算计，在未来的时间里不再尝试［演说］也许会更好；而是开始写作，既然［他］可以为［他］的书获得一些材料。”（8th Apr. 1840；L. –B.，488）“英雄和英雄崇拜”系列演说结束之后，卡莱尔从未进行过任何演说活动。

《英雄和英雄崇拜》的成书过程极其艰辛。1840 年 6—9 月，卡莱尔重写演说稿。6 月，第一讲“神明英雄”完成，同时第二讲的重写准备就绪（15th Jun.；to Mrs. Aitken；Let.[3]，Ⅰ，196）。7 月，第三讲的重写完成（15th Jul.；to Dr. Carlyle；199）。至 8 月末，第五讲“文人英雄”彻底完成，而第六讲“帝王英雄”已经开始（25th Aug.；to Mrs. Aitken；207）。9 月 3 日，全部重写任务完成。他在信中告知母亲，“两天前我完成了最后一讲［的重写］”（5th Sep.；208）。重写期间，他曾经产生怀疑，认为演说稿毫无成书的价值。“我的演说对于我自己看起来毫无价值。”（1st Aug. 1840；to Dr. Carlyle；201）他如此绝望的根源在于，文字“缺少通过声音和面部表情表达出来的个人虔敬的润色”，因而“在纸张上看起来非常沉闷无聊”（Ibid.）。即使卡莱尔本人对书稿存在一定的不满，但是《英雄和英雄崇拜》依然是他最为重要的作品之一，是解读他思想的主要文本。

作为一条思想线索，英雄崇拜在卡莱尔的思想体系中有一个发展过程。早在《歌德》（“Goethe,” 1828）中，某些英雄崇拜的思想要素便已表现出来。歌德被描述为“一个几乎一跃而成为全部欧洲最负盛名的人；通过不断的进步渐渐在国人的敬仰中站稳脚跟；半个世纪之后［……］，依然毫无争议

① Shepherd, *Memoirs*, Vol. Ⅰ, p. 216.

② Shepherd, *Memoirs*, Vol. Ⅰ, p. 216.

地占统治地位，阅历丰富而荣誉更多；依然为自己的使命奋斗，依然带着国王般的仁慈，促进本国文化可以受益的对象”（Wks.，XXVI，200）。这一歌德形象与文人英雄之间存在一定的相似性。《席勒》（“Schiller，”1831）中甚至可以找到英雄崇拜理论的雏形。“伟人是人类漆黑的朝圣路程中的火柱；他们就像神圣的标志，是过往事物永生的见证，是未来事物预见性的记号，是人类本性被启示的、被表现的可能。”（XXVII，166－167）这与英雄作为神性的表现一脉相承。在《鲍斯威尔的〈约翰逊传〉》（“Boswell's Life of John，”1832）中，相关思想表现得更为明确。“这些便是我们所谓的人，我们所谓的伟人；他们是愚众的向导，——根据不可抵抗的规定，众人跟随着他们。”（XXVIII，89）伟人的品质在于“了解和相信；他们存在的本质是，他们的生活不以道听途说，而以清晰的视觉为基础”（Ibid.）。伟人可以“洞见事物本身”，因而“他们的存在具有现实性”（Ibid.）。可见，英雄的品质和存在状态在此得到了一定程度的阐释。《旧衣新裁》中同样存在有关英雄崇拜理论的论述。其中，“［人］的敬畏机能”，英雄作为“神性的启示”以及“英雄崇拜”作为“任何政体的基础”等思想均得到表达（Sar.，251）。在卡莱尔后期几乎所有的社会批评作品中，英雄崇拜依然是一条贯穿的线索。“他后来所有的社会论述的主导原则是强硬的领袖、即英雄，以及崇拜他的主题的原则。”①

在维多利亚时期，英雄崇拜是一个具有一定普遍性的思想潮流。在一定意义上，英雄崇拜可谓“一个19世纪现象”。②“在1830年后的50年时间里，对英雄的崇拜是英国文化中的一个主要因素。”③ 维多利亚时期的英雄崇拜思想潮流有多方面的来源。“当维多利亚时代开始的时候，所有英雄崇拜的先决条件都已经在场：热情的秉性、有关超凡人物的构想、荷马神话和中世纪民谣的复兴、伟大的艺术与华丽的风格之间的等同、司各特与拜伦的流行、拿破仑式的士兵与水手的存在。”④ 所有这些因素对于英雄崇拜思潮的形成均起

---

① 威廉斯：《文化与社会》，第113页。

② Houghton，op. cit.，p. 305.

③ Houghton，op. cit.，p. 310.

④ Houghton，op. cit.，p. 310.

到不同的作用。其中，浪漫主义的天才（genius）理论可谓维多利亚时期英雄崇拜思潮的理论先导。在天才理论视角下，伟人与普通人之间的差异是本质性的。伟人是“半神”，“拥有最高的智慧和超凡的行动能力”。[①] 曼弗雷德（Manfred）和普罗米修斯（Prometheus）可谓浪漫主义天才人物的代表。卡莱尔式的英雄与浪漫主义天才之间存在一定的关联和相似性。

卡莱尔的英雄崇拜作为一个理论具有许多原创性。首先，他的英雄崇拜理论具有丰富的历史维度。在他看来，英雄崇拜不是一个单一的理论，而是人类历史发展所表现出来的总体趋势。在这一视角下，历史根据英雄崇拜的类型被分期。最终，历史发展表现为英雄崇拜的发展。这样，历史成为英雄史。总体而言，历史是卡莱尔考察英雄崇拜的背景。如韦勒克所言，“卡莱尔作为一位文学历史学家和批评家的功绩在于他为歌德、席勒和让·保罗所做的肖像，在于有关鲍斯威尔和彭斯的散论，而不在于更加宏大的历史设计”。[②] 可见，英雄崇拜理论居于卡莱尔历史研究的中心。其次，他在最大限度上扩大了英雄的类型。“英雄和英雄崇拜”系列演说共六讲，对应于六种主要的英雄类型。从斯堪的纳维亚神话到伊斯兰世界的穆罕默德，从但丁（Dante）和莎士比亚（Shakespeare）到路德（Luther）和诺克斯（Knox），从约翰逊和彭斯到克伦威尔（Cromwell）和拿破仑（Napoléon），形形色色的人物被纳入卡莱尔的英雄谱系。另外，他的英雄崇拜理论具有明显的现实依据。卡莱尔始终从英雄崇拜的角度对现时代的社会进行观察。在这一视角下，现时代的社会处于不再进行英雄崇拜的状态。这被认为是现代社会顽疾产生的根源所在。可见，英雄崇拜理论的背后隐藏着卡莱尔强烈的社会意识。最后，英雄崇拜理论带有明显的德国思想因素。如上所述，歌德的泛神论和费希特的文人理论对于卡莱尔英雄崇拜理论的形成具有重要的借鉴意义。此外，英雄崇拜理论中也含有他本人融入有德国思想要素的形而上学思想。在某种程度上，英雄崇拜理论可谓卡莱尔思想的发展。

卡莱尔英雄崇拜理论的基础在于个体和民族之间的关联。在他看来，个

① Houghton, op. cit., p. 306.

② Wellek, “Carlyle and the Philosophy of History,” p. 97.

体，特别是那些杰出的个体人物，即伟人或者英雄，是民族性格的集中体现。对伟人进行研究，也就是对民族性格进行研究。早在1822年，这一认识便在通信中被表达出来。“［他］的意图［……］是关于内战，关于英联邦写成一篇论文——不是写作历史——而是尽［他］所能展现民族性格表现在克伦威尔、劳德、福克斯、弥尔顿以及海德等这些宏大舞台上最杰出的表演者身上的一些特点。”（27th Apr.；L. – B.，110）他甚至特别指出，“［他］可以在描写作品中插入一些思想，这些思想［他］可以从宇宙中任何方面获得”（Ibid.）。非常明显，伟人在此被认为与万事万物之间存在关联。这样，伟人成为民族性格的集中表现。在这一宏观认识的内部，还存在微观认识。伟人的性格只能实现局部的认识。然而，“人的精神本性，人的内在生命力，本质上是同一个东西，是不可分割的；我们称之为想象力、幻象力、理解力等，不过是洞察能力的不同形态，它们全都是相互联系、不可分割的，即使它的外表也是相互联系的”（H. & H.，106）。基于这一判断，“我们可以从其局部看到全局”（Ibid.）。这意味着，对伟人性格的认识可以通过伟人某一品质的认识而最终实现。这又是一个以点带面的解决办法。在所有品质之中，卡莱尔主要选择了德性（morality）作为研究对象。“德性，即我们称之为一个人的道德品质，是人赖以生存和工作的生命力的另一侧面的表现。”（Ibid.）这样，对伟人的研究最终归结为对伟人德性的研究。伟人的道德品质和道德行为，可谓卡莱尔英雄崇拜理论的核心内容。

卡莱尔的英雄崇拜理论与现代思想之间存在一定的关联。这一关联一方面存在于他与尼采之间。卡莱尔的英雄崇拜理论与尼采的超人学说之间具有一定的相似性。“卡莱尔直接导向尼采”，而且“［尼采］的超人是［卡莱尔的］英雄的进一步发展”。① 然而，这一关联不宜被过分夸大。“卡莱尔的伟人和英雄不要被误读：他们不是尼采式的超人，在道德秩序之外，超越善恶，而是上帝意志的工具，是一个不是他们自己所选择的命令的执行人，不去实现他们的个体目的。”② 总体而言，只有将“［卡莱尔和尼采］各自对于他们

① Grierson，*Carlyle and Hitler*，p. 47.

② Wellek，op. cit.，p. 100，

在宗教或者文学领域里所扮演的独特而又毫无先例的预言角色所形成的认识，他们特殊的在社会领域里的分离状态以及他们对废嫡、传统的丢失和社会混乱的不同寻常的反应”纳入思考，[①] 两人的相关理论才可以得到正确的理解。

另一方面，卡莱尔的英雄崇拜理论与希特勒（Adolf Hitler）之间存在一定的关联。他被认为是现代法西斯主义的理论先驱。“希特勒的先驱”和“超人英雄的崇拜者”等，[②] 成为他的称号。甚至奥威尔（George Orwell）也持有这一观点。在他看来，“卡莱尔是权利和成功现代崇拜的奠基人之一，他热烈地赞扬德国第三次侵略战争”。[③] 这样的观点影响了对他思想的解读。他被看作是“一位有着对我们这代人而言险恶的信息”。[④] 特别是“他有关社会和政治问题的观点”，最“表明在本质含义上是一个法西斯主义者的观点”。[⑤] 然而，卡莱尔与纳粹之间的关联是反历史的。如卡西尔（Ernst Cassirer）所说，“若要卡莱尔为由他的理论所导致的后果负责，这样的做法有悖于历史的客观性”。[⑥] 事实上，《英雄和英雄崇拜》“并没有将独裁者当作偶像”。[⑦] 希特勒也不会成为卡莱尔式的英雄。“卡莱尔不会将希特勒当作克伦威尔，就像柏拉图不会将他当作哲学王一样。”[⑧] “‘不列颠法西斯主义者’的小团体”虽然存在，但是可谓“与卡莱尔长久以来几乎被人忘记的观点毫无关系”。[⑨] 事实上，《英雄和英雄崇拜》以及“他的晚期作品”并不可被看作是“专制统治理论的辩护”。[⑩] 罗素的相关评价比较公允。“历来有两派自由主义，这两派不妨区分为‘冷头脑派’和‘柔心肠派’。”[⑪] 其中，“‘柔心肠派’按另外一

---

① LaValley, *Carlyle and the Idea of the Modern*, p. 298.

② Wellek, “Thomas Carlyle,” p. 92.

③ *Essays*, p. 551.

④ Schapiro, “Thomas Carlyle, Prophet of Fascism,” p. 97.

⑤ Schapiro, “Thomas Carlyle, Prophet of Fascism,” p. 97.

⑥ *The Myth of the State*, p. 216.

⑦ Rosenberg, *Carlyle and the Burden of History*, p. 115.

⑧ Willey, “Thomas Carlyle,” p. 130.

⑨ Trevelyan, *Carlyle*, p. 5.

⑩ Trevelyan, *Carlyle*, p. 5.

⑪ *History of Western Philosophy*, p. 584. The Chinese translation is from He Zhaowu（何兆武）, Li Yuese（李约瑟）and Ma Yuande（马元德）'s version（Beijing: The Commercial Pr. , 1976）.

些逻辑阶段，经过费希特、拜伦、卡莱尔和尼采，发展到希特勒”。① 罗素在此指出，“这个说法过于简括，不够十分正确，但只可算一种帮助记忆的指掌图”。② 可见，卡莱尔的英雄崇拜理论与希特勒之间存在一定的关联，但是不宜夸大。

卡莱尔对时代的影响主要表现在英雄崇拜理论之上。如梭罗（Henry David Thoreau）所说，“卡莱尔所有的作品都可以纳入《英雄和英雄崇拜》这一标题之下”。③ 甚至可以毫不夸张地说，“在这一领域里，他是世界大学的首席教授，甚至会远远超过普鲁塔克（Plutarch）”。④ 通过英雄崇拜理论，“卡莱尔将精神性的视觉恢复给［他所在］的时代，这个时代正因为精神性视觉的缺失而衰亡”。⑤ 当然，英雄崇拜理论也有反对者。萨克雷（William Makepeace Thackeray）的名篇《名利场》（*Vanity Fair*）有一个意味深长的副标题。“一部没有英雄的小说”可谓反对立场的集中表现。

至此，有必要进入卡莱尔英雄崇拜理论的内部。本章分四部分对之进行解读。研究对象分别是英雄崇拜的社会依据、制度依据、理论本身和文人英雄。

第一节　社会依据

统治者的失责，是英雄崇拜理论的社会现实基础。19 世纪 20 年代前后，卡莱尔开始对现实社会进行观察。在他的观察中，英国社会主要处于一种被统治者与统治者相互分离的状态。一方面，被统治者处于剧烈的疾苦之中；另一方面，统治者无所事事。早在 1819 年，他便在通信中（11th Nov. 1819; to John A. Carlyle）提到，“下层阶级大多处于贫困之中”，而统治者大多只是“无所事事之徒”（Let. 1，Ⅰ，245）。同样的状况在 1820 年被再次提到。“普通人处在水深火热之中”，与此相对，“当地殷实的资产阶级和空虚的君主论

① *History of Westem Philosophy*，p. 584 .

② *History of Westem Philosophy*，p. 584 .

③ Seigel，*The Critical Heritage*，p. 298.

④ Seigel，*The Critical Heritage*，p. 298.

⑤ Willey，*More Nineteenth Century Studies*，p. 299.

者”不但全然无视，甚至“以武装实现镇压的目的”（26th Jan. 1820；271）。这种情况只能让这位未来的社会先知勉强地“压下关于人的自私和愚蠢的苦笑”（271－272）。很明显，此处所谓的“人”专指统治阶级。所谓的无所事事也得了一定程度的澄清，是未能针对问题给出有效解决方法之意。同年（1st Mar.），情况的恶化令他愤怒。“关于贫穷，或者几乎可以说饥饿的非常有根据的抱怨在政府方面仅仅遭遇了冷漠或者冷血的嘲讽。”（L.－B.，277）这一次，他将矛头直接指向了统治者。除非“国王和他的大臣们［……］采取一系列完全不同的措施”，否则“更加可怕和更加集中的反抗将会产生”，甚至“英国”会失去其“海上霸主”的地位（Ibid.）。可见，对统治阶级失职的抱怨开始占据主要地位。有效统治的缺失，导致情况的进一步恶化。“黑人的不安”、“物质和道德上的痛苦”以及“激进的起义”等此起彼伏（5th May；to John Johnstone；Let.[1]，Ⅰ，302－303），可谓“在不列颠历史前所未见”（302）。1822年，他对统治阶级的失望转化为更为具体的表达。“立法机关需要为农业的利益做一些持久有益的事情；这是农村的迫切需要”（5th Feb. 1822；to James Carlyle；Let.[1]，Ⅱ，45）。然而，即使在这种情况下，统治者依然毫无作为。此后，他的重心开始转向德国思想研究。30年代前，他少有有关时局的论述。不过，这一时期关于英国统治阶级的失责所形成的印象深刻地影响了卡莱尔的社会批评。

对统治阶级失责的根源进行解释是卡莱尔下一阶段主要的思考对象，也是英雄崇拜理论的深化。关于统治阶级失责的根源，他形成了比较独到的思考。他认为，失责的直接原因在于统治阶级对于自身所承担责任的无视。这一视角贯穿于他30年代主要的社会批评作品。《时代的征兆》的主要话题虽然在于人的机械化，但是人的机械化的根源在很大程度上也是统治阶级失责的根源所在。一种因为“思想问题”而产生的“精神疾病”（Wks.，XXⅦ，80），① 是人和时代机械化产生的根源。同样，统治阶级也是因为“审视”的方式出现了严重的问题，才会“屈从于外在事物，不能自拔，失去了自主能

① 引文参见乔修峰译本（《世界文学》2018年第4期，第285—313页）。为行文方便，引用时略有改动。下同。

力”（80－81）。可见，统治阶级的失责被归结为一个认识问题。同一观点在《特征》之中得到了一定程度的扩展。卡莱尔以目的和手段之间的关系对人进行理解。“事实上，在任何地方有生命力的行动都完全是一个手段，而不是一个目的；生命被赋予给我们不是简单为了生存，而是为了一个隐匿的外在的目的的实现。”（XXⅦ，3）显然，统治阶级失责的根源在于他们只是囚禁于自我，而忘记了外在的更加高等的目的。他们忘记了“无限的名字是善、是神”，忘记了他们“在地球上是士兵，在一个异域里战斗”（43）。很明显，对上帝作为目的、对自身作为手段的遗忘是统治阶级失责的根源所在。英雄崇拜理论在此已初见雏形。《谷物法歌谣》（“Corn Law Rhyme,”1832）的论述更为具体。统治阶级的失责在其中被明确地描述为“低俗的无所事事”（Do－Nothing）（140）。“那些如腓特烈大帝或者拿破仑一样的人物在成长时［……］没有被赋予发现他们天职（vocation）的眼睛；相反，他们的目光移向他处。”（Ibid.）对天职的无视，是英国统治阶级职责的根源。卡莱尔甚至更进一步，声称他所赞许的领袖是“一个在个性（在其范围内是清晰、虔敬的）、洞见力、勇气和心脑可控力等方面均得到良好发展的人”（141）。这些与卡莱尔式的英雄所具有的品质已经相差无几。

卡莱尔在40年代完成的社会批评作品，在更大的程度上实现了合题。社会危机和统治阶级的失责被联系在一起，后者被明确地看作是前者的根源。《宪章运动》在系列演说“英雄和英雄崇拜”前一年发表，在很大程度上是英雄崇拜理论的先声。《宪章运动》开宗明义，指出研究“英格兰现状问题”的迫切。“有一种感受非常普遍：目前工人阶级的状况和情绪已经非常危险，应该站出来说点什么，做点什么了。”（XXIX，118）① 宪章运动产生的根源，在表面上被归结为生活的困苦。“宪章运动意味着痛苦的不满情绪，也即英国工人阶级所受的不公正待遇或愤忿的情绪，已经变得更加严重乃至疯狂。”（119）宪章运动产生的根源在于统治者的失责。这是“一个无所事事的引导［者］”在“一个有所作为的世界”之中所造成的问题（186）。为实现问题的

① 第一章“英格兰现状问题”的引文参见乔修峰译本（《世界文学》2018年第4期，第313—319页）。为行文方便，引用时略有改动。下同。

解决，统治者一定要成为“真正意义上的领袖”，“贵族和神职人员”有必要“在一定的合适程度上发现世人对他们的期待，发现这些如果缺失世界便无法运作的事物”（Ibid.）。只有统治者“发现［上帝指派给他们的任务］，一切才会幸福安康；如果他们不能，那么其他人就有必要且一定要［发现］”（Ibid.）。可见，卡莱尔关于统治者失责的认识在此实现了明确的深化。所谓的失责并不是简单的一事不做，而是本职不明之意。议会出台的《贫穷法案》（*Poor Law*）以及相关的修正案等不是完全意义上的无为，而是未能完成上帝赋予他们的天职之意。此处，作为上帝意志的解读者以及统治权神授的思想被明确地表达出来。这是英雄崇拜理论最为基础的思想。在此基础之上，《宪章运动》进一步对现行统治制度产生疑问。工业社会所奉行的“自由主义”（*Laissez-faire*）被讽刺地称为“自我取消的无为主义”（Donothingism），被看作“所有苦难的根源”（167）。正是因为自由主义成为统治方法，统治者才会“仅仅关注一件事情，即他们自身的利益”（Ibid.）。这是卡莱尔的社会批评向制度批评的转折。在此转折中，英雄崇拜被视为理想的替代制度。这一思路一直延续到40年代末的爱尔兰之行。“［爱尔兰］再也没有任何种类的领主；甚至假领主也不带着他们的土地收入来到这里。”（Rem.[2]，55）可见，即使是在爱尔兰社会问题的观察上，统治阶级的失责也是卡莱尔主要的视角。

综上可见，卡莱尔的英雄崇拜理论具有明确的社会现实依据。他所在的社会是一个被统治者与统治者之间出现严重脱离的社会。被统治阶级生存状况的恶化，在很大程度上是统治者失责的后果。卡莱尔初期将失责主要理解为无所事事，统治者的放任自流被认为是社会危机产生的根源。后期，他对同一问题的理解有了明显的深化。所谓的无为是统治者对自身天职认识的缺失，是对上帝所赋予的使命的无视。英雄崇拜理论的雏形在以上社会批评过程之中表现出来。卡莱尔式的英雄是一个具有超凡洞见力的人物，不但可以解读上帝的意志，还可以传达给众人，使得整个社会作为一个整体成为实现上帝意志的手段。可见，英雄崇拜理论在很大程度上来源于卡莱尔的社会批评。

第二节　制度依据

在社会现实基础之上，英雄崇拜作为一个理论还具有制度依据。同在社会批评中表现出来的过程一样，英雄崇拜与卡莱尔的制度批评之间具有紧密的关联。理解卡莱尔的制度批评，有必要理解当时英国的现行制度，即功利主义原则（utilitarianism）。功利主义与英国经验主义哲学传统一脉相承。两者均重实践而轻形而上学思辨，都可谓是实践的哲学。“在有关实在作为一个整体的科学或者理论这一意义上，英国哲学弱于形而上学思辨。”[①] 如果欧陆哲学，特别是德、法哲学的“主流是形而上学”的话，[②] 那么英国哲学传统的长处在于对实践（practice）的促进。在英国哲学中，即使是极具形而上学特色的认识论也是实践性的。根据博尔特（Edwin A. Burtt）的观点，英国传统中的“形而上学被典型地简化为认识论（epistemology），而且是带有强烈实践色彩的认识论”。[③] 知识“并没有被当作理论问题”，并未用于“实在的系统研究”，相反，而是被当作“为他们聚焦于实践问题进行辩护的手段”，专门“证明理解终极真理的尝试是无效的”。[④] 这样的注重实践的哲学“在提供处理人的方法的心理学方面是伟大的，在管制人的行为的伦理学方面是伟大的，在为与政治学和政治经济学同样具有实践特征的科学奠定哲学基础方面是伟大的”。[⑤] 从培根（Francis Bacon）到霍布斯（Thomas Hobbes），从洛克到休姆，英国哲学家或者投身于科学实验或者聚焦于建设理想的政治共同体，或者否认先天的理念（innate ideas）或者极端到甚至否认全称概念（general ideas）的存在。

功利主义在英国有根深蒂固的传统和一段漫长的发展历史。功利主义紧承英国经验主义哲学传统，可谓“以英国［哲学］精神之中的实证主义和现实主义倾向为基础”。[⑥] 功利主义在 17 世纪之前的最为重要的代表，是英国国

---

① Burtt, *The English Philsophers*, Intro., p. xvii.
② Dibelius, *England*, p. 150.
③ Burtt, op. cit., Intro., p. xvii.
④ Burtt, op. cit., Intro., pp. xvii – xviii.
⑤ Dibelius, op. cit., p. 150.
⑥ Cazamian, *L'Angleterre Moderne*, p. 40.

教功利主义（Anglican utilitarianism）。盖伊（John Gay）、布朗（John Brown）、杰宁斯（Soame Jenyns）、劳（Edmund Law）、图克尔（Abraham Tucker）、卢瑟福斯（Thomas Rutherforth）和佩里（William Paley）等是早期功利主义的代表人物。在他们的思想之中，两点内容占据主导地位。其一，是“知识、美德和健康等所有的事物只有在提升快乐和抵消痛苦的意义上才是有价值的”。[①]这一认识在很大程度上可以上溯至伊壁鸠鲁（Epicurus）的学说。其二，是“行动对错的判断取决于对公共好处，亦即最大的快乐所造成的效果”。[②] 这一点的现代表达来源于侃博伦（Richard Cumberland）的《自然法则论》（*A Treatise of the Law of Nature*）。早期功利主义者的贡献在于，他们实现了“两个思想潮流的合题”。[③] 在这一点上，侃博伦和洛克的功绩最大。侃博伦从自然法（natural law）理论之中推论出“上帝的法则可归结为一点”，即“提升有理性的行动人的共同利益（common good），也就是上帝的荣耀和人的幸福”。[④] 洛克则彻底地抛弃了侃博伦学说中所有关于上帝的论述，而是直接将人的幸福作为唯一的思考对象。洛克从人的本性开始讨论幸福。“幸福可以还原为快乐和痛苦的不在场”，人“无一例外地具有根据其获得快乐而避免痛苦的欲望行事的动机”。[⑤] 由此，追求幸福成为人本性的要求。18 世纪，功利主义得到了一定的发展。伯克利（George Berkeley）、哈奇森（Francis Hutcheson）和休姆等均在洛克基础之上，对这一学说进行了不同的发挥。19 世纪初，功利主义迎来了学说的集大成者。

边沁（Jeremy Bentham）的功利主义学说紧承传统。最大多数人最大的利益作为对错衡量的标准以及普遍幸福的实现等，这两项功利主义的基本公理早在《政府片论》（*A Fragment on Government*）中便得到清晰的表达。[⑥] 人的动机（motives），是边沁功利主义学说的基础。《道德与立法原理导论》（*An*

① Heydt, “Utilitarianism before Bentham,” p. 17. It needs to be acknowledged that my discussion of pre – Benthamean utilitarianism is largely based upon Heydt's work here cited.

② Heydt, “Utilitarianism before Bentham,” p. 17.

③ Heydt, “Utilitarianism before Bentham,” p. 17.

④ Heydt, “Utilitarianism before Bentham,” p. 18.

⑤ Heydt, “Utilitarianism before Bentham,” p. 21.

⑥ Crimmins, “Bentham and Utilitarianism in the Early Nineteenth Century,” p. 39.

Introduction to the Principles of Moral and Legislation）从主观和客观两个方面对快乐和痛苦作为人的动机进行论述。在主观上，人被认为“［处］于两位主公——快乐和痛苦——的主宰之下”（§1.1）。[①] 两者对人的主观感受而言，不是简单的名称（names），而是真正的实体（entities；§6.6N）。作为实体，快乐和痛苦决定了人的应然和未然行为，决定了人的“所行、所言、所思”（§1.1）。在客观上，快乐和痛苦表现为功利性（utility）。“功利是指客体的一种性质”，或者“给利益有关者带来实惠、好处、快乐、利益或幸福”，或者“防止利益有关者遭受损害、痛苦、祸患或不幸”（§1.3）。利益不但包括“个人的幸福”，而且涵盖“共同体的幸福”（Ibid.）。在此基础之上，实现快乐而避免痛苦既是人的主观动机，也是人的客观动机。把快乐和痛苦看作人动机的来源，是功利主义的根基。“功利主义承认这一被支配地位，把它当作旨在依靠理性和法律之手建造福乐大厦的制度的基础。”（Ibid.）快乐和痛苦被进一步看作判断道德行为的标准。“功利原理是指这样的原理：它按照看来势必增大或减小利益有关者之幸福的倾向，亦即促进或妨碍此种幸福的倾向，来赞成或非难任何一项行动”，而且不仅包括“私人的每项行动”，甚至还有“政府的每项措施”（§1.2）。可见，边沁的功利主义学说的实质是将快乐和痛苦看作人动机的来源，以此为基础对人的个体和社会道德行动进行促进。

以边沁学说（Benthamism）为骨干内容的功利主义，在维多利亚时期成为规范社会的制度。功利主义作为社会规范的制度被普遍接受，在很大程度上决定于其与英国经验主义哲学传统之间所存在的渊源和继承关系。与英国哲学在近代以来所表现出来的主要倾向一样，边沁学说同样将复杂的人类行为简单地归结为某一或者某些普遍要素作用的结果。经历这样的归化之后，原本表现为复杂的对象在本质上表现为简单，极具可控力和可预见力。特别是在应用于人和社会之后可以取得十分理想的效果。人的道德和社会实践所表现出来的不可控性和不可预见性，在归化之后可以实现向反题的有效转化。这对正在处于工业化起始阶段的英格兰而言，可谓理想的社会规范制度。

---

① 引文参见时殷弘译本（商务印书馆2000年版）。为行文方便，引用时略有改动。下同。

然而，以边沁学说为骨干内容的功利主义存在深刻的问题。这些问题不仅是穆勒等边沁学派成员（Benthamite）思考的焦点，也是卡莱尔抨击和否定的对象。穆勒思考的焦点在于个体快乐向最大多数人最大利益之间的转化。边沁主要从量（quantity）的角度对快乐进行衡量。若以量量之，则推针（push - pin）与诗（poetry）所实现的快乐毫无差异。“如果抛弃掉偏见，则推针游戏与艺术和科学、与音乐和诗具有同等的价值。”[①] 而且，快乐的量决定了对象的价值。“推针游戏如果可以提供更多的快乐，那么就要比其他两者更具价值。”[②] 非常明显，这将导致量对质（quality）的取消。所有在质上占优而在量上处劣的快乐，将被取消价值。在这种情况下，所有高尚的道德行为将与玩乐无异，而且在价值上甚至会低于玩乐。游戏将比耶稣（Jesus）的行为更有价值。对此，穆勒将质看作衡量标准。如果“一种快乐除了在数量上较大之外，还有什么能使它比另外一种快乐更有价值，我想可能的答案只有一个”，[③] 这便是质。质决定了快乐的等级。一种快乐无论在量上占据何等的优势，只要在质上处于劣等，将不被认为具有更多的价值。“做一个不满足的人胜于做一只满足的猪；做不满足的苏格拉底胜于做一个满足的傻瓜。”[④] 质决定了快乐的价值。可见，穆勒主要从功利主义学说内部逻辑出发，对其中的缺陷进行适当的补充，使之完整，从而具备更强的包容性和解释力。穆勒对功利主义学说所做的修正，与他的亲身经历具有紧密的关联。他的思想危机来源于对人生终极目的的思考。“假设你人生所有的目的都实现了；所有你所盼望的制度和观念上的变革在这一刻完全实现了：这对于你就是最大的快乐与幸福吗?”[⑤] 显然，思想（intellect）不能取代情感（emotion）。边沁不能代替柯尔律治。[⑥] 思考维度的增加让穆勒从质的角度重新评估快乐的价值。

---

① Bentham, *The Rationale of Reward*, p. 206.

② Bentham, *The Rationale of Reward*, p. 206.

③ Mill & Bentham, *Utilitarianism and Other Essays*, p. 279. The Chinese translation is from Xu Dajian（徐大建）'s version（Beijing: The Commercial Pr., 2014, p. 10）. All Chinese translations quoted in this book hereafter are from this edition.

④ Mill & Bentham, *Utilitarianism and Other Essays*, p. 281.

⑤ Mill, *Autobiography*, p. 112.

⑥ Cf. Mill's "Bentham" and "Coleridge".

卡莱尔对功利主义的攻击最为激烈。在很大程度上，英雄崇拜是对功利主义作为现行规范制度的替代。将人的动机简单地归化为快乐和痛苦，是卡莱尔最为诟病的内容。他否认快乐和痛苦以及建立在两者基础之上的利益和损失的平衡是人的动机来源。“核查和比较盈亏得失，从来没有成为人类的左膀右臂；盈亏得失之虑，急功近利之求，从未让人焚膏继晷，全力以赴。”（Wks.，XXⅦ，70）卡莱尔直指功利主义学说的理论核心。“边沁的功利主义以得失定善，把上帝创造的世界变为没有生命、没有理性的蒸汽机，把人的无限神圣的心灵，当作称量干草和蓟花、愉快和痛苦的天平”，这些边沁学说的根基被视为“关于人类及其在宇宙中命运的观点［最］可鄙、［最］荒谬的”观点（H. & H.，76）。在此，快乐和痛苦作为人动机的来源被彻底否认。动机来源的明确导向人目的的明确。“人在尘世主要的目的”并不是快乐的获得和痛苦的避免，不是“通过加减法将［正义和邪恶决定于这两个方面能给人以多少终极愉快］整体计算，得出最终的答案”（75）。可见，实现最大多数人最大的利益在卡莱尔看来并不是人的目的所在。英雄崇拜的基本主题，再次得到表现。

卡莱尔对人动机的来源持有自己的意见。在人的动机来源问题上，他与功利主义的观点截然相反。这意味着，行动的来源绝不可以是个人利益盈亏的算计。与功利主义观点不同，人的动机有两个主要来源。这两个主要来源对应于人的物质和精神要素。在结构上，人“的身上包含着物质性的和精神性的两种力量”（Sar.，118）。人的精神性因素表现为灵魂（soul），物质性因素为身体（body）。这样，人可谓“灵魂与身体之间的二元对立”（Wks.，XXⅧ，4）。精神和物质因素在人动机的产生方面具有的作用不同。精神和物质对应于“人行动的两个单元”（XXⅦ，73）。如果精神对应于“人类命运和天性［中的］动态的层面”，那么物质则对应于其中的“机械的层面”（68）。前者“探究并切实应对人类原始的、天生的力量和能量，包括引发爱惧、惊奇、热情、诗歌和信仰的那些神秘源泉，它们都有真正的生命力，都是无限的”；而后者“探究上述力量和能量在后天有限的发展，即直接的‘动机’，如期待回报或担心惩罚”（68－69）。这两个层面“相互渗透，相互作用，盘根错节，密不可分”，而“只有妥善调和二者，大力推动二者共同发展，才是正道”（73）。动态层面的过分强化会导致“误入徒劳、空幻、不切实际的歧路，在蒙昧时代还会引发迷信和狂热，带来一系列臭名昭彰的恶果”，而机械学部分的过度开发“虽然不会立即看到坏处，短时期内甚至会有不少好处，但从长远来看，却必定会破坏道德力量，即一切力量的源头，带来更加不可救药的恶果”（Ibid.）。很明显，动态和机械层面被共同看作人动机的来源。两者有必要处于平衡和协作状态。

卡莱尔进一步对人行动的理想状态进行考察。缄默（silence）或无意识（unconsciousness）是人的行动处于理想状态的标志。“身体状况完美的标志是，整体的机体活动好似一体；不是表现在分离的单一行动之上，而是表现为整体所共同完成的活动。”（XXVIII，1）同样，作为人动机的来源，动态层面和机械层面之间的“统一、配合永远是缄默的、或者轻声的”；只有两者之间的“无序才通过噪声而显现”（1－2）。只要人动机来源的两个层面“相互彼此合适，便可以产生像和谐弦乐一样的运动，这就是旋律和统一”（2）。可见，缄默是人的行动处于理想状况的标志。同样，如若人的行动处于理想状况，则人处于一种对理想状态无觉察的状态，即所谓的无意识状态。就像“不是健康的人，而是患病的人才会觉察他们的健康状况”一样，“所有的生命能量无论在什么地方，只要处于健康状态，就是一个看不见的、无意识的能量”（10）。无意识也标志着人的行动处于理想状态之中。然而，理想状态无法真正实现。“实践上的完美就像思想上的完善一样，只能接近，不能实现。”（38）这决定理想状态只能是一种接近（approximation），而不是实现（realization）。这样，人的行动向理想状态的发展成为一个无限接近而无法完成的过程。

缄默和无意识是卡莱尔考察人行动状况的依据和标准。根据他的考察，在历史上人的行动状况处于完美之中。就像维吉尔（Virgil）的田园诗《牧歌》（*Eclogae*）中所描写的农夫一样，“在那些时光里，健康与疾病是无关紧要的异域传统；[人]的整个存在是统一的，作为整体的人就像一个得到表现的意志”（2）。这种表现在农夫身上的统一状态便是理想状态。理想状态是人行动状态的上限。“无论人处于停歇还是处于持续不断的劳动之中，但愿我们的生命会永远如此，是一首纯粹的、永恒的、无所顾忌的音乐；是一道完美的白光，使得所有的事物都变得可见，但自身不可见，因为这是完美的白色，任何无序的阻碍都没有将它打断为其他色彩。”（Ibid.）此处，理想状态是愿望的对象。可见，人行动最为完美的状况便是处于理想状态。这决定卡莱尔对人行动状况所进行的考察其实是以缄默和无意识作为标志的理想状态为最高标准，通过人的行动与理想状态之间的背离程度的确定来确定人的实际状况的过程。

根据他的考察，现实之中人的行动状态不但没有处于理想状态，反而是一种危机的表现。“如果我们现在通过实践性的医学视角以无意识为标准对我们时代的状况以及人在其中的命运进行考察，那么我们所得到的诊断结果令人担忧。”（18）总体而言，人在现实之中并没有处于无意识状态下，反而“对于很多事情过于有意识”（3）。人不再表现为统一。“多数情况下，生命是中断和抽搐刺耳的噪声，无论我们意愿如何，这都不能忽视。”（Ibid.）就像只有病人才会对健康状况有所觉察一样，处于危机状态之中的人对自身状态的觉察便是危机的暴露。在此意义上，“知识［便］是紊乱的症状”（Ibid.）。可见，卡莱尔对时代症状所开出的诊断结果是，时代处于深刻的危机之中。如果将时代症状纳入历史发展进行考虑，那么非常明显，危机是一个现代问题。在此意义上，卡莱尔对时代问题的分析其实也是他对维多利亚时代的现代性（modernity）所进行的思考。

卡莱尔进一步指出，以边沁学说为主要内容的功利主义是时代危机的根源所在。在动态和机械层面，人的行动有两个来源。然而，功利主义将物质看作唯一的来源。“这个时代的哲学家是斯密、狄龙、边沁之流，他们［认为］不仅幸福完全取决于外在境况，心灵的力量和尊严，竟然也是外在境况的产物和结果。”（XXⅦ，67）这种完全将物质因素看作人动机来源的理论，必将导致动态和机械层面之间平衡的破坏。“物质王国受到了前所未有的崇拜和关注，精神王国却受到了前所未有的轻视和冷落。”（Ibid.）严重的机械化问题随之产生。“倘若非要用一个词来形容当今时代，我们不会说这是一个英雄的、虔诚的、哲学的、道德的时代，而首先是一个机械的时代。”（59）在机械化时代里，机械层面超越自身适用范围而进入动态层面，成为动态层面的规范制度。“机械的研究正侵入各个领域”，不但“物质研究全靠机械理论”，而且在“精神研究”之中情况同样如此（66）。这是对动态和机械层面相互协作配合的严重背离，也是人的行动相对于理想状态的背道而驰。

基于以上判断，卡莱尔为时代病症开出药方。这一药方的实质便是以英雄崇拜替代功利主义。如果功利主义作为规范制度导致了严重的时代机械化问题，那么只有以英雄崇拜替代功利主义，精神因素才可以成为人行动的来源，所有的时代问题才会迎刃而解。在人行动的来源问题上，英雄崇拜与功利主义构成正反论题。如果功利主义将物质因素看作人行动的来源，那么英雄崇拜则将精神因素看作人的动机之本。可见，英雄崇拜不是一个简单的理论，而更是卡莱尔为解决时代问题所开出药方和所给出的解决方案。英雄崇拜中的许多理论细节，可以在卡莱尔对功利主义的批评和反对中反映出来。

第三节　英雄崇拜理论

卡莱尔的英雄崇拜理论是对功利主义作为规范制度的替代。为论证替代的合理性，英雄崇拜被赋予历史的维度。历史发展的实质被看作英雄业绩的表现。“世界历史就是人类在这个世界上所取得的种种成就的历史，实质上也就是在世界上活动的伟人的历史。”（H. & H.，1）世界史归结为伟人史的根源在于伟人的塑造力。伟人“是民众的领袖，而且是伟大的领袖，凡是一切普通人殚精竭虑要做或想要得到一切事物都由他们去规范和塑造”，因此“从广义上说，[伟人] 也就是创造者”（Ibid.）。在此意义上，如果套用叔本华（Arthur Schopenhauer）的名作《作为意志和表象的世界》（*Die Welt als Wille und Vorstellung*）的标题，世界在卡莱尔看来表现为英雄的意志。“世界上存在的一切成就，本是来到世界上的伟人的内在思想转化为外部物质的结果，也是他们思想的实际体现和具体化。”（Ibid.）这样，历史的复杂性被取消。整个历史发展可以归结为伟人意志的表现。“整个世界历史的精华，就是伟人的历史。”（Ibid.）历史被归结为伟人史。

世界历史被归结为英雄史使得卡莱尔从历史角度对现时代进行判断成为可能。非常明显，现时代是一个以功利主义为规范制度的时代。这是对历史发展趋势的背离。现时代是一个“否认当今时代伟人的存在”的时代，是一个“否认对伟人的需要”的时代（12）。在现时代，伟人不再是崇拜的对象。

如果“向评论家举出一位伟人”，他们“不是对他崇拜”，而是“对他进行所谓的‘描述’”，甚至“从各个方面加以评头论足，使他变为一个微不足道的人物”（Ibid.）。在这种时代氛围下，路德（Martin Luther）无论在历史上多么伟大，也仅仅沦为“时代的产物”而已（Ibid.）。这也是彭斯所处的时代。“他没有处于一个英雄主义和宗教的时代，而是处于一个怀疑论、自私和琐碎的时代，其中真正的高贵无人理解，却被一个肤浅、破碎、完全贫瘠和无果的傲慢原则取而代之。”（Wks.，XXⅥ，311）英雄没有得到应有的崇拜。这样，英雄崇拜不再有效开展。甚至卡莱尔本人也“充分注意到，有人认为英雄崇拜，即［他］所谓的英雄崇拜，在现今已经过时了，终于不存在了”（H. & H.，12）。在这种设计下，功利主义作为规范方式不是简单地与英雄崇拜对立，而更是与历史发展潮流相违背。

现时代所产生的问题，同样获得历史的解释。在英雄崇拜被赋予历史维度之前，包括时代的机械化在内的所有时代问题均是制度问题。问题产生的根源在于功利主义作为规范的制度被确定下来。在获得历史维度之后，对时代问题进行历史的解释成为可能。时代问题的产生不仅仅是一个制度问题，更是现时代与历史发展之间的协调问题。

一方面，时代问题的历史维度表现在现代性的获得之上。事实上，卡莱尔可谓“第一个将生活在一个新时代，生活在可以被真正叫作 19 世纪的感受带给他的读者的作家”。[1] 现时代不同于以往任何历史时代。这是时代问题现代性的集中体现。时代问题的现代性表现为问题的不可理解（incomprehensibility）。具有现代性的时代问题极难理解，甚至被称为“命运之谜”（P. & P.，13）。解决这一问题的关键在于理解现代性，即厘清“［英吉利民族国家］的奇怪的新的今天的意义”（Ibid.）。以诗意的方法表达，也就是“看看我们脚下这个凌乱的舞台”的现实状况（Wks.，XXⅦ，59）。理解现代性的关键在于理解现时代的根本特征。“如果我们够聪明，就能觉察到真正的时代征兆，了解时代的缺陷和优势，从而合理调整自己的位置。”（Ibid.）只有现代性得到理解，时代问题才可以获得解决的方法。“细看［时代征兆］之后，

① Tillotson, “Carlyle,” p. 60.

有些乱象会消失不见，有些独有的特征和深层的趋势则清晰显现出来。”（Ibid.）现代性理解之后，“我们也就更容易看清自己与时代的关系，看清我们在这个时代的真正目标和任务”（Ibid.）。可见，历史维度赋予时代问题以强烈的现代性。

另一方面，时代问题的历史维度决定现代性问题的历史解决。具有强烈现代性的时代问题产生的根源在于现时代违背了历史发展的要求。这一点集中地表现在功利主义作为规范制度取代了英雄崇拜。如上所述，英雄崇拜在卡莱尔看来是历史发展的实质。英雄崇拜被功利主义取代，这意味着现时代背离了历史发展的要求。于是，对现代性的理解从对时代特征的理解转化为对历史要求满足状况的判断，即对英雄崇拜开展状况的判断。非常明显，英雄崇拜在现时代的开展状况糟糕至极。“总体而言，我们英雄崇拜的开展比世界上任何民族国家在任何历史时期都要差。”（P. & P.，39）这意味着时代发展背离了历史发展的要求，也意味着现代性问题解决的方法在于恢复英雄崇拜为规范制度。卡莱尔直言不讳，“我们一定要学会更好地开展我们的英雄崇拜；［英雄崇拜］开展得越来越好，意味着民族国家的灵魂从窒息之中的觉醒，意味着天堂般的被保佑的生活的回归”（Ibid.）。在此，现代和历史合流于英雄崇拜。英雄崇拜理论丰富的外部结构表现出来。

英雄崇拜作为一个理论除具有丰富的外部结构之外，还有复杂的内在构成。在内，英雄崇拜集中地表现为对英雄品质的探讨。总体而言，英雄是人与上帝之间的中介。英雄被看作“神秘莫测的上帝派遣的使者，带着信息来到人间”（H. & H.，45）。只有英雄才可以启示上帝的意志，因此英雄的“言论［是］一种‘天启’”（46）。与此相对，普通人无法实现对于上帝意志的认识。普通人在卡莱尔看来永远是“黑暗的大众，产生黑暗，只能放射出黑暗、贪婪、下流”（Skh.，41）。普通人“虽然具有人的形体，却比大多数的动物和猿类都要不幸”（Ibid.），因为他们无法获得神意。普通人所能获得的最高智慧，便是苏格拉底式的无知之知。“我们在这个世界上的生活不过是梦幻、梦游；其中绝大多数人无疑在游荡，就好像他们可以将右手同左手区分开来；然而只有知道自己什么都不知道的人才是明智的。”（Sar.，54）可见，在有关神意的知识获得方面，英雄与普通人之间存在本质性的差别。认识能力上的优越，是英雄的主要表现。

英雄与普通人之间在认识能力上所表现出来的差别，主要决定于上帝的存在方式。在实然的真理所描述的事实之中，万事万物作为上帝的象征而存在，对上帝进行表现。但是，启示（revelation）和隐匿（concealment）共同统一于象征（219）。这样，自然在对上帝进行启示的同时，也发挥了隐匿的作用。如果将自然看作“书卷”，那么“上帝是其中的作者和写作人”（258）。人首先需要具有有关“［书卷］的字母”以及“［书卷］的单词、句子、描写篇章”等知识（Ibid.），才可以通晓。这些前提条件决定，普通人不具有解读上帝意志的能力。事实上，“即使是先知也会因为关于［这卷以神圣的象形文字书写而成、其中满是神圣文字的书卷］在这儿读懂一行、在那儿读懂一段而感到满意”（Ibid.）。人在认识能力上的局限，决定于人性与神性之间所存在的矛盾。人性是有限的（finite），而神性是无限的（infinite）。人对上帝的意志进行认识，便是以有限作为手段去实现认识无限的目的。非常明显，属性上的不对等决定了手段与目的之间的不对等。人认识能力的局限集中表现在对作为上帝的象征而存在的自然的超越性（transcendence）之上。“对于最为聪明的人来说，即使他的视野非常广阔，自然依然深度无限、广度无限；人所有的经验都局限于可以计算的世纪和可以丈量的平方之中。”（257）在此意义上，人性无法实现对于神性的认识。甚至卡莱尔本人在对无限进行表达的时候，也感受到了有限的词语的局限。他坦言，“如果要将我所有要说的内容表达给你［即约翰·穆勒］，这几页纸已经无法容纳，更何况一张简单的便条”（L. –M.，75）。在这种情况下，“笔无法传达万千的思想；言辞也无法再现一隅”（Ibid.）。“我们只要说出第一个字，就是开始出错”（Ibid.），歌德的名句可谓人认识能力的局限最好的表达。

英雄作为上帝意志的解读者具有特殊的秉性。总体而言，虔敬（sincerity）是卡莱尔式的英雄的主要品质。“虔敬，即一种深沉的、崇高而纯洁的虔敬，是各种不同英雄人物的首要特征。”（H. & H.，45）英雄的虔敬是一种自发状态，表现为无知无觉。因此，“虔敬并不是自封的”，“那种自封的虔敬［……］是肤浅而有意识的自我吹嘘，主要是自命不凡”（Ibid.）。相反，真正的“虔敬是［英雄］自己无法言传的东西”，是“［英雄］没有意识到的东西”（Ibid.）。在此意义上，英雄的“虔敬并非取决于他自身，是不以他的意志为转移的”（Ibid.）。非常明显，卡莱尔对虔敬的认识非常类似于苏格拉底对于哲学的认识。与苏格拉底式的“热爱智慧”（φιλοσοφια）非常相似，卡莱尔式的虔敬并不是一个抽象的品质，而是一个存在的状态和生活的风范。虔敬是英雄的品质，更是英雄的状态。因此，就像“热爱智慧”表现在苏格拉底的所有言行之上，虔敬表现在卡莱尔式的英雄的所有言行之上，“是伟人和他的一切言行的根基”（Ibid.）。

虔敬作为英雄的主要品质和存在状态表现在英雄发展史之中。世界历史被归结为英雄历史之后，历史发展便表现为不同历史时期所对应的英雄类型的交替过程。如卡莱尔所说，“英雄崇拜在不同的历史时代具有不同的表现”（P. & P.，39）。他在英雄发展史之中共区分出六种类型的英雄，分别是神明（divinity）、先知（prophet）、诗人（poet）、教士（priest）、文人（man of letters）和帝王（king）英雄。这六类英雄在现代性方面具有不同的表现。这样，英雄发展史表现为这六类英雄类型之间的前后交替。虔敬作为英雄的主要品质和存在状态表现在所有六种类型的英雄之上。神明英雄崇拜在本质上与“斯堪的纳维亚的神话”一样，是一种“人类与其周围世界中那种显然在起作用却看不见的神秘力量进行虔敬的交流”（30）。虔敬是穆罕默德作为先知英雄在性格上的主要表现。“他的性格”可谓“严肃而虔敬”（53）。同样，诗人英雄“不能不是一个虔敬的人”（81）。在路德“那畏惧的思念中，可以看出他是最衷心的、最虔敬的”（141）。文人英雄亦然。“由于他的虔敬，也由于他在某种程度上道出了自然的心声，虽然用的是流行的虚饰方言，但约翰逊是一位先知。”（180）最后，帝王英雄也是虔敬的。克伦威尔便被认为“有粗犷的洞察力，有质朴的虔敬感情”（217）。卡莱尔虽然没有如此推论，但是虔敬作为英雄的主要品质决定英雄史可以进一步归结为虔敬史。这样，他对英雄史所进行的考察在很大程度上可以转化为对虔敬史的考察。

虔敬决定了英雄的存在状态。如上所述，虔敬不但是一种属性，更是一种存在状态。虔敬作为英雄的存在状态决定英雄通神（enthusiasm）的可能。人性与神性之间在属性上的矛盾是人不能认识上帝意志的主要根源。虔敬使得英雄获得神性成为可能。内在事实构成英雄的存在范围。“存在的伟大事实对他是重要的”，虽然英雄“想自由翱翔，但他不能摆脱现实世界对他的严厉约束”（45）。内在事实是英雄的存在空间。英雄“直接来自万物的内在事实；他每天与之交往时置身其中，而且必须置身其中”（Ibid.）。这样，万事万物的内在事实对于英雄而言不是封闭的，而是开放的。“他来自于世界的核心；他是万物主要实在的一部分。”（46）这种特别的存在状态使得英雄在一定程度上获得了神性。英雄“有直接来自上帝的无穷力量”（13）。神性的获得使得英雄有能力解读上帝的意志。作为“灿烂夺目的光源”，英雄“不仅像盏明灯，更像上帝赐予的日月光辉；［……］这是一种体现天赋创见、豪迈刚毅和英勇崇高品德的永不熄灭的光源”（2）。在此意义上，英雄才是崇拜的对象。英雄“总是值得敬仰的，实际上，此外再没有值得敬仰的东西了！在人们的胸怀中，没有什么比这种对高于自己的人产生的敬仰更高贵的感情”（11）。

英雄的认识内容便是卡莱尔的融合有启蒙和德国思想因素的加尔文主义信仰。第一，上帝的存在是英雄最为重要的认识内容。“世界上存在着上帝”（199），可谓英雄的要义所在。这个上帝并不是昭显的，而是隐匿于物质世界。“在一切事物之中和它们之上，存在着唯一的上帝。”（56）物质世界是对上帝的表现。“他先是创造了我们，然后是供养我们，我们和万物都不过是他的影子，是他永恒光辉的一个暂时外套。”（Ibid.）在级别上，上帝优越于其他一切存在。“只有这个上帝才是伟大的，此外再没有伟大的东西了。”（Ibid.）在实在性上，上帝是唯一实在的存在。只有上帝“是真实的存在，［……］是真实的”（Ibid.）。可见，对物质的否定以及普遍表现等思想融汇于英雄的认识。第二，上帝的作为法则而存在。“世界上确实有一条公正的法则，虽然它是深奥难测，然其实质是善。”（Ibid.）作为法则而存在的上帝要求所有人的服从。“我们必须服从上帝，我们的全部理想寓于对他全心全意的服从，听从他为我们安排的一切，无论今生今世，还是来世，都应如此。”（Ibid.）只有服从法则，上帝才会与人为善。“最聪明的人不只是服从必然性——诚然，必然性会使人服从——而是要善于理解和相信必然性所安排的严峻的事物是最聪明、最好的东西。”（Ibid.）在此，加尔文主义信仰中的服从思想再现于英雄的认识。综上可见，卡莱尔的英雄崇拜理论在很大程度上重复了他几经修改的加尔文主义信仰的主要内容。

英雄崇拜与信仰的等值进一步表现在卡莱尔对崇拜所持有的理解之上。总体而言，崇拜即信仰。对英雄所表示的“一切忠诚［……］和宗教信仰相似”，因为“信仰是对某个有灵感的导师，对某个高尚的英雄表示的忠诚”（12）。可见，崇拜被卡莱尔等值为信仰。宗教与信仰之间的等值取决于两者之间的生成关系。“所有宗教的最终结果［都是］实际的英雄崇拜。”（P. & P.，233）英雄崇拜“是宗教的基础，不仅异教如此，而且更高更纯洁的宗教——迄今已知的一切宗教，都是如此”（11）。甚至基督教同样以英雄崇拜为来源。“英雄崇拜，即以无比炽热之情，衷心敬仰与膜拜一位神一般的最崇高的人物——这［……］就是基督教的萌芽。”（Ibid.）在信仰生成于崇拜这一意义上，信仰与崇拜之间的等值在合理性方面获得辩护。

最后，英雄崇拜的最终目的在于人行动的实现。如上所述，卡莱尔反对功利主义将幸福的获得和痛苦的避免看作人动机的来源。据他看来，人是“一个穿着马裤的杂食性两足动物”，但更是一个精神性的存在（Sar.，65）。在时代语境下，不但动态和机械两个层面有必要平衡协作，精神要素作为人行动的来源更要得到凸显。他放眼历史发展，“欧洲十字军”、“宗教改革”、“英国的革命”以及“法国大革命”等人类行动的产生，除依靠物质因素之外，更依赖于精神因素。“只有那不可见的无限目标，才能令人赴汤蹈火，在所不辞。”（Wks.，XXVII，70－71）在此，历史成为精神要素作为人行动来源的合理性的辩护。卡莱尔进一步将人的精神看作获得上帝意志的媒介。“不可见的世界并未消失，它就栖居在人的心灵之中。”（81）这样，“上帝曾经显灵的神殿［……］可以修复，可以重建”（Ibid.）。人可以通过精神获得上帝的意志，进而通过行动实现上帝的意志。在此意义上，所有人的劳动成果，即使是“一间棚屋”，都是“一个思想的可见表现”，都是“不可见事物的可见记录”（220）。这样，人的动机来源于对上帝的崇拜。又因为普通人无法直接获得上帝的意志，因而英雄崇拜成为人与上帝之间的中介，崇拜上帝即崇拜英雄。最终，英雄崇拜成为人行动的来源。“‘世界的神圣理念’在［普通人］心中挣扎，但是不会在任何地方得到可见的表现。”（Wks.，XXVIII，31）这样，他们只有“他们需要为自己实现一种崇拜”（Ibid.），才可以实现行动。可见，英雄崇拜最终落实为人行动的来源。

以上便是时代背景下卡莱尔英雄崇拜作为一个理论的概貌。在外部，英雄崇拜是功利主义作为规范制度的替代。为实现替代的合理性，历史维度被赋予英雄崇拜。世界历史的本质被看作是英雄言行的记录。这样，世界历史被英雄史替代。世界历史作为英雄史决定英雄崇拜不仅仅是一个替代制度，更是历史发展的要求。在此意义上，功利主义作为现时代的规范制度也不仅是一个制度确定的问题，而更是一个现代性违背历史发展趋势的问题。在历史维度下，英雄崇拜替代功利主义成为规范制度具有极强的必然性。

在内部，英雄崇拜作为一个理论还具有极其丰富的内容。对英雄品质的探寻是英雄崇拜内在内容之中最为重要的一个。总体而言，英雄被卡莱尔看作是人和上帝之间的中介。这一设置具有深刻的认识论根源。万事万物作为上帝的象征既具有启示功能，又具有隐匿功能。特别是人性与神性在品质上所存在的矛盾决定，人性无法实现对于神性的认识。在此意义上，人性有必要融入有神性才可以实现对于上帝意志的认识。这样，英雄崇拜理论发展为对英雄品质的探寻。虔敬被看作是英雄最为主要的品质。虔敬不但赋予英雄以新的品质，更决定了英雄的存在状态。虔敬使得英雄存在于万事万物的内在事实。这样，神性在一定程度上被赋予英雄。由此，英雄成为上帝意志的解读人。

概而论之，卡莱尔的英雄崇拜理论在内容上是他融入有启蒙和德国思想的加尔文主义思想的表达。与他的加尔文主义信仰如出一辙，对上帝存在的强调是最为重要的内容。上帝的潜在性（immanence）、实在性（reality）和超越性（transcendence）等在英雄崇拜理论之中再次得到重复。另外，上帝作为法则而存在也是主要内容之一。人对上帝意志的服从以及服从所具有的必要性（necessity），几乎是他加尔文主义信仰的翻版。最后，英雄崇拜的最终目的在于人行动的实现。普通人在英雄的指引下去实现上帝的意志，这是卡莱尔英雄崇拜理论的最终目的。可见，英雄崇拜对功利主义的替代是卡莱尔的信仰对现实规范制度的替代。

第四节　文人英雄

在卡莱尔所列出的英雄谱系之中，文人英雄是其中之一。卡莱尔关于文人英雄的讨论极具价值。"'文人英雄'在《英雄和英雄崇拜》之中占据着十分重要的地位，部分因为其中包含了卡莱尔关于自己在社会分工中所扮演角色的反思，部分因为这一主题代表着系列演说中有关英雄主义的现代解读。"① 卡莱尔对文学和诗的理解在很大程度上表现在他对文人英雄的论述之上。理解文人英雄崇拜理论对于理解卡莱尔的文学和诗学理论具有重要的价值。

卡莱尔对英雄崇拜发展史有一个简单的新旧区分。如果"神明英雄、先知、诗人和教士，都是旧时代英雄的不同形式，他们产生于极其遥远的过去"，那么"文人英雄完全是新时代的产物"（154）。如果不同的历史时期对应于不同的英雄崇拜类型，那么非常明显，前四类英雄崇拜的类型"早就失去存在的可能"，甚至"再也不会在这个世界上出现"（Ibid.）。文人英雄的状况与此截然不同。"只要奇妙的书写艺术，或者说快速书写，即我们称之为印刷术存在着"，那么文人英雄"就会作为一切未来时代主要的英雄形式继续下去"（Ibid.）。可见，文人英雄崇拜是现时代英雄崇拜的主要样式。

文人英雄崇拜作为现时代英雄崇拜的主要开展样式决定于文学的认识能力。作为"一首英雄主义之歌、也许也是虔诚之曲"（Wks.，XXⅧ，15），文学被看作"神圣之物的新启示"（41）。很明显，文学是启示上帝意志的手段。卡莱尔接受了费希特有关文学的观点。他将文学看作"是一种'自然的启示'，是'公开秘密'的启迪"（H. & H.，163）。特别是费希特有关文学与市民之间关系的观点，对他颇有启发意义。文学是"费希特非常恰当地命名的神性在市民百姓中的'连续的启示'"（Ibid.）。可见，文学是文人与市民之间的中介。文学作为神性的启示具有必然性。"一切真正的天才歌唱家和演说家正是有意无意这样做的。"（Ibid.）同样，文学作为神性的启示可以在程度上区分出差别。"时而用这种语言，时而用另外一种语言［将那永远存在着的神性］表达出来。"（Ibid.）语言的不同决定了启示的不同。

文学作为启示神性的手段决定了文人的存在状态。同卡莱尔笔下其他类型的英雄一样，文人处于万事万物内在的实在空间之中。文人的"生命是自然本身永恒心灵的一部分"（155）。很明显，文人贴近自然的本质。真正的文

---

① Salmon, "Thomas Carlyle and Luminous Author," p. 54.

人英雄“是生活于事物的内在境界，也就是生活在真实、神圣和永恒的境界之中，而大多数的凡夫俗子是看不到这些深层次东西的存在”（Ibid.）。可见，文人存在于内在本质的范围之内，使得文人与众人区分开来。文人英雄的存在状态可谓紧承其他先前类型英雄的存在传统。作为英雄的一种类型，文人英雄同样存在于内在事实的空间之中。存在状态决定文人在一定程度上具有神性。“真正的文人，不论其是否被世人公认，总有这种神性。”（157）这是文人启示上帝意志的基础。

文人英雄的存在状态决定文人英雄可以启示上帝的意志。文人因为处于事物内在的实在空间，因此“能看透事情的真谛”（156）。作为“永恒的教士”，文人“一代一代向所有的人们宣传上帝依然存在于他们的生命之中；一切‘现象’，不论是在世界上看到的任何东西，都是‘世界神圣理念’的一种外表，因为‘它存在于现象深处’”（157）。[①] 可见，文人所启示的内容就是卡莱尔的融入有启蒙和德国思想的加尔文主义信仰。在此，文人成为他信仰的代言人。这样，文人被称为“不断向人们显示神性的教士”变得易于理解（Ibid.）。文学同样被卡莱尔纳入他的宗教体系之中。

卡莱尔主要从宗教角度对文学进行理解。总体而言，文学被他纳入宗教之中。文学与宗教之间存在紧密的关联。与“艺术”一样，“文学”被认为“与宗教有着紧密的联系”（Wks.，XXⅦ，94）。[②] 就好像“围栏与拱桥”，“内在世界的制高点”通过文学“逐渐将自身与一般平面联接起来，并由此畅通无阻”（Ibid.）。可见，文学是内在世界的表达。据此，文学被纳入宗教。“文学是宗教的一个分支，并一直具有宗教的特征。”（XXⅧ，23）在现时代这个宗教出现严重危机的时代，文学甚至有取代宗教的趋势。文学是“唯一还表现出些许绿意的支脉”，甚至“有朝一日还会成为主干”（Ibid.）。文学由此成为现时代宗教的主要样式。

---

① Cf. a similar point of view in “State of German Literature.” “Literary Men” are said to be “the appointed interpreters of this Divine Idea; a perpetual priesthood, standing forth, generation after generation, as the dispensers and living types of God's everlasting wisdom, to show it in their writings and actions, in such particular form as their own particular times require it in” (Wks., XXⅥ, 58).

② 引文参见刘鑫译本（商务印书馆 1999 年版，第 231—242 页）。为行文方便，引用时略有改动。下同。

文学作为宗教的分支来源于文学与宗教之间的生成关系。文学被认为起源于崇拜。与“其他事物”的起源一样，“《伊利亚特》以及大多数其它诗性的、特别是史诗性的东西与祈祷拥有一样的起源”（P. & P.，133）。无论是“希腊伟大的《伊利亚特》”，还是“英格兰的《罗宾汉的花环》”，所有这些文学作品都是“在其所在世纪和国家中的英雄歌谣不可知庞大的废墟中精编过的‘精选的美’”（Ibid.）。所谓的精选的美是崇拜之意。这样，文学记录的内容都是崇拜。事实上，第一个进行崇拜的人被卡莱尔称作一位诗人。人的崇拜来源于事物的不可知性。“第一个人以开放的灵魂看着这个令人敬畏的天地，这美和敬畏之物，我们把它叫做自然、宇宙等，其本质永远难以名状。”（132）宇宙的不可名状激发了人的崇拜。“第一个看着［宇宙］的人跪倒下来，带着敬畏。”（Ibid.）第一个进行崇拜的人是“一位诗人”（Ibid.）。可见，诗最初的表达内容便被看作是崇拜。如上所述，崇拜被等同为宗教。这样，文学起源于崇拜意味着文学起源于宗教。

文学作为宗教的分支决定了文学的表现内容。非常明显，宗教或者与宗教等同的崇拜是文学的表现内容。文学应该“为我们描绘人类从自然精神那里获得连续的启示，描绘他哪些方面抓住了并竭力表现出那无法言说的美的一瞥，这种美在其最清晰的时候就是宗教，是预言家的灵悟，而且或多或少启发了每个真正的歌唱者，假如他的题目并不太卑微的话”（Wks.，XXVII，94）。文学所表现的对象不仅仅是一个静态的对象，也是一个动态的过程。通过文学，“我们应当看到，人类如何一步一步地走向圣堂；如何接近它；又是由于怎样的不幸而长期背离了它，匍匐伏在头上没有音乐的平地上，或者盲目挣扎着走向其他高度”（Ibid.）。可见，文学的表现对象是人进行崇拜的整个过程。在此意义上，文学是宗教或者崇拜的记录。

卡莱尔对诗的论述在很大程度上与他对文学的论述一致。与文学一样，诗被认为是启示上帝意志的手段。事实上，卡莱尔甚至“试图将作为洞见者的诗人看作最高类型的思想家”。[1] 诗认识能力的基础在于诗所具有的旋律性（metricality）或音乐性（musicality）。一方面，旋律性或音乐性是万事万物的

① Gross，*The Rise and Fall of the Man of Letters*，p. 44.

内在本质。“一切内在的东西，都是有旋律的，它本能地以歌曲表达自己。”（H. & H.，83）旋律性所呈现的和谐一致是事物存在的根源所在。“内在的一致和谐是事物的灵魂，他决定事物有权利存在于这个世界。”（Ibid.）旋律性或音乐性作为万事万物的本质决定万事万物表现为歌。“一切深刻的东西都是歌。”（Ibid.）甚至人也表现为歌。“由于某种原因，歌似乎成了我们真正的核心本质，其余的一切好像都是一些覆盖和装饰的东西。”（Ibid.）另一方面，旋律性或音乐性是诗的主要品质。旋律性被看作是诗的定义的主要内容。“以往对诗的那种通俗看法是颇有意义的，即认为诗的特征是旋律，其中有音乐，是一首歌。”（Ibid.）音乐性的存在决定诗的存在。“如果一定要下个定义的话，那就应该说：如果人们的描写真正具有音乐的和谐，这种音乐的和谐不仅表现在字面上，而是涵盖在核心与实质中，体现在它的一切思想和表述中，参透在它的整个观念中，这就是诗，否则，就不是。”（Ibid.）万事万物与诗在本质上均表现为旋律性或音乐性，这决定诗可以表现万事万物的本质。“一种音乐和谐的思想是发自心灵的思想，他渗透在事物最深处的核心，它觉察到了事物最深刻的奥秘，即隐藏在事物深处的旋律。”（Ibid.）基于以上判断，诗成为启示上帝意识的手段。

诗作为启示上帝意志的手段决定了诗人的存在状态。诗人在一定程度上具有神性。诗是诗人实现认识的手段，这是诗人神性存在的根源。如果“诗［可以］称作富有音乐的思想”，那么“诗人就是以这种方式进行思维的人”（83－84）。诗人凭借诗进行认识。诗允许诗人透视事物内在的本质。“要是有深远的目光，才能发现音乐的和谐，自然界内心处处都有音乐，只是看你能否找到它。”（84）很明显，诗人凭借诗可以实现这样的认识深度。诗人杰出的认识能力赋予诗人以神性。“诗人身上有一种无限性；他们能把一种 *Unendlichkeit*，即一种无限特性灌输到他所描绘的所有作品中去。”（82）可见，无限性是诗人身上神性的表现。诗人的存在状态将他从众人区分开来。“［诗人］比别人更接近［神圣的奥秘］。”（81）这样的存在状态甚至具有一定的必然性。“他认为自己生活于其中，而且必须生活于其中。”（Ibid.）可见，诗人处于事物内在事实的存在状态是一种必然状态。必然性的存在决定，启示上帝的意志是诗人的天职。“［诗人］是被某种力量推动去理解［神圣的奥秘］的，无须他的同意。”（Ibid.）

诗人是上帝意志的启示人。与先知和其他英雄一样，诗人“已经洞察了这个神圣的奥秘，他是派来教育人们加深对它的认识”（80－81）。对上帝意志的启示甚至被看作“始终是［诗人］的使命”（81）。诗人的使命甚至被赋予强烈的现代性。“当人们忘掉［神圣的奥秘］的时候，［诗人］却理解它。”（Ibid.）可见，诗人的生存环境与卡莱尔所在的时代之间具有强烈的相似性。他们都生活在一个对上帝的存在失去信仰，对上帝的意志失去认识的时代。在这样的时代，重申上帝的存在以及强调上帝的意志不但是卡莱尔本人最为重要的命题，也是他赋予包括诗人在内所有类型英雄的使命。以此观之，卡莱尔再一次将个人信仰赋予英雄崇拜理论。

以上便是卡莱尔文人英雄崇拜的主要内容。文人英雄在认识方式、认识能力和存在状态等方面与其他类型的英雄表现出强烈的一致性。与先知等早期英雄不同，文人英雄被认为是现时代最为主要的英雄类型。文人英雄由此被赋予强烈的现代性。在此意义上，文人英雄可谓英雄发展史上最为重要的一个环节。如果将卡莱尔本人的文人身份纳入思考，那么文人英雄具有极强的映射力。事实上，卡莱尔本人便是他笔下的文人英雄。他是一代人的“先知和导师”，特别是“对于年轻人来说，对于慷慨的人来说，对于每一个认真对待生活、希望其生活崇高并对无所事事和挣取金钱不能感到满足的人来说，他的话语就好比重见的天日一般”。[①] 他的话语起到振聋发聩的作用。“在四十年前的矛盾、争论、疑惑、蜂拥而至的不确定性中，卡莱尔的声音对于年轻一代的英国人来说就好像‘一万把号角’在他们耳边的声响一样。”[②] 卡莱尔所传达的信息就是他的英雄所启示的神意。“卡莱尔第一个让我们看到他［即上帝］现在在这处于运作中的世界的运动的、真实的存在。”[③] 可见，卡莱尔就是一位真正的文人英雄。

卡莱尔对文学的理解具有极强的被动性。所谓的被动性指，文学不在于

---

① Froude, *Life in London*, Vol. Ⅰ, p. 248.

② Froude, *Life in London*, Vol. Ⅰ, p. 249.

③ Froude, *Life in London*, Vol. Ⅰ, p. 250.

创作（to create），而在于再现（to represent）。所谓再现是将对象的原始面貌不加任何修饰而直接地表现出来的意思。在很大程度上，卡莱尔对文学的理解仅仅停留在再现这一内容之上。文学以及诗被认为是上帝意志的启示手段，这一内容可谓再现的集中表达。对再现的强调使得卡莱尔的文学观疏远于浪漫主义文学和诗学理论。对诗人想象力和创造性的强调在卡莱尔的认识之中几乎完全缺失。在此意义上，卡莱尔的文学观更加类似现实主义文学理论。然而，现实主义文学所再现的对象是现实，特别是社会现实。与此相比，卡莱尔的文学再现的对象只是他加尔文主义信仰的内容而已。再现对象的不同将卡莱尔的文学观同现实主义文学理论区分开来。可见，卡莱尔的文学观是处于浪漫主义和现实主义文学理论之间的过渡状态，在很大程度上可谓现实主义文学理论的准备。

再现作为卡莱尔文学理论的主要内容来源于他对同感（sympathy）的认识。所谓同感是怀有相同的（sym－）情感（－pathy）的含义。[①] 同感是认识的前提。“要认识事物，即我们说要有知识，首先要热爱事物，与它建立同感，也就是说，要公正地对待事物。”（107）同感是认识的必要条件。一个人“所以能完全识别对象，或者说，能抓住事物极其重要的典型，首先在于他有我们称之为对事物的同感，——能赋予事物以由衷的同感之情”（93）。同感的有无决定了认识的成败。认识主体“必须对事物有虔敬；必须具备真诚和同感；一个没有价值的人，就不能表述任何事物的真相；他只能停留在一切事物粗浅的表面现象、谬误和琐细的传说之中”（Ibid.）。同感表现为一种洞见。“对万物怀有的深厚同感”被认为是一种“深刻的洞察力，深入事物的本质，去驾驭事物”的能力（217）。同感也是洞见的前提。“同感［……］是导致洞见首要的本质性［要素］。”（Rev.，368）卡莱尔赋予同感以极其重要

① 同感的英语原文是“sympathy”，本应翻译为“同情”，但汉语的同情多有“可怜”“怜悯”之意，这与卡莱尔的所谓的“sympathy”具有较大差别。英文“sympathy”来源于古希腊文“συμπαθεια”，为“fellow－feeling”之意，其中，“συμ”为“συν”，为“伴随（along with；together with）”之意，而“παθεια”来源于“παθος”，为“经历（experience）、情感（feeling）”之意，两者合成一词则为“相同的经历、相同的情感”之意，故翻译为“同感”。卡莱尔以“同感”来解释人的认识过程，即人只有以被认识之物的情感为依据和基础才可以实现对于被认识之物的认识，所以他所谓的“同感”是“怀有相同的情感”之意。

的认识意义。

卡莱尔对同感的理解主要来源于他早期对容纳（tolerance）的认识。在早期认识之中，容纳同样被认作是认识的前提条件。容纳作为认识的前提来源于传记写作的启发。在为伏尔泰立传时卡莱尔指出，“如果我们真的愿意理解任何事情的真理，而不是如同普通的平常状况一样，仅仅屈从于我们业已形成的观念，仅仅满足于这个或其他的偏见以及恶意，那么容纳可以看作所有先决条件中最不可缺少的因素；容纳是［认识的］真正进步可以实现的唯一的条件”（Wks.，XXVI，405）。同样，在传记写作中容纳也是认识的前提。“性格只有首先被带着某种不但是容纳、而且是同感的情感看待，才可以被正确理解。”（Ibid.）可见，容纳不但可以避免偏见，更可以促进认识。容纳的实质是对认识对象原始面貌的再现，在传记写作中即是对立传对象原始状态的接受。“如果我们要正确判断一个人的性格，我们就一定要既以我们的视角、更要以他的视角看待；我们一定要与他建立同感，将他看作一个同类，一句话，热爱他，否则他真正的精神本质就会永远被我们误解。”（406）在此，容纳与同感等义。两者均是在承认认识对象原始面貌的前提下，对对象进行再现的含义。

同感也好，容纳也罢，对认识对象原始面貌的再现贯穿卡莱尔早期的写作。在对歌德的作品进行解读时，他提出这一原则。“只有我们看到作者的对象，无论它是什么，就像他看到的那样，我才算阅读一个作者”（150）。很明显，接受原作者初始写作对象的原始面貌是实现解读的必要条件。这是一个深入认识对象内在空间的过程。“我们应该理解使得他的头脑认为真实、或者劝说他进行写作的情况，因为他知道写作内容是虚构的。”（Ibid.）只有这种具有强烈同感特征的方式才可以实现认识。“如果以任何其他方式进行判断，这都是不公正的。”（Ibid.）这种从文学解读所获得认识手段被卡莱尔最终推广到传记写作中去。在《论传记》（“Biography,” 1832）中，传记写作与文学解读等同起来。“在我们欣赏《主显圣容》、或者在我们研读《伊利亚特》的时候，我们总是试图想象拉斐尔的精神状态；想象荷马的思维形式，其中蕴含着艾莉希安之光和达达里亚之晖，那古老的世界因此而形成，这些翠绿的文字不过是微弱却持久的抄件而已。”（XXVIII，45－46）非常明显，这是读者与作者之间的同感。在同感中，作者的主题成为读者的认识对象。两者甚至交融在一起。“画家和吟诵诗人与我们同在；就在此时，我们部分地成为这位画家以及这位吟诵诗人。”（46）对主题的无条件接受实现作者和读者的融合。

以上便是卡莱尔对同感的理解。总体而言，同感是对认识对象原始面貌无条件地接受与再现。这种实现与对象具备相同的情感的认识手段不要求任何主观上的创造，而是要求以客观代替主观，使得客观的状态同样融入主观。同感来源于卡莱尔对宽容的认识。宽容是他解读文学作品，特别是德国作家的主要标准。德国文学，尤其是浪漫派文学对于英国读者的理解存在一定的障碍。宽容原则主要在这一语境下提出。在此语境下，宽容要求读者不以英国的文学品位为标准，反而以德国文学自身的内容为评判依据。这样，宽容的含义变得易于理解。宽容被卡莱尔进一步应用于传记写作。在他一系列的传记作品之中，设身处地地深入写作对象的境况成为他主要的写作依据。

卡莱尔有关同感的认识建立在他的加尔文主义信仰基础之上。如上所述，卡莱尔式的知识是上帝的法则。作为法则而存在的知识（to know）不是认识，而更是服从（to obey）的对象。这种以服从为主要目的的知识主要以“要义”和“秘义”等形式呈现。这赋予知识以强烈的神秘主义色彩。“无论何时信使被派来，对天堂的不服从是、并依然是不可能的。”（P. & P.，284）知识的产生不是认识的结果，而更是启发的作用。这种知识要求人的服从。作为“这个宇宙秘密的新的更深层次的启示”，真理“本质上是来自上天的一个启示，对它必须而且要愿意服从”（H. & H.，193－194）。在此，知识被看作是启示的结果。知识与神启（inspiration）等同。很明显，这种通过神秘的手段而获得神性的知识只能是服从的对象。

认识被进一步转化为信仰。卡莱尔知识论的实质是取消认识。如果知识无须认识，那么认识便失去存在的价值。认识不再是实现知识的手段。相反，认识反而会导致知识的丧失。卡莱尔信仰危机产生的根源便在于知识的积累与增加。认识被取消之后，知识的定义被卡莱尔转化为信仰（to believe）。“真理仅仅是相信之意，或者是被相信，或者是被信仰之意。”（Wds.，87）这样的观点可谓是对知识的背叛。在此，知识让位于信仰。对于卡莱尔而言，“一个人的信条是他的依靠，他的所有”（Nt. B.，21）。信仰可以满足卡莱尔所有的需要。“有一条笔直的大路为我们准备好，即使这是一条错误的路，穿越这事物混乱的荒原——也比当我们永远找不到一条正确的路之时等待寻找这条正确的路要好。”（Ibid.）可见，卡莱尔对于空间的离散性以及光速的恒定性等纯粹知识并无需求。相反，实现行动是他的主要需求。行动作为主要需求决定认识可以被取消。这样，知识被信仰置换。

至此，卡莱尔文人英雄崇拜理论的全貌已经表现出来。文人英雄崇拜理论建立在他的文学观基础之上，而文学观进一步建立在他对同感以及容纳所形成的认识之上，后者又以他的知识论为基础，而知识论不过是加尔文主义信仰的表现。总体而言，文人英雄崇拜理论是卡莱尔文学观的逻辑推演。理解文学观所针对的对象是理解卡莱尔文学观的关键。在他看来，在现时代文学热爱的对象出现了问题。“我们没有对于伟大的热爱，而只有对于伟大热爱的热爱。”（Wks.，XXⅧ，23）有基于此，现时代的文学才出现了严重的问题。“无限的矫揉造作、纷扰由此而产生；在所有情况下，谬误不可避免。”（23－24）可见，现时代的文学背离了卡莱尔加尔文主义信仰的内容。在他的信仰里，文学是信仰和宗教的表现。背离本质的要求，是现时代文学产生问题的根源。在这种情况下，他的文学理论是对现时代文学状况的否定，而文人英雄崇拜是他为实现文学病症开出的药方。这位集病理确定者、诊断人和药剂师于一身的医生再一次将自身的治愈过程普遍化，使之成为时代问题解决的良方。

不过，信仰作为文学的表现内容存在问题。文学表现为复杂，任何单一因素作为文学的对象都是对文学复杂性的替代，而替代的结果必然是谬误。即使是卡莱尔的上帝，任何内容也不能成为文学的唯一。卡莱尔的文学观具有一定的进步性。他察觉到时代文学状况所表现出来的问题。特别是文学对象的低等导致文学的退化。然而，以一唯一内容（信仰）取代所有内容，这让他最终陷入无可挽回的一元论。卡莱尔的文学审查制度甚至可以想象。在这样的制度之下，信仰将成为文学唯一的内容，对上帝的意志进行表现将成为文学唯一的表现对象，文学对信仰的任何叛离都将成为否定和批评的对象。这样的文学只有凋零的余地。

第三章　历史观

卡莱尔是维多利亚时期最为重要的历史学家之一。“历史不能概括他的全部，但是他作品的绝大部分被历史性的叙事或评论占据；历史作为真理的首要评判标准以及仲裁的依据是他所有思想的基础。”① 《法国大革命》、《克伦威尔书信及演说集》和《腓德烈大帝》等是他主要的历史作品。卡莱尔对法国大革命的关注由来已久。早在1829年，他便已经创作完成《伏尔泰》。1833年，《狄德罗》（“Diderot”）完成。同年年底，《加里奥斯特罗伯爵》（“Count Cagliostro”）发表。所有这些作品可谓《法国大革命》的先导。特别是《加里奥斯特罗伯爵》，这一作品堪称“在表现力、洞见力、对比方法、分组类型和幽默等方面是即将完成的伟大历史作品的引导”。② 这一年，他在通信（1st Oct；to Dr. Carlyle）中提到，“［他］最为关注的主题之一就是法国大革命，事实上这依然是最为重要的主题”（Let.[2]，Ⅱ，120）。定居伦敦（1834）后，有关法国大革命的写作计划被彻底制订，这是“下一部作品的主题”。③ 1834—1837年，他潜心阅读研究相关文献。其中的一大批由穆勒提供。④ 1835年，《革命》的第一卷手稿被不幸焚毁（L.－M.，106）。同年9月，新稿完成。与“旧稿相比”，新稿“欠生动性，但是设计和结构更加完善”。⑤ 次年4

① Grant, *English Historians*, Intro., p. lviii.

② Shepherd, *Memoirs*, Vol. Ⅰ, p. 138.

③ Froude, *First Forty Years*, Vol. Ⅰ, p. 352.

④ Hanson, *Necessary Evil*, p. 187.

⑤ Hanson, *Necessary Evil*, p. 201.

月，第二卷完成。1837 年 1 月，第三卷写就。至此，《革命》彻底完成。此外，卡莱尔还写有《钻石项链》（“The Diamond Necklace,” 1837）、《米拉博回忆录》（“Memoirs of Mirabeau,” 1837）和《法国大革命议会史》（“Parliamentary History of the French Revolution,” 1837）三篇相关作品。《革命》得到了穆勒的大力称赞。作品被誉为“既是法国大革命的历史，又是法国大革命的诗”。① 只有“一位伟大的诗人——他具有创造性的想象力，他可以在分散的线索和混乱的见证中选取材料［……］最后将这些编织成一个整体”才可以写出这样的作品。②《革命》中的历史写作极其鲜明形象。如奥丽芬（Margaret Oliphant）所说，“卡莱尔不是一个 *raconteur*［转述者］，而是一个观察家，在这些混乱的、具有悲剧性的事件出现、形成并扩散，之后就像天上的风暴再次解体为碎片的时候，在血雨腥风肆虐、魑魅魍魉游荡以及大屠杀发生在街头的时候，他在观察”。③《革命》在文体上存在一定的问题。这部作品“依赖文体转化的基本原则，因为它承认文体规则，但是并不遵从”。④ 这导致《革命》的文体极具多样性和不确定性，同时也成就了作品独特的艺术风格。

《克伦威尔书信及演说集》是卡莱尔第二部重要的历史作品。卡莱尔关于英国内战的关注更有来历。早在 1822 年，他便开始有意识地阅读相关材料。在通信中，他透露了写作计划。“［他］的意图［……］是关于内战，关于英联邦写成一篇论文——不是写作历史——而是尽［他］所能展现民族性格的一些特点。”（27th Apr.；L. – B.，110）同年 4—5 月，他在笔记中再次明确写作目的。“［本书］一定是联邦时期英国民族性格的总体素描。”（Nt. B.，28 –29）虽然这一写作计划长期未能得到实现，但是他在 20 多年的时间里从未中断过对内战的关注（Skh.，pref.，vi）。1843—1844 年，他开始动笔，并完成了一定数量的历史速写。⑤ 然而，作品未能最终完成。与此同时，《书

① *Early Essays*, p. 271.

② *Early Essays*, p. 278.

③ “Literature of the Last Fifty Years,” p. 405.

④ *Cumming*, *A Disimprisoned Epic*, p. 51.

⑤ See *Historical Sketches of Notable Persons and Events in the Reigns of James* Ⅰ. *and Charles* Ⅰ (ed. Alexander Carlyle, London: Chapman and Hall, 1902).

信集》的写作准备也在进行。1839—1842 年，他收集并阅读相关材料（Let.[3]，Ⅰ，147，148 - 149，213 - 214，217，219，226，246 - 247，272）。1842 年 9 月，他甚至亲自赶往克伦威尔的故居，获得深刻的感受（269）。1843 年 10 月，经过多次尝试失败，卡莱尔终于开始了《书信集》的写作。1845 年 8 月，作品的第一版完成。作品被认为是“对英国历史最为重要的贡献”，而卡莱尔也成为“打破自复辟以来有关克伦威尔主题偏见，以及使得克伦威尔和克伦威尔的时代为人所知的第一人”。① 在很大程度上，《书信集》是“一种新的‘认识的’或者‘心理的’历史，聚焦于历史人物的意图、欲望、动机、感受以及心理状态等”。② 此外，他还写有《盟约人巴里》（“Baillie the Covenanter,” 1841）和《长期议会选举》（“An Election of the Long Parliament,” 1844）等两篇相关主题的作品。

《腓德烈大帝》是卡莱尔最后一部，也是篇幅最长、耗时最久的历史作品。早在《书信集》第一版完成后，卡莱尔便开始了相关的阅读。“［他］带着许多思考阅读了［《腓德烈大帝》］，并有意关于此人进行更多的调查”（8th Oct. 1845；L. - W.，218）。1851—1852 年，他的阅读更加系统（Let.[3]，Ⅱ，117，，118，124）。1852 年秋季，他决定前往德国，为写作做最后的准备。1853—1865 年，他处于写作的过程之中。其间，于 1858 年秋，他再次因写作需要前往德国。1865 年初，《大帝》正式完成。因为这部作品，他先后分别于 1865 年当选爱丁堡大学名誉校长，于 1874 年获得普鲁士颁发的勋章。然而，与他所付出的努力不相匹配，《大帝》可谓“在卡莱尔的主要著作中读者最少，并且看起来即使是在将来，也不会获得更多的读者”。③ 即使如此，《大帝》对于解读卡莱尔的思想依然具有很大的意义。首先，在“某些个人环境和品质”方面，卡莱尔与腓德烈大帝之间具有强烈的共性。④ 在某种程度上，腓德烈大帝可谓卡莱尔的“alter ego［另一个自我］”。⑤ 其次，《大帝》

① Froude, *Life in London*, Vol. Ⅰ, p. 305.

② Fermanis, “A ‘Poor Crotchety Picture of Several Things’,” p. 97.

③ Le Quesne, *Carlyle*, p. 89.

④ Adrian, “Frederick the Great,” p. 178.

⑤ Adrian, “Frederick the Great,” p. 178.

中的修辞技巧具有很大的研究价值。“不但一些关于卡莱尔本人的问题，而且关于历史写作的本质问题”均与此相关。①

除以上主要作品外，卡莱尔还写有一些短篇历史作品。② 这些作品包括两篇理论性的论文。分别是《论历史》（“On History,” 1830）和《再论历史》（“On History Again,” 1833）。其中，《论历史》来源于未完成的《德国文学史》的引论部分。作品原以《历史感想》（“Thoughts on History”）为题，于1830年8月前后被寄给《弗雷泽杂志》（6th；to Dr. Carlyle；Let.[2]，Ⅰ，227），11月发表。③《再论历史》原以《所知为何》（“Quæ Cogitavit”）为题发表于1833年5月版的《弗雷泽杂志》。《二百五十年前》（“Two Hundred and Fifty Years Ago,” 1850）是一部应求之作。在《雷·亨特杂志》（*Leigh Hunt Journal*）主编的请求下，卡莱尔创作该作品。这部作品创作并发表于《晚近文集》之后，标志着他的兴趣点向历史领域的回归。《君主遇劫》（“The Prinzenraub,” 1855）发表于《威斯敏斯特评论》（*Westminster Review*）。《挪威早期帝王史》是卡莱尔最后一部历史作品，连载于《弗雷泽杂志》。④

历史作为真理的载体，是卡莱尔历史思想的根基。对于他而言，“历史是人发现真理尝试的记录”，是“真理以例子被教授的表现”。⑤ 这一根基性的思想在他所有的主要历史著作之中具有体现。《革命》“在作者的心目中绝不仅仅是一部事件实录，此书体现了他最深刻的道德与宗教信念”。⑥ 在很大程度上，《革命》可谓“一位先知召唤罪人进行忏悔的激越呼号”。⑦ 同样，卡莱尔“运用克伦威尔的事业”的目的在于“向时代表现其运行模式中存在的错误”。⑧ “情感和政治实践力在克伦威尔身上的结合”以及“他有关忠诚、

---

① Peckham, “Frederick the Great,” p. 199.

② For Carlyle's minor historical writings, see *Thomas Carlyle: Historical Essays* (ed. Chris R. Vanden Bossche, The Norman and Charlotte Strouse Edition of the Writings of Thomas Carlyle, Berkeley & Los Angeles: Univ. of California Pr., 2002).

③ Cf. Ger., Intro., p. XXXVn.

④ See *Fraser's Magazine* 61, pp. 1 – 16; 62, pp. 135 – 155; 63, 273 – 288.

⑤ Harrold, *Carlyle and German Thought*, p. 153.

⑥ Gooch, “Carlyle and Froude,” pp. 324 – 325. The Chinese translation is from Geng Danru（耿淡如）'s version (Beijing: The Commercial Pr., 1989).

⑦ Gooch, “Carlyle and Froude,” p. 325.

⑧ Neff, *Carlyle*, p. 209.

议会、律师、平民以及有组织的帝国主义政策等”，则是卡莱尔理想的表现。[①] 在《大帝》中，“腓德烈大帝的英雄主义是一个确定不移的事实，只有尊重这个历史事实，才能最接近于认识到 18 世纪历史中得到展现的神圣公平天意”。[②] 可见，历史事实成为天意的载体。

历史作为真理的载体，这一根基性的思想主要来源于卡莱尔的德国思想研究。在德国，莱辛（Gotthold E. Lessing）是历史作为真理的载体这一思想的先驱。据他理解，“世界历史是人学习终极真理的学校”。[③] 世界历史“对于人类种族而言就像普通教育对于个体；世界历史，或称人类过去的经验，令人可以更快地学习”。[④] 历史作为真理的载体以及作为人学习的对象，这与卡莱尔的历史思想之间具有一定的相似性。与莱辛相比，卡莱尔与赫尔德在历史思想方面表现出更强烈的相似性。首先，“对于两人而言历史（在许多方面与自然类似）在内部是一个有机的整体”。[⑤] 其次，“人类历史（依然与自然相似）启示神性；但是（与自然一样）这一启示只是部分的”。[⑥] 历史作为有机性的整体以及作为神性的部分启示，是卡莱尔历史观的主要内容。事实上，卡莱尔对赫尔德的《人类历史哲学的概念》（*Ideen zur Philosophie der Geschichte der Menschheit*）具有比较理想的理解。虽然他无法接受“万事万物作为环境和组织的效果”以及“生命是光与电程度更高的凝练”等思想（Nt. B.，72），但是依然表示有进一步阅读的必要（73）。卡莱尔的历史思想受席勒启发最为深刻。“历史中的断代无法填补；历史不过是片段的集成而已；只有无限的精神可以审视全部历史；只有目的论，即有关历史中一个内在的、活动的目的的理论，可以使得历史具有解读性；只有哲学性的历史学家，而不是常规的、毫无灵感的事实收集者，可以希望把握并再创过去”等所有这些思想，[⑦] 既构成卡莱尔历史思想的细节，也是历史作为真理的载体这

① Neff, *Carlyle*, p. 209.
② Le Quesne, op. cit., p. 90.
③ Harrold, op. cit., p. 156.
④ Harrold, op. cit., p. 156.
⑤ Shine, “Carlyle's Early Writings and Herder's *Ideen*,” pp. 20 – 21.
⑥ Shine, “Carlyle's Early Writings and Herder's *Ideen*,” p. 21.
⑦ Harrold, op. cit., p. 158.

一根基性思想的逻辑分化。

历史作为真理的载体是卡莱尔形而上学思想的延续。历史作为真理的载体可谓物质作为精神的表现这一思想在历史领域里的延续。若以“衣服哲学”的术语表达，则历史是真理的衣服。若以“自然超自然论”的术语表达，则历史是真理的象征。可见，同一形而上学思想延续到历史领域。“卡莱尔对于历史哲学的杰出贡献便是衣服隐喻，通过衣服隐喻他的历史哲学得以表达”。① 与卡莱尔形而上学思想之中所存在的问题一样，历史作为真理的载体同样建立在类比基础之上。历史（H）相对于真理（T）就像衣服（C）相对于穿衣服的主体（S），即

$$H: T = C: S$$

这样，就像衣服是主体的表现一样，历史也可以看作是真理的表现。然而，以上等式成立的关键在于历史相对于真理的关系（H：T）与衣服与主体的关系（C：S）是同一范畴。非常明显，此处合理性的证明再一次依靠修辞，即依靠类比实现。这又是将新现象纳入旧有知识体系的过程。与形而上学思想一样，卡莱尔历史观的重点同样不在于逻辑起点的缜密，而在于在承认逻辑起点合理性的基础之上实现后续的逻辑推演。他历史研究的目的不在于历史本身，而在于历史的作用。

卡莱尔历史研究的目的在于理解现时代的社会。在他的历史思想之中，周期论（periodicity，periodicism）是一个相对明显且重要的因素。卡莱尔式的历史周期论指“历史发展处于（1）进步时代和（2）倒退时代之间的周期性循环之中”。② 历史发展所表现出来的周期性是历史发展规律的基础。很明显，周期性可以看作规律性（regularity）的一种表现。历史的周期性发展可谓历史发展规律的表现。卡莱尔式的历史发展规律虽然不能被严格定义为一种“抽象的法则，即时间中的变化的一般性的认识”，但是依然“强调［……］社会生活以及历史生活的历史发展”。③ 在历史的视角下，社会发展

① Culler, “Mill, Carlyle, and the Spirit of the Age,” p. 62.

② Shine, *Carlyle and the Saint – Simonians*, p. 1N.

③ Young, *Carlyle and the Art of History*, p. 91.

表现出强烈的时间性。社会发展由此被纳入历史发展。社会现状是历史发展的最新阶段，而历史发展是理解社会现状的基础。这样，社会发展最终被纳入处于所谓的进步时代和倒退时代之间的钟摆运动之中。在此意义上，历史思想可谓卡莱尔理解社会发展的理论背景。

卡莱尔的历史观深刻地影响了他历史写作的语言。历史学家的写作对象不是简单的历史事件，而是历史所启示的真理。“对于他而言，历史学家的主要任务在于发现宇宙中产生作用的因素，因为具有生命力和永恒性的要素可以在其中发掘出来。”① 这样，历史学家的语言需要精心的设计。“历史不是文明的记录；历史是文明本身，过去通过历史学家的声音与现在和未来对话”，因此，“如果没有生动的语言，就不会有历史”。② 事实上，卡莱尔历史写作的语言特色主要来源于历史作为真理的载体这一根基性的思想。“卡莱尔关于象征性的对象潜在于现实世界之中的特别关注使得他在文体风格上最具创新性。”③ 与麦考莱（Thomas Babington Macaulay）的历史写作风格完全不同，卡莱尔的“叙事方法在两个视角之间剧烈地转换”，其一，运用“现在时使得读者真实地处于历史人物的环境之中”，其二，“同人物之间拉开不可衡量的距离”。④ 这种带有强烈动态效果的写作方法与麦考莱静态的方法完全相反。“麦考莱与卡莱尔之间的分歧十分重要：对于前者而言，我们关于全体的印象来源于描述的凝练程度；对于卡莱尔而言则完全相反，效果完全来源于审视主体的解释原创性。”⑤ 可见，叙事视角的剧烈变化是卡莱尔实现历史写作效果的主要手段。

本章以卡莱尔的历史思想为解读对象。共分三部分。其一，解读历史结构，其二，解读历史发展与社会发展，其三，解读时间、历史和历史决定论。

第一节　历史的结构

总体而言，历史作为教义（teaching）是卡莱尔历史观的核心思想。“哪

---

① Sanders, “Thomas Carlyle,” p. 167.

② Rosenberg, *Carlyle and the Burden of History*, p. 15.

③ Jann, “Thomas Carlyle,” p. 49.

④ Cronin, *Romantic Victorians*, p. 50.

⑤ Jones, *Lost Causes*, p. 25.

里黑格尔认为是一个理念，那里卡莱尔以一种英雄主义情感取而代之。”① 就像黑格尔在历史之中启示理念一样，卡莱尔在历史之中探寻英雄崇拜。这样，真理被置于历史的内部。历史不是简单的历史事件，而是隐匿性真理的启示。历史作为教义深刻地影响了卡莱尔对历史的理解。对于他而言：

> 历史是教导的文字，老一辈人写下了这样的教导文字，传给新一代人；或者可以这样说，更加普遍地说，历史是说出的或者写下的信息，所有的人都传给所有人；历史是唯一说出的交流（因为没有说出的和无言的交流——无论是否可以理解——如此奇怪地通过我们存在的每一个纤维、行为的每一个步骤，就在我们周围、就在我们之上）过去和现在、远方和近处共有这唯一的交流。（Wks.，XXⅧ，167）

可见，历史在此被理解为含有教义的文字。历史作为教义的载体进一步深刻地影响了卡莱尔对于历史学的理解。他认为：

> 作为一种有限而且唯一可以实践的形态，真正的历史学，即处理重大历史事件的那部分历史学，无论在古代还是近代都被视为最高的艺术；也许今天它的威望比以往任何时候都高。因为古代历史学的魅力主要在于满足我们对神奇和未知事物的渴望；它所履行的是一位吟游诗人、一位故事讲述者的职能。而今天，它进一步扮演的是一位中学女教师，用教授知识的方式来满足人们的兴趣。（XXⅦ，84）

可见，与历史作为教义的载体一脉相承，历史学被认为是最具价值的学科。不仅如此，历史的教义在此甚至被赋予现代性。现时代的历史学不但继承了以往历史学的全部传统，而且还满足现实的特殊需要，是知识的主要来源。这便是卡莱尔历史观的概貌。理解卡莱尔的历史观，有必要从他关于历史的结构的认识入手。

历史在卡莱尔看来并不是一个简单的单层结构，仅仅表现为历史事件在

---

① Taine, *L'Idéalisme Anglais*, p. 146.

时间顺序上的先后排列。相反，历史被认为是一个具有内外双层结构的事物。在历史事件的背后隐匿着历史内在结构的剧烈运动。在很大程度上，历史事件仅仅是内在结构运动的表现而已。内在结构才是历史的本质。卡莱尔历史研究的目的在于通过透视历史事件获得对于内在结构的认识和把握。对历史结构的认识深刻地影响了卡莱尔对历史的定义。历史在他看来是一个含有要义的对象。获得历史的意义是他全部历史研究的目的所在。基于此，历史被看作一部圣经。“人的历史以及人类的历史［……］是一个永恒的福音。”（Sar.，254）然而，这部历史福音的含义并不是显露的，而是隐匿的。因此，“所有的历史”也是“都是一部无言的圣经”（Wks.，XX，325）。虽然历史具有深层次的含义，但是隐匿是历史的首要表现。历史“以某种隐晦、复杂的手段对这个较为低等的世界上的神圣表象在进行启示”（Ibid.）。所有的历史事件都是神圣表现的启示，都具有神意。“因为上帝的确创造了这个世界，并永远支配它；声响巨大的时间织机以法国大革命、犹太革命的形式‘编织着你可以看见［上帝］的衣物’。”（325－326）甚至所有的传记也是神圣表象的启示。“所有人的传记与任何历史或者民族国家的传记一样，都包含有天堂的信息。”（326）然而，即使所有历史现象均对神意进行启示，这并不意味着所有人都可以获得历史的启示。“这个宇宙之所是、上帝法则之所是、每个人的生命都会将其教授给你；所有人、所有事物的生命”，所有这些“传达给倾听的耳朵，也传达给不倾听的耳朵”（Ibid.）。很明显，同所有的象征一样，隐匿是历史的主要表现。

卡莱尔有关历史结构的认识深刻地影响了他对历史写作（historiography）的判断。历史内外结构的区分使得历史写作的对象得以确定。非常明显，写作对象不再是简单的历史事件，而是历史内部所隐匿的启示性内容。对此，卡莱尔对两类历史写作进行了区分。这两类历史写作对应于两类历史写作者。“历史学中的艺术家”可以同“历史学中的匠人”区别开来（XXⅦ，90）。区分的根源在于两类历史写作者对历史的把握层次不同。“有的人在一个部门从事机械劳动，看不到整体，也不觉得有整体；有的人以整体的观念使一个卑微的领域变得崇高起来，为人们所熟悉并且习惯性地认识到，唯有在整体中部分才能得到正确的认识。”（Ibid.）可见，只有历史的艺术家对历史内部所隐匿的启示性内容具有一定的认识。卡莱尔本人历史写作的理想变得十分显然。“工匠”、“学者”以及“事件记录者”等集于一体并不是他的理想，而“艺术家”、“先知”、“哲学家”和“历史学家”所构成的“四位一体”才是他的愿望所在。[①] 事实上，卡莱尔最反对仅对历史事件作为写作对象，而对历史内部所隐匿的启示性的内容毫无觉察的写作方法。他对伏尔泰的历史阅读所作的批评便根源于这一观点。伏尔泰“没有带着一个虔诚观察者或者评论者的眼睛阅读历史；而是仅仅通过一对反对天主教的眼镜”（XXVI，414）。在这一视角下，“历史不是一出伟大的剧作，在无限的剧场里上演，太阳是灯光，永恒是背景；剧作的作者是上帝，主旨和无尽的寓意在于将我们引导向上帝宝座，‘因为光亮无限而无法发现’”（Ibid.）。卡莱尔立场在批评之中变得更加明显。他历史写作的目的在于表现隐匿于历史内部的启示性内容。

历史作为启示性内容的载体影响了卡莱尔对历史学的理解。根据他的认识，如果任一学科以某一特定知识为研究对象，那么历史学则以普遍真理为研究对象。历史学的研究对象包容其他所有学科的研究对象。这样，历史学包容其他所有学科。“历史不仅仅是唯一最为合适的研究［对象］。而且也是唯一的包括所有其他任何研究［对象］的研究［对象］。”（XXVIII，168）在某种程度上，所有其他的学科都以历史为研究对象。“所有的学生，所有那些求知的心灵，不论层次的高低，都围聚在［历史］的讲台前，满怀敬意地思考和聆听［历史］的教诲，把它视为智慧的真正基础。”（XXVII，84）这种兼收并蓄的气质不但将历史与其他学科区分开来，也使得历史获得高度的开放性。历史被卡莱尔类比为一个帝国（empire）。“诗歌、神学、政治学、物理学，都有其支持者和反对者；每个知识小行会都要为自己的领地展开攻战与守卫；而历史学则是一个自由的帝国，在那里一切好战者都将偃旗息鼓，和平共处。”（84－85）就像众多民族可以统一于帝国一样，众多的思想类型也可以融入于历史。“无论感伤主义者还是功利主义者，怀疑论者还是神学家，都异口同声地劝告我们：借鉴历史吧，那是‘经验的哲学教诲’。”（85）可见，卡莱尔认识之中的历史作为一个学科具有极强的包容性。

---

① Harrold，“Carlyle and Novalis，” p. 58.

包容性使得历史成为最具价值的研究对象。历史研究包容其他所有研究对象，这意味着对历史研究即是对所有其他学科进行研究。作为所有其他学科的学科，历史最具研究价值。“历史有资格被推荐为所有研究之中最为有益处的：的确，特别是对于人作为一种存在而言——人出生，需要学习、劳动，过一些年之后又要离开，留下后代和事迹，以这种方式证明自己是人类之中的有机一体——没有更为合适的研究对象。”（XXⅧ，167）包容性赋予历史以充足性（sufficiency）。历史研究是自给自足的。研究历史意味着不再需要研究其他任何学科。“精通历史之人理解、看到并知道亚当整个家族目前为止所有之所是和之所为，精通一切学识或者可能之学识；因此他不再需要研究任何其他对象；因此他不需要做任何事情，而仅仅需要是他自己、做他自己，而其他人则以此创造历史，向他学习。”（168）精通历史即精通所有学问。历史学家成为最为博学的研究者。

历史结构的改变导致历史发展（development）的改变。如果仅仅具有单一结构，那么历史不过是历史事件在时间顺序上的定向排列。然而，如果历史表现为双层结构，且内在结构控制并主导外在表现，那么历史便会随之表现出明显的规律性（regularity）和目的性（purposiveness）。外在结构与内在结构之间的偏离与吻合是历史发展规律性的根源。一般而言，历史发展会被规定在一个外在结构一段时间符合、一段时间背离内在结构的要求的循环往复的过程之中。这样，历史发展表现出极强的规律性。这也是历史发展规律的基础。然而，外在结构与内在结构之间的偏离与吻合并不是同样处于主导地位。很明显，吻合会被规定为是主要的。这样，历史发展总会表现为外部结构一定要符合内部结构的要求。这是历史发展目的性的根源所在。历史发展的目的在于符合内在结构的要求。一定阶段的历史使命的合理性来源于历史发展的目的性。所有的历史使命均以取消偏离、实现吻合为主要内容。在此意义上，历史被历史的内在结构取代。历史不再是主要的研究对象。历史的内在结构取代历史成为关注的焦点。很明显，这是对历史的背叛。“与历史解释的细微要点相比，卡莱尔的兴趣更在于历史的作用，只要他主要满足于表现一个内在结构性理念存在于世界历史之中，那么何种组织原则塑造了历史事件的流动变得无足轻重。”[①] 卡莱尔历史研究的目的不在于历史本身，而在于历史的作用。历史之作用（use）只能导向历史之滥用（abuse）。卡莱尔历史的滥用开始于对历史内在结构的探寻。

历史发展在卡莱尔看来是某一内在理念的表现。作为历史发展的内在结构，所有历史事件均是对这一内在理念的表现。事实上，卡莱尔将内在理念看作世界历史的表现对象。

> 这些理念是如何实现，又是如何巧妙地游走于混乱无序的现实之外的呢？如果说世界历史对我们有所教诲的话，那就是世界历史要教给我们的：这些理念如何经过长期暴风骤雨版的酝酿、成长，结出举世无双的成熟果实，然后迅速（因为花期是短暂的）惨然地凋零、萎谢，最后纷纷飘落，哗然或悄然地失去踪影。花期苦短如是，如一些百年生的仙人掌花，经过一个世纪的等待，只璀璨闪耀几个小时而已！（Rev.，10）

可见，全部世界历史无论具备怎样的多样性与复杂性，在此被简单归结为某一理念的表现。这一理念是世界历史发展的动力，而全部世界历史是这一理念的表现。相对全部历史的时间长度，理念实现的时间范围极其有限，就像仙人掌花的花期一样弥足珍贵。很明显，这样的设置说明，在历史发展的大部分时间里，外部结构处于符合内在结构要求的过程之中。这样，促进历史的发展，即通过一定的形式促使外部结构在尽量短的时间里符合内部结构的要求，是卡莱尔历史研究另外一个比较重要的主题。

历史发展的内在理念主要通过有选择性的历史写作（selective historiography）而得到表现。有选择性的历史写作需要在一定程度上进行辩护。历史写作的选择性（historiographical selectivity）在卡莱尔看来是合理的。这一合理性来源于人认识的局限。总体而言，人无法实现对于历史作为一个整体的认识。“任何种类的完美都不是人类的运气：但是在所有超自然的完美品质之中，历史的完美（可以被轻易想象）也许是最具有传奇色彩的。”（Wks.，

① Dibble, *The Pythia's Drunken Song*, pp. 73 – 74.

XXVIII，168）历史领域中认识上的完美甚至被喻为“一匹毫无瑕疵的怪兽”，这样的东西“世人不会看到，甚至纸上也无法见到”（Ibid.）。卡莱尔对人认识上的局限还有更加深刻的思考。他认为：

> 而且如果我们对过去事件的洞察力从来就不完善，那么我们观察这些事物的方式与它们实际发生的方式就有着根本的差异；因此，他的观察（且不说它的其他不足之处）就必定是连续性的。而实际发生的事情常常是同时性的。实际发生的事情不是一个序列，而是一个组群。这个组群并不在已发生的历史之中，正如它并不在书写的历史之中一样：现实事件之间的关系绝不像父子关系那样简单，每个单一事物的原因都不只一个。它是所有其他或更早或同时事件的共同结果，而它又反过来与其他事件结合造成新的事件：这就是存在的亘古常新和永远变动着的混沌状态；在这里，形形色色的事物从它数不胜数的元素之中产生。这种混沌状态，正如人们的栖息和绵延一样地无限，正如人们的心灵和命运一样地深不可测。就是这个东西，历史学家要通过几根粗略的线条加以描绘或科学地测度！（XXVII，88）

人的认识方式与历史的发生方式在性质上不同。认识是连续的，而历史是同时的。性质上的不同决定，人不可能实现对于历史全貌的认识。同一思想在他的笔记中也有表现。“历史学家一定要以线进行写作；但是每一个事件都是一个面；如果我们调查一下其中的根源，事件也是一个体。”（Nt. B.，124）可见，历史写作与历史事件的发生之间在性质上存在差异。“因此，在叙事艺术之中存在着一个首要的且几乎不可逾越的缺陷。”（Ibid.）历史写作无法完全再现历史事件。非常明显，卡莱尔的否定对象是历史全貌的认识，而不是有关历史的某些认识。他进一步论证：

> 因为尽管［历史的］整体的意义超出我们认识的范围，但是在这部复杂的手稿中（它全是些无形的、错综复杂而又难以辨认的文字，而且它是一种可以擦掉的羊皮纸手稿，但它包含的那些预言文字仍然隐约可辨），某些字母、某些文字仍然可以辨出；即便没有完整的哲学，这儿或

那儿也结集着一些智慧的格言可资利用。同时还要理解，我们已辨认的只是很小的一部分，大部分仍然有待解释。历史是一真实预言的手稿，任何人都不能充分解释。（Wks.，XXⅦ，89－90）

人虽然不能实现对于历史全貌的认识，但是依然可以认识历史的局部。非常明显，局部性的认识是选择性的认识。人认识能力的局限最终成为历史写作选择性的合理性的辩护。由此，卡莱尔有选择性的历史写作是合理的。

历史写作的选择性不但是合理的，也是必要的。历史写作选择性的必要性主要表现在，选择性的缺失意味着历史写作的失效。历史写作只有依靠选择才可以最终实现。“高等历史学家一定要有一个真正地选择性的眼睛”,[①] 这是卡莱尔坚持的立场。如没有这种选择性，历史学家就会成为一个“对大小事件均会留意的驯服的摄像师”。[②] 很明显，这种没有选择性的记录将无分巨细。这将最终导致历史的失效。卡莱尔如此论证选择的必然性：

我们需要留意，仅仅通过自然倾向，就像无人预先设计一样，一种选择的合理性变得不可避免，甚至在很大程度上都是不可避免的。完全无价值的选择不会存在，如果没有比这条规则更好的规则作为指导：人永远只是说出在范围之内、在周围处于活动之中的事物。因此，可以产生结果的事物，结果依然会造成结果的事情，这些才被选择成为记录和书写的对象；只有这样的事情才是伟大的，是值得记录的。（XXⅧ，174）

可见，选择性是历史写作产生和展现的根源所在。伴随着历史写作的产生，选择性融入其中。同样，历史写作的展现过程也是选择性的表现过程。作为历史写作的一部分，选择性具有必然性。选择性不但对于历史，甚至对于所谓的世界历史或者普遍历史同样具有必然性。世界历史或者普遍历史如此产生：

---

① Stewart，“Carlyle's Conception of History，” p. 572.

② Stewart，“Carlyle's Conception of History，” pp. 572－573.

> 历史在成为普遍历史之前，最有必要进行压缩。如果历史没有经典化的过程，一个人的记忆无法超过一周时间。如果没有这一过程，如果将压缩完全排除，我们的记忆不能超过一个小时，或者根本不会记忆：因为时间就像空间一样，可以被无限分割；一个小时及其事件、感受和情感可以被延长，覆盖整个记忆领域，将所有其他事情推出记忆边缘。(172)

此处，选择性相对于世界历史或者普遍历史所具有的必要性来源于时间的空间性，即时间的无限可分性。与空间一样，时间也可以无限分割下去。显然，时间的无限可分性对于卡莱尔而言意味着事件的无限复杂性。无限复杂的事件不可能实现记录。在这种情况下，历史写作将不具有可能性。然而，时间的无限可分性并不必然导致事件的无限复杂性。事件可能在时间上可以无限分割，但是在复杂性上依然在可把握的范围内。而且，即使事件非常复杂，这并不意味着所有程度上的复杂性都需要纳入思考。显然，卡莱尔过分夸大了时间的无限可分性与时间的无限复杂性之间的关联。无论怎样，他依然据此实现了具有卡莱尔风格的世界历史或者普遍历史的建立。

为构建自己的世界历史或者普遍历史，卡莱尔对历史进行了选择。他所选择的历史事件是历史的外部结构违背内在结构要求的事件。在解读这些事件之前，有必要先对卡莱尔的历史发展规律进行一定的解释。如前所述，卡莱尔式的历史发展规律主要表现为历史发展的规律性和目的性。卡莱尔首先区分出两个类型的历史时期。其一，是外部结构符合内部结构要求的时期，即“信仰时期”。其二，是外部结构不符合内部结构要求的时期，即“否定时期”。“有否定时期，即怀疑时期［……］也有肯定时期，即信仰时期”。[①] 这两个时期处于交替性的循环之中。“历史发展可以认为是（1）进步时代和（2）退步时代的周期性交替。”[②] 事实上，卡莱尔更加强调两个时期的周期性（periodicity）。这两个历史时期的循环交替就像四季变化一样具有周期性和规

① Carré, op. cit., p. 179.

② Shine, *Carlyle and the Saint - Simonians*, p. 254.

律性。“就像在长久的收缩和长久的舒张一样，信仰时期和否定时期一定交替出现；各种观点、精神呈现和创造的夏日繁荣一定跟随着秋日的腐败、冬日的瓦解。”（Sar.，112）历史时期之间的转化也可以像季节转变那样具有诗情画意。总体而言，卡莱尔对两种历史时期的留意并不是均等的。在他看来，历史的外部结构不符合内部结构要求的时期，即所谓的否定时期才是关注的焦点。“认为生活的普遍内在性在所有时代都是相同的，唯有对共同的天赋与天命的重大偏离，特别是外在生活形态偶尔经历的重大变更才需要记录下来——这对我们并没有多大益处。”（Wks.，XXⅦ，86）虽然他曾经否定过这样的观点，但是他本人的历史写作均以否定时期为主要对象。法国大革命是欧洲历史上最为动荡的时代，克伦威尔当政之时正值内战之际。“虽然卡莱尔在人类历史之中看到了上帝的印记，但是卡莱尔一次又一次暗示混乱是人的历史经历和时空经验不可避免的一个维度。”[①] 可见，历史的外部结构与内在结构之间的背离时期是卡莱尔有选择性的历史写作主要的涉及对象。

在所有历史的外部结构违背内在结构要求的历史时期之中，法国大革命是卡莱尔有选择性的历史写作最为突出和重要的对象。法国大革命被放在历史发展规律之中进行解读。在这一视角下，法国大革命不再是一个简单的历史事件，而是历史的外部结构违背内在结构要求的表现和反映。可见，法国大革命爆发的根源在于历史发展的目的性开始发挥强制作用。“法国大革命是历史延续性变得必要的一次中断。”[②] 在此意义上，法国大革命被看作“近一千年以来进入到现实空间的最为残忍的预兆”（P. & P.，229）。面对这样的历史事件，只有“带着敬畏的、忏悔的心致敬”，只有“把它看作上帝声音的再现，虽然这是一个愤怒的上帝”（Ibid.），这样才可以解读法国大革命的真正含义。在他的理解中，法国大革命是历史的外在结构违背内在结构要求的表现：

> [法国大革命] 的确是我们时代伟大的作品（一个最痛苦、贫瘠和无

---

① Lamb，“A ‘Chaos of Being’，” p. 25.

② Vitoux，op. cit.，p. 20.

> 果的作品，这一作品对于我们依然有影响，我们已经经历而且还在经历着)：对于我们所有重要的可能的知识都投入其中，都用于对法国大革命的正确理解［……］［我］应该理解所有这些分割的混乱、传统的宣传、断头台屠杀、不伦瑞克崩溃；这些含义却超出我的理解！你无法理解；因为它是一个燃烧的事实；永恒的深度穿透令人震撼的时间单元的裂隙看出来；——好像穿透了所有的时间单元，只有模糊的眼睛才看不见。对于我而言，经常是这种情况，法国大革命正确的历史（我通过历史所表示的那个不可能之物）是我们时代的伟大诗歌；可以写出法国大革命真理的人，价值抵得上所有其他的作家和诗人。(L. –M.，70 –71)

很明显，法国大革命在卡莱尔看来并不是一个简单的历史事件，而更是一个隐匿着启示含义的象征。正因为法国大革命的意义在结构上不是单一的，卡莱尔才会一时间找不到解读的正确手段。不过他的历史直觉在第一时间告诉他，这是一个可以启示真理的历史事件。这样，他对法国大革命历史（H）的研究变成对真理（T）的探寻，即：

$$H\rightarrow T$$

如果将他对知识所进行的改造纳入思考，那么结果一目了然。就像知识被纳入信仰一样，历史最终只会成为信仰的辩护。

在卡莱尔的解读中，英雄崇拜是法国大革命所启示的真理。为实现这一解读，选择性被应用于历史写作。卡莱尔所选择的对象都是一些小意义事件(insignificant events)。他称这样的选择是疯狂的。“在所有的历史选择和挑选之中，最疯狂的工作在进行着。”（Wks.，XXⅧ，171）然而，这样疯狂的选择依然被认为具有合理性。“甚至最值得认识的事件也许就是最不被人说起的事件；甚至有些人说，这种事件的本质即是如此。”（Ibid.）在法国大革命一系列伟大的历史事件之中，卡莱尔并没有在米拉博（Mirabeau）政改、雅各宾派（Jacobin）专政、热月政变等事件中解读出历史所启示的真理。相反，按照许多评判标准，他选择的事件过于微不足道。在一次巴黎市民的起义之中——

> 穿着叮当作响的盔甲、手持利刃的野蛮人，将由盾牌保护的宝座上的最前者高高举起，郑重而真诚地说：让汝做我们公认的最强者吧！这个时刻并非小题大做。对于这种公认的最强者（又可称为国王，*Könning*、*Can－ning*,[①] 或能人）来说，现在，这是一个对于他们这些野蛮人来说多么举足轻重、与世界命运多么息息相关的符号！一个真正回归仁爱、顺从原则的符号。如果他知道那是人的首要需求就好了。这个符号可以用神圣来形容，因为在尊重比我们更高尚的价值的同时，难道不存在坚不可摧的神圣吗？在这方面，也有人说，公认的最强者有神圣的权利，因为无论其是否是公认的，人们肯定也在考虑是谁使他成了最强者。所以，在困惑和难言的矛盾之中（因为任何成长都是令人困惑的）产生了王权，以及围绕着王权的忠诚。王权的成长神秘莫测，既咄咄逼人又兼收并蓄（因为这是生命的法则），最后也变得和这个世界一样伟大，并成为我们现实生活的关键事实。（Rev.，9－10）

很明显，卡莱尔所选取的历史细节是英雄崇拜正在被实现的一幕。基于此，英雄崇拜被看作历史发展目的性的表现。这意味着英雄崇拜是历史的内在结构。如奥拉尔（A. Aulard）所言，“在这本书［即《法国大革命》］中，卡莱尔的目的在于穿越文本和事件，直抵法国人内心的深处，发现推动他们如此生存、如此死去的动机所在”。[②] “在我们当时的人民中间，他发现了一种英雄主义的情感。”[③] 可见，发现英雄崇拜是卡莱尔研究法国大革命的根源所在。然而，与他的精神信仰恢复一样，这又是一场自编自导的闹剧。一个以带着明确目的进行历史研究的人一定可以在研究之中实现他的目的。同样，以将英雄崇拜设置为历史内在结构为目的的卡莱尔一定可以在历史之中选择出这样的细节。历史领域被迫融入大量的主观思想。历史不是目的，而是成为辩护的手段。这便是历史的滥用。在此意义上，维多利亚时期最伟大的历史学

① Carlyle's discussion of "king" as derived from "konning" or "canning" seems to be inspired by the old English word "kyninga".

② "Carlyle," p. 201.

③ "Carlyle," p. 201.

家之一也是历史的背叛者。

至此，世界历史或者普遍历史被归结为英雄史已成定局。无论何物，一旦被定义为历史的内在结构，这便意味着全部历史发展可以归结为此物的表现。同样，英雄崇拜与历史内在结构等同之后，世界历史归结为英雄史只是最自然、最简单的逻辑推演。在如此必要的时刻，卡莱尔依然没有放弃证明的机会。“诚然，从古代斯堪的纳维亚的奥丁到英国的赛米尔·约翰逊，从基督教神圣的创始人到百科全书派已衰落的领袖，不论何时何地，英雄都受到崇拜。”（H. & H.，15）在此，英雄崇拜被赋予空前的普遍性。最终，世界历史或者普遍历史被等同为英雄史：

> 因为就我所知，世界历史就是人类在这个世界上所取得的种种成就的历史，实质上也就是在世界上活动的伟人的历史。他们是民众的领袖，而且是伟大的领袖，凡是一切普通人殚精竭虑要做或想要得到的一切事物都由他们去规范和塑造，从广义上说，他们也就是创造者。我们所见到的世界上存在的一切成就，本是来到世上的伟人的内在思想转化为外部物质的结果，也是他们思想的实际体现和具体化。可以恰当地认为，整个世界的精华，就是伟人的历史。(1)

这便是《英雄与英雄崇拜》第一讲的开篇最为重要的部分。事实上，全部系列演讲便是围绕这一中心思想而进行展开的。在演讲中，卡莱尔勾勒了一幅英雄崇拜从最原始的时期一直发展到现时代的历史画卷。一代又一代的英雄前赴后继，构成历史发展的动力。一代又一代的民众顶礼膜拜，形成英雄崇拜的伟大传统。然而，卡莱尔历史研究的目的不在于历史，而更在于以历史为视角实现对于社会，特别是现时代的社会的认识。理解他的历史观，有必要将社会维度纳入思考。

以上便是卡莱尔有关历史结构的论述。在他的理解中，历史是一个具有外部和内部双层结构的对象。内外结构可谓历史的本质和表现，处于被表现与表现的关系之中。历史作为上帝的启示便建立在双层结构基础之上。

一方面，这一双层结构是卡莱尔从外部理解历史的依据。历史的双层结构深刻地影响了他对历史写作所持的观点。他的写作的对象并不是简单的历史事件，而是历史事件背后所隐匿的具有启示性的内容。据此，历史写作的艺术家和匠人被区分开来。历史作为具有启示性内容的载体影响了卡莱尔对于历史的认识。在他看来，历史既高于，又包括其他所有学科。在此意义上，历史是学科的学科，是最值得研究的对象。

另一方面，双层结构是卡莱尔对历史的内部进行理解的主要角度。历史的发展模式为之改变。内部与外部结构之间的符合与背离是历史发展的两大主要趋势。其中，外部结构符合内部结构的要求是主要趋势。这样，全部历史发展被认为是某一理念的表现。为实现这一理念的表现，选择性被赋予历史写作。人认识的连续性和历史事件的同时性之间的矛盾，是有选择的历史写作的合理性的根据。建立在时间的无限可分性基础之上的事件无限复杂性，是选择性的必然性所在。卡莱尔的历史写作主要选取了外部结构背离内部结构要求的历史时期。他所选取的对象均不是重大历史事件，而仅仅是一些小意义事件。在对这些时期以及事件的解读中，他将英雄崇拜看作历史的内在结构。最终，世界历史或者普遍历史被归结为英雄史。

卡莱尔对历史结构的认识存在问题。历史的内在结构是问题的集中表现。历史是一个具有高度复杂性的对象。其实，卡莱尔本人对于这一点也有所认识。然而，面对复杂性，他的选择是将之归结为某一单一元素。这种简化的基础是他的信仰。很明显，历史在此被纳入他的信仰。同自然和人一样，历史也是上帝意志的表现。解读历史不过意味着解读卡莱尔的信仰。很明显，具有高度复杂性的历史不能简单地被归结为信仰。如他同时代的历史学家麦考莱所说，理性和想象在历史中占据同样重要的地位。与之相应，修昔底德（Thucydides）和希罗多德（Herodotus）的历史作品各占其一。“一个完美的历史学家必须具有足够的想象力，才能使他的叙述既生动又感人。但他必须绝对地掌握自己的想象，将它限制在他所发现的材料上，避免添枝加叶，损害其真实性。”[①] 如果将卡莱尔的信仰也理解为想象的一种，即宗教想象，那

① *Critical*, *Historical*, *and Miscellaneous Essays and Poems*, Vol. Ⅰ, p. 270. The Chinese translation is from Liu Xin（刘鑫）'s version（Beijing: The Commercial Pr., 1999）.

么显然，他并没有将信仰限制在事实之内。相反，全部历史事实被用以诠释他的信仰内容。这是信仰对历史的颠覆。

第二节　历史发展与社会发展

卡莱尔历史研究的目的不仅仅在于厘清历史的发展脉络和内部结构，而更在于通过历史实现社会预言。“卡莱尔对未来的关注可以在乌托邦文体中得到理解，或者如果将语境纳入思考，也可以在预言文学的样式中得到理解”。[①] 历史在他看来是预言的基础。“如果过去没有以这样亵渎的方式处理，预言未来、打理现在不会成为如此不可能的事情。”（P. & P.，239）可见，历史的恰当处理意味着预言的可能。在此，历史研究同预言未来联系在一起。两者实现联系的关键在于，两者处于共同的发展脉络之中。一条隐匿的人类发展模式作为一条脉络如同一条地下暗流，从历史发源而来，向未来流动而去。这样，历史和未来贯穿在一起。很明显，预言未来的方法与历史研究一样，都是对这一地下暗流进行发掘。

英雄崇拜便是历史和未来之间贯穿的主线。英雄崇拜作为贯穿的主线表现在两个方面。一方面，这一贯穿性表现在空间之上。英雄崇拜是万事万物存在的根源。“英雄崇拜是一切根源中最深刻的根源，是主根，其余一切，在很大程度上是从中汲取养分而发展起来的。”（H. & H.，11）英雄崇拜表现在万事万物之上。可见，英雄崇拜在空间上具有极强的普遍性。另一方面，这一贯穿性表现在时间上。“无论何时何地，只要有人类存在，像‘黄金’般的英雄崇拜就会存在。”（12）在此，英雄崇拜被赋予时间维度。英雄崇拜的发展贯穿人类的发展。这样，英雄崇拜在时间上具有极强的延续性。很明显，英雄崇拜时间上的延续性以空间上的普遍性为基础。

英雄崇拜作为贯穿的主线主要表现在社会发展之上。与自然和人一样，社会在卡莱尔看来也是英雄崇拜的体现。他认为：

> 每一个社会、每一个国家组织，都有一个精神法则；社会是某一理

① Sussman, “The Condition of Manliness Question,” p. 71.

> 念的体现，无论体现是暂定的，还是或多或少不完整的：社会所有的运动倾向、风俗习惯的特性、法律、政体和整个程序（就如某些像孟德斯鸠一样的人通过数不清的表层阻扰部分看到的那样）都由这一理念决定、从中自然发展而来，就像运动从运动之源发展而来一样。无论是对于一个人或者一个阶级的人、对一个信条、对一个体系，或者甚至像在更加远古的时期对一片土地的忠诚，这一理念都是真正的忠诚；其中具有宗教性的、至高无上的、无限的特征；这是国家的灵魂、生命；同其他形式的生命一样神秘，同它们一样悄然运作，深度超越意识之外。（Wks. XXVIII,13 – 14）

在此，社会被看作是某一理念的体现。风俗习惯、法律以及政体等所有社会的因素均由这一理念决定，并从中发展而来。这一生成关系被类比为运动和运动源之间的关系。这一理念被认为是忠诚。从忠诚所具有宗教性、至高无上性和无限性等特征可以推出，所谓的忠诚就是崇拜之意。“作为一切社会不可缺少的忠诚，就是源于英雄崇拜的产物，即对真正的伟人表示顺从和敬仰。”（H. & H.，12）事实上，卡莱尔将英雄崇拜看作社会的基础。“社会是建立在英雄崇拜的基础之上的。”（Ibid.）英雄崇拜相对于社会的创建地位说明，英雄崇拜便是社会所表现的理念。

社会发展被进一步赋予时间维度。很明显，社会的时间维度来源于英雄崇拜。英雄崇拜是具有时间维度的。整个历史发展均是对英雄崇拜的体现。作为社会的基础，英雄崇拜将自身的时间维度传递给社会。卡莱尔认为：

> 社会有疾病和健康，青春、成年、衰老、瓦解和新生的阶段；我们在任何时间、在所有我们居住的地点发现社会处于其中的一个阶段；就在此时此地，无论配合还是抗拒，作为健康的成员还是有病的成员，可喜可悲，我们成为社会的一个部分。社会的实际情况如何？这个问题在最近一段时间非常不幸，变得十分重要。这一问题关涉我们所有的人；但是对于大多数有些想法的人，问题真正的答案就是实际情况，这几乎是我们最为需要的东西。与此同时，因为真正的答案，即，完全和根本

> 的回答的解决，就像人们要求的一样，无从得出，其实，根据本质也是不可能的，任何类似答案诚实的接近都有其价值。最微弱的光，甚至不过是对于黑暗的承认都是受人欢迎的，因为这是获得光芒的第一步。（Wks.，XXⅧ，13）

在此，社会被类比为人的身体，具有从青春到最后的瓦解之间的发展和过渡。这样的发展赋予社会以时间维度。可见，卡莱尔所谓的社会的时间不是简单的时间的先后关系，而更是一种类似于身体，或者有机体的成长。这显然是一种社会的发展观。卡莱尔对现实社会的理解便以社会的发展为背景。现实社会是社会发展的最新阶段。这样，现实社会与社会发展之间获得关联。理解现实社会不仅仅是理解社会的现状，更是理解在社会发展之中所处的阶段（stage）。如前所述，历史发展处于信仰时代和否定时代之间的循环交替之中。这样，社会发展同样处于一段时间符合、一段时间不符合英雄崇拜要求的过程之中。现实社会所处的历史阶段只能是两者中的一个。

现实社会被定义为处于一个过渡阶段（transitional stage）之中。总体而言，现实社会处于一个英雄崇拜的要求并没有得到满足的阶段。卡莱尔本人也“充分注意到，有人认为英雄崇拜，即［他］所谓的英雄崇拜，在现今已经过时了，终于不存在了”（H. & H.，12）。很明显，这是英雄崇拜的要求没有得到满足的标志。在这种情况下，现实社会处于否定时期。然而，卡莱尔有关现实社会所处阶段的判断并非如此简单。一方面，现实社会处于否定时期；另一方面，肯定时期处于正在实现的过程之中。肯定时期存在的根据在于英雄崇拜。英雄崇拜是社会的本质，而本质不灭。“社会［……］并没有死亡：那具被你叫作死亡的社会的尸体不过是社会蜕下的外皮，目的在于获得一个更好的；社会本身穿越无限的变形，在越来越好的发展之中永生，直到时间汇聚于永恒。”（Sar.，236）可见，社会本身不会死亡，而社会的表现处于不断更新的过程之中。“无论哪里，只要两三个活人聚集在一起，那里就有社会。”（Ibid.）社会不灭的根据在于人与人之间通过崇拜聚集在一起，从而形成社会。可见，现实社会之中存在两个趋势，处于过渡阶段之中。“我们多难时代的特征全在于此：人已经永远地放弃了恐惧，这不过是低级阶段；但是人还没有进入永恒的崇拜，这才是更高和最高阶段。”（251）英雄崇拜正在逐步实现，这是过渡阶段的标志。

新旧之间的交替是现实社会所处阶段过渡性的表现。通过以上分析可以看出，卡莱尔所谓的过渡阶段是一个旧制度尚未完全瓦解，而新制度尚未完全建立的阶段。“在整个社会构造下面，蕴藏着一场根深蒂固的斗争，新旧两种力量在永无休止地剧烈碰撞。”（Wks.，XXⅦ，82）新旧之间的交替是过渡的主要内容。卡莱尔主要以两个意象对过渡阶段进行描述。其一，是蛇的蜕皮。“在活着的生命体中……变化是逐渐发生的：因此，当蛇退去旧皮的时候，新皮已经在下面形成了。”（Sar.，244）“就在旧皮蜕下之前，新皮已经在旧皮之下形成。”（253）与蛇的蜕皮非常相似，在处于过渡阶段的社会之中，新旧两种因素交织在一起。其一，是凤凰的重生。这也是一个比较主要的意象。

> 你根本不知道像凤凰一样的世界的燃烧，如果你认为凤凰一定要首先烧尽，成为一堆死灰；从中年轻的凤凰通过奇迹出现，向天堂飞去。绝对不是这样！在那火旋风中，创造和毁灭同时进行；旧事物的灰烬被吹散的时候，新事物的有机丝线在神秘地自我编织：在那旋风元素的冲撞和起伏之中传来了有旋律的死亡歌曲，死亡歌曲只有在更有旋律的生命歌曲之中才会结束。(244－245)

与蛇的蜕皮一样，凤凰的重生同样伴随着新旧两个趋势的交融。至此，卡莱尔对过渡阶段的理解变得更加明显。他所理解的过渡不是单向的转变，而是具有一定复杂性的双层结构。这个双层结构一方面表现为旧有制度的瓦解，另一方面表现为全新制度的建立。两者交织在一起共同构成现实社会所处阶段过渡性的表现。

现实社会处于一个过渡阶段，这可谓卡莱尔对维多利亚社会所作出的宏观理解。除他之外，穆勒对维多利亚时代状态的理解有异曲同工之妙。在《时代精神》（“The Spirit of the Age”）一文中，穆勒同样以时代状况为研究对象。他认为，“现时代首要特征的第一点便是，这是一个过渡时代”。[①] 过渡作为现时代的首要特征，这便是穆勒对维多利亚社会所在的时代状况所做出的判断。他做出这一判断的依据在于，“人类已经脱离了旧有的制度和旧有的信条，但是依然未能获得新的”。[②] 可见，与卡莱尔的判断极为相似，当代社会处于一个过渡阶段的根源在于新旧之间的交替。两位维多利亚时期的伟大思想家对时代格局做出近乎相同的判断，这不能不表明某些发生在维多利亚社会中的变化。事实上，维多利亚社会处于从“旧有的”和“祖先的”（ancestral），即“中世纪的”和“封建的”，向工业的和现代的时期的过渡之中。这是最为主要的时代精神，也是卡莱尔最为宏观的思想背景。

过渡迹象在很大程度上可以在社会状况之中发觉。在卡莱尔看来，这些过渡的迹象甚至是昭显的。“在我国和其他国家，的确出现了一些鼓舞人心的迹象。这些迹象表明，机械不可能永远当我们的工头，对我们颐指气使，终有一天也会成为我们的仆人，对我们百依百顺，一个崭新而又光明的时代正徐徐走向人间。”（Wks.，XXVII，81）这是功利主义不再发挥规范作用，正在被英雄崇拜取代的迹象。如果这一迹象更加侧重功利主义的被取代，那么另外一些迹象则侧重表现新时代的主要特征。“甚至就在我们看向四周的时候，天亮的迹象已经出现在东方；黎明正在来临；当时间期限圆满之后，白天就要来了。人向所有的最高等、最崇高事物的更加高等、更加崇高发展的进步不但可以被预言给信仰，而且像文字一样写下来可以通过眼睛观察，我们只要能走就可以看到。”（XXVIII，37）这明显是一位乐观的预言家所看到的未来视阈。他看到了一个历史的内部结构的要求被满足、英雄崇拜被实现的未来。伴随着视野的扩大，更加显著的迹象也被发觉：

> 这的确非常显著，永恒的事实到处都开始被辨认出来，人类事务中有一个上帝一样的存在；上帝不但创造了我们、看着我们，而且存在于我们、在我们周围；现在就是奇迹的时代，同以往一样。我们可以在所

---

① *The Spirit of the Age*，*On Liberty*，*The Subjection of Women*，p. 5.

② *The Spirit of the Age*，*On Liberty*，*The Subjection of Women*，p. 5.

> 有方面、在所有国家发现这样的迹象：这样的迹象在每一个国家有其自身的方式。(42)

伴随着预言的升级，预言的宗教色彩更加显著地表现出来。至此，卡莱尔所看到的未来世界已经和他的宗教无法分清界限。很明显，他所预言的未来是一个上帝的存在被普遍接受的时代，上帝的法则以英雄崇拜为主要形式成为社会的规范方式。这样，预言与信仰等同。预言在很大程度上成为信仰的伸张。

卡莱尔对过渡阶段存在的合理性有一定的论述。他主要以人的习惯对旧制度的存在进行说明。在他看来，人有保存旧有事物的习惯：

> 保存法则对于人来说是最为深刻的：人在本性上痛恨变化；直到他的房子在现实中已经在他耳边倒下，他才会离弃自己的房子。因此，我已经看到神圣仅仅剩下仪式、神圣的象征被当作无用的装饰，直到已经过了三百年，甚至过了三百年以上的时间，所有的生命和神圣性都从中消失殆尽。(Sar.，237)

无论卡莱尔是否意识到，他这里所谈的问题其实远远超越习惯，包括传统、习俗、规定和公约等在内的要素均具有极强的维持力，不过他依然对旧制度的存在给出了解释。一言以蔽之，人性使然。人有保存旧有事物的习惯，旧制度同样在被保存之列。甚至在旧制度已经远远过时的时候，保存习惯仍然有效。“严格意义上的社会几乎灭绝；仅仅是群居情感和以往继承下来的习惯在这一环节上使我们没有陷入分散和普遍的民族战争、内战、家庭和个人战争。”（231－232）可见，即使社会已经瓦解，习惯依然可以维持群居生活。人的习惯赋予旧制度以坚韧性。这种坚韧性使得更加符合要求的新制度不会立即取代旧制度。这样，新旧制度会在一定的历史阶段处于制衡之中。新旧之间的制衡是过渡阶段存在合理性的来源。

过渡阶段决定了现实社会所应负有的历史使命（historical missions）。卡莱尔对现实社会所处的过渡阶段进行研究的目的不仅仅在于认识现实的阶段性，而更在于在此基础之上明确现实社会的历史使命。“也许，细看之后，有些乱象会消失不见，有些独有的特征和深层的趋势则清晰显现出来。我们也就更容易看清自己与时代的关系，看清我们在这个时代的真正目标和任务。”（Wks.，XXⅦ，59）可见，明确历史任务是卡莱尔主要的认识目的之一。非常明显，与过渡阶段两方面趋势相对应，现实社会的历史使命也是双重的。一方面，旧制度需要实现最终的瓦解；另一方面，新制度需要实现最终的建立。“旧有的、有病的社会应该任由它燃尽（啊，燃料绝对不应该是香料）；[……] 社会是一只凤凰；一个新的、从天堂诞生的、年轻的社会将从她的灰烬中发展而来。”（Sar.，237）新制度的诞生伴随着旧制度的灭亡。实现或者加速新制度的诞生以及旧制度的灭亡，这便是现实社会所负的历史使命。

在历史使命的两项内容之中，旧制度的灭亡主要由功利主义完成。功利主义是现实社会的规范方式。作为规范方式，功利主义造成了严重的社会弊病。这导致宪章运动和曼彻斯特起义等众多社会运动的爆发。这些在卡莱尔看来是社会处于瓦解过程之中的表现。在此意义上，功利主义对社会具有破坏作用。“尤迪丽塔利亚（Utilitaria）这匹怪兽因为有鼻环、笼头、脚镣以及每一种可以想象的捆绑方法而被控制住，无法暴虐，本应该任她完成她的任务——以她宽大的蹄子践踏旧的破败的宫殿和庙宇，直到所有的一切都被踏平，这样新的更好的事物可以建立起来。”（236）可见，旧制度的瓦解是新制度建立的前提。在此意义上，功利主义作为社会的规范方式是历史任务完成的必经阶段。这样，功利主义也被纳入卡莱尔的历史思想体系之中。

旧制度的建立具有必然性。这一必然性固然可以通过英雄崇拜作为历史的内在结构进行论证，但是卡莱尔在此主要以人的保存习惯为针对对象。在他看来，即使人具有保存旧制度的习惯，旧制度作为历史发展的阻碍并无法被真正保存，只有淘汰的余地。他以规劝的口吻写道：

> 啊，我保守的朋友们，你们依然叫自己，并努力证明自己是“保守的”，但愿我可以让你们知道这同世界一样古老的事实，相比之下，命运也不具有更多的确定性，那就是只有真理和正义才能被“保留”和保存！不是正义的东西、没有符合上帝法则的东西，你可以在上帝的宇宙中尝试保存吗？它很古老，你说？是的，因此你更要赶快行动，你不要让它

继续古老下去了！但是你心中微弱的声音告诉你这不公平——赶快，为了保守主义，严格地证明它，如果它是有罪的就要立即并永久地放弃它。你怎样保存，又怎能保存它呢，这不是正义的东西？“不可能”标记在上有上千次了。(P. & P.，165－166)

旧制度不符合上帝的法则。这决定旧制度不应该成为保存的对象。即使作为保存的对象，旧制度也不能得到真正的保存。可见，旧制度的灭亡具有强烈的必然性。

新制度的建立主要通过英雄崇拜而完成。与旧制度的灭亡一样，新制度的建立同样具有必然性。崇拜在卡莱尔看来是人最为基本的情感，深入人的本质。这样，对英雄进行崇拜成为人的本质要求。由此，英雄崇拜成为社会的规范方式获得必然性。卡莱尔对此深怀信心，他甚至发出这样的豪言：

不可见的世界并未消失，它就栖居在人的心灵之中，而心灵犹在。上帝曾经显灵的神殿已经破败不堪了吗？可以修复，可以重建呀。先人的智慧和英雄气概，我们丢了，可还能找回来呀。虽然现在的贵族经常是一副玩世不恭、游手好闲的样子，但人们仍然仰慕往日的贵族，终有一天会争相效仿那时的高贵风范，人类也将恢复往昔的模样，而且会超越以往。这绝不是白日做梦，而是确有可能，也是我们在当下的希望。在我国和其他国家，的确出现了一些鼓舞人心的迹象。(Wks.，XXVII，81)

可见，人所怀有的崇拜之情是英雄崇拜成为规范方式必然性的基础。一方面，普通人一定会对英雄进行崇拜；另一方面，英雄也一定会成为崇拜的对象。旧制度的必然灭亡和新制度的必然建立，这两点可谓卡莱尔时代预言的主要内容。

最后有必要指出，卡莱尔预言的对象不是确定的时间，而是大体的趋势。事实上，他本人也无法给出过渡完成的确切时间。“你不需要问，这样的凤凰火葬在哪一幸运年里可以完成。”（Sar.，237）旧制度的瓦解和新制度的建立的时间是不确定的。“凤凰的生死循环最终需要多长的时间决定于不可见的偶发事件。”（Ibid.）过渡时期的持续时间长度也是不可确定的。这说明卡莱尔的预言不具有精确性。与物理学之中的预言（测）不同，在给出所有条件的前提下，卡莱尔所预言的内容只是一个大体的趋势。这使得他的预言参考价值在很大程度上受到限制。很明显，一个长期的社会政策很难仅仅建立在趋势判断的基础之上。

以上便是卡莱尔有关社会发展与历史发展所持有的观点。总体而言，他将社会发展纳入历史发展。现实社会由此成为历史发展的最新阶段。社会发展历史维度的基础在于英雄崇拜。作为社会的基础，英雄崇拜具有极其明确的历史维度。这样，社会通过英雄崇拜被纳入历史发展之中。在历史视角下，现实社会被认为处于一个过渡阶段。旧制度的瓦解与新制度的建立共同交织在现实社会之中。旧制度的存在，特别是旧制度的尚未瓦解的根源在于人的保存习惯。即使存在人的保存习惯，旧制度的瓦解和新制度的建立具有必然性。在必然性基础之上，卡莱尔做出预言。他主要预言了旧制度的必然瓦解和新制度的必然建立。这是一个不具有很大精确性的趋势预言。

第三节 时间、历史和历史决定论

卡莱尔历史观的概貌在以上分析过程之中表现出来。首先，他历史观的基础在于时间的连续性（temporal continuity）。具有连续性的时间作为一个整体而存在。时间是“过去、现在和未来在连续体中的彼此相互联系”。[1] 过去、现在和未来三个主要要素通过相互联系共同构成时间。流动是卡莱尔用以说明时间连续性的主要意象。在时间的流动之中，任何一个时间点都“位于无穷的过去与现在两个永恒的交汇之处，潮流从最遥远的过去汹涌而来，又朝最遥远的未来奔腾而去”（Wks.，XXⅦ，59）。在这种具有连续性的流动之中，过去、现在和未来统一于时间。时间由此获得连续性。

时间的连续性是卡莱尔预言合理性的基础。连续性赋予过去和现在之间以紧密的关联。“现在与过去并不是没有必要地联系在一起。”（Sar.，47）在时间的流动中，现在是过去的表现和效果。“现在是整个过去的活着的全部。”（Wks.，XXⅧ，39）可见，现在作为最新阶段而存在。“［现在］从过去中生

① Keating, *The Victorian Prophets*, p. 18.

长而来，就像一棵树一样，树根并不同树干纠缠在一起，却平静地深埋于地下。”（Ibid.）在此，树的意象比流动更进一步，在表现现在是时间的最新表现的同时，更好地表现了过去相对于现在的生成作用。这样，过去成为贯穿时间的主线。过去的贯穿作用使得卡莱尔以历史为依据对现时代进行预言成为可能。过去甚至一直贯穿到未来。“过去是一个模糊的、不可怀疑的事实：未来也是一个事实，只是更加模糊而已；其实未来是同一事实的不同表现和不同发展阶段。”（P. & P.，42）。这样，以历史为依据对未来进行预言同样成为可能。

此外，卡莱尔历史观的基础还在于人存在的时间性（human temporality）。总体而言，人的存在是时间性的。狄奥根尼在刚刚出生的时候被称为“时间精神（*Zeitgeist*）”（Sar.，87），在成人之后依然被称为“时间之子”（121）。可见，时间性是卡莱尔对人进行理解的主要视角。时间性也是人存在的根本属性。“［人］的整个物质存在建立在时间基础之上，由时间建造而成；完全是一个运动，是一个时间驱动；时间是其作者，是其材料。”（127）人所有的行动表现出明显的时间性。在此意义上，时间性可谓人的基本属性。时间性作为人的根本属性使得卡莱尔从时间的角度对人进行理解获得合理性。从时间的角度对人进行理解，即是从人的根本属性对人进行理解。这是对人的本质所进行的理解。人存在的时间性强烈地影响了卡莱尔对历史的理解。在本质上，“历史是一种人类的产品，是人类行动的领域和时间中的事件，同时也是这些行动和事件的记录”。① 这样，人与历史紧密地结合在一起。这一方面使得历史的人性成为可能，另一方面使得人的历史性获得合理性。

最后，卡莱尔历史观的基础在于人的历史性（historicity）。一方面，卡莱尔主要从人的行为对人的历史性进行理解。在他看来，任何一段人的行为过程同时也是一段历史过程。这样，人的任何行为均表现出历史性。历史性由此被赋予人。他的具体论述如下：

> 记述历史的才能，可以说是我们与生俱来的；它是我们的主要禀赋。

① Frye，“History as Biography，Biography as History，” p. 133.

> 在某种意义上，人人都是历史学家。哪一种记忆不是写满了编年史，其中有哀乐相间，兴衰交替？哪一个“内在王国”的命运，无论它有否自己的哲学，其“内政”与“外交”是没有牢不可灭的记载的？我们的语言就奇怪地有一种记述的功能。你会发现大多数人的说话都是记述，而不是为了表达思想——它确乎只是一个微不足道的部分，是为了表达他们的见闻经历；这种经历，如果他们健谈。就会是一个没有穷尽的话题。如果离开叙述，交谈的溪流，即便在最聪明的人中间也会干涸，变成一掬死水，而在愚蠢的人中间就会完全枯竭。因而，我们所作所为都是在演示历史；我们说话只是记叙；而且在最广泛的意义上，我们全部的精神生活都是建立在记叙基础上。因为，严格说来，一切知识都是记录下来的经验和历史的产品；因而在历史知识中，推理和信念与行动和激情一样，都是根本的东西。(Wks.，XXⅦ，83－84)

这段论述非常详细。历史性可谓表现在人行动中的任何一个环节。记忆是历史的表现，言辞是历史记录，甚至人所有的一切行动都是在“演示历史”。这样，历史性相对于人的行动具有极强的普遍性。在此基础之上，历史性被看作人的主要品质之一。不难看出，卡莱尔所谓的历史性与时间性具有紧密的关联。如果时间性表现在过去、现在和未来三方面因素，那么历史性仅仅表现在过去之上。历史性作为人的主要属性是卡莱尔对人的时间性认识的深化。在此，历史（过去）成为认识人的主要依据。

另一方面，卡莱尔从人的存在状态对人的历史性进行理解。表面上，人存在于现在。然而，若将现在与过去之间的关联纳入思考，那么十分明显，人也是过去的产物。在此意义上，人决定于历史。卡莱尔认为：

> 你需要将历史的开端看作延伸向漆黑遥远的时间；从黑暗的神秘永恒之中发展而来：历史的末端在此时将我们笼罩，因此，我们在此时既作为行动者又作为联系者组成了历史的部分！在形式上我们可以将历史叫作数学之中的双曲渐近线；趋向无限的曲线在我们周围有限的空间之内变得窄小：在我们身后的无限空间内变得越来越窄小。在本质和意义

> 上，历史被叫作“真正的史诗和普遍神圣的经文，其‘全部启发’没有人（无论是精神错乱还是没有错乱）可以怀疑”。(XXⅧ, 176)

如果可以运用一句具有隐喻性的话语说明，那么时间的连续性使得人处于时间的洪流之中。这样，人在时间上不仅仅具有现在的维度，而更被赋予了历史的维度。在此意义上，人是历史的继承者和效果。最终，人在时间维度上的存在状态将历史性赋予人。

卡莱尔历史研究的对象不是历史，而是历史性。历史与历史性之间存在深刻的区别。“历史与历史性相区分，就像自然现象从思维活动中相脱离一样。如果历史是关于过去的研究，那么历史性就是历史学家关于过去概念性的经验。总而言之，历史学家如果以其自身历史存在意义为研究对象，那么毫无疑问便以历史性为研究对象。”① 显然，历史与历史性之间的区分是客体与主体之间的区分。如果历史以具有个体性的历史事件，那么历史性则以具有主体性的历史思维为研究对象。显然，卡莱尔历史研究的对象并不是历史本身，而是历史存在的意义，即历史的作用。历史对于卡莱尔而言最大的作用在于使他明确了历史的发展规律。历史性对于卡莱尔的历史研究具有重要的意义。第一，过去通过历史性成为历史。历史性是历史学家的一种视角。在这一视角下，不同的历史事件获得相同的品质。相同品质的获得使得过去成为历史。“历史性是历史学家在过去之中所寻求之物，或者更是他带入过去的东西，是他将过去变为历史的主动性原则。”② 同样，卡莱尔也在过去之中发现了英雄崇拜作为共同的品质。过去因表现出相同的品质而成为历史。第二，历史通过历史性而表现出规律性。历史事件本身表现为复杂，但是通过历史性则表现为统一。历史性是“从杂乱无章向井然有序、从布朗［即无规则］运动向有规律的过程的转变。”③ 卡莱尔通过历史性将历史发展变成英雄崇拜的发展，历史发展由此表现出强烈的规律性。

卡莱尔的历史思想具有明显的历史主义（historism，organology）特征。

---

① Natanson, “History, Historicity, and the Alchemistry of Time,” p. 81.

② Aymes, “Historicités,” p. 65.

③ Aymes, “Historicités,” p. 65.

卡莱尔的历史主义思想主要来源于德国思想。“德国的辩证形而上学”是“卡莱尔的［历史主义思想］的来源”。[①] 历史主义的经典定义来源于克罗齐（Benedetto Croce）。他认为“根据这一词汇的科学用法，‘历史主义’的内容在于肯定生活是生活，现实是历史、而且除了历史不是其它的东西”。[②] 可见，历史主义在本质上是将历史看作唯一的解释基础和依据。在历史主义的视角下，万事万物均是历史的表现，均可以获得历史的解释。历史主义在卡莱尔的思想之中表现出来。历史作为隐匿的真理的启示便是历史主义的表现。“因为人生存在时间之中，他的整个凡间存在、努力和命运都以时间为他呈现：只有在短暂的时间象征之中我们以之为基础的永远不动的永恒才得到表现。”（Sar.，112）在此，卡莱尔对历史所进行的夸大一目了然。正因为历史性是人的唯一主要属性，历史才成为真理的来源和解释的唯一角度。这种对历史的夸大便是卡莱尔历史思想中历史主义特征的表现。

卡莱尔的历史思想还具有明显的历史决定论（historicism）的特征。历史决定论的含义是“通过凝想历史我们可以发现人类命运的秘密、本质。历史决定论的目的在于发现人类注定要经历的发展过程；在于发现历史的线索［……］或者历史的意义”。[③] 实现历史预言（historical prophecy 或者 historical prediction）是历史决定论的最主要特征。在此意义上，历史决定论是“一个认为历史预言是主要目的、认为这一目的可以通过发现潜在于历史进化之中的‘节奏’或者‘模式’、‘法则’或者‘趋势’而导致社会科学的方法”。[④] 卡莱尔在历史之中同样发现了历史的发展规律，并根据这一规律对现时代进行分析。他的历史研究同样以实现社会预言为目的。“卡莱尔在历史之中看到了对未来进行思考和对当代社会批评进行写作的基础。”[⑤] 历史在他的思想中是认识和把握未来的基础和依据。“只有知道曾经发生过什么的人，才可以知道什么是应该的、什么是将要发生的。”（Wks.，XXVIII，169）他甚至将历史

① Wellek, “Carlyle and Philosophy of History,” pp. 86 – 87.

② “La Naissance de l'Histoirisme,” p. 603.

③ Popper, *Open Society and Its Enemies*, Vol. Ⅱ, pp. 297 – 298.

④ Popper, *The Poverty of Historicism*, p. 3.

⑤ Childers, “Carlyle's *Past and Present*,” p. 247.

和预言混淆在一起。“预言……是历史的一种新的形式。”（170）综上可见，卡莱尔的历史思想具有历史决定论特征。

卡莱尔的历史观有片面之处。他的确创造了一个庞大的历史世界。在这一世界里，所有的一切都是历史。历史性是所有一切事物的唯一品质。人、社会、政治、经济等都是历史。甚至所有的文献都是历史文献。“因此，所有的书——无论是诗歌集还是数学文献——总体而言都是历史文献，——就像所有的言辞本身都是历史文献一样。”（167－168）。这样的历史世界得以建立的基础在于复杂性的简单化。这样的简单化必然会造成认识上的局限和偏颇，甚至是错误。与卡莱尔相比，尼采意识到了历史的局限。“他意识到……‘历史感如果推向逻辑极限就会毁灭未来，因为他会毁坏幻想，并剥夺存在之物赖以生存的唯一氛围。’他认为‘历史文化其实是一种继承下来的苍白。’这财产以‘战争、苦难和疲惫’将人湮灭。”因此，“生命因为历史的泛滥而残废和退化，此后历史的退化也会到来。”[①] 历史不是所有一切的唯一主要品质。因此，也不能作为认识和把握所有一切的唯一基础和依据。一种“非历史的感官”（unhistorical sense）在认识上发挥着同样重要的作用。作为“认识人类生命不变和永恒的意义的能力”，[②] 非历史的感官同样用以认识和把握卡莱尔笔下的人和社会，甚至可以揭示出某些被忽视的内容和细节。

卡莱尔所发现的历史发展规律同样存在问题。英雄崇拜被认为是历史发展的内在结构。历史发展与英雄崇拜之间一段时间符合而另一段时间不符合的关系构成了历史发展的模式。历史发展一定要求符合英雄崇拜的要求则构成了历史发展的主要趋势。“历史决定论者在所谓历史的事件序列中所发现的‘方向’或者‘趋势’并不是法则，这些如果是某些东西，也不过是倾向而已。”[③] 同样，卡莱尔所发现的历史发展规律也不是法则，而不过是对历史事件进行高度概括所得到的必然逻辑结果而已。历史事件作为整体并不能进行高度概括，因为任一历史事件都是独一无二的，都具有与其他任何历史事件

---

① Farrell, “Matthew Arnold and the Middle Ages,” pp. 324－325.

② Farrell, “Matthew Arnold and the Middle Ages,” p. 325.

③ Popper, op. cit., p. 110.

相互区分的品质，都可以以此与其他任何历史事件相互区分。社会发展也不能简单地纳入历史发展。如波普尔所说，“至于人类社会的历史［……］我们的论点以这样的语言［……］已经制定：人［……］在历史之中发现了某一情节、节奏、预定的模式［……］我却只能看到一个突发事件紧跟另外一个突发事件［……］只有一个伟大的事实，既是独一无二的，也不能进行高度概括”。① 社会发展没有预定的模式可以遵循。英雄崇拜不过是高度概括的逻辑结果，社会发展并不决定于英雄崇拜。

有选择性的历史写作同样存在问题。卡莱尔对历史事件的解读并非以历史事件本身为目的，而以证明英雄崇拜作为历史发展内在结构的合理性为目的。这样的解读必然会造成偏差和错误。他对法国大革命的解读便存在问题。如哈罗德所说，“卡莱尔的《法国大革命》可以看作构成他资源主体的回忆录和历史片段构成的巨大杂烩。那些没有用于有关革命、民族或者其他问题的当场评论的部分是各种无聊或者及其有偏见的观点的卡莱尔式的展示，因为色彩和戏剧性而得到选择，根据高潮或者对比而得到排列，为了保证所需结果——一个‘火焰图像’——而得到表现”。② 法国大革命根据英雄崇拜作为历史发展的内在结构而得到了刻意的安排，可以实现这一目的的事件得到研究，而不能实现这一目的的事件则被忽视。这不是历史写作，而是历史重组。强烈的选择性也造成了《法国大革命》这部历史作品的文体确定问题。“《法国大革命》在本质上既不是史诗也不是悲剧，而是一部浪漫主义讽刺作品，许多问题混淆其中。”③ “他的《法国大革命》开始看起来是装作历史的文学，而不是文学作为历史”。④ “它经常被认为是文学，而不是历史。”⑤《法国大革命》并不是历史作品，这恐怕是对作为历史学家的卡莱尔最大的讽刺。

卡莱尔的历史观是一种历史的思维习惯（historical habit of mind）。与维多利亚时期的思想倾向一致，他相信“思想若要得到完全的理解，则一定要具

---

① Popper, op. cit. p. 100.
② Harrold, “Carlyle's General Method in *The French Revolution*,” pp. 1150 – 1169.
③ Ryals, “Carlyle's *The French Revolution*,” p. 18.
④ Pyke, “History as Literature,” p. 96.
⑤ Ben – Israel, “Carlyle and the French Revolution,” p. 127.

有历史的、而不是逻辑的存在方式。"① 这样的思维方式促使他通过历史获得真理。其实，历史作为真理的来源是他历史观的预设。在此意义上，他的历史研究并不是对这一思想的证明，而是直接承认思想的合理，并在此基础之上给出进一步的阐发。他对历史事件所进行的研究不过是对这一思想的合理性所进行的辩护而已。最终的结果必然是某物成为历史发展的内在结构。他的特别之处在于选择了英雄崇拜，因为英雄崇拜更是中世纪的社会规范方式。"对于大多数维多利亚人而言，如果的确有进步存在，进步就是中世纪思想和制度的瓦解。法国大革命对于他们而言……在本质上是对中世纪传统的打击。"② 卡莱尔同样感受到了时代的变革。然而，他选择了为中世纪传统进行辩护和捍卫。英雄崇拜作为历史发展的内在结构便是他所进行的努力。他的特别之处还在于选择了从历史角度对中世纪传统进行捍卫。由此，历史成为真理的来源、对现实进行认识和把握的依据、对未来进行预言的基础，历史之中蕴含着法则和规律，人类的命运在其中可以得到解读。

历史的思维习惯在卡莱尔所在的时代非常普遍。他的历史观得到了同时代评论家的认可和赞扬。文德尔班（Wilhelm Windelband）的意见极具代表性。"没有人像卡莱尔这样对世界历史观的本质进行如此深刻地把握［……］［以及］热情地阐释。"③ 从历史角度对现实进行认识、对未来进行预言的思想不为卡莱尔独有。勃朗宁（Robert Browning）同样"注意到了对过去进行新的阐释的需求"，他也"通过毫无畏缩地选择代表相互矛盾的历史事件观点直面历史写作的问题"，并"试图通过想象复活过去"。④ 斯密（Goldwin Smith）"虽然批评卡莱尔将过去变成了对现在不光明的控告，但是他［……］本人同样倾向于以现在为着眼点对过去进行解释"。⑤ 穆勒与卡莱尔最为接近。他甚至发现了某种历史发展规律，认为"历史发展规律同人性法则融合在一起。人性在历史发展规律之中得到表现"。⑥ 历史思维习惯的背离和例外体现

① Bruns, "The Formal Nature of Victorian Thinking," p. 905.

② Farrell, op. cit., p. 322.

③ *A History of Philosphy*, p. 640.

④ Baker, "The Diamond Necklace and the Golden Ring," pp. 32, 34, 36.

⑤ Wallace, "Goldwin Smith on History," p. 226.

⑥ Bouton, "John Stuart Mill," p. 570.

在阿诺德的思想之中。"阿诺德与卡莱尔并不一样，他不是一个历史决定主义者。'希伯来主义'和'希腊主义'在其效力上更是文化性的，而不是普遍性的，这就意味着它们的能力不是决定性的，而决定于具体社会的特征"。[①]

历史作为真理的来源在维多利亚末期不再得到接受。历史思想的发展在维多利亚末期发生了变化。"从卡莱尔向弗里曼的思想转变表现了维多利亚后期历史思想最为重要的唯一特征：历史背后有某些更大的真理或者目的的信仰的丢失。对于弗里曼而言，坚持实事不过是职业责任；对于卡莱尔而言，事实是更伟大真理的表现。"[②] 甚至不必等到世纪之末，这一信仰的丢失在麦考莱的历史作品之中即有体现。卡莱尔也注意到了他们历史作品之间的巨大差异。他将麦考莱看作"一个强壮的年轻人［……］一个有重点、热切、真正有说服力的人；但是非常不幸，他没有神圣的理念"（Nt. B.，236）。神圣的理念是卡莱尔与麦考莱思想之间的区别所在。神圣的理念在卡莱尔的历史作品之中得到了表现，而在麦考莱的历史作品之中则彻底消失。因此，他如此评价麦考莱：

> 目前他是世界上最具活力的年轻人。他最终可能成功，或者根本不会，这要根据时局而定：此时，他价值的限度可以辨认出来。他身上没有伟大的事物。他满足于作为一个评论者，对于属于他的任何力量都没有需求，他本可以凭借这些做些什么；他没有获得任何信仰，显然也不因为没有信仰而痛苦，这就是他的致命点所在。我认为这个人的道德本质非常平庸；因此，他的智力本质也不会不同，同样可以认为非常平庸。此时，他是唯一有天赋的年轻人，又是一个辉格党；这是另一个特征。人们可能听说过他，他也会受欢迎；但是听说是什么？只要一个人敲鼓也会被听到。让我们希望 M.［麦考莱］会获得更好的视角，一个清晰的、强健的基础，成为他之所能："一个衣服和屏障之中的人。"（276－277）

卡莱尔对麦考莱的评价反映了两种历史观之间的差别。前者在历史之中发现

① Bruns, op. cit., p. 909.

② Tuman, " 'Irritant Poison'," p. 415.

了历史发展的内在结构，而后者则只发现了独一无二的、不可高度概括的历史事件。卡莱尔预言了麦考莱历史观的失败，而历史发展则宣告了卡莱尔历史观的没落。在维多利亚时代末期，历史思想之中已经不再蕴含有所谓的神圣的理念。

历史并不是普遍真理的来源。如罗素所言，“当历史被认为教授着某些普遍的哲学教条时，其危害最大……所有这些教条都需要精心挑选地点和时间——甚至更糟——需要价值的伪造才可以得到支撑。这一危害最著名的例子就是卡莱尔”。[①] 历史之中并没有蕴含任何普遍真理，而任何对历史之中普遍真理的发现都是“想象性真实的教条式运用”。[②] 这样的真理的获得都是对历史有意的安排和刻意的选择的结果。卡莱尔在历史之中所发现的普遍真理存在同样的问题。他所发现的真理同样是历史所展示的普遍法则，同样需要对历史事件进行高度的概括和抽象才可以得到，同样需要为了在历史之中获得真理而进行有意的安排。其实，这样的普遍真理可以造成严重的错误。任何违背真理的现象都需要被消灭，任何不符合普遍法则的对象都要被清除，甚至是某一人群、阶级和种族。历史上希特勒（Adolf Hitler）也发现了某些类似于历史之中所蕴含的真理，结果他屠杀了难以计数的犹太人。

其实，所谓的“历史是一个变化的、有问题的话语，其表面上有关世界、过去的一个方面，由一群具有现代思想的工人（在我们的文化中即为领工钱的历史学家）生产，他们工作的方式可以被轻易辨认，因为他们在认识论上、方法论上、意识形态上和实践上都有其立场，他们的产品一旦流通就有被使用和滥用的可能，这在理论上是无限的，他们的产品事实上与一系列存在于任何时间的权利基础相对应，这些权利基础在一个其起决定作用又处于边缘的范围内决定并分配历史的意义”。[③] 任何历史都是一定立场、一定视角和一定思维方式的产物。卡莱尔的历史同样如此。他的历史是英雄的历史，是英雄崇拜作为普遍法则而获得合理性的历史。其实，历史上不同的思想家看到

① “On History,” p. 502.

② Jann, *The Art and Science of Victorian History*, p. vii.

③ Jenkins, *Re-thinking History*, pp. 31-32.

了不同的历史，也发现了不同的历史发展的内在结构。卡莱尔的英雄史只是其中一员而已。

卡莱尔通过历史真理所要实现的最终目的其实是进步（progress）。他历史思想的基本思路是历史处于进步之中，而发现了历史发展的内在结构就可以把握实现进步的手段，从而实现进步。然而，"'历史'并不会实现进步；只有我们——作为人类的个体——才可以实现进步。我们还可以更好地实现进步，如果我们可以更加全面地意识到进步决定于我们、决定于我们的努力、决定于我们对于我们目的把握的清晰度和目的选择的现实性。[……] 进步不是事实，而只是我们的决定和行动而已"。① 卡莱尔实现进步的手段也许存在错误，但是他实现进步的愿望值得肯定。在卡莱尔所创造的庞大历史世界之中有一个独特的存在，这就是他所在的维多利亚社会。维多利亚社会是历史和现实之间的连接点，也是过去和未来的交汇处，卡莱尔创造庞大历史世界的目的在于认识和把握他所在的维多利亚社会、在于站在历史的顶峰俯视他所在的现实。虽然卡莱尔已经将社会发展纳入历史发展、已经确定了维多利亚社会的历史阶段和历史使命，维多利亚社会依然有其独一无二的特征需要进一步的讨论。卡莱尔也需要带着他从历史中所发现的真理进入他所在的维多利亚社会，在那里批评、否定，成就一代先知的身份和地位。

① Popper, *After The Open Scoiety*, p. 81.

第四章　社会研究

卡莱尔是维多利亚时期著名的社会批评家之一。在他的作品和思想之中，社会批评是一条明显的线索。《时代的征兆》是他第一部重要的社会批评作品。在这部作品中，"德国思想的影响是明显的"。① 甚至"还有其他许多观念、片语只言，也同样可以在这些德国影响中追根溯源"。② 《时代的征兆》确定了他此后社会批评的基本思路。其中的"普遍看法成为卡莱尔此后一切作品的基础，而且屡见于其他许多作家的思考之中"。③ 《特征》是另外一部比较重要的社会批评短文。该作品可谓"卡莱尔思想最为深刻、风格上最为完美的表现之一"（Rem. 3，76）。《特征》"颠覆了个体主义的政治学和经济学，是卡莱尔社会理论基本原则的陈述"。④ 作品"将有关健康的认识应用于一系列话题，特别是应用于当前的思想氛围，即时代精神"。⑤ 在此意义上，《特征》"既是一份诊断，也是一份预断，还是一份药方"。⑥ 在以上两部作品中，"卡莱尔扮演了社会批评家这样一个新角色"。⑦ 这是他从哲学研究向社会批评转向的标志。

卡莱尔的社会批评甚至贯穿于《法国大革命》之中。《法国大革命》虽

① 威廉斯：《文化与社会》，第 107 页。

② 威廉斯：《文化与社会》，第 107 页。

③ 威廉斯：《文化与社会》，第 107 页。

④ Neff，*Carlyle*，p. 142.

⑤ Haley，"Obeying the Laws of Life，" p. 71.

⑥ Haley，"Obeying the Laws of Life，" p. 71.

⑦ Le Quesne，*Carlyle*，p. 26.

然主要是一部历史作品，但是依然有卡莱尔社会批评的表现。作为历史事件，法国大革命为卡莱尔的社会批评提供了理想的题材。“《法国大革命》既是一部社会预言，也是一部历史作品，对于卡莱尔而言这一主题的魅力在于为他提供了描写处于混乱之中的社会的机会。”① 在他看来，大革命是法国社会瓦解的标志。“法国大革命对于卡莱尔而言是一个社会的终结，这个社会的灵魂已经死亡。”② 卡莱尔进一步对法国社会瓦解的根源进行分析。在《法国大革命》中，他“将一个民族所不可避免的危险展现出来，他们的社会秩序建立在阶级特权和古代的不义基础之上”。③ 在许多方面，大革命时期的法国对应于现时代的英国。在作品的“历史背景的描述中，经常出现与英国当时社会状况的对照，一般来说，这并不引人注目，但敏锐的读者不会看不出这种不祥的对照”。④ 可见，法国大革命是对现时代英国社会的警示。法国大革命被认为验证了卡莱尔的社会预言。“卡莱尔的青年时期与法国大革命重合，这场伟大的革命对于他而言是他社会理论实现的标志。”⑤ 总体而言，法国大革命既是历史，也是社会现实。对法国大革命进行研究，便是对社会进行研究。

《宪章运动》是卡莱尔社会批评的新起点。与之前的作品不同，《宪章运动》聚焦于一个具体的社会问题。该作品“是对本运动第一份严肃的分析，这一运动使得一部分社会成员兴奋，另一部分恐惧”。⑥ 在卡莱尔的解读中，宪章运动“是深层危机的表现，不能通过令人恐慌的措施被镇压，也不能被普遍选举以及经济手段抚慰”。⑦《宪章运动》同样蕴含了卡莱尔此后社会批评的主要思路。特别是“关于金钱交易关系的观点［在《宪章运动》一书中］还仅仅是一个轮廓，但却是一个具有远大发展前景的理论观点，可以说它已经形成了对资本主义的也许至今仍然是最强烈的道德谴责的基础”。⑧ 在

① Shelston, *Thomas Carlyle*, pp. xi – xii.
② Cazamian, “L'Idéalisme Philosophique,” p. 1072.
③ Roe, *The Social Philosophy of Carlyle and Ruskin*, p. 62.
④ Le Quesne, op. cit., p. 42.
⑤ Schulze – Gaevernitz, *Thomas Carlyles Welt – und Gesellschaftsanschauung*, pp. 105 – 106.
⑥ Chapman, “Thomas Carlyle,” p. 83.
⑦ Chapman, “Thomas Carlyle,” p. 83.
⑧ Le Quesne, op. cit., pp. 50 – 51.

许多方面，《过去与现在》是卡莱尔社会批评最为杰出的作品。艾默生称之为“卡莱尔的新诗，是他有关英国苦难的《伊利亚特》”。[①]《过去与现在》被进一步誉为“一个强大的、有成就的思想家的作品”，是“最接近于现代历史的作品”。[②] 在这部作品中，卡莱尔“将［英国社会的危机］看作是最具紧迫性的问题”，并将“预言家的声音同好争论的新闻工作者的声音融合在一起”，[③]从而实现了理想的表意效果。《过去和现在》产生了强烈的影响。这一影响可谓“不可预期地广泛”。[④] 恩格斯（Friedrich Engels）对这一作品格外推崇。“与其他任何评论家相比，［恩格斯］在提升作品名誉方面所做的努力最大”。[⑤]《晚近文集》是卡莱尔最后一部重要的社会批评作品。与之前的作品相比，“这些小册子中几乎充满了虚无主义的否定的观点”。[⑥] 甚至“除了斯威夫特的作品以外，很难想象还有其他任何作品能像这套丛书一样，如此有力地表达出对英国社会的强烈的和普遍的不满”。[⑦]《晚近文集》之后，卡莱尔再次转向历史写作。他虽然从未中断对当代社会状况的关注，但是未有重要作品问世。

卡莱尔所面对的现代社会是一个处于转折之中的社会。转折甚至可谓维多利亚时代最大的特征。时代处于转折之中“是关于这段时期基本的、甚至几乎是普遍的认识”。[⑧] 维多利亚时期对于自身所处的转折阶段有着清醒的认识。“虽然所有的时代都是转折时代，但是人们从未”像维多利亚人一样，“认为他们自己的时代是一个从过去向未来变化的时代”。[⑨] 时代的转折性由多方面因素造成。“转折的动因是工业化、民主以及纯粹的科学等，这些导致了政治、经济和思想上的革命。”[⑩] 在所有这些因素之中，工业化的作用可谓

---

① Seigel, *The Critical Heritage*, p. 219.

② Seigel, *The Critical Heritage*, pp. 219, 220.

③ Altick, “Past and Present: Topicality as Technique,” p. 112.

④ Stange, “Refractions of Past and Present,” p. 106.

⑤ Stange, “Refractions of Past and Present,” p. 107.

⑥ Le Quesne, op. cit., p. 79.

⑦ Le Quesne, op. cit., p. 79.

⑧ Houghton, *Victorian Frame of Mind*, p. 1.

⑨ Houghton, *Victorian Frame of Mind*, p. 1.

⑩ Neff, *Carlyle and Mill*, p. 54.

最为明显。“英格兰是工业化的摇篮，而工业化的影响最为深远。”① 在某种意义上，“现代英国赖以形成的经济因素便是 18 世纪以来工业和商业的发展。”② 19 世纪，“英国社会行为的特征表现在处于主导地位的工业之上”。③ 在工业化开始之初，“直到大约 18 世纪结束之前，英格兰是一个农业占主导地位的国家”。④ 1800—1830 年，英国的工业得到了蓬勃的发展。在这段黄金岁月里，“分工和重组创造了手工业；机械在工业领域里的应用，先是水，再是蒸汽，对这些自然资源价值的肯定，产生了现代工厂”。⑤ 工业化彻底改变了英国社会的整体面貌。时代处于转折之中作为一个可见的事实被确定下来。工业化改变了社会生活秩序。随着工业化的深化，大量的农村人口“开始涌向国内的工业区”，随之“一种新的生活秩序开始产生”。⑥ 与原有的农业生活相比，工业造成了雇主与工人之间的分裂。“［雇主］远离［雇工］，生活在自己的房子里，在不同的社会氛围里。”⑦ 这一点特别集中地表现在贵族的失责之上。面对工业化所造成的社会疾苦，贵族或者兴修住所，或者吃喝玩乐，完全忽视了自身对社会所承担的责任。⑧ 理解工业化所带来的社会变革，是卡莱尔社会批评的主要内容。

本章分三部分以卡莱尔的社会批评为研究对象。主要涉及他对社会现状问题的分析、对功利主义批评以及对英雄崇拜实现的论述。

第一节　社会现状问题

卡莱尔社会研究的基础和依据在于真理所规定的社会的理想状态。理想社会是一个所有组成内容均对宗教作为社会本质进行表现的社会，这样的社会处于缄默和无自我意识之中。因此，缄默和无自我意识成为判断社会状况

---

① Neff, *Carlyle and Mill*, p. 54.

② Cazamian, *L'Angleterre Moderne*, p. 19.

③ Cazamian, *L'Angleterre Moderne*, p. 19.

④ Dibelius, *England*, p. 110.

⑤ Cazamian, *Le Roman Social en Angleterre*, p. 23.

⑥ Trevelyan, *Illustrated English Social History*, Vol. Ⅳ, p. 12.

⑦ Trevelyan, *Illustrated English Social History*, Vol. Ⅳ, p. 13.

⑧ Altick, *Victorian People and Ideas*, p. 22.

的标准。他认为：

> 在身体政治之中，就像在动物身体之中一样，正常表现的标志是无自我意识。这就是“社会的人为状态”这一词语的含义所在；人为状态相对于自然状态而言，人为状态要比自然状态低等好多。在所有有生命的事物上，人们可以区分出一个人为状态和一个自然状态；我们对于这一真理有某些模糊的认识，并在此坚持：人为状态是有自我意识的、机械的；自然状态是无自我意识的、运动的。因此，就像我们有人为的诗，却只认为自然的诗有价值；由此，我们也有人为的道德、人为的智慧和人为的社会。人为社会正是知道自身结构、自身内在功能的社会；社会的健康并不在于注意、知道这些内容，而在于外在地工作以实现目的。(Wks.，XXⅧ，13)

显然，缄默和无自我意识在此是对社会状态进行评价和衡量的依据和基础。社会处于缄默和无自我意识之中则处于理想状态之中，否则社会则出现严重的问题。维多利亚社会便是一个没有处于缄默和无自我意识状态之中的社会。卡莱尔对此有如下评论：

> 如果我们现在以实用医学的视角、以同样无意识的标准检验我们时代的状况，以及人在其中的生活，我们的诊断结果绝对不会令人满意。我们时代的社会状况，在所有可能的状况之中，是最不无自我意识的状况：在我们的时代里，人存在曾经不被感觉到的、无自我意识的层面都得到了各种各样的调查，这些调查好像占据了思想的全部领域。(18)

维多利亚社会不但没有表现出缄默和无自我意识的特征，反而在“所有可能的状况之中，是最不无自我意识的状况”。甚至人存在中一直以来无自我意识的领域都得到了调查和研究。所有这些症状均是社会没有处于理想状态，甚至还存在严重问题的表现。卡莱尔进一步对维多利亚时代的社会问题进行研究。

维多利亚的社会问题有多方面表现。这一问题不仅表现在物质领域，也表现在精神领域。“对于我们来说，社会的精神状况与物质状况比较来说同样病入膏肓。”（22）可见，维多利亚社会在物质和精神两方面领域之中均存在严重的问题。社会物质领域所存在的问题被叫作“社会外在的、物质的疾病”（20）。可见，这又是以疾病类比社会问题。在物质领域，贫富差距问题和机械化问题是卡莱尔关注的焦点。贫富差距问题主要表现为财富的积累并没有实现任何人的幸福。“19 世纪开始于一个残忍的矛盾：科学和工业进步并没有实现社会问题的解决。古典主义政治经济学所表达的思想与事实刚好相反：经济进步当然实现了国家财富的增长；但是并没有实现劳动力阶级生存状况的改进。”① 财富与幸福的脱离是维多利亚社会的一个普遍现象。维多利亚社会在物质财富上实现了巨大的进步。甚至可谓人们“已经征服了这个星球，这是他的居住地和财产；但是并没有从胜利当中收获利益”（21）。物质财富的积累没有实现人的幸福。相反，物质财富的积累产生了深刻的矛盾。“英格兰充满财富，充满种类繁多的产品，可以满足人各种各样的需求；不过英格兰却遭受虚乏。”（P. & P.，1）一方面是物质财富的不断增长，另一方面任何人的幸福并非因此而得到满足。这种不能实现幸福的财富被叫作“被诅咒的财富”（10）。“英格兰成功的工业，还有其过多的财富，没有使任何人富裕；这是一个被诅咒的财富，不属于任何人。”（Ibid.）面对这样矛盾的物质财富进步，卡莱尔发出质疑：

> 那么，对于谁来说，英格兰的财富才是财富？这财富保佑了谁；使谁更加幸福、更加明智、更加美丽、以任何方式变得更好？谁占有了这财富，使得它为自己拿来送走，就像一个真正的仆人，而不是一个假仆人；给他带来任何真正的服务？然而，没有任何人。我们所拥有的财富比其他任何国家曾经拥有的都多；我们从中获得的利益比其他任何国家曾经获得的都少。我们成功的工业目前并不成功；如果我们就此停下，这是一个奇怪的成功！在过量的财富之中，人们灭亡；没有人对于金墙、满仓感到安全或者满意。（11）

① Martinoia，“L’‘Ère Marshallienne’，” p. 93.

在卡莱尔所提出的问题之中可以看出他将分配问题等同为社会问题，而社会问题其实包含更加复杂、更加广泛的内容。可见，在此他再一次将复杂性简单化，从而将社会纳入他的研究范围。

物质财富的积累进一步造成了贫富之间差距的加深。维多利亚社会所实现的物质财富使得一部分人获得了巨大的利益，而绝大部分人并没有从中实现幸福。这造成了贫富之间差距的加深。卡莱尔将贫富之间的差距类比为两极之间的差距。“财富已经大量积累；贫穷，以同样的数量，不可逾越地同财富分离；两者相互对照、没有联系，就像处于正极和负极的力量一样。”（Wks.，XXⅧ，20）贫富之差如南北之极，差距显然可见。贫富之间的差距被看作表现在国家和个人之间。物质财富的积累仅仅实现了国家的利益，而个人的幸福并没有得到实现。

> 这看起来非常令人伤心：在文明的最高阶段，十分之九的人类需要在野蛮人或者甚至像动物一样的人的最低等斗争中挣扎，即抗争饥饿的斗争。国家是富裕的，在各种方面的增长都是繁荣的，出类拔萃：但是这些国家的人却是贫穷的，比以往更加需要所有的外在的和内在的滋养；需要信仰、知识、金钱、食物。（21）

在此，个人和国家被置于贫富差距的两极。贫富矛盾被理解为国家和个人之间的矛盾。可见，贫富问题不是一个简单的个人问题，而是被赋予更深刻的社会背景。贫富问题由此被纳入社会问题。

在社会贫穷问题之中，卡莱尔对工人的生存的状况进行了特别的关注。维多利亚社会所实现的物质财富增长同样没有实现工人的利益。工人的生存状况不但没有因为物质财富的增长而得到改善，反而在对比之中显得更加悲惨。工人生存状况的恶化是不争的事实。“这件事无须争论，对于任何人来说都毫无疑问。你走到下层阶级的任何地方，市镇也好，郡县也罢，无论你走哪条路……只要你睁开眼睛看，同样的悲惨情景就会展现出来：你不得不承认富裕英国的劳动主体已经沦落了，或者迅速沉沦到从任何方面考虑都是一种无与伦比境地。”（P. & P.，9）卡莱尔对工人的生存状况进行了大量细致的描写。他借一位“风景旅行者”的视角对工人的生存状况进行了直接的观察：

> 我看到五十甚至更多的人坐在木凳上，就在他们巴士底狱的前面，处于围墙和栅栏之中。他们身体健硕而高大，大多数都是青年或者中年人；他们面容诚实，许多人心思缜密，甚至拥有智慧。他们坐在彼此之间，处于麻木和令人心痛的沉默之中。他们处于沉默之中；然而，他们又能说些什么？大地延展在他们的周围，呼喊着，来啊，耕耘；来啊，收获；——然而我们中了邪，坐在这里！这些人眉宇之间最为凄凉的表情不是气愤，而是痛苦、羞耻和许多无法言传的悲痛和疲倦。他们也看着我，眼神似乎在说，“不要看我们。我们中了邪，坐在这里，我们也不知道原因。太阳在照耀，大地在召唤；然而，因为英格兰的统治权利的无能，我们无法响应召唤。他们告诉我们，这不可能！”看到他们让我想起了但丁的地狱；我赶快离开了。(8)

可见，工人生存状况恶化的根源在于无工可做。整个世界在卡莱尔看来是人工作的空间。然而，因为社会的规范方式未能实现有效的协调，工人作为一个阶级在劳动力上产生了巨大的浪费。由此观之，财富问题并不是一个简单的分配问题。所有社会问题均指向社会规范方式的失败。

事实上，在工人问题的解决上，卡莱尔主要以社会的规范方式为针对对象。工人问题在他看来已经十分严重。“有一种感受非常普遍：目前工人阶级的状况和情绪已经非常危险，应该站出来说点什么，做点什么了。”（Wks.，XXIX，118）然而，即使在这种情况下，严重的问题并没有得到合理的解决。英国政府对此也出台了一些解决方案，但是并没有实现应有的效果。这些解决方案在卡莱尔看来不过是“临时的应对方法”（P. & P.，8），只是“镇痛剂”（Ibid.），而不是“解药”（9）。针对工人生存状况恶化所出台的解决方案最终沦落为“《贫困法》监狱”和“工房巴士底狱”（8）。在此情况下，工人的精神状态极其低迷。在工房内，他们“吃痛苦的面包，喝痛苦的水［……］而不需要任何一点英雄气概”（Wks.，XXIX，130）。可见，解决工人问题的关键在于实现工人的英雄气概。这只能通过英雄崇拜才可以实现。最终，工人问题被转为社会规范方式的转变问题。

除贫富差距问题之外，机械化是另外一个比较重要的社会问题。机械化是维多利亚社会物质领域问题的集中表现。机械化被看作卡莱尔所在时代的标记。“根据卡莱尔，现代世界的标志是倦怠、精神麻痹、地平线的狭小、萎缩、一个完全机械化的世界的图景。”① 他的描述更为具体生动：

> 倘若非要用一个词来形容当今时代，我们不会说这是一个英雄的、虔诚的、哲学的、道德的时代，而首先是一个机械的时代。无论从字面还是比喻意义上说，这都是一个机械的时代。它全力以赴地推动、传授、践行着一种使手段适应目的的伟大艺术。现在，没有什么能够直接做成或手工完成，一切都得遵循特定规则，借助精密的机械。哪怕最简单的操作，都有工具器械随时待命，都有省时省力的窍门可供使用。古老的劳作方式受到了质疑，被丢到一旁。各行各业活生生的手艺人都被赶出作坊，速度更快却毫无生命的机械取而代之。梭子从织工手中滑落，掉进了能让它更快速运动的铁手之中。水手也收起船帆，丢掉船桨，指挥着力大如牛且不知疲倦的仆人，插上蒸汽的翅膀，在水上飞驰。汽船已经穿越了大洋，伯明翰的火轮也抵达了神秘的东方。（Wks.，XXⅦ，59－60）

这便是卡莱尔对时代做出的整体性判断。机械化可谓时代的总体特色。在卡莱尔的描述中不难看出，机械化表现在时代的任何一个方面。特别是物质生产，几乎整个领域都处于机械化的统治之下。

时代的机械化有其成因。总体而言，机械主义（mechanism）超越物质领域而进入精神领域是时代机械化的根源所在。机械主义本是物质领域的规范方式。在物质领域，人可以以机械主义为规范方式，甚至可以以此在物质财富上取得一定的成就。“我们向原始的大自然开战，只要搬出无坚不摧的机

① Brée，“Rencontre avec Carlyle，” p. 292.

器，必将无往不胜，满载而归。”（60）但是，在维多利亚时代，机械主义超出自身适用范围而进入精神领域，甚至成为精神领域的规范方式。与物质领域一样，精神领域同样根据机械主义原则进行规范：

> 不过，我们还是暂且放下这些问题，看看我们时代的机械精神如何渗透进了那些迥然不同的领域。如今，不仅外在的、物质的层面受机械控制，内在的、精神的层面也未能幸免。没有什么事情还能顺其自然，也没有什么事情还能用古老的自然方法完成。无论做什么，都有精巧的工具和预先准备的器械，都不再用手工，而是用机械完成。(60－61)

可见，机械主义不仅仅是物质领域的规范方式，还成为精神领域的规范方式。精神领域同样有大量机械主义的现象存在。“教育机械”“宗教机械”等现象(61)，便是精神领域机械化的表现。同样，集体性质的精神活动也表现出机械化的倾向。

> 任何人，任何团体，如果想宣讲一个真理，或完成一项精神任务，绝不会只用身体器官立马去做，而是先召开一个公开会议，任命委员会，发布计划书，一起聚个餐。一句话，就是要通过设立机构来宣讲，使用机械来完成。没有机械，他们就灰心丧气，束手无策，活像一群蹲坐在兰开夏郡腹地的印度织工。(Ibid.)

在此，机械不仅仅是机器。思想表达需要符合的规章制度等也被纳入机械的范畴。可见，卡莱尔所理解的机械具有更大的包容力。

作为精神领域的规范方式，机械主义造成了更为严重的社会问题。机械主义原本是物质领域的规范方式。作为精神领域的规范方式，机械主义深刻地改变了人的生存状态。人被机械化，并表现出强烈的机械主义特征。根据卡莱尔的观察，人的生存方式因为机械主义而发生了巨大的变化。他认为：

> 虽然我们只是蜻蜓点水地说了说，但并不意味着这些现象不重要，它们标志着我们的整个生存方式发生了剧变。这种习惯不仅控制了我们

> 的行为模式，也控制了我们的思维和情感模式。不仅手变机械了，心和脑也变机械了。人们不再相信任何人力或自然力量。人们殷切盼望并孜孜以求的，不是内在的完美，而是外在的联合、组织、机构和体制，也即各种各样的机器。人们所有的行为、喜好和观点，都转向了机器，并带有了机器的性质。(62－63)

机械化深刻地改变了人整个的存在方式。人的心脑结构开始机械化。机械性的对象成为人的追求。甚至人本身都带有强烈的机械化特征。在所有涉及对象之中，人的精神领域是卡莱尔对机械化进行观察的主要领域。在这一领域，他同样发现了强烈的机械化倾向。他观察到：

> 这种情形在我们时代的各个重要领域都有。知识方面有，包括最受宠的那些学问及其研究方法；实务方面也有，包括政治、艺术、宗教和道德；精神方面的所有源头和全部潮流都有，丝毫不亚于物质方面。(63)

可见，机械化的倾向表现在人精神领域的所有方面。政治、艺术、宗教和道德等均被机械化。机械主义成为人精神活动的规范方式。“个人也不例外。那些与生俱来的能力，都失去了用武之地。现在没人愿意舍弃机器，单枪匹马去完成哪怕最微不足道的任务。他必须求助于现有的组织，借他们的牛来犁自家的地。”(61) 机械主义特征表现在人精神领域的所有内容之上。“哲学、科学、艺术和文学，无不依赖机械。”(Ibid.) 人精神领域的机械化造成了严重的问题。精神领域不再产生精神成果。在自然哲学和科学领域，“即便牛顿在世，也不可能通过苦思冥想，从掉落的苹果中发现世界的规律。现在有的是和牛顿迥然相异的人，站在博物馆或科学机构中，面对整套的蒸馏甑、煮解器和电池，专横地‘拷问自然’，却不急于给出答案”(61－62)。在艺术领域，“我们固然没有拉斐尔、米开朗基罗和莫扎特，可我们有皇家绘画学院、雕塑学院和音乐学院，足以提振日渐消沉的艺术精神，正如官办的厨房必然有更多珍馐佳肴”(62)。在文学领域，“文学也有连锁机制，包括生意宴请，编辑的秘密会议，以及出自私心的吹捧。因此，书不仅是由机器印刷的，很大程度上也是由机器来写作和销售的”（Ibid.）。精神领域机械化所造成的最严重后果，是精神和灵魂的丧失。“机械主义的才分对人造成的窒息比任何噩梦都要严重；直到灵魂几近窒息，只有一种消化的、机械的生命留存下来。”（Sar.，221）机械主义使得人忽视精神和灵魂的存在。人仅仅在意物质存在，彻底沦为机械。

以上便是卡莱尔在维多利亚社会所发现的贫富差距问题和机械化问题。这两个问题均发生在物质领域，是社会问题在物质领域里的集中表现。其中，机械化问题不但涉及物质领域，而且还表现在精神领域。作为物质领域的规范方式，机械主义超越自身适用范围进入精神领域，甚至成为精神领域的规范方式。由此，精神领域表现出强烈的机械化特征。精神领域的机械化导致人整个存在状态的彻底改变。总体而言，卡莱尔对社会问题进行描述的同时，也对社会问题的成因展开了一定程度的探讨。他认为，社会问题的产生主要是社会的规范方式的失效造成的。最终，社会问题转化为社会规范方式的有效性问题。

在明确社会问题在物质领域的表现之后，卡莱尔进一步对精神领域的表现进行探讨。总体而言，物质领域和精神领域在他的认识里具有不同的重要性。与物质领域相比，精神领域更为重要。这样，社会问题在很大程度上可以被归结为一个精神问题。精神领域问题的解决意味着全部社会问题的解决：

> 还是让我们向内看看吧，看看社会的精神状况，看看这一领域的特征和前景。毕竟，只有在精神领域里整体的秘密和起源才可以找到：社会的物质紊乱不过是精神紊乱的影像和印记；当心脏健康的时候，所有其他的疾病都是表面的、暂时的。错误的行动是错误思想的结果；如果社会的精神自由并强壮，也就是说，如果真正的原则激发社会的成员，那么紊乱就不会在行动中积累；每一种紊乱都会被立刻、真实地调查，一旦出现就得到解决。（Wks.，XXⅧ，22）

在此，精神紊乱被看作是一切紊乱的根源。精神紊乱的解决意味着一切紊乱的解决。非常明显，这一观点与卡莱尔有关精神和物质之间关系的观点相一致。精神领域里的问题在他看来是社会的主要因素。社会问题的解决依赖于精神领域问题的解决。这样，社会问题最终被归结为精神领域的问题。

维多利亚社会精神领域所出现的问题集中表现在信仰领域。宗教信仰在维多利亚社会几近消亡。“这就是降临在我们这个时代人上的痛苦。信仰几乎从世界上消失殆尽。”（29）信仰的缺失是卡莱尔所在时代的主要特征。狄奥根尼便将他所在的时代叫作一个“无信仰的时代”（Sar.，112），一个“无神论的世纪”（184）。在卡莱尔的解读中，宗教信仰的丧失被赋予现代性。信仰的丧失是一个现代问题。只有在现时代这特殊的时代环境里，宗教信仰才会成为一个问题。卡莱尔对今昔进行了对比：

> 年轻人在这个神奇的宇宙上醒来，却不能找到任何理论解释其中的神奇。过去是这样的，当他问自己，什么是人，什么是人的责任？答案对于他来说就在那里。但是现在古老的“所有的基础计划”在同现实碰撞的时候都成为了虚假的东西；教堂母亲最多成为一个被废黜的继母，无人顾及她的教诲；或者被摒弃、被轻蔑地否定。对于那些年轻的、怀有英勇之气的人，还有那些渴望行动的人，没有理想的骑士精神召唤他们成就英雄主义，告诉他们什么是英雄业绩：人古老的理想已经过时，新的理想对于我们依然是不可见的，我们在黑暗之中探寻它，一个人抓住了这个幽灵，另一人抓住了另一个幽灵。（Wks.，XXⅧ，29）

在对比中，今昔的差距一目了然。在过去，信仰给予人以确定性。人可以确认自己的责任以及为履行责任所需付出的行动。在现在，信仰的丧失造成行动的盲目。在这种环境下，无人可以实现真正的卓越。

在社会领域，信仰问题产生的根源同样在于机械化。如上所述，机械主义超越自身适用范围进入精神领域。在这一僭越的过程中，机械主义甚至被应用到信仰领域，成为信仰领域的规范方式。在机械主义的规范下，信仰领域开始凋零：

> 我们可以发问，宗教消失在什么地方？[……] 依然徘徊于这些被叫作，或者叫自己有宗教的人心的同一宗教的本质是什么？这是一个健康

> 的宗教，有生命力，对自身无自我意识；自发地在工作，或者在言的布道中自发地显现吗？非常不幸，不是这样。［……］宗教，同其他事物一样，变得［……］越来越机械化。作为整体而考虑，最近的基督教持续自我瓦解成形而上学；就像河流一样，现在有在贫瘠沙漠中消失的危险。（22－23）

在对时代信仰状况所做的高度概括性的分析中，卡莱尔直接指出问题的根源在于信仰的机械化。信仰不再是自发的，不再是无意识的。相反，机械主义成为宗教的规范方式。在这种情况下，宗教甚至有瓦解为形而上学的危险。

信仰的丧失将会导致社会的瓦解。如前所述，宗教在卡莱尔看来是社会的基础。信仰的瓦解意味着社会基础的瓦解。这将最终导致整个社会的瓦解。事实上，根据卡莱尔的观察，现实社会处于正在瓦解的过程之中。他认为：

> 你把那东西叫作社会［……］那里不再存在任何社会理念；连公共之家的理念都没有，却只有一个普通的、拥挤寄居所的理念？那里每一个人都是孤立的，不顾他人，与他人对立，能得到什么就抓紧什么，叫嚷“我的！”并名之曰和平，因为在抢钱包和割喉的争夺中只有阴险狡诈可以派上用处？那里友谊、交流都变成了不可相信的传统；你最神圣的圣餐不过是烟熏的客舍餐点而已，厨子成了传道者？那里牧师的舌头只用于舔盘子：你的导师和督管不能引导；他们只能听到自由主义到处得到激烈的鼓吹；你们还是不要引导我们为好，这样的光亮比黑暗还要漆黑；拿走你们的薪金，沉睡吧！（Sar.，232）

可见，社会形成的根源在于所有人都怀有相同的宗教信仰。在此意义上，社会是一个信仰理念的表现。在现时代，信仰的丧失直接导致社会的瓦解。社会不再是人通过信仰形成的联合体，而是成为人聚居的场所。

卡莱尔对信仰的丧失有比较独特的理解。在他看来，信仰来源于人的崇拜。崇拜是人的本性要求。这样，信仰不会消灭。在此意义上，所谓的信仰的丧失是信仰的表现失效的含义。这一点表现在他有关宗教的观点之上。宗教并没有瓦解，真正瓦解的是所谓的宗教的衣服，即宗教的表现。卡莱尔的观点如下：

> 与此同时，就在我们这个世界的时代里，这些同样的教堂衣服已经在肘部痛苦地消失干净；不，甚至更加糟糕，其中的许多已经变成不过空洞的形式或者面具而已，其中没有任何鲜活的形体或者精神；只有蜘蛛和不净的甲壳虫，以恐怖的数量，经营着它们的产业；面具像鬼一样假装具有生命力，依然以玻璃的眼睛向你发射出光芒。(216)

可见，瓦解的只是所谓的“教堂衣服”。与此相对，宗教作为社会的本质会永远持续下去，而且保持不变。

以上便是卡莱尔对维多利亚社会问题在精神领域里的表现所进行的思考。社会问题在精神领域里的表现被认为是问题的关键所在。与物质领域一样，精神领域问题产生的根源在于机械主义。作为规范方式，机械主义造成了精神的机械化。特别是信仰领域，机械主义造成了更加严重的问题。信仰的丧失造成了社会的瓦解。可见，与物质领域一样，卡莱尔对精神领域的分析同样针对规范方式的失效。最终，他对社会的问题的讨论转化为对现行规范制度的批评和否定。

第二节　功利主义

在社会问题上，卡莱尔对现行规范制度的批评与否定以功利主义为针对对象。在他看来，只有在问题产生的根源得到清晰认识的基础之上，全部社会问题才可以得到根本的解决。“有了真正的洞见”，“也就等于找到了解决的办法”（Wks.，XXIX，122）。可见，正确的认识是解决问题的关键。在这一认识基础之上，卡莱尔进一步对社会问题产生的根源进行探讨。他认为社会问题之所以产生是因为——

> 他们招惹了神圣的力量——他们同宇宙永恒的内在事实相分离，并追随了宇宙暂时的外在表象；因此他们才会沦落到**这种境地**。这就是所有不幸的人和不幸的国家的秘密。如果他们知道了自然的正确真理，自然的正确真理会给他们带来自由。他们中了邪；在咒语的控制下乱步，

在灾难的边缘行走，因为他们不够明智。他们忘记了正确的内在真实，以外在虚假真实为伴。他们错误地回答了斯芬克斯的问题。愚蠢的人不能回答正确！愚蠢的人将暂时的表象误解为永恒的事实，将迷失得越来越远。(P. & P.，14)

可见，社会问题产生的根源在于社会未能符合法则的要求。这是卡莱尔应然的真理的规定。违背这一真理意味着违背上帝的意志。事实上，作为法则而存在的真理的实现具有必然性。在此意义上，对社会问题产生的根源进行认识变得更有必要：

如果你不能将永恒的正义同暂时的权宜之计相区分，如果你在内心深处不知道正义是光芒照耀的、仁慈的，就像全胜的光元素一样，正义在本质上就是一个全胜的火元素，将所有种类的私利和最为坚硬的铁炮熔化，好像这些就是柔软的蜡，正义长期处于统治地位，并不允许任何其他东西统治——那么你就在说不可能的事情！(24)

正义的实现具有必然性。只有认识正义的要求，全部社会问题才可以真正解决。正义在此被认为是昭显的。就像光一样，正义是普世可见的。这样，只需借助于一般的视力，人便可以实现对于正义的认识。

在维多利亚社会之中，功利主义被认为是违背正义要求的主要因素。如上所述，功利主义将快乐的实现和痛苦的避免看作人动机的来源。功利主义作为规范方式意味着对快乐和痛苦的权衡成为整个社会的运行机制。在维多利亚社会之中，功利主义不但是社会的规范方式，甚至深入宗教领域。宗教所发生的巨大变化便由功利主义造成：

在大多数国家，宗教都已经不再是原来的样子，也不再是它应该有的样子。其实，所有国家都存在这个问题，只是程度不一。宗教不再是心中向上帝千吟百唱的赞美诗，不再是真、善、美的源泉，也无法再从真、善、美的表象中看到，却在很大程度上成了一种纯粹基于计算的圆滑世故，和现今的其他事务一样，权衡利害，计算功用，自然也会为了

> 丁点尘世之乐，牺牲许多天国之乐。因此，宗教也成了一种只图回报的收益，由崇敬变成了庸俗的期盼或恐惧。（Wks.，XXⅦ，76 –77）

在功利主义的规范之下，宗教发生了严重的质变。宗教同样变成对快乐的实现和对痛苦的避免。快乐和痛苦之间的权衡与算计，成为宗教的主要内容。可见，规范方式的错置是宗教领域产生问题的根源。

功利主义也是贫富差距问题的根源。在维多利亚社会，贫富之间差距的加深以及由此而爆发的社会运动是社会瓦解的直接表现。根据卡莱尔的观点，贫富差距问题由功利主义造成。功利主义以个人幸福最大化取代社会责任。“卡莱尔对功利主义的憎恨来源于他相信，根据功利主义原则，绝对价值并不存在。个人幸福的数量是衡量任何事物唯一的标准，人由此局限于幸福之中，而这仅仅是个人的幸福而已。这样，除了虚伪、自我满足之外别无他物，而虚伪的问题在于虚伪将灵魂囚禁于自我之中，而自我的本质则因为一种更高妙的事物、值得敬畏的事物而完整。”① 社会责任意识的丧失造成了统治者的失职。“对于卡莱尔而言，社会的道德和物质健康——文化健康——是统治阶级的责任……统治阶级的首要责任在于为大众提供工作。”② 然而，统治者因为接受功利主义原则而没有履行责任。在功利主义的影响下，“统治阶级既不会管制，也根本不知道他们应该管制，不知道人们期待他们的管制”（P. & P.，152）。无为成为他们的行动原则。这样的统治阶级“在行动上毫无作为，在言辞上一言不发”（Ibid.）。统治者所负有的责任被忽视。这样的失职最终造成了严重的财富分配不公。特别是功利主义所倡导的自由竞争，进一步加深了贫富之间的差距。“自我销毁的无为主义和自由竞争竟然深入到我们的行动，这是所有痛苦的根源。”（Wks.，XXIX，167）

功利主义是导致时代机械化的根源。功利主义仅仅强调人物质方面，而忽视精神方面的内容。根据功利主义原则人不过是“穿着马裤的杂食性两足动物”而已（Sar.，65）。功利主义以过分简化的方式看待人，从而导致“人

---

① *Stawell*, “Goethe's Influence on Carlyle. Ⅰ,” p. 181.

② Swift, “Thomas Carlyle, ‘Chartism’, and the Irish in Early Victorian England,” pp. 69 –70.

的情感和关系被简化为建立在得失——现金交易关系——算计基础之上可度量的量和机械互动，进而以经济、财政责任取代人的精神、社会责任等”。[①]功利主义忽视人的精神因素。因此，宗教信仰被取代，不再作为社会的规范方式。同样，人所有的精神内容均被忽视。甚至宗教信仰也表现出强烈的机械化特征。这最终造成了整个时代的机械化。

卡莱尔针对功利主义进行批评和否定。他对功利主义深恶痛疾，并将之叫作“猪哲学”（Wks.，XX，315）。与功利主义不同，他对人有不同的理解。“对于卡莱尔就像对于他的浪漫主义先驱一样，人是一个丰满并有可能是崇高的感官、感觉、想象和心智的混合物；对于实用经济学家而言，人不过是一个经济单位，是对数据整体的添加数字而已。”[②] 在卡莱尔看来，人的精神因素与物质因素之间存在巨大的区别。其中，精神因素是人“潜在的、无限的能力”，控制人的“想象和内心”；而物质因素是人“浅显的、表面的能力”，控制人的“自爱和算数性的理解”（Sar.，225）。两者分属不同领域，具有不同的功能。因此，人不能仅仅以物质领域的规范方式进行规范。“人不是没有灵魂而处于需求控制之中的机械，人是神圣理念的表现、是反射神圣理念的镜子、是肯定神圣理念的行动；人的精神组成永恒的思想，参与庄严的现实。我们归根结底只有一个现实：理念的现实。”[③] 可见，功利主义不能成为人唯一的规范方式，更不能成为人精神因素的规范方式。

卡莱尔反对功利主义作为人的规范方式。对人本质的不同理解决定了对人规范方式的不同理解。卡莱尔对功利主义作为人的规范方式倍加反对。“［没有人］认为人可以通过‘制度’进行管制；可以通过有史以来最为精巧的自我利益机械、通过所有可以想象出的收支平衡的设计进行管制。”（Wks.，XXⅧ，41）他甚至动用历史，从历史角度对功利主义不能成为人的规范方式进行证明：

> 不仅如此，甚至可以说，人类所有的伟大成就，乃至一切影响深远

---

① Heffer, *Moral Desperado*, p. 194.

② Altick, *Victorian People and Ideas*, p. 137.

③ Carré, *Goethe en Angleterre*, pp. 168 - 169.

> 的运动，也都源自人性的动态层面。尽管看似不可思议，但只要细思历史，就不难发现，核查和比较盈亏得失，从来没有成为人类的左膀右臂。盈亏得失之虑，急功近利之求，从未让人焚膏继晷，全力以赴；只有那不可见的无限目标，才能令人赴汤蹈火，在所不辞。欧洲十字军起于宗教，他们的可见目标从商业的角度说一文不值，他们真正向往的是不可见的世界，那里的熊熊火光令可见世界如纸卷般皱缩。这场浩大的运动，不是机械的，也用不着机械手段。不需要共济会酒馆的聚餐和其他一系列现代机构，也不需要妥善协调各种“既得利益”，只需要一人慷慨陈词，炽热的灵魂透过双眸迸射出来，枕戈待旦的欧洲勇士就会热血沸腾，随他南征北战。后来的时代也不例外。宗教改革有一个不可见的、神秘的、理想的目标，其结果固然体现在外，但其精神和价值却是内在的、不可见的、无限的。我们英国的革命也是起于宗教。那时候，人们的确在为良心而非金钱而战。其实，这一点至今未变。法国大革命并不只是为了便宜面包和人身保护令，它还有更高的目标，也涉及一种理念，一种动态而非机械的力量。尽管是一场盲目并最终走向疯狂的斗争，却仍是为了捍卫权利、自由、国家的无限性和神圣性。(XXⅦ, 70 –71)

通过历史可以知道，其实功利主义并不是人和社会的规范方式。在历史之中，人一直以来都以宗教信仰为规范方式。人的行动来源于上帝的启发。这一点在十字军、宗教改革、英国革命和法国大革命等重大历史事件之中均可以得到表现。可见，功利主义取代宗教信仰不是一个简单的规范方式的替换问题，而更是一个社会发展违背历史发展的问题。

卡莱尔尤其反对机械主义成为人的主要规范方式。他认为，只有物质因素才可以通过机械主义进行规范。而且，物质因素在人的整体利益之中只占有很小的比例。“但稍作回顾或反思就不难发现，现在和未来都有可能是另外一种样子，因为以前人们认为，机械的领域［……］只涉及一小部分人类利益，而且绝不是最重要的部分。”（68）可见，只有在现时代功利主义才成为规范方式。“不是通过机械主义，而是通过宗教信仰；不是通过自我利益，而是通过忠诚，人才被管制，或者可以被管制。”（XXⅧ, 42）卡莱尔特别反对功利主义成为精神领域的规范方式。特别是宗教信仰，尤其不能成为功利主义的规范对象。卡莱尔主要以基督教为例说明：

> 不妨再举一个至高无上的例子——基督教。不管信不信它，也不管如何阐释它，都应把它看作我们整个现代文化的最大荣耀，甚至是生命和灵魂。基督教是怎样兴起并传播的呢？借助了组织机构和严密有序的机械体系？恰恰相反。在古往今来所有为此而建的机构中，基督教的神性都毫无例外地出现了衰落。基督教源自人的灵魂深处，通过“宣讲圣言”，通过简单的、纯粹自然的个人努力传至四方，就像薪薪相传的圣火，净化并启迪众生。它的圣洁光芒如日月星辰，永远照耀人类的黑暗命运。这跟机械没有关系，人类的最高成就是由动态而非机械的层面实现的。（XXVII，70）

可见，基督教的传播和交流依靠人与人之间精神的联系。在历史之中，宗教信仰的传播手段表现得十分明显。所有这些情况说明，功利主义不可成为人精神领域的规范方式。特别是信仰领域，更不能成为功利主义的规范对象。

综上可见，在卡莱尔的认识里，功利主义主要违背了真理的要求。社会以宗教信仰为规范方式，这是真理的要求。然而，功利主义取代宗教信仰而对社会进行规范，这是对真理要求的背离。卡莱尔将功利主义作为规范方式看作对法则的违背：

> 边沁激进派在我们的时代中是最让人感到痛苦的一派人。自然惧怕真空——的确这样！她不会让一个邪恶的、没有同情心的、骨瘦如柴的无神论和利己主义在她的世界上成功，而是回答它说——“够了，你这个骨瘦如柴的无神论！去你的吧，好吗？”①

功利主义在社会中的存在，就像真空在自然界的存在一样。两者都违背法则的要求。在此基础上，功利主义的未来变得可以预测。非常明显，一个违背

---

① Froude, *Life in London*, Vol. Ⅰ, p. 148.

法则要求的对象只能被最终淘汰。事实上，卡莱尔的预言包括功利主义的未来发展。他预言道：

> 功利主义者是这个时代“登峰造极的仁慈”：是好多趋势——在现在整个智力和道德之上向下伸展、向旁边传播——的顶峰（现在开始出现在人们的视野）。渐渐地，云会散去，我们会看到它在赤裸和野蛮之中；功利主义这个怪兽会带着巨大的声响死去。你不这么认为？——人的理性能永远被感官踩在脚下；我们身上的野兽能永远战胜天使吗！（Nt. B.，145）

可见，在卡莱尔的预言之中，功利主义终将被淘汰。作为法则而存在的真理的必然性在此表现得一目了然。就像人的理性终将战胜感官一样，人的精神因素一定会主导物质因素。在此过程中，功利主义将不再作为规范方式。

功利主义的存在具有一定的合理性。功利主义违背真理的要求。这样，功利主义存在的合理性有必要得到一定的说明。卡莱尔认为，功利主义存在的根源在于人并没有意识到人所存在的精神实质。这一问题被他叫作人的“精神困境”（Wks.，XXⅦ，80）。精神困境的解决办法仅仅在于转变审视对象的视角。所有的一切“只是因为舆论出了问题。既然我们是被自己打造的锁链缚住了，自然也能把它们扯断。我们屈从于外在事物，不能自拔，失去了自主能力。这不能怪大自然，只能怪我们看待自然的方式太愚蠢”（80－81）。精神因素是人的本质，并对物质因素起决定作用。然而，在维多利亚时期，精神因素被忽视，而物质因素成为人的全部。功利主义由此成为人的规范方式，并获得存在的合理性。

功利主义尚有历史使命需要完成。功利主义在卡莱尔看来不但有存在的合理性，还有需要完成的历史使命。“功利主义、激进主义、机械主义哲学或者无论叫作什么名字的这些东西，依然还有其任务需要完成。”（XXⅧ，41）功利主义的历史使命同维多利亚社会的历史使命联系在一起。维多利亚社会作为一个过渡社会而存在。一方面，一个不以英雄崇拜为规范方式的社会形式需要瓦解；另一方面，一个以英雄崇拜为规范方式的社会形式需要建立。

其中，旧有社会形式的瓦解通过功利主义而完成。如前所述，功利主义造成了贫富之间差距的加深。社会运动由此而产生。这些社会运动在卡莱尔看来是社会处于瓦解过程之中的表现。“这些人——自由主义者、功利主义者或者无论叫作什么——将最终实现他们的目的，分解、摧毁目前存在的社会体制，这看起来是一件在一段时间里不再可以怀疑的事情了。”（Sar.，233）可见，功利主义会最终造成旧有社会制度的瓦解，完成历史使命。

以上便是卡莱尔在社会领域里对功利主义所进行的批评。他认为功利主义违背了作为法则而存在的真理的要求。这是他批评的基础和预言的依据。卡莱尔特别反对功利主义成为信仰领域的规范方式。快乐和痛苦之间的权衡代替宗教成为社会的规范方式被认为是所有社会问题产生的根源所在。在此基础之上，贫富差距问题和时代机械化问题被看作功利主义造成的后果。历史是卡莱尔审视功利主义的主要视角。在历史中，人的行动并非来源于功利主义，而是来源于宗教信仰。然而，功利主义在现时代的存在主要来源于人对精神因素的忽视。在完成历史使命之后，即在实现旧有社会制度的瓦解之后，功利主义终将被淘汰。

第三节　英雄崇拜的实现

至此，卡莱尔的历史研究和社会研究实现了统一和融合。在历史研究之中，他主要将维多利亚社会定性为一个违背历史发展规律的社会，并对所处历史阶段和所负历史使命进行了规定。在社会研究之中，他指明维多利亚社会违背历史发展规律的具体原因在于功利主义成为社会的规范方式，而维多利亚社会的一部分历史使命主要通过功利主义而得到完成。历史和社会的融合使得维多利亚社会问题可以从历史角度得到解决。历史的发展表明，所有的社会形式都是对英雄崇拜的表现。这样，社会发展符合英雄崇拜的要求成为任何社会得以发展的手段：

> 发现能人并授予他以能力的象征，即赋予尊严、崇拜（值得尊敬的品质）、王权、王位，等等，从而他可以切实行使他那种指导者的才能——无论其任务完成好坏，这是世界上一切社会秩序必须要做的事情！

> 议会竞选讲台上的演说、议会动议、选举法修正法案、法国大革命等的核心问题，不是别的，就在于此。一个国家中能发现最有才能的人，把他提到至上的地位，忠诚地崇敬他：这个国家就有了完美的政府……它就处于完善的境界，是一个理想的国家。最有才能的人也意味着心地最真诚、最公正、最高尚的人。他教导人们做的，是最明智、最恰当的，人们在任何地方、任何情况下都应记取的——人们应该以非常忠诚的感激之情毫不犹豫地照办！这样，就政府的调节作用范围来说，人们的事业和生活，就能安居乐业，这就是政府体制的理想。（H. & H.，196 - 197）

可见，社会发展的关键在于选取合适的英雄进行崇拜。只要将合适的英雄选举出来，并赋予其权力，社会就可以实现良性的发展。同样，维多利亚社会的发展需要符合英雄崇拜的要求。英雄崇拜的开展状况直接关系到维多利亚社会的发展：

> 英格兰或者学会这些，或者不再在民族国家之中存在。英格兰或者学会崇拜英雄，并同伪英雄、侍者以及全身充满虚假气的小人物区别开来；学会将他们当作空洞的口号和暂时的市场叫嚷中的可听见的上帝的声音，学会带着真诚的忠诚对他们说，“你成为我们的国王、牧师、福音以及引导”：否则英格兰就会一直崇拜永远更新的假象——无论弹性和恢复能力如何，长此以往，英格兰一定会沦为虚假之父！（P. & P.，219）

可见，维多利亚社会需要发现可以崇拜的英雄并对其进行崇拜，将权利赋予他们。事实上，英雄崇拜理论是卡莱尔为解决时代问题所开出的药方。“正是在英雄之中他看到了宇宙之谜的答案，看到了所有这些严重的形而上学、道德、政治或社会问题的最终解决办法。”① 这样，维多利亚社会的发展才可以符合真理的要求。

事实上，卡莱尔将英雄崇拜理论在社会领域推向了极限。建立一个神权

---

① Basch, *Carlyle*, p. 202.

政体（theocracy）是他最终的社会理想。他认为：

> 神权政体、上帝政府正是因为它奋斗的！一切先知、热忱的教士，都是为了实现这个目标，希尔德布兰德想望过神权政体，克伦威尔也一样，并为它而战，穆罕默德则获得了它。不仅如此，凡是热情的人，无论是教士，还是先知，或者是别的什么称号的人，实际上，不都在想望，而且必须想望吗？正义和真理，也就是上帝的律法，至高无上地统治着人们，这是神圣的理想（"上帝意志"的一种启示，在诺克斯时代流行，也能沿用于一切时代），宗教改革家坚持认为人们越来越接近这个目标。我说过，凡是真诚的宗教改革家，因他的教士本性，都力图实现神权政体。（H. & H.，152）

神权政体是理想的社会形式，是历史上所有英雄的奋斗目标，也是卡莱尔本人的终极社会理想。他一方面意识到了理想社会的存在，另一方面意识到了理想社会不可能得到实现。他认为人不可能实现理想社会的建立，但是理想社会的存在将作为一个目标对人进行引导，从而不断实现社会的进步：

> 理想的事物绝不可能完全体现在现实中。理想与现实总是隔着非常大的距离，任何向理想的适度接近，我们应该由衷地感到满足！正如席勒所说，但愿没有人在我们这个贫穷的世界上，过分要求"用一台准确的天平来衡量现实的贫乏产物"。那样的人是不聪明的，人们会把他看作不健全的、牢骚满腹的愚人。然而，另一方面，绝不能忽视理想的事物确实是存在的。如果认为人们一点也不能接近理想，人类的整个事业就会破灭！这是千真万确的。（197）

理想社会不能在现实之中得到完全的实现，但是将作为一个终极理想而存在。这里，卡莱尔所设计的社会发展模式是一个不断完善、不断向理想模式靠近的过程。社会将永远处于符合英雄崇拜要求的过程之中，而英雄崇拜也将永远对社会发展发挥决定作用。

最后，卡莱尔在理想社会和现实社会之间实现了妥协。维多利亚社会毕竟是一个工业社会，英雄崇拜成为社会的规范方式意味着需要与工业社会的社会现实相适应。卡莱尔在产业工人中发现了实现英雄崇拜的机会。他将工人对工头进行崇拜看作实现英雄崇拜的现实模式。“工头可以号令工人，可以从工人中获得工作成果，工头已经是一个非同小可的人物。工头不是普通人，我在他们身上看到可贵的和万分可贵的迹象；他们是贵族，并开始感觉他们一定作为贵族而行动：所有的人都拥向工头，工头是目前英格兰的希望。”（P. & P.，207）在工业社会中，工头可以扮演英雄的角色。工人可以对工头进行英雄崇拜。这样，英雄崇拜可以在工业社会的现实环境中实现。妥协反映了卡莱尔对工业社会的观点。他所反对的对象并不是社会的工业化。这一点在他对机械主义作为人物质因素的规范方式的赞同，以及对维多利亚社会在物质财富上所实现的进步的赞扬中便可以看出。“他在机械的年代之中发现了物质进步的因素。但是他的核心主题是机械年代的后果将机械化的模型强加给了整个社会关系。”① 他所反对的对象其实是功利主义取代旧有的宗教信仰成为社会的规范方式。社会规范方式的改变被认为带来了社会结构的改变。统治阶级与被统治阶级之间出现裂隙，甚至统治阶级中不再出现英雄人物。机械化甚至改变了整个时代的特征。这“不是一个英雄主义和宗教的年代，而是一个怀疑主义、自私和琐碎的年代，这个年代里无人知晓真正的高尚，取而代之的则是肤浅分裂、完全空虚无效的傲慢法则”（Wks.，XXVI，311）。他对社会结构由此所发生的变化更加感到悲哀。这是“一个没有高尚的时代，一个没有高级品德、没有天才迹象的时代；一个昏暗的、矫揉造作的、自欺的、充满怀疑主义和各种揶揄的时代”（465）。卡莱尔赞成社会的发展，但是他认为社会在发展的同时需要保持旧有的结构。作为社会的本质，普通人对英雄的崇拜不容改变。在此意义上，他在变化（change）之中寻找不变（rest）的因素，只是这一次他在社会的变化之中找到了英雄崇拜作为不变的因素。

卡莱尔社会研究的基础是社会的本质。在他的思想之中，社会处于永恒的变化之中。但是，社会的本质表现为不变，并对社会发生决定作用。社会

① Vitoux，“Carlyle et le Culte du Héros，” p. 21.

的变化围绕本质进行。这样，处于变化之中的社会获得不变的因素。社会研究由此成为可能。研究社会即研究社会的本质。对此，卡莱尔的观点是：

> 社会［……］并没有死去：你所谓的死亡社会的尸体不过是她已死的躯壳而已，她脱掉才可以获得更好的躯壳；社会经历永恒的变化，处于不断的进步之中，直到时间成为永恒。无论哪里，只要两三个活人聚集在一起，那里就是社会；社会及其精巧的机制和庞大的结构将笼罩这小小的地球，上达天堂，下抵地狱：因为一直以来，社会只有两种表现，或表现为上帝，或表现为魔鬼；或表现为卜道坦，或表现为绞刑架；或为前者，或为后者。（Sar.，236）

社会的外在形式是暂时的、变化的，而社会的本质是永恒的、不变的。认识和把握了社会的本质意味着认识和把握了社会。

英雄崇拜作为社会的本质存在问题。在卡莱尔的思想之中，社会的本质来源于人的本质。社会是人与人之间的联合。这样，人的本质成为社会的本质。人的本质是精神，社会的本质同样是精神。英雄崇拜都是人最基本的精神活动，并由此成为社会的本质。如前所述，卡莱尔主要通过类比和隐喻实现精神作为人的本质。但是，修辞只能实现旧有知识的重新整理，不能实现新知识的获得。如果精神作为人的本质已经存在严重的问题，那么英雄崇拜作为社会的本质更加无法获得合理性的证明。事实上，只要按照“社会—社会的本质”二元关系对社会进行研究就一定可以获得社会的本质。在历史中，社会的本质可以表现为理念、意志、权利意志以及功利等。不同思想家按照不同的思想过程得到了不同的社会本质。这样，甚至社会本质也表现为变化。卡莱尔社会的本质表现为英雄崇拜存在必然性。他主要从历史的角度对社会的本质进行探寻，认为社会在历史中诞生于英雄崇拜。英雄崇拜由此成为社会的本质。然而，这一过程不过是先有思想获得合理性的辩护而已。

卡莱尔通过社会本质实现社会问题解决的方法存在问题。维多利亚社会是一个处于巨大社会变革之中的社会。这一巨大的社会变革在他看来表现为工业主义取代封建主义而成为社会的规范方式。“他们给我们准备了工业主义和最明智的人的统治以代替封建主义。”(118)。工业主义造成了旧有社会结构的变化，带来了人的机械化，加深了贫富之间的差距。严重的社会问题由此而产生。对工业主义进行批评是他作品的主题之一。卡莱尔尤其反对功利主义。在他看来，功利主义是所有社会问题产生的根源。“他将最终毁灭创造性活动并将人变成机械的劳动分工、建立在算计基础之上的边沁派功利主义、特别是两个与之相联系的趋势——向符合数量法则‘体制化机械’的政治运动——还有瓦解为仅仅通过数量关系在一起的人类集合的社会作为攻击的目标”。[①] 他的社会研究在他所在的时代产生了一定的反响。他向同时代人阐明了社会现状，使得他们意识到了工业社会的问题之所在。“他将他们从冷漠和安全的迷梦——边沁的功利主义哲学使得他们陷入这样的迷梦——中唤醒”。[②] 卡莱尔对工业社会的研究甚至对马克思（Karl Marx）也有启发作用，只是他们的解决方案之间存在区别。“马克思和卡莱尔同向这一问题进军：对于前者，根源在于物质；对于后者，根源在于道德。”[③] 最终，道德成为卡莱尔解决工业社会问题的主要方法。

卡莱尔的英雄崇拜理论可以在他的社会批评之中得到更好的解读。英雄崇拜是真理的内容、上帝意志的体现和历史发展规律的要求。维多利亚社会现实是英雄崇拜理论得以产生的现实基础。卡莱尔其实通过英雄崇拜理论规定了一个与他所在的现实社会相对立的社会模式。英雄崇拜作为社会的规范方式以功利主义作为社会的规范方式为针对对象。“卡莱尔将英雄主义生命观同功利主义道德相对立。[……]‘得失的德性’不是约定的价值，灵魂的统一和尊严才是人类生命伟大的动力。功利主义道德忽视灵魂的永恒需求，而灵魂才是人之所以是人的根源。功利主义唤醒人对好运的美梦和诡计的崇拜，因此使活力萎靡、产生平淡而犹豫不决的性格、使受苦的荣耀不为人知，因此将社会置于危险的境地。”[④] 功利主义以人的物质因素为关注点，而英雄崇

① Vitoux, “Carlyle et le Culte du Héros,” p. 21.

② Davey, *Darwins*, *Carlyle*, *and Dickens*, p. 49.

③ Woody, “Of History and its Method,” p. 178.

④ Yandell, *Thomas Carlyle*, pp. 19 – 20.

拜则以人的精神因素为关注点。卡莱尔进一步通过英雄崇拜理论对整个维多利亚社会进行认识。“英雄主义的气质被发展到所有领域，以抵抗大众运动的自然主义和社会事务伦理之中的功利主义；像引发创造性行动的福音一样，英雄主义既与民主政治、资本主义又与被美学化和具有思考性的自我满足相对立。”① 这样，整个社会成为卡莱尔社会研究的对象。卡莱尔最后将英雄崇拜理论神圣化。英雄崇拜成为真理的内容、上帝的意志和历史发展规律的要求。这样，他便把握“正义”于手中，而他对维多利亚社会的批评和否定都是“正义的”。他的社会批评获得绝对的合理性。

虽然英雄崇拜理论在合理性上存在问题，但是卡莱尔试图通过真理进行社会研究反映了他所在时代的思维方式。维多利亚时代是一个相信真理的时代，真理不但是绝对的，而且可以被人认识并把握。“维多利亚人相信真理不但是绝对的，而且真理可以获得。真理一旦获得，就会被当作教条而接受。先知不会争论，或者考虑相反的思想或信仰。他以确定的言辞告诉你，腔调也不会谦虚，因为他毕竟不在给出一个意见，他其实在表明一个教条。”② 真理在维多利亚时代主要表现为规律和法则，认识真理即认识规律和法则。“维多利亚的思维方式总体而言相信绝对法则。政治、道德、历史、经济、艺术、教育——所有这些都被认为由在所有时间和地点都真的普遍法则或者原则控制；因此，可以被任何知道其所是的人带着神圣的权威进行陈述”。③ 卡莱尔的思想体系便诞生在这样的思想氛围之中。他也相信真理是绝对的。因此，他将真理看作上帝的意志。他也认为真理可以为人认识并把握，他本身便对真理进行探寻并通过洞见（insight）和灵感（inspiration）发现了他的真理。卡莱尔的真理也作为规律和法则而存在。真理是历史发展所表现出来的规律并作为历史发展规律而存在。他也相信万事万物都是真理的控制对象，并以真理为基础和依据对维多利亚社会进行研究。在此意义上，卡莱尔的思想体系是他所处时代的产物并迎合了时代的思维方式。因此，他才产生了巨大的

---

① Troeltsch, “Le Dix－Neuvième Siècle,” p. 31.

② Houghton, *The Victorian Frame of Mind*, p. 144.

③ Houghton, *The Victorian Frame of Mind*, p. 145.

影响，成就了一代思想家和先知的地位。

根据卡莱尔的研究，维多利亚社会的历史使命包括两部分内容，一方面需要实现一个以功利主义为规范方式社会模式的瓦解，另一方面需要实现一个以英雄崇拜为规范方式社会模式的建立。如果功利主义可以完成维多利亚社会的第一部分历史使命，第二部分历史使命尚需要通过其他因素得到实现。在卡莱尔的思想之中，这一其他因素便是工作。工作是真理最终得以实现的手段。

第五章　真理与工作

所谓卡莱尔式的真理的实现，是上帝意志获得物质表现形式之意。在卡莱尔的世界观之中，整个世界是上帝的创造。上帝是不可见的，并通过可见的、被创造的物质形式获得表现形式。这一过程在卡莱尔看来便是上帝意志的实现过程。作为上帝意志表现形式的物质世界，是上帝的象征。可见，象征是“任何通过感官可以察觉到的存在、任何将精神表现给精神的事物”（Sar.，74）。上帝的意志可以在象征之中得到表现。“在真正的象征之中，即在我们所谓的象征之中，或多或少清晰地和直接地，都有对于无限事物的表现和启示；无限事物同有限事物混杂在一起，变得可见，而且触手可及，就像被规定的那样。”（220）上帝意志的实现过程是精神获得物质表现形式的过程。这一过程对应于象征的创造过程。这样，卡莱尔所谓的真理的实现是对物质世界的改造。

第一节　工作观

卡莱尔所谓的工作是上帝通过物质世界对人进行召唤、人服从上帝的召唤而对物质世界进行改造并实现上帝的意志的整个过程。工作绝对不是简单的物质生产过程。工作的来源是上帝与人之间召唤与服从的关系。工作的过程是人服从上帝的召唤并实现上帝意志的过程。工作的效果是物质世界得到改造并成为上帝的表现形式。这样的工作是人在物质世界之中建设“天堂之国”的行动（P. & P.，25）。在此基础之上，卡莱尔将工作理解为“是同自然进行的交流；完成工作的欲望本身可以将一个人逐渐引导向真理，引导向自然的任命和规管，而这些就是真理”（196）。总之，工作是实现真理的手段。

卡莱尔所谓的工作是精神发挥主导作用的工作。他将作为精神而存在的人看作工作的主体。“人是他在工作时的精神。”（Sar.，203）人的精神因素在工作之中对物质因素发挥决定作用。“手永远被意识神秘的运行机制引导。”（35）事实上，精神因素在工作之中的主导作用是卡莱尔强调的重点。他认为：

> 精神因素是实践因素的亲源和第一原因，这一点经常被说起，但是并未得到足够的考虑。任何地方精神因素都产生实践因素，并进行塑造、创造：这样，在人之中，即使最为悲惨的外部条件也是更为悲惨的内部条件的证据。就像思想是行动的生命源泉和动机灵魂，因此，人类世界的任何一个领域，任何将自身呈现给眼睛的外在之物不过是不可见的内在之物的衣服或者形体；内在之物试图对自身进行表现，在所在的既定环境之中发现它能够并可以以这种方式表现自身。（Wks.，XX，296）

精神因素在工作过程之中发挥主要作用，这与卡莱尔实然的真理的内容一脉相承。人在他看来作为精神而存在。“我们的整个日常生活都是精神性的（*geistig*）：我们所做的一切都源自精神这个秘密，这个不可见的力量。”（Sar.，172）同样，虽然工作涉及物质，但是工作之中的人同样表现出精神因素的决定作用。

卡莱尔所谓的工作是宗教信仰。他认为“所有真正的工作都是宗教”（P. & P.，201）。人只要工作就是在进行宗教信仰活动。“人在世界上所有的工作就是一个具有象征性的说出的或者做出的祈祷。”（228）同样，工作无论是高尚还是粗劣，都是宗教信仰。“所有真正的工作都是神圣的；在所有的工作之中，即使只是真正的手工活，都有某些神圣因素。工作，同地球一样宽广，顶峰在天堂之中。”（202）工作和宗教信仰进行等同的基础在于两者之间的渊源关系。宗教信仰是工作产生的根源。“每一个崇高的工作起先都是‘不可能的’。的确，因为对于崇高的工作来说不可能性将会通过无限的空间而扩散；只有对于宗教信仰，工作才是有言的、才可以被发现。”（198－199）同样，人也只有通过宗教信仰才可以成就伟大的工作。“信仰是所需之物；有了信仰，本是弱小的殉难者可以愉快地忍受屈辱和十字架；没有宗教信仰，俗人通过自杀在繁华之中耗尽病态的存在。”（Sar.，159）工作来源于宗教信仰，两者因此可以等同。

卡莱尔所谓的工作也是英雄崇拜。他认为“*Laborare est Orare*，工作就是崇拜”（P. & P.，201）。英雄崇拜在卡莱尔看来是真理的主要内容。英雄崇拜与工作发生等同更加深刻地改变了工作的含义。人只要在工作便是进行英雄崇拜，因此便是在实现真理：

> “工作就是崇拜”：是的，在某种意义上的确如此［……］谁清楚地了解了这一点，谁就了解了整个未来的预言；这是最后的福音，其中包括其他所有的福音。其教堂的穹顶是无限的空间——你曾经见过：上面镶嵌着银河；铺着陆地和海洋绿色的马赛克；永恒的星座是祭坛！祈祷和赞美诗是崇高的行动、英雄主义的工作和忍耐，以及全人类中勇敢者发自内心的真正呼声。和声是古老的风声和海声，声音低沉，含混不清，却是命运和历史最真实的声音，同古时一样崇高。(230－231)

人只要在工作就是在进行英雄崇拜，而人进行英雄崇拜意味着社会以英雄崇拜为规范方式。卡莱尔真理所规定的应然社会形式由此实现。这样，工作还有实现社会过渡的作用。在此，卡莱尔的社会理想同他关于工作所持的观点联系在一起。他预言了一个以英雄崇拜为规范方式的社会形式的建立，而这样的社会形式通过人的工作而实现。

工作不是一个一次性的过程，而是一个连续性的过程。精神与物质之间存在矛盾。虽然物质是精神的表现形式，但是物质是暂时的、时间性的，而精神是永恒的、非时间性的。这意味着任何物质形式作为象征永远处于变化的过程之中。“因为所有的事物——甚至天上的发光体，还有大气状的流星——都具有兴起、高潮、衰亡的阶段。”（Sar.，225）物质的时间性决定任何象征都会经历新旧转变的过程。“然而，总体而言，就像时间给象征增添了神圣性，时间同样在流逝过程之中最终消灭、甚至将它们去神圣化；象征像所有凡间的衣服一样，变得陈旧。”（224）陈旧的象征不再是上帝意志的物质表现形式。此时上帝的意志需要全新的物质形式作为象征而得到表现。这样，工作的过程成为一个淘汰旧象征、产生新象征的连续过程。

卡莱尔根据工作的连续性对人的工作提出要求。在卡莱尔的思想体系之中，“从象征的形而上学思想演绎出责任的形而上学思想”。① 从象征的时间性可以推导出工作的连续性。因为象征的时间性，他认为人应该连续不断地、随时随地地进行工作。工作是一个具有连续性的过程，这决定人应该连续不断地工作：

> 农神，或者克若诺斯，或者我们叫作时间的东西，吞噬他所有的孩子：只有通过不断的奔跑，通过不断的工作，你才可以（在差不多七十年的时间里）逃脱他；最终他也会吞噬你。[……] 因此，这就是我们整个的责任，就是移动、工作——在正确的方向上。难道我们的身体和我们的灵魂不是处于连续的运动之中，无论我们愿意与否；处于持续的消耗之中，需要持续的修复？我们整个外在的、内在的需求的最终满足不过是一段时间内的满足而已；因此，我们完成的所有事情就是完成了，对于我们来说就此消灭了，我们永远都需要前进并重新开始。(127)

物质世界的时间性决定人的工作效果不会永远作为上帝的象征而存在。人的时间性决定人也不会永远作为上帝意志的实现者而存在。这样，人有必要连续不断地进行工作。工作作为一个具有连续性的过程进一步决定人应该随时随地地工作。卡莱尔认为：

> 然而，难道我们不能说，精神解放的时刻是这样的：当你的理想世界——在理想世界之中整个人一直都在模糊的挣扎并不言传地希望工作——得到启示、显现之时；你发现——带着足够的惊奇，就像《威廉·迈斯特》中的洛塔里奥一样——你的“美洲新大陆就在这里，或者哪里也没有”？没有责任、没有理想的情况从来没有被任何人遭遇过。是

① Barthèlemy, *Thomas Carlyle*, p. 158.

> 的，这里，你的理想就在这里，这贫穷、苦难、被束缚、可鄙的现实，你现在的处境，就在这里，不在别处：在现实之中实现你的理想；在实现的过程之中，相信、生活、获得自由。傻瓜！理想就存在于你本身，阻碍也存在于你本身：你的境况不过是你将实现同一理想所用的材料：只要你给予它的形式是具有英雄气的、是诗意的，这材料是这类或者那类又有什么意义？啊，如果你在现实的囚禁之中憔悴，如果你向神灵痛苦地哭泣，向他寻求一个可以统治和创造的王国，你应该知道这个真理：你所寻求的东西就在你的身上，“就在这里，或者哪里也没有”，你能看到该有多好！（196 – 197）

人是工作的主体，物质世界是工作的对象，任何地方都成为人工作的场所。因此，人应该随时随地地工作。

卡莱尔关于工作的观点来源于他所在的维多利亚社会。维多利亚社会是一个工业社会，工人问题被认为在其中是最为严重的社会问题。维多利亚时代“见证了英国在工业领域的崛起，英国成为‘世界工厂’。资本主义得到了自由的发展，并成功地建立起有利于新兴权利阶级——资产阶级——的政治、社会和经济制度。工业工人阶级——比欧洲的其他工人阶级数目更大，组织更好——对新秩序普遍强烈反对。卡莱尔的英格兰第一次感受到影响了劳动力的社会问题”。[①] 他主要将维多利亚社会问题归结为工作问题，并认为工作在工业社会之中受到了严重的阻碍。大量劳动力出现剩余，这是社会问题的集中表现：

> 不过，即使我们会怀疑，人的确在此；不是问问题，而是做工作：如果他的行动机能处于沉睡之中，并只有怀疑的询问发生作用，这就是最大的罪恶，在此时是这样，在所有时候都是这样。这样，无论谁看一看这个世界，将过去和现在进行对比，都会发现现在人的实践条件是最悲惨的；人处于痛苦之中，程度无与伦比。（Wks.，XXVIII，28）

① Schapiro，“Thomas Carlyle，Prophet of Fascism，” p. 99.

解决工作问题成为解决社会问题的关键。他进一步对人在维多利亚社会工作受到阻碍的根源进行探寻，并将工作问题产生的根源归咎于人没有发现上帝。他的具体论述如下：

> 并没有因为穷人的劳作我才感到悲伤：我们所有人都需要进行劳作，或者偷盗（无论我们如何命名我们的偷盗），这更加糟糕；没有忠诚的工人认为自己的任务是一个消遣。穷人忍饥挨饿；但是他依然拥有食物和水：他负重而疲劳；但是天堂也将睡眠——甚至是最深的睡眠——送给他；在他满是灰尘的茅屋里，湿润的困倦将他笼罩；还有美梦断断续续的闪光，但是我悲伤的内容是他的灵魂之灯竟然熄灭；他没有任何天上的或者甚至地上的知识；恐惧和不安就像两个幽灵在可怕的漆黑之中与他为伴。啊，他的身体宽大而黝黑，但是他的灵魂瞎了眼睛、聋了耳朵、变得愚蠢、几近消亡！啊，他的灵魂是上帝的呼吸；是来自天堂的馈赠，只是在凡间永远不会得到启示！——如果这种情况一分钟之内发生二十次，而且根据计算其的确如此，一个有获得知识能力的人竟然死于无知，我将这叫作悲剧。(Sar.，228 - 229)

人是上帝实现意志的手段。实现上帝的意志是人的责任。人没有发现上帝意味着人没有发现其与上帝之间召唤与服从的关系。这在卡莱尔看来是工作问题的根源所在。这样，工作问题的解决就变成了使人在物质世界之中发现上帝。

卡莱尔关于工作的观点以机械主义作为工作的规范方式为否定和批评对象。如前一章所述，维多利亚社会以功利主义为规范方式。物质生产领域主要奉行机械主义原则。人被安置在机械关系之中进行工作，结果造成了人的机械化。卡莱尔关于工作的观点主要以此为否定和批评对象。他以人与上帝之间的召唤与服从关系取代机械主义工作关系，并试图以此将人从机械化的工作关系之中解放出来。在他看来，工作来源于上帝的召唤，而非来源于机械主义：

> 所有的工作［……］是［……］真正的宗教性活动；工作没有宗教

> 就无法开展。以其他方式你无法工作［……］人以往完成的工作或者可以完成的工作都具有宗教性；即使是可怜的力工的工作、衣服的编织者、鞋的缝纫者的工作都具有宗教性。所有的人，如果他们没有在一个伟大的工头眼下工作，就会错误工作，对于他们自己和你都会不幸地工作。（P. & P.，206）

人的工作是人服从上帝召唤的结果，任何工作均对人与上帝之间的召唤与服从关系进行表现。工作只能来源于上帝，而不能来源于机械主义。

工作问题可以通过英雄崇拜得到解决。工作问题只是工业社会出现的社会问题，工作只有在工业社会之中才受到阻碍。与工业社会不同，工作在历史之中可以顺利进行。这样，工作问题的解决依赖于在历史之中发现工作的来源。工作在历史之中来源于英雄崇拜：

> 在以往的日子里，行动是简单、自发的，因为人的神圣价值为人所共知；思考是全面的，因为思考将自身列为行动的婢女；不能将自身列为行动婢女的思考在本质上就因为人的忽视而灭绝了。忠诚依然使得服从神圣，使得统治崇高；依然有些值得表示忠诚的对象：神圣的事物在人的利益和事务之中作为象征而得到表现；有限之物表现无限之物；在时间之中可以看到永恒。人的生活被天堂之光耀包围、笼罩，就像人的住处被蓝色的苍穹笼罩一样。（Wks.，XXⅧ，30）

可见，工作在历史之中来源于英雄崇拜。现时代被卡莱尔看作历史的延续。在这一认识基础之上，现实社会之中的工作可以通过英雄崇拜而实现。

卡莱尔关于工作的观点改变了工作的目的。维多利亚时代以功利主义为规范方式。物质生产的目的在于实现个人利益的最大化，结果造成了贫富之间差距的加深，并带来了无法解决的社会问题。卡莱尔的观点与此完全相反。他认为工作的目的并不在于实现个人利益的最大化。“幸福不是我们在这个世界上的最终目的。”（L. -J.，Ⅰ，12）他甚至认为实现上帝的意志比获得幸福更加重要，“没有人有权利请求幸福的获得，人可以没有幸福。有比幸福更加美好的东西”（Lec.，212）。工作由此成为人可以获得的唯一幸福。“一个好人可以劳烦自身请求的唯一幸福就是完成工作的幸福。[……] 幸福也好、不幸也罢，所有这些就是你的工钱；[……] 现在就工作，你的工作在哪里？快点，完成工作；让我们看看你的工作。”（P. & P.，157–158）最终，卡莱尔以人相对于上帝的责任取代个人的物质利益。以上帝意志的实现取代个人利益最大化的追求，这是他对功利主义作为衡量工作目的标准的批评和否定。

卡莱尔关于工作的观点也改变了工作的结构。功利主义在社会组织领域奉行自由主义。自由主义造成了统治阶级和被统治阶级之间的裂隙。两者之间进行关系维系的纽带发生了断裂。工人的生存状况异常恶化，工人运动不断爆发，社会开始瓦解。针对这一情况，卡莱尔认为统治阶级与被统治阶级之间同样存在召唤与服从的关系。普通人不能直接获得上帝的召唤，他们需要通过英雄作为中介才可以服从上帝的召唤。这样，统治阶级与被统治阶级之间的关系是英雄与普通人、被崇拜与服从之间的关系。事实上，他以英雄崇拜为模式对工作进行了重新建构。“我［狄奥根尼］敬重两类人，没有第三种。”（Sar.，227）第一种是普通人，他们主要进行物质性的工作，是“拿着在地球上做的工具勤奋地征服地球并将其变成人的地球的辛苦的工匠”（Ibid.）。物质性的工作具有重要的意义：

> 吃苦耐劳的兄弟！为了我们你的背如此弯曲，为了我们你笔直的腿和手指如此畸形：你是我们的征兵，任务落在你的身上，因为进行我们的斗争你才被如此毁坏。因为在你的身上也有一个上帝创造的形体，但是它并不能得到展现；它一定要同劳动紧密联系在一起，承受劳动的磨砺：你的身体就像你的灵魂一样，并不知道自由。然而，继续劳作，继续劳作：愿意就可以摆脱，但是你在履行你的责任；你为了完全不可缺少的、为了每日的面包而劳作。（227–228）

第二种是英雄，他们主要进行精神性的工作，因此，“我［狄奥根尼］敬重第二类人，而且更加敬重：我们看见他为了不可缺少的精神事物而劳作；不是为了日常面包、而是为了生命面包而劳作的人”（228）。精神性的工作具有更加重要的意义：

难道他不也在履行他的责任；尝试到达内在的和谐；无论高等还是低等，通过行动还是言语，通过他的外在尝试对此进行表现？当他的外在和内在尝试统一的时候，这就是最高等的情况：当我们叫他艺术家；不仅仅是凡间的工匠，而是受到启发的思想者，他以上天制作的工具为我们征服了天堂！如果可怜卑微之人的劳作给我们带来了食物，难道那高等荣耀之人不也为他而劳作吗，他由此才得到光明，得到引导、自由、不朽？（Ibid.）

工作涉及精神性的和物质性的两类工作。英雄和普通人承担不同的工作，两者都需要参与工作。卡莱尔特别强调精神性的工作需要同物质性的工作相互结合。物质性的工作需要以精神性的工作为基础，并对精神性的工作进行表现：

然而，当我发现两种高贵的品质联合在一起的时候，这是无法言说地令人感动；为了最为低等的人类需求而进行外在劳作的人，同时也为了最为高等的人类需求进行内在劳作。我不知道如果在任何地方这样的人可以遇见，我不知道在这个世界上还有什么能比一个农民圣人更加神圣的。这样的人会将你带回拿撒勒；你会看到天堂的光彩从地上最卑微的路上跳动出来，就像在黑暗之中闪耀的光一样。（Ibid.）

这样，工作过程最终成为英雄崇拜实现的过程。人在现实社会之中通过工作被纳入英雄崇拜的框架之内，卡莱尔以此实现了对工作的重新建构。

工作作为实现真理的手段决定人可以通过工作而实现真理。其实，卡莱尔对工作寄予了深切的希望，他认为：

你指给我一个实干的民族；他们喘着粗气、挣扎着、全力以赴；他们的心跳飞快，每一块肌肉都绷紧，带着人的能量和意志——我就指给你一个可以预言有所事事的民族；如果他们的努力可以继续，各种各样的功绩对于他们来说都是确定的。通过工作，他们会知道；他们同安泰一样，脚已经跨入了真理之门：他们一定可以知道的！（P. & P.，207）

卡莱尔进一步将真理的实现寄托在回归过去的状态之上。维多利亚时代是一个否认上帝存在的时代，也是一个不进行英雄崇拜的时代。这样的时代不能实现卡莱尔的真理。他认为只有回归过去的状态，真理才可以实现：

> 然而，这些实情，过去比现在更易感受。人类幼年时期的人们既有童稚般的新奇感，又有成年人的认真和深沉。他们不认为仅仅科学名词便可通晓天地万物，而是只能以敬畏和惊奇的神情直接凝视它们，他们更能感受人和自然中的神性——他们并非发狂而崇拜自然，而且崇拜人胜过自然中的其他任何事物。正如上述，崇拜就是无限敬仰，他们只要充分运用自己的官能和心灵的全部真诚，便能做到这一点。（H. & H.，11）

可见，人在历史之中可以在自然之中发现超自然因素，可以对英雄作为上帝召唤的获得者进行崇拜。这样，只有回归过去的状态，人就可以成为卡莱尔工作的主体。他们被认为可以实现真理的内容。

工作是上帝对人进行的召唤。非常明显，卡莱尔便是他笔下可以直接获得上帝召唤的英雄。他认为上帝通过物质世界作为象征对人进行召唤。人服从上帝的召唤聚集在象征周围从而象征社会。然而，并不是所有的象征都可以对上帝进行表现。"然而，我需要进一步对象征进行说明，它们具有外在的和内在的价值；大多数情况下仅仅具有前者。"（Sar.，222）这决定，大多数象征"没有内在的、必要神圣性，或者价值；而获得了外在价值"（223）。而仅仅少数象征才可以对上帝进行表现。只有具有内在价值的象征才可以成为社会建立的基础：

> 然而，当你的象征具有内在意义，并适合人在周围联合起来，这就是另外一件事情了。让神圣的事物向感官进行表现，让永恒或多或少看透时间形体（*Zeitbild*）！这样人在那里联合才合适；在这样的象征前一起进行崇拜；一天又一天，一个时代又一个时代，将新的神圣性添加在上面。（Ibid.）

人只能在具有内在价值象征的周围联合起来。这样，只有少数象征才是社会建立的基础。然而，普通人不能直接获得上帝的召唤。因此，普通人也就不能对象征进行区分。与此不同，英雄可以直接获得上帝的召唤。因此，英雄可以对象征进行区分。卡莱尔认为对旧象征和新象征的判断通过英雄得以实现：

> 因此，我们把他叫作教主、世界的教皇、诗人和受到启发的创造者；他就像普罗米修斯一样，可以塑造新的象征，将新的火焰从天堂带来，固定在那里。这样，我们就不会总是缺乏新的象征；也许我们现在也不缺乏新的象征。与此同时，随着事情的进展，我们把他看作立法者和智者，他可以判断什么时候一个象征变得陈旧，并轻轻地将之移除。(225)

非常明显，卡莱尔对新旧象征进行了区分。功利主义在他看来便是不能对上帝的意志进行表现的象征。社会不能建立在功利主义基础之上。英雄崇拜则是可以对上帝进行表现的象征。社会可以建立在英雄崇拜的基础之上。这样，卡莱尔成为他笔下的英雄。他直接获得了上帝的召唤，并传达给普通人。他呼唤普通人通过工作实现上帝的意志。

普通人也的确听从了作为英雄的卡莱尔的呼唤。工作在维多利亚时代变成流行词汇，“除了‘上帝’，维多利亚词汇中最受欢迎的词语就是‘工作’”。[①] 作为维多利亚社会流行词汇的工作是经过卡莱尔改造之后的工作。“他把他自己的不可调和的积极态度融汇在工作之中。他倡导工作的责任和崇高，非常具有说服力，使得闲散之徒不再闲散，轻浮之人以轻浮为耻。他以感动心灵的语调倡导我们在凡间真正的价值和幸福在于劳作，无论多么卑微。”[②] 工作在维多利亚社会不是简单的物质生产，而是人通过改造物质形式实现上帝意志的行动。“世俗背景下的工作是宗教信仰的对应物，工作的效力被认为是绝对可靠的教条。‘勤奋’和‘工作’在当时的词汇中是神圣的词语，两者所体现的道德效果被卡莱尔同信仰相等同，并被他提高为现实的第

① Houghton, *The Victorian Frame of Mind*, p. 242.

② Greg, “Kingsley and Carlyle,” p. 171.

十一条戒律。”① 卡莱尔的工作产生了深刻的影响。他本人成为一代人崇拜的英雄。其中的根源在于他迎合了他所在时代的思维方式。“当卡莱尔说‘人的目的不是一个思想而是一个行动’，他说出了一个一直以来对安格鲁－撒克逊种族都非常珍贵的思想，因为这个种族一直都短于思考而长于行动。”② 卡莱尔把握了安格鲁－撒克逊人的民族性格。他的思想符合他们的思维习惯。在此意义之上，他的确是值得崇拜的英雄。

卡莱尔关于工作的观点存在问题。总体而言，人在他的思想之中仅仅是一个手段而已，人是实现真理的手段，人存在的目的并不在于人本身，而在于人之外的真理。然而，人并不是手段，而是最终的目的。人本应该成为卡莱尔所谓的真理的最终目的。虽然这一真理的目的在于上帝的天堂之国在人间的实现，然而，天国的实现的最终目的其实还在于人的幸福。人可以在所谓的天国之中实现美好的生活。在此意义上，人是真理的目的。任何不以人为最终目的的理论都会给人造成巨大的伤害。作为手段的人甚至可以以牺牲生命为代价而实现某一目的。同样，为了实现卡莱尔所谓的真理、为了实现所谓的天堂之国，作为手段的人可以不惜生命而实现这一目的。这样的结局恐怕不是卡莱尔的愿望。

另外，卡莱尔主要通过实现真理激发人的工作，这样的做法也存在问题。工作的动机可以有很多。从生活的维持到习惯的决定、从家庭的建立到资本的增殖，所有这些都可以激发工作。卡莱尔激发人工作的方式非常特别。他认为工作产生于上帝与人之间召唤与服从的关系。工作的过程是上帝的意志获得表现的过程。工作的结果是真理的实现。这样，真理的实现最终成为人工作的动机。然而，真理的实现同普通人之间的距离非常遥远。他所谓的上帝甚至需要通过将物质看作精神才可以发现。所谓的天堂之国更是虚无缥缈。以实现真理作为动机而激发人的工作恐怕只能给工作的产生造成更大的障碍。

卡莱尔关于工作的观点同样具有一定的意义。工作的来源原本体现为多元性。所以，对任何一种因素作为工作来源的肯定以及对其他因素作为工作

① Altick, *Victorian People and Ideas*, p. 168.

② Mackenzie, “La Philosohie Contemporaine en Grande－Bretagne,” p. 595.

来源的忽视或者否定都会造成偏颇和错误。维多利亚社会奉行功利主义。个人利益的最大化成为工作的唯一来源。机械主义成为规范工作的制度。自由主义成为协调工作关系的原则。这样的做法是对单一因素的肯定。结果必然造成对其他因素的忽视和否定。卡莱尔关于工作的观点以此为批评和否定对象。他将宗教信仰看作工作的来源，将上帝意志的实现作为工作的目的，将英雄崇拜作为工作的关系。虽然他的做法是以一单一因素取代另一单一因素，但是他依然对单一因素作为工作来源提出了挑战。也许他没有最终实现工作来源的多元化，不过他的确做出某种改变的尝试。

第二节　工作与真理的实现

卡莱尔将工作看作实现真理的手段。真理的实现是上帝的意志获得物质表现形式的过程。在人的层面之上，这一过程对应于人的工作。工作也是精神因素获得物质表现形式的过程。卡莱尔以此将工作看作实现真理的手段。他认为“我们的工作是一面镜子，精神从中首先看到它的自然轮廓”（162）。他甚至认为人所有的工作都是对上帝意志的实现：

> 难道他所做的一切不都是具有象征含义的；不都是将人所具有的神秘的、上帝给予的力量对感官的表现；不都是“自由的福音书”，人是“自然的弥赛亚”，尽可能通过行动和言说进行布道？人所建造的一间茅屋都是一个思想的表现；其中含有对于不可见事物的记录；在超验意义上，是既具有象征含义又真实的。(220)

人所有的工作都是真理的实现的过程。这样，卡莱尔思想之中的工作不是简单的物质生产，而是真理的实现手段。

工作是上帝赋予人的责任。卡莱尔认为整个物质世界都是上帝的象征。“所有可见的事物都是象征。”（72）上帝通过物质世界作为象征对人进行召唤。“这样，人通过象征被引导和被命令，感到幸福或感到痛苦。”（220）人服从上帝的召唤。“无论有意识还是没有意识，人在象征中并通过象征生存、工作并获得存在。”（222）上帝召唤人进行工作。人需要对物质世界进行改造从而使之成为上帝的象征。因此,“人的使命是工作”(92)。工作则成为上帝赋予人的责任。“这也就是我们全部的责任,也就是[……]工作。”这样,人只要进行工作便是在履行上帝赋予的责任,便是在实现上帝的意志。工作作为上帝赋予人的责任来源于人作为上帝的象征而存在。上帝是全在的上帝。这样的上帝是“一个包括万物的大爱,既涵盖了天使、也涵盖了萤火虫”(Wks.,XXⅥ,424)。这样,人也是上帝的象征,也作为上帝的象征而存在。“无限世界存在于人。”(Sar.,190)在此意义上,人被认为是“飘浮在神圣天空中的光亮”(55),是“神圣的存在”(65)。人作为上帝的象征甚至表现在人的所有方面内容之上:

> 但是,如果我们现在不论见到什么事物都把它看作是至高无上的上帝对我们显示的象征,那么,我应当补充说人是比任何事物更主要的象征。人们知道圣·克里索斯托在谈到希伯来人的舍金纳或约柜即上帝显明的启示时有句名言:“真正的舍金纳是人!”是的,的确如此。这并非空话,而是真正符合实情。我们的本质,我们自称为“我”的内在奥秘——啊!用什么言辞来表达这些东西呢?——应该说是上帝的气息,是至高无上的上帝在人身上的显示。人的躯体、各种官能和生命,所有这一切不全是那无名之物的外罩吗?虔敬的诺瓦利斯说:“宇宙只有一座神殿,这就是人的躯体。没有比这崇高的形式更为神圣的东西。对人的膜拜就是对肉体中蕴含的天启表示崇敬,当我们把手放在一个人身上,也就是接触了上帝。”这些话听起来似乎只是华丽的辞藻,其实不然。只要认真思索,就会知道这本是科学的事实;这种言论表述揭示了事物实在的真理。我们是奇迹中的奇迹——上帝非常玄妙难测的奥秘。我们不能理解它,也不知道怎样表述它。但是,只要我们愿意,就能感知和体验,情况确实如此。(H. & H.,10-11)

人作为上帝的象征而存在,这深刻地改变了人的生命过程。卡莱尔认为人的生命过程是人履行上帝赋予责任、实现上帝的意志的过程。“如果你仔细考虑,人本身以及他整个的凡间生活不过是一个象征;是神圣自我的表现和可见衣服，他的神圣自我就像一个光子，从天堂送到人间。因此，我们才说他通过身体得到表现。”（Sar.，73）这样，人成为上帝的象征。人生命的意义在于上帝意志的实现。

工作的前提是人在物质世界之中看见上帝。虽然上帝通过物质世界作为象征对人进行召唤，但是人首先需要在物质世界之中看见上帝，卡莱尔认为：

> 自然同人的灵魂是一样的：创造的起初是——光。在眼睛获得视觉之前，整个肢体在捆绑之中。要有光！这句话被说起的时候——在人的被暴风雨折磨的灵魂之上，就像曾经在激荡翻滚的混沌之上——就是神圣的时刻。对于曾经感受到这一时刻的最伟大的人来说，这难道不是奇迹和上帝的宣告吗？对于最简单和最渺小的人来说，这也是奇迹和上帝的宣告，只是形式上比较简单罢了。疯狂的、原始的无序平息了；混杂的、相互冲突的元素组织在一起成为不同的天空：深深的、沉默的岩石基础在下面建造起来；穹顶带着永恒的光亮出现其上：不是一个黑暗的、废弃的混沌，我们有了一个美丽的、肥沃的、天堂环抱的世界。(197)

人需要首先在物质世界之中发现上帝的存在，之后才可以获得上帝的意志，从而进行工作，履行上帝赋予的责任。然而，人在物质世界之中发现上帝存在一定的困难。整个物质世界作为上帝的象征而存在。然而，象征既具有表现作用，又具有隐匿作用。一方面，物质世界是上帝的表现形式，这是表现作用；另一方面，物质世界具有本然形式，这是隐匿作用。这样，物质世界作为象征具有表现、隐匿双重作用：

> 象征奇妙的作用在于同隐匿不可估量的影响属于同类，同更加伟大的事情联系在一起。在象征之中既有隐匿又有启示；因此，在这里，通过缄默和言说的共同作用，一个双重意义得以实现。如果言说本身是高昂的，缄默又是合适的、崇高的，他们的联合多么有表现力！因此，在许多粉饰的器物，或者简单的象征封印中，最普遍的真理也会通过全新的着重得到宣扬。(219)

物质世界具有双重作用。这意味着物质世界一方面对上帝进行表现，另一方面又对上帝进行隐匿。象征的隐匿作用决定人不会直接发现所表现的上帝，而需要借助一定的手段才可以实现对于上帝的认识。

在物质世界之中发现上帝的手段是将物质看作精神。上帝是客观存在的精神。整个物质世界是这一客观精神存在的表现形式。人只有将整个物质世界看作精神才可以在其中发现上帝。“你真正的起点和天父在天堂之中，你以肉体之眼永远不会看到，你只有通过精神之眼才可以看到。”（86）卡莱尔将这样的认识方法叫作“精神之眼”，以及“纯粹理性之眼”和“哲学之眼”等，这些都是相对于“外在之眼”“低俗逻辑之眼”“凡人之眼”而言（65）。通过“精神之眼”，物质发生了巨大的变化。物质成为精神的表现。这样，将物质看作精神的人可以发现上帝的存在，因为——

> 物质创造不过是一个表象，一个典型的影子，其中神灵将自身表现给人。不可见的世界不但有真实性，而且是唯一的真实性：其他所有的一切不但在隐喻意义上，而且在文字意义和严格的科学意义上是“一个表现形式”；以诗人的话说，是 *Schall und Rauch umnebelnd Himmels Gluth*，即“遮盖了天堂光彩的喧嚣和烟尘”。不可见的世界就在我们周围；如果肉体的羁绊可以从灵魂上移除，那么不可见之物的光耀甚至现在就在我们周围；就像古人关于天界音乐的传说一样。因此，不但在语言上，而且在真理和信仰上，他感觉被上帝包围；在思想的每一个层面都感觉到，“在上帝之中他生活、移动并获得存在”。（Wks.，XXⅦ，27－28）

将物质看作精神即看到了作为精神而存在的上帝。因此，将物质看作精神的手段可以实现在物质世界之中发现上帝。卡莱尔将所谓的“精神之眼”叫作“有锐利观察力的眼光！正是这种观察力，揭示了事物内在和谐；揭示出大自然的蕴含，以及大自然包含在往往是粗糙外表中的音乐般的理念。大自然确实蕴含着某些重要的东西，对于锐利的观察力来说，某些东西是不难识别的”（H. & H.，105）。可见，所谓的“精神之眼”是可以看到上帝的方法。

卡莱尔主要将“精神之眼”应用于时间和空间。在他的思想之中，时间和空间是人和物质世界最基本的存在方式。人对于时间和空间的审视方式决定了人能否在物质世界之中发现上帝。“总体而言，我们关于永恒的概念［……］依赖于时间［和空间］的概念。”（Nt. B.，221－222）时间和空间表现为物质性。这样，人将时间和空间看作物质存在。因此，人没有在物质世界之中发现作为精神而存在的上帝。卡莱尔认为时间和空间的物质性造成了人认识上的失误。“但是，同样的空间，还有其兄弟时间，最初就是我们洞穴迷梦的制造者；或者不如说是帆布（上面的经纱和纬纱），我们所有的迷梦和生活视觉就画在上面。”（Sar.，55）这样，将物质看作精神的手段应用于时间和空间具有必要性。只有这样，人才可以在物质世界之中发现上帝。“时间是哲学最长久的内容，现代哲学已经取得了关于时间的伟大胜利。如果你相信根本就没有空间、没有时间，好多自相矛盾就会融合。”（Nt. B.，222）如果将时间和空间看作精神，人就可以在物质世界之中发现上帝。所谓的将时间和空间看作精神指将两者看作上帝的创造：

> 如果时间和空间在我们头脑之外没有绝对的存在，那么我们神学的门槛上就移除掉了一个羁绊的阻碍。因为在此基础之上，当我们说神灵是全在的、永恒的，说对于上帝而言空间和时间是普遍的空间和时间，我们并没有说出什么神奇的东西：我们只是说他同样创造了时间和空间，时间和空间不是上帝存在的法则，而仅仅是我们存在的法则。［……］自然起源和存在的整个问题一定会得到极大的简化：物质的旧有敌意就此结束，因为物质本身被消除了，而那黑色的幽灵，即无神论，“带着它令人作呕的露水”，永远化为无物。（Wks.，XXVII，26）

时间和空间同是上帝的创造，同样具有精神性。两者可以作为精神而看待。人看到时间和空间的精神性意味着人看到了上帝的创造。这样，人最终发现上帝的存在。“当观察者站在神圣的无限空间和永恒时间之上的时候，他们就可以辨别［上帝的存在］了：所有的民族都认为他们的上帝是普遍存在的、永恒的，存在于普遍的空间、永恒的时间之中。”（Sar.，55）最终，将时间和空间看作精神实现了在物质世界之中发现上帝。

时间和空间都是精神存在。在卡莱尔看来，时间和空间并不是物质存在。两者依赖于人的精神，都是人精神的产物。“空间和时间同我们的思想神秘地联系在一起，不过是思想表面的、人间的依附而已［……］仔细想一想，你也会发现，空间不过是我们人类感官的一种方式，时间同样如此；没有空间，也没有时间。”（Ibid.）时间和空间依赖于人的精神而存在。因此，两者具有精神性。事实上，卡莱尔以极端的灵实论看待时间和空间。两者对于他而言甚至只是人精神的某种存在方式。“时间和空间不是外在的实体、而是内在的实体：它们没有外在的存在，在意识之外既没有时间，也没有空间；它们只是人精神存在的形式而已，只是人的思考本质所遵循的法则而已。”（Wks.，XXⅦ，25－26）在这样的极端的灵实论之中，时间和空间甚至只作为人的认识方式而存在。两者完全依赖于人的精神，脱离精神时间和空间都不可能存在。

卡莱尔最终实现了在物质世界之中发现上帝。时间和空间都是精神存在，人看到了时间和空间即看到了作为客观精神而存在的上帝，他认为：

> 抛弃掉时间的幻觉；如果你有眼睛，你就可以从近处的运动看到远处的制动者：那来自整个一系列弹球的动力，如果最后一个球只是被弹一下、飞出去了，这动力就不是动力了吗？啊，如果我可以（带着消除时间［和空间］的帽子）将你从起点直接带到终点，你的眼睛就会开启，你的心会在神圣奇妙的光海中燃烧！你会看到这个美丽的宇宙，即使只是其中最为贫穷的部分，其实就是布满星星的上帝之城；上帝的荣耀通过每一颗星星、通过每一片草叶、通过每一个活着的灵魂发出光亮。但是，自然这上帝的时间衣服，向聪明人启示上帝，把上帝从愚蠢人的眼睛中隐藏起来。（Sar.，264）

上帝创造了整个物质世界，这样，人通过将物质看作精神甚至可以在物质世界的任何地方看到上帝的存在：

> 你可知道世界的任何角落，那里没有力量？你从你潮湿的手上抖落

> 的水滴，并没有留在它掉落的地方，而在明天你发现它已经被移动了；已经乘着北风的翅膀，正在靠近北回归线。水滴怎么可以蒸发，而不是静止地留在原地？你认为所有的一切都是静止的；没有力量，完全死寂的？（71）

在这样的世界里，人只要睁开眼睛便可以看到上帝的存在。“如果我们能够放开思路和视野，不是也能通过每一颗星，通过每一片草叶看见上帝吗？［……］每一物体中都有一种神圣的美，每一物体缺失仍是‘一个可以窥见无限本身的窗口’。”（H. & H.，10）最终，卡莱尔通过这种极端的认识方式实现了在物质世界之中看见上帝。

人在物质世界之中发现上帝对于卡莱尔而言更意味着人发现与上帝之间的关系。人是上帝的象征。上帝通过物质世界作为象征对人进行召唤。在此意义之上，人在物质世界之中发现上帝更意味着人发现人是上帝的象征。在此，物质世界是人与上帝之间的中介。一方面，上帝通过物质世界对人进行召唤；另一方面，人对物质世界进行改造从而使其成为上帝的表现形式。卡莱尔对物质世界的中介作用进行了进一步的具体说明：

> 物质仅仅作为现象而获得存在：如果我们不在那里，物质就不会在那里；物质仅仅是一个关系，或者更是我们的灵魂同伟大的第一动力之间关系的结果；其表现品质决定于我们的身体和精神器官；物质本身没有内在的品质，是——这个词的普通含义——无物。树是绿色的、是坚硬的，这并不是自身自然品质的结果，而仅仅因为我的眼睛和我的手具有这样的构造，可以在这样那样的条件下发现这样那样的表现。［……］事实上，那里［……］没有树；只有某个不是我的力量的表现。所有物质自然，整个可见的宇宙，还有其中的运动、图形、事件和品质的情况同样如此；所有的一切都是某个与我不一样的东西给我造成的印象。（Wks.，XXVII，24－25）

物质世界不过是人与上帝之间的中介，本身并没有存在意义。物质世界作为上帝的象征存在的唯一意义在于向人表现上帝的存在。

最后，人通过在物质世界之中发现上帝而进行工作。上帝通过物质世界作为象征对人进行召唤，人服从上帝的召唤而对物质世界进行改造。这样，人在物质世界之中发现上帝的最终目的在于实现工作。“［一个人的存在］不但要转化为一个思想，还要转化为一个行动。”（Sar.，143）人是上帝意志实现的手段，这只有通过工作才可以得到实现，因此，卡莱尔将工作看作人的最终目的，“人的目的在于行动，而不在于思想”（Sar.，155）。上帝的意志通过人的工作获得其物质表现形式。最终，真理也在这一过程之中得到实现。

结　论

卡莱尔的真理观具有一段复杂的发展史。真理观的形成与确立与他的生平之间具有紧密的关联。他出生于具有浓郁加尔文主义思想氛围的家庭环境。父母未经理性检验过的信仰直接被幼时的他接受，不但是他行为的准则，更是他观察一切外在对象的视角。卡莱尔所接受的加尔文主义信仰以直接承认上帝存在的合理性为基础。这一点进一步转化为对虔敬的强调。对物质世界进行改造、使之成为上帝意志的表现被认为是检验信仰的标准。总体而言，上帝的存在是这一真理的核心内容。

卡莱尔的真理观与他所接受的启蒙教育出现冲突。卡莱尔所接受的教育，特别是大学教育，具有强烈的启蒙特征。数学、哲学、逻辑学以及矿物学等学问的积累和增加极大地养成了他的理性思维。理性要求一切逻辑推理有必要建立在第一原则基础之上，而根据启蒙传统，尤其是根据英国经验主义哲学传统，第一原则是可以被感官感知的物质因素。在理性原则视角下，上帝的存在在合理性方面出现严重的问题。非常明显，上帝的存在不能被感官感知。这样，卡莱尔的信仰发生了严重的危机。在此，他将信仰问题转化为知识问题。上帝的存在在他看来不是一个简单的相信上帝存在的问题，而更是获得上帝存在的知识的问题。在这一认识基础之上，他主要以认识的手段实现信仰的目的。这也是他真理观的最大特征。

德国思想研究对于卡莱尔全新的真理观的建立具有重要的意义。从放弃法律学习到定居伦敦，卡莱尔经历了漫长的德国思想研究阶段。这一时期是他的精神发展史最为重要的阶段。他首先接触了席勒、歌德、里希特、施莱格尔兄弟和诺瓦利斯等德国古典文学家和浪漫派的作品。其中，特别是歌德的思想为他实现信仰的恢复提供了大量的思想要素。在德国文学作品的解读过程中，他认识到哲学研究的必要性和意义。他先后研究了康德、赫尔德、费希特和谢林等哲学家的思想。超验唯心论，特别是康德的时空唯心性学说和费希特的文人理论，是他最为主要的借鉴思想。在德国思想资源之中，卡莱尔接受了大量具有灵实论的内容。这些思想被认为对于实现上帝存在的物质证明具有重要的辩护作用。他全新的真理观融入有大量的德国思想因素。然而，研究目的严重影响了他哲学研究的精度。知识被简单地等同于信仰。卡莱尔真理观的主要特征再一次表现出来。

卡莱尔全新的真理观融入有加尔文主义思想、启蒙思想和德国思想等要素。所有这些内容汇聚在一起，共同塑造了他的真理观。总体而言，卡莱尔的真理观可以区分出实然和应然两个部分。实然真理是对对象的描述和再现。在实然的真理中，卡莱尔描述了一个物质普遍对精神进行表现的世界结构。这其实也是灵实论思想在本体论方面的应用和推广。在此基础之上，万事万物被认为是上帝的物质表现。卡莱尔的“衣服哲学”和“自然超自然论”等理论可谓这一思想的体现。卡莱尔未能对灵实论思想进行合理的证明。他主要从认识论角度证明物质作为精神的载体，从而混淆了认识论和本体论。可见，他的真理观在逻辑起点上具有强烈的非理性特征。

在应然的真理中，卡莱尔主要将实然真理所描述的世界结构设计为应然状态。在此，知识被转为法则。真理不是简单的知识，而是成为具有强烈必然性的上帝的意志。在此设计中，真理成为外部世界的规范原则。外部世界不但有必要遵从真理的规定，还需要在不符合真理规定的条件下转而满足真理的要求。然而，知识，特别是真理在卡莱尔看来具有强烈的隐匿性。除非是少数的类似于上帝的选民的杰出人士，否则真理不对大众开放。这导致应然的真理的实现有必要借助于少数的中介。这便是卡莱尔的英雄崇拜理论的来源。

英雄崇拜理论是卡莱尔真理观的集中体现。这一理论一方面有现实依据。卡莱尔在大学毕业后便开始对现实社会进行观察。他看到一个统治阶级严重失责的社会现状。英雄崇拜理论中的某些内容，便以社会现实为针对和否定对象。这一理论一方面有制度依据。维多利亚社会是一个以功利主义为规范方式的社会。功利主义将快乐的获得和痛苦的避免看作人行动的来源。这在卡莱尔看来造成了严重的制度问题。英雄崇拜在很大程度上是对功利主义的替代。卡莱尔首先赋予英雄崇拜以历史的维度，认为是历史发展的要求。他进而对英雄的品质进行认识。认为英雄是少数可以获得上帝意志的杰出人士。最终，英雄成为人与上帝之间的中介。英雄崇拜由此获得合理性上的辩护。在卡莱尔所列出的英雄谱系之中，文人英雄同样是崇拜对象。这一设计在很大程度上来源于他将文学（以及诗）看作是认识真理的手段。文人作为英雄、作为崇拜的对象，在很大程度上是卡莱尔对自身地位的评估。

卡莱尔主要从历史角度对英雄崇拜理论进行理解。他首先将全部历史归结为英雄史。历史事件发生时的属性与人认识方式的属性之间存在矛盾。这样，历史写作的选择性是必要的。卡莱尔主要选择那些历史发展的要求没有被满足的时刻。在这样的时刻里，英雄崇拜作为历史发展的要求表现出来。他进一步将社会发展纳入历史发展。社会发展在他看来是历史发展的最新阶段。社会发展一段时间符合、一段时间不符合历史发展要求的模式是卡莱尔历史发展规律的主要内容。现实社会被认为不符合历史发展的要求和处于符合历史发展要求的过渡之中。卡莱尔以此对现实社会进行预言，认为现实社会终将符合历史发展的要求。卡莱尔的历史观以时间的连续性和人存在的时间性为基础。人存在的时间性被进一步转化为历史性。这样，历史成为认识和理解人的根本属性。总体而言，卡莱尔的历史观具有强烈的历史主义特征。历史性被认为是所有的一切的基本属性。历史由此成为解释的角度。卡莱尔的历史观同样具有强烈的历史决定论特征。实现预言是他历史观的主要内容。他主要预言了一个符合英雄崇拜要求的未来格局。

卡莱尔的社会研究是英雄崇拜理论在社会领域的应用和推广。在卡莱尔的认识中，贫富差距问题和机械化问题是社会问题的集中表现。两个问题造成了严重的后果。维多利亚社会被认为处于瓦解的过程之中。在社会批评中，卡莱尔主要将功利主义作为否定对象。功利主义过分强调人的物质因素，从而忽视精神因素，特别是忽视人的信仰。这在卡莱尔看来是一切问题的根源所在。他认为功利主义不能作为现实社会的规范方式，英雄崇拜应该取而代之。在社会领域，英雄崇拜的实现具有必然性。一个以英雄崇拜为规范方式的社会终将建立起来。

工作是真理实现的手段。卡莱尔所谓的工作是人对物质世界进行改造，使之成为上帝的物质象征的过程。在此意义上，工作与崇拜等同。由此，工作成为英雄崇拜的表现。这样，人只要在工作便是在进行英雄崇拜。卡莱尔对这样的工作寄予厚望。他认为工作是上帝对人的召唤，是上帝赋予人的使命。人实现这种具有神性特征的工作的前提是认识。人有必要首先在物质世界之中认识到上帝的存在，之后再将认识转化为实际行动。他甚至在工业社会之中发现这种工作已经实现的迹象。工人在工头的指挥下进行工作，这被认为是现代英雄崇拜实现的形式。

以上便是卡莱尔真理观的全貌。总体而言，卡莱尔并没有对纯粹的知识产生兴趣。他所谓的知识在内容上并没有建立在全新的现象的观察基础之上。相反，知识不过是旧有的信仰内容的再现而已。这是对知识的背叛。与此相对应，卡莱尔求知的方法同样存在问题。因为他的最终目的并不是求知，所以他在很大程度上以求知的虔敬替代了求知本身。在他的理解里，求知态度上的虔敬便是知识获得的标志。这样的认识在很大程度上不过将信仰直接移植到知识领域。卡莱尔式的真理的结果可想而知。所有的知识将被信仰取代。在此意义上，他更是一个先知，而不是学者。

卡莱尔从历史的角度对知识的合理性进行论证的做法同样存在问题。知识的合理性并非来源于历史。如果是真正意义上的知识的话，知识具有强烈的普遍性、必然性和确定性，具有极强的描述力、解释力和预见力。就像万有引力定律一样，知识的合理性不在于历史，而在于知识本身。从历史的角度对知识的合理性进行论证，这是对真理的效力没有信心的表现。真正意义上的真理将接受，而且将承受得起所有事实的检验。很明显，这种历史的做法不但是多余的，而且是不可靠的。

即使这样，卡莱尔的真理观依然有其意义。他的真理并不是一个简单的知识体系。真理的背后是强烈的现实意识。真理所构建的理想对应于一个存在严重问题的现实社会。如果抛开卡莱尔式的真理中所有的不合理内容，那么他的真理观的最大意义在于从某一个方面诠释出一个真实的、历史的维多利亚社会的面貌。这是一个处于工业化过程之中的社会。各种各样的社会问题突如其来。卡莱尔也许在求知方面存在各种局限，不过在社会观察方面拥有着无限的潜能。他所看到的社会现状不但在当时具有警醒意义，于今日的发展同样具有一定程度上的借鉴作用。可以说，在新知不能获得的前提下，认清旧有知识体系的问题同样具有意义。卡莱尔真理观的意义便在于此。

“合上你的拜伦，打开你的歌德”，这是卡莱尔的名言。他本人的作品何时能被现代人打开，这一问题颇有魅力。

附录一　卡莱尔的社会批评思想对《荒凉山庄》的影响[①]

在维多利亚时代的作家之中，卡莱尔和狄更斯构成极为典型的师徒关系。在他们于1840年首次相见之际，[②] 卡莱尔已颇赋名望，向“切尔西的圣贤”稳步靠近，[③] 而狄更斯已经开始他的文学生涯，因《匹克威克外传》［《匹》］（*Pickwick*，1837）、《雾都孤儿》［《雾》］（*Oliver Twist*，1838）和《尼古拉斯·尼克贝》［《尼》］（*Nicholas Nickleby*，1839）等作品而声名鹊起。狄更斯“对卡莱尔的敬佩与年俱增”，“在人生的后半期最钦佩、最瞩目他”，希望他成为《圣诞颂歌》（*A Christmas Carol*，1943）的首位读者。[④] 《艰难时世》［《艰》］（*Hard Times*，1854），这部“最具‘卡莱尔特色的’小说”，[⑤] 被题献给他。“我想在首页写下，本书题献给托马斯·卡莱尔。”[⑥] 虽然这一行为有“职业发展”的考虑，但是“强烈的个人感激之情”鲜明可见。[⑦] 在“爱德华·爱（Edward Eyre）事件”的争论中，他拥护卡莱尔的立场，并成为

---

① 本文曾以《卡莱尔的社会批评思想对〈荒凉山庄〉的影响——卡莱尔和狄更斯结构批评研究》为题发表于《语言教育》2019 年第 1 期，第 86—91 页。

② Christian，“Carlyle's Influence upon the Social Theory of Dickens（Part One：Their Personal Relationship），” p. 28.

③ Tennyson，*A Carlyle Reader*，Intro.，p. xiii.

④ Froude，*Life in London*，Vol. Ⅰ，p. 236；Vol. Ⅱ，p. 137.

⑤ Storey，*Dickens*：*Bleak House*，p. 11.

⑥ Dickens，*Selected Letters*，pp. 278－279.

⑦ Kaplan，*Dickens*，p. 91.

“辩护委员会”的一员。① 卡莱尔在初次见面时即对这位后辈怀有好感。② 虽然他对虚构类文学作品持怀疑和批评立场，但是《双城记》［《双》］（*A Tale of Two Cities*，1859）仍被认为是一部“杰作”（Let.[3]，Ⅱ，205）。对于狄更斯的去世（9th Jun. 1870），他表示深切的哀悼，认为意味着“所有民族快乐”的“消失”。③

在社会观点方面，狄更斯受卡莱尔的影响最为深刻。卡莱尔可谓“狄更斯最大的思想影响”。④ 这一影响开始于 19 世纪 30 年代，在 40 年代变得明显。⑤ 在社会改革问题上，狄更斯仅接受过边沁（Jeremy Bentham）和卡莱尔二人的观点。⑥ 他初期相信“功利主义的普遍原则”，认为“社会改革可通过制度改革实现”，⑦ 后接受卡莱尔的批判态度，将功利主义看作“算计的、决定论的、机械论的”，⑧ 无法实现社会问题的解决。特别是功利主义“将所有的关系归结为个人利益”“自由主义”作为唯一的经济运营模式以及将“工资体系建立在统计学基础之上并仅由市场控制”等做法，甚为诟病。⑨ 放弃功利主义原则，堪称狄更斯思想发展史上最为重要的事件。此后，他在议会改革、权力重组、教育、卫生和移民等方面全面接受卡莱尔的相关主张。⑩

在狄更斯以社会批评为主题的小说之中，卡莱尔的影响清晰可见。“狄更斯对卡莱尔社会理论的依赖”，甚至贯穿“从《雾》到《德鲁德疑案》（*The Mystery of Edwin Drood*，1870）”的全部写作过程。⑪《匹》、《雾》和《尼》等早期作品虽然创作于他们相见之前，但是卡莱尔在《伏尔泰》、《时代的标记》、《特征》、《旧衣新裁》和《法国大革命史》［《革命》］等作品中的社会

① Kaplan，*Dickens.*，p. 481.
② Kaplan，*Thomas Carlyle*，pp. 260 – 261.
③ Shepherd，*Memoirs*，Vol. Ⅱ，p. 292.
④ Storey，op. cit.，p. 2.
⑤ Oddie，*Carlyle and Dickens*，p. 5.
⑥ Engel，*The Maturity of Dickens*，p. 172.
⑦ Goldberg，“From Bentham to Carlyle，” p. 62.
⑧ Storey，op. cit.，p. 2.
⑨ Storey，op. cit.，p. 2.
⑩ Cf. Goldberg，“From Bentham to Carlyle，” pp. 64 – 69.
⑪ Tarr，“The ‘Foreign Philanthropy Question’ in *Bleak House*，” p. 275.

理念在其中有明显的体现。[1]《艰》虽然在“结构”上未见“卡莱尔的影响”，不过对理性主义的批判这一主题来源于“这位时代最重要的反理性主义者”。[2]《双》与《革命》在主题上极为相似。“在制度与人文目的不相符合的时代对个人能力社会化方式的探寻”，[3] 贯穿两部风格迥异的作品。包括《荒凉山庄》[《荒》]（*Bleak House*，1853）和《小杜丽》（*Little Dorrit*，1857）在内，卡莱尔社会观点的影响体现在所有这些晚期小说作品之中。[4] 与卡莱尔一样，“社会批评”同样构成狄更斯晚期作品最为主要的主题之一。[5]

《荒》是狄更斯晚期作品中最为重要的一部。相关创作构想产生于1851年。[6] 同年的通信中（to Mary Boyle，21st Feb.）提到，“一个全新故事的某些影子已经以诡异的方式萦绕于我周围”。[7] 此后，狄更斯在致友人信件中多次提到创作过程。[8]《荒》于1852年3月至1853年9月连载，[9] 1853年以书的形式出版。虽然狄更斯本人持保守态度，认为与《大卫·科波菲尔》（*David Copperfield*，1850）相比，《荒》在人物塑造上远远不及，[10] 而且时论亦多贬低、诟病和指责之词，[11] 但是无论在主题设计还是在谋篇布局，无论在人物塑造还是在叙事多样化等方面，《荒》均具有极强的解释潜力，甚至堪称狄更斯最为优秀的小说作品。[12]

在主题上，《荒》明显地体现了卡莱尔的影响。创作期间，狄更斯反复阅读《革命》，甚至“无论走到哪里都怀揣一册”。[13] “这部神奇的作品”，他

---

① Christian，“Carlyle's Influence upon the Social Theory of Dickens（Part Two：Their Literary Relationship），” p. 11.

② Oddie，op. cit.，pp. 42，41.

③ Marcus，“The Carlylean Vision of *A Tale of Two Cities*，” p. 56.

④ Christian，op. cit.，p. 17.

⑤ Johnson，*Charles Dickens*，p. 342.

⑥ Forster，*The Life of Charles Dickens*，Vol. Ⅱ，p. 118.

⑦ Dickens，op. cit.，p. 227.

⑧ Cf. Dickens，*Bleak House*，pp. 885 – 889；*Selected Letters*，pp. 248，259.

⑨ Cf. Dickens，*Bleak House*，pp. 885 – 886.

⑩ Forster，op. cit.，Vol. Ⅱ，pp. 127 – 128.

⑪ Collins，*Charles Dickens*，pp. 275，281，283 – 284，287 – 289，297 – 298，298 – 299.

⑫ Storey，op. cit.，p. 17.

⑬ Froude，op. cit.，Vol. Ⅰ，p. 80.

"再次阅读一遍，这已经是第500次了"。[①] 虽然这样的说法有夸张之嫌，但是他对《革命》的推崇毋庸置疑。《革命》强烈地影响了《荒》的主题。与《革命》一样，《荒》"描述了社会制度从旧向新"这一"社会和经济权利结构的转变"。[②] 此外，对"海外人道主义计划无情的讽刺"，是《荒》中另外一个明显的卡莱尔式的主题。其程度堪与"卡莱尔在《黑人问题》（'The Nigger Question,' 1949）中对约翰·罗素勋爵援助西印度群岛黑人计划的抗议"媲美。[③]《荒》中"对杰利比夫人（Mrs. Jellyby）和帕迪戈尔夫人（Mrs. Pardiggle）的具有讽刺性的描写"，是"最鲜明影响"的体现。[④] 最后，对"无为主义"（dilettantism）的批评，是另外一个借鉴主题。[⑤] 狄更斯对戴德洛克爵士和夫人（Sir & Mrs. Dedlock）的批评，[⑥] 与卡莱尔对"贵族沦落为享乐派"所持的观点极为相似。[⑦] 总体而言，《荒》是狄更斯紧承卡莱尔"控诉英格兰今夕现状的苦难"这一主题，对"功利主义价值观"的"具有启示性的回应"。[⑧]

在《荒》中，卡莱尔的影响不仅仅体现在批评主题，更表现在批评结构之上。卡莱尔的社会批评除主题批评（thematic criticism）之外，还有结构批评（structural criticism）这一层次。结构批评建立在卡莱尔的社会结构构想之上。社会在结构上被分为本质（essence）和表现（appearance）两方面内容。社会本质决定社会表象，而社会表象对社会本质进行表现。社会表象对社会本质的表现程度，决定一个社会的运行状况。社会批评主要以社会表象与社会本质之间出现的裂隙与分歧为对象，以实现两者的弥合和对接为目的。总体而言，结构批评是主题批评的基础和前提，主题批评是结构批评在某一方面的具体体现。卡莱尔式的结构批评被狄更斯借鉴，表现在《荒》的社会批评之中。

---

① Forster, op. cit., Vol. Ⅱ, p. 72.

② Arac, "Narrative Form and Social Sense in *Bleak House* and *The French Revolution*," p. 59.

③ Christian, op. cit., pp. 17, 18.

④ Tarr, op. cit., p. 276.

⑤ Christian, op. cit., p. 18.

⑥ Christian, op. cit., p. 18.

⑦ Goldberg, op. cit., p. 65.

⑧ MacKenzie, *Dickens*, p. 248.

本文以卡莱尔和狄更斯的结构批评为研究对象，分两部分。其一，研究卡莱尔式的结构批评，其二，研究《荒》中的结构批评。

一　卡莱尔的结构批评

卡莱尔式的结构批评，以他的社会结构构想为基础。他对社会结构的理解，具有极强的拟人论（anthropomorphism）特征。社会被类比为人的身体，是一个机体性的（organic）结构。如果“政府”构成“外在的皮肤”，“工艺协会”以及“联盟”等机构是“肌肉和骨骼组织”，那么“宗教”则是“最内在的心包和神经组织”（Sar.，216）。在此，社会被分为内外两方面。与人的身体一样，社会的内外构成具有不同的作用。“若没有［心包和神经组织］”，“（工业的）骨骼和肌肉就无法活动，只有通过电流的刺激才表现出生气；皮肤就会变成枯萎的皮毛，或是快速腐烂的生皮”（Ibid.）。可见，社会的内在构成起主导作用，外在构成仅起辅助作用。

社会内外构成作用的不同，决定两者地位的不同。具有主导作用的内在构成，被认为是社会的本质。这一点明显地表现在宗教对于社会的生成（generation）所具有的作用之上。“只有通过宗教，社会才变得可能。”（215）“只有通过仰望天堂……我们所谓的……社会等才可以实现。”（214）非常明显，宗教是社会之所以成为社会的根源所在。在决定社会的生成这一意义上，社会内在构成是社会的本质。与此相对，社会外在构成因不具有主导作用，故不对社会的生成产生影响。包括所有社会机构在内的外在构成，作为社会的表象而存在。

社会的外在表象和内在本质处于表现和被表现的关系之中。这一表现与被表现关系在《特征》中有详细的论述。在社会“无意识状态”（Unconsciousness）的论说中，卡莱尔指出：

> 任何社会、任何政体都有一个精神原则；是一个理念具有尝试性的，或者多少完备的表现：其所有的行动取向、风俗特征、法律、政治以及程序……均由这一理念决定，从中自然发展而来，就像运动从动力源产生出来一样。（Wks.，XXⅧ，13－14）

社会在外表现为“行动取向、风俗特征、法律、政治以及程序”等，在内则表现为“精神原则”。前者是后者的“表现”，两者之间的关系可以类比为“运动”和“动力源”之间的关系。非常明显，这是社会的外在表象和内在本质之间的表现和被表现关系。

社会的外在表象和内在本质之间表现和被表现的关系，对于理解卡莱尔的结构批评具有重要意义。首先，这种关系决定了现实（actual）社会的理想状态。当外在表象完全表现内在本质时，即当外在表象与内在本质一致时，现实社会处于理想状态。对于社会理想状态的界定，卡莱尔的认识有一个变化的过程。如上所述，宗教被看作社会的内在本质。现实社会的理想状态是与宗教相一致。在此意义上，“任何可以想象的社会……可以看作一座教堂”（Sar.，215）。至演说集《论历史上的英雄、英雄崇拜和英雄业绩》出版，宗教被理解为“英雄崇拜”。“信仰是对某个有灵感的导师，对某个高尚的英雄表示的忠诚。”（H. & H.，12）据此，与英雄崇拜相一致，是现实社会的理想状态。“任何地方的社会都是英雄崇拜……有等级的表现。”（14）这一认识上的变化并无前后矛盾。宗教和英雄崇拜之间存在一定的关系。“[英雄崇拜]是宗教的基础，不仅异教如此，而且……一切宗教，都是如此。”（11）可见，英雄崇拜是宗教的深化。总体而言，现实社会的理想状态是与宗教相一致，作为宗教的完全表现而存在。

另外，这种关系决定了现实社会可能状态的范围。如果理想状态是现实社会可能状态的上限，那么下限则是外在表象与内在本质完全不一致的状态。若以“危机状态”称之，则现实社会的可能状态处于从理想状态到危机状态的范围之间，即：

现实社会 = [理想状态，危机状态]

然而，卡莱尔并不认为现实社会可以处于理想状态。“不完美的人类社会”只能是“完美的某些接近”而已（P. & P.，26）。相对于理想状态，现实社会只能接近（approximation），而无法实现（realization）。这样，理想状态对于现实社会而言永远是封闭的。理想状态不在现实社会可能状态的范围之内，即：

现实社会 = （理想状态，危机状态]

现实社会永远不能与宗教或者英雄崇拜相一致，而只能处于无限接近两者的过程之中。这是一个现实社会无限接近理想状态的张力性（tensional）社会发展模式。

现实社会对于理想状态的接近程度（degree of approximation），是卡莱尔社会批评的对象。现实社会对于理想状态的接近，有程度上的区别。概而言之，接近可分为两类。其一为“可忍受”（supportable），其二为“不可忍受”（Ibid.）。接近程度与可容忍程度成正比，即

$$接近程度 \propto 可容忍程度$$

接近程度高，则可容忍程度高。反之亦然。社会的存亡决定于可容忍的程度。“人面对可忍受的接近可以保持耐心”，但是如若发展到“不可忍受的阶段”，则“国家本身在走向自杀性的死亡”（Ibid.）。在可容忍的范围内，社会可以保全。超越可忍受而进入不可忍受的范围，则社会瓦解。在不可忍受的范围内，大规模的社会危机爆发。“曼切斯特起义、法国大革命以及成千上万的大小现象，急声宣告有必要提升［外在表象的接近程度］。”（27）可见，在卡莱尔对社会危机现象观察和批评的背后，存在他对社会理想状况的企望。

卡莱尔结构批评的主要内容在以上分析中表现出来。总体而言，结构批评以社会的理想状况为依据（ⅰ），对现实社会的实际状况进行考察（ⅱ），主要对现实社会接近程度低于可忍受范围的危机情况进行批评和否定（ⅲ），以实现接近程度的不断提升为最终目的（ⅳ）。非常明显，与通常的平面式的社会批评模式相比，卡莱尔的结构批评不仅对社会的现实情况进行考察（ⅱ）以及对危机状况进行否定和批评（ⅲ），其中还有社会理想状态的探讨（ⅰ）和社会发展终极目的的实现（ⅳ）等维度的存在。简而言之，这是一个以理想（ideality）为依据、对现实（actuality）进行考察的张力性批评结构。理想与现实之间的张力性（tensionality），是卡莱尔结构批评的主要特征。

卡莱尔的结构批评并非仅仅停留在理想与现实之间的张力性结构之上，而是进一步以实在性（reality）对两者进行理解。理想被认为是实在的（real），而现实则是非实在的（unreal）。这一点明显地表现在他对英国社会结构的认识之上。在结构上，英国社会可分为“事实（Fact）的内在范围”和“外表（Semblance）的外在范围”两部分（18）。所谓的事实是“英雄崇

拜”，而所谓的“外表”是“自由主义”、“供求关系”和“金钱关系”等（38）。非常明显，所谓的“事实”对应于“理想”，而所谓的“外表”对应于“现实”。两者在实在性上的表现颇为不同。只有事实才是实在的，只有以事实为依据所谓的“正义”（Justice）才可以实现（19）。最终，理想与现实之间的张力性结构被转化为实在（reality）和非实在（unreality）之间的结构。卡莱尔的结构批评是以理想的和实在的（the ideal - real）为依据，对现实的和非实在的（the actual - unreal）进行否定和批评。

理想—实在与现实—非实在之间的张力性批评结构，表现在卡莱尔社会批评的所有方面。在对时代特征的整体判断中，“机械时代”被置于与“英雄的、虔诚的、哲学的或者道德的时代”之间的对比之中（Wks.，XXⅦ，59）。对“机械时代”的批评最终发展为对“一个崭新的、更加明亮的精神性时代”到来的预言（81）。同样，功利主义（utilitarianism）的“盈亏哲学”与“信仰”构成对比（Sar.，159）。对功利主义作为社会规范方式的否定，是对“一个可以洞见事物内在的真正英雄”的呼唤。[①] 在对机械论（mechanism）的批评中，“［卡莱尔］社会批评的主要魅力之一便是他看到‘机械’的内在和外在意义、理解科技变化和情感效果”。[②] 可见，结构批评普遍存在于卡莱尔的社会批评之中。

二　《荒》中的结构批评

《荒》中的社会批评主要针对大法官庭制度（Chancery）所造成的弊病。[③] 作品开宗明义，以伦敦一场漫无边际的大雾象征诉讼制度的腐朽和黑暗。“腐败的大法官庭本身和它的陈旧而烦琐的条文与程序”，[④] 在批判中暴露无遗。特别是“运用象征、比喻手法对生活进行宏观的把握”的写作方式，“显示了狄更斯的小说艺术又有了重要的发展”。[⑤] 除大法官庭制度外，人道主义的滥

① Welch，“Thomas Carlyle on Utilitarianism，” p. 385.

② Sussman，“Transcendentalism and the Machine，” p. 35.

③ Ford，*Dickens and his Readers*，p. 104.

④ 狄更斯：《荒凉山庄》，序，第1页。

⑤ 薛鸿时：《浪漫的现实主义》，第167页。

用以及贵族制度的没落等同样构成比较重要的批评对象。

如果以上内容是《荒》结构批评中的现实维度，那么理想维度则表现在女主人公埃丝特（Esther Summerson）对现实社会的观察、感受和体验之上。埃丝特怀有的仁爱（sympathy）思想，是理想维度的主要内容。所谓的仁爱，是与他人怀有相同的（sym－）情感（－pathy）之意。同感的实现是家庭建立的基本条件。初次见面之时，埃丝特便与同样是孤儿的婀达（Ada Clare）和理查德（Richard Carstone）建立起兄妹之情（Bk. H.，30）。[①] 同感进一步将贾迪思先生（John Jarndyce）纳入他们的情感世界。他好像“慈父”一般（60），与本来应该在法庭上相见的对手组建起一个与家庭非常相似的情感共同体。同感对于社会关系同样具有维系作用。埃丝特通过同感成为凯蒂（Caroline Jellyby）的知己（43－44）。贫民窟之中的女子“由于遭受这种悲惨命运而相爱相怜”，“相依为命”（101）。相反，若无同感，即使是家庭也只能有名无实。戴德洛克夫人终日一副冷面，对所有的一切都毫无情趣，“厌烦得要死了”（11）。可见，《荒》结构批评中的理想是一个以同感为基础、与家庭结构类似的社会共同体。

同感并不是一个简单的情感效果，而是具有一个明显的发展和深化过程。移情（empathy）是前提。移情即进入（em－）他人情感（－pathy）世界之意。从自我情感范围超越出来并进入异己的情感世界的愿望，是幼年时期埃丝特的本能。这个“非常胆怯”，“不大敢跟人说话，也从来不敢把心里的想法说出来”的“小姑娘”有一个属于自己的情感天地，“喜欢默默地观察眼前的事物，希望更深刻地了解这些事物”（17）。这种了解非我对象的愿望，便是移情的主要表现。埃丝特对移情始终怀有强烈的需求。她自以为“没有经验，对于那些生活在不同环境里的人，[她] 不善于设身处地地去想他们所想的事情，也不善于从适当的观点出发去和他们交谈”（96）。然而，正是这种类似于苏格拉底式的无知之知的意识，让她始终可以实现移情。

移情是同感的前提条件。移情的缺失，可以导致同感的失效。杰利比夫

---

① 本文所有《荒》的引文来自诺顿评论本（Dickens, *Bleak House*, New York: W. W. Norton, 1977）。页码直接在引文后标示。引文参考黄邦杰译本（上海译文出版社 1998 年版）。

人因缺乏移情的愿望，甚至在家庭生活完全失序的情况下依然热衷于非洲的慈善事业。“非洲的规划占了［她］的全部时间”，“需要［她］全力以赴”(38)。正是这种盲目的仁爱，致使家庭成员生活困苦。杰利比先生性格犹豫自闭（41），女儿终日“抄抄写写”（44）。凯蒂“希望非洲毁掉”的心声(43)，可谓对这种“望远镜里的慈善事业”的巨大嘲讽。帕迪戈尔夫人同样缺乏移情的愿望。即使面对烧砖工人赤裸裸的贫困，她依然固执己见，口若悬河，进行毫无意义的道德说教（98）。这种以“大大扬名”为目的的“贪得无厌的慈善事业”(93)，根本无法治愈工业社会的顽疾。

与以上情况形成鲜明的对比，埃丝特可以高效地实现移情。移情主要表现在她的感受力和体验力之上。相见之初，移情让她发现“［婀达］的举止落落大方，富有魅力”，发现“［理查德的］态度坦诚，笑起来非常动人”(30)。这种入微的体验实现了兄妹之情的建立。在杰利比府上，移情使她在第一时间注意到杰利比一家的缺失。一个母亲应负的责任，一时间由她承担。受伤的啤啤（Peepy）被她安慰（36），杰利比小姐对失责母亲的控诉由她倾听（43－44）。在帕迪戈尔夫人虚伪的慈善事业面前，她可以深入烧砖工人一家的情感。她可以直接地“意识到，在我们和这些人之间，隔着一堵铜墙铁壁，而［帕迪戈尔夫人］是不可能把它拆掉的”(99)。同样，在首次与生母相见之时，她可以透视戴德洛克夫人冷漠的外表，直接感受到迟到的母爱。“［戴德洛克夫人］脸上有一种表情，是［她］小时候就梦见的，是［她］在别人脸上从未见过的，也是［她］在［戴德洛克夫人］脸上从未见过的。”(448)

移情来源于爱人的意志（the will to philanthropy）。如埃丝特所言，“当［她］热爱一个人的时候，［她］似乎就心明眼亮起来”（17），可以进入他人的情感世界。爱人的意志是移情的前提。她的这种意志曾经受到过压抑。幼年的她生活在具有浓郁清教（puritan）色彩的家庭氛围里。她的出生被认为是罪过的开端，生命的目的在于赎罪（19）。作为唯一的家庭成员，教母与她毫无情感交流，她也“始终没有爱过［教母］”（18）。即使经历这样的压抑，她的爱人的意志依然没有被消灭。她虽然“始终不能像［她］所希望的那样爱［教母］”（18），但是依然怀有强烈的爱人意志。教母去世后，爱人的意志可以自由地实现满足，移情成为她始终如一的行为准则。

以上便是《荒》结构批评中理想维度的全貌。这一理想维度在宏观上是一个以同感为基础、与家庭结构类似的社会共同体，在微观上则是建立在爱人欲望基础之上的移情诉求。以同感为基础的社会理想与现实社会构成鲜明对比。这一对比集中体现在对大法官庭制度的讽刺和批评之上。大法官以及相关法律从业者毫无同感之念，根本未能体会争讼双方的情感诉求。他们有意拖延诉讼周期，专营私利。身在其中“那就像在一个慢慢转动的磨子里被碾成齑粉；就像在用文火烤炙；就像被一只只的蜜蜂螫咬；就像被一滴滴的水淹没；就像长年累月一点一滴地发疯”（52）。在微观层面上，这一理想维度以爱人意志为基础，因而融入有直观的体验和感受，具有强烈的实在性。与此相比，全部法律争讼过程则表现得虚幻荒诞。“贾迪思控告贾迪思”案件的结局，竟然是遗产全部耗尽。这样具有强烈讽刺性的结局与深入他人情感相比，毫无实在性可言。

三　结语

综上可见，卡莱尔和狄更斯的社会批评并非对社会弊病简单的暴露和揭发。社会现实否定和批评的背后，明显隐藏着他们所怀有的社会理想。社会理想构成他们社会批评的基础和依据，是社会批评的起点。社会批评是社会理想的应用和践行，最终目的在于社会理想的实现。这种现实与理想交织在一起所构成的张力性的批评结构，便是本文所谓的结构批评。结构批评是一个二维的批评结构。在结构批评中，现实的批评往往伴随着理想的弘扬，而理想的诉说往往意味着现实的否定。结构批评对于理解卡莱尔和狄更斯的社会批评，对于理解他们之间的思想借鉴关系具有重要意义。

除卡莱尔和狄更斯之外，结构批评对于理解现实主义（realism）文学同样具有一定的价值。在一部分现实主义文学之中，对现实（或实际）的描述、展示和体现伴随着理想的辩护、投射和伸张。在此意义上，现实主义文学并非理想主义（idealism）的对立。相反，现实主义是理想主义的扬弃。在宏观上，对现实的再现贯穿现实主义文学；在微观上，对理想的弘扬潜在于现实主义文学之中。现实主义文学放弃了对理想的直接描绘和陈述，但是没有失去对理想的隐匿编织和追求。这种现实和理想交织在一起所构成的张力性现实主义，是现实主义文学的一种重要表现，对于理解现实主义文学的全貌具有重要意义。

附录二　卡莱尔生平、著作和思想年表[①]

1795 年	托马斯·卡莱尔于 12 月 4 日在苏格兰的埃克尔费亨出生
1801 年	简·芭丽·威尔士（Jane Ballie Welch）于 7 月 14 日在爱丁堡附近的哈丁顿（Haddington）出生
1802 年	就学于霍坦姆村（Hoddam）的教区学校
1805 年	就读于安南文法学校（the Grammar School of Annan）
1806 年	入学安南学院（Annan Academy）
1809 年	在爱丁堡大学开始接受教育
1812 年	暑期，留校读书。阅读书目主要包括苏格兰常识学派作品和伦理哲学，涉及休姆、吉朋和莎士比亚等
1813 年	入三一学堂学习，目的在于满足他父母的期望，他未来将从事神职职业

① 本年表主要参考《英雄和英雄崇拜》（*On Heroes, Hero-Worship, and the Heroic in History*, The Norman and Charlotte Strouse Edition of the Writings of Thomas Carlyle, ed. Michael K. Goldberg, Joel J. Brattin & Mark Engel, Berkeley & Los Angeles: Univ. of California Pr., 1993）、《论历史上的英雄、英雄崇拜和英雄业绩》（商务印书馆 2010 年版）和《平民的先知》（台湾大学出版中心 2011 年版）等完成。

续 表

1814 年	大学毕业，返回安南学院教授数学
1816 年	遇见以教师和牧师为业的爱德华·欧文（Edward Irving）。开始在爱丁堡附近的科尔卡迪（Kirkcaldy）的教会学校教书
1817 年	与欧文游览高低地区和西部苏格兰。写作文章，为报刊供稿，偶尔以科学和哲学话题写诗。不再考虑担任神职。读斯塔尔夫人的《论德国》，深受影响
1818 年	初患消化不良症。年底，与欧文辞去科尔卡迪的教职
1819 年	移居爱丁堡。开始学习德语。思想上开始对宗教产生怀疑。开始学习法律
1820 年	3 月，与第一位女友玛格丽特·戈尔登（Margaret Gordon）终止恋情。做法文翻译。写作一系列的百科全书词条
1821 年	欧文介绍卡莱尔与简·威尔士相识。在欧文的帮助下，卡莱尔成为查尔斯和亚瑟·巴勒（Charles & Arthur Buller）的家庭教师，收入基本得到保证。7—8 月，在爱丁堡附近的雷丝路（Leith Walk）经历宗教信仰的恢复。在此过程中，不是信仰或者神学，而是工作或者行动的首要性和重要性被看作是个人自我认识的关键所在
1822 年	在弟弟约翰的帮助下，翻译勒让德（Legendre）的《几何基础》（*Éléments de Géométrie*）。《论〈浮士德〉》发表
1823 年	翻译歌德的《威廉·迈斯特》。《席勒生平》在《伦敦评论》发表。文章被进一步扩充为《席勒传》
1824 年	从 6 月开始，在伦敦游历。主要在巴勒和欧文人际圈中活动，并涉足伦敦的文学圈，结识柯尔律治和兰姆（Charles Lamb）
1825 年	翻译德国作家的多部作品。受歌德影响深重
1826 年	10 月 17 日，与简·芭丽·威尔士成婚。开始写作自传体成长类小说《沃顿·赖因福莱德》（*Wotton Reinfred*），未能完成
1827 年	《爱丁堡评论》（*Edinburgh Review*）的编辑弗朗西斯·杰弗瑞（Francis Jeffrey）成为卡莱尔的资助人和好友。包括《让·保罗·里希特》在内，卡莱尔在《爱丁堡评论》发表一系列评论文章，主要关于德国文学和思想，并在苏格兰和英格兰获得一定的名望。四卷本译作《德国故事集》发表

续　表

1828 年	因未能获得合适的职业，卡莱尔一家移居邓斯科尔（Dunscore）附近的一处叫作克拉普托奇（Craigenputtoch）的遥远农场
1828—1829 年	在《爱丁堡评论》发表《彭斯》和《时代的征兆》两篇文章。在《国外评论》（*Foreign Review*）发表多篇有关德国文学的文章，其中包括《伏尔泰》
1830 年	致函歌德。在《弗雷泽杂志》（*Fraser's Magazine*）发表《论历史》。开始《旧衣新裁》的创作
1831 年	再次赶赴伦敦。重新融入巴勒和欧文社交圈，并与约翰·斯图尔特·穆勒（John Stuart Mill）结交友谊。未能为《旧衣新裁》找到出版商。《特征》在《爱丁堡评论》发表。《十四十五世纪德国文学》（“German Literature of the XIV. and XV. Century”）在《国外评论》发表
1832 年	父亲詹姆士·卡莱尔（James Carlyle）去世。为此，托马斯写作回忆录一部，后收入《回忆录》中。返回克拉普托奇
1833 年	1833 年 11 月至 1834 年 8 月，《旧衣新裁》在《弗雷泽杂志》上连载。受穆勒启发和鼓励，写作《钻石项链》这一有关法国大革命题材的作品。《再论历史》发表于《弗雷泽杂志》。8 月，艾默生到克拉普托奇拜访。他们之间长久的友谊由此开始。卡莱尔考虑移民美国，未果
1834 年	卡莱尔一家迁居伦敦，住在切宁街 24 号。此后，他们终身未改变居住地址。爱德华·欧文去世。9 月，卡莱尔开始写作《法国大革命》
1835 年	3 月，唯一的手稿（完成三分之一）在约翰·穆勒的保存下被意外焚毁，卡莱尔被迫重新写作。遇见骚塞（Southey）和华兹华斯（Wordsworth）。与约翰·斯特林结为好友。未来五年里，朋友圈进一步扩大，将雷·亨特（Leigh Hunt）、哈利艾特·马蒂诺（Harriet Martineau）、伊拉斯谟·达尔文（Erasmus Darwin）、蒙克顿·米尔内斯（Monckton Milnes）、约翰·福斯特（John Forster）、狄更斯、萨克雷、丁尼生（Alfred Tennyson）、菲茨杰拉德（Fitzgerald）和勃朗宁（Robert Browning）等纳入进来
1836 年	《旧衣新裁》首次以书的形式在波士顿出版
1837 年	从 5 月开始，进行有关德国文学的七个系列公共演说。《法国大革命》出版
1838 年	十二讲有关欧洲文学系列演说完成。《旧衣新裁》以书的形式在伦敦出版。在艾默生的协助下，《批评杂文集》在波士顿出版

续 表

1839 年	六讲有关欧洲现代革命系列演说完成。准备赴美演说，未成。《宪章运动》发表。在伦敦图书馆的创建过程中扮演重要角色
1840 年	六讲有关英雄崇拜的系列演说完成。在苏格兰度过夏季，此后一直延续这一习惯。计划写作克伦威尔的传记
1841 年	《英雄和英雄崇拜》出版。受邀游历约克郡
1842 年	在参观圣埃德蒙墓地期间，产生写作《过去和现在》的计划
1843 年	《过去和现在》出版
1844 年	《长期议会选举》发表于《弗雷泽杂志》。约翰・斯特林去世
1845 年	4 月，高雯・杜菲（Gavan Duffy）与青年爱尔兰运动的领袖至伦敦访问卡莱尔。《奥利弗・克伦威尔书信和演说集》出版
1846 年	8 月，因友相邀偕游比利时五天
1847 年	艾默生在访英期间拜访卡莱尔一家。9 月，与高雯・杜菲访爱尔兰六天
1848 年	观察宪章运动。遇见约翰・皮尔爵士（Sir John Peel）。卡莱尔表示赞赏，并支持他在废除《谷物法案》过程中的领导地位。5 月，与穆勒开始交恶
1849 年	6 月，遇见弗劳德（James Anthony Froude）。在高雯・杜菲的陪伴下游历爱尔兰，发现英国政策对于爱尔兰状况负有责任。写出《我的爱尔兰之旅回忆录》，死后于 1882 年出版。发表论文和批评表达对英国政局和文化状况的不满，其中包括发表于《弗雷泽杂志》的《黑人问题偶论》。考虑以有关民主、物质主义和性宽容等的负面效果为话题写作一部作品
1850 年	《晚近文集》出版，包括八篇有关现代不列颠状况的讽刺性文章。罗斯金（John Ruskin）首次拜访，成为卡莱尔的弟子。与年青一代的思想人士结交友谊，包括威廉・埃林汉姆（William Allingham）和约翰・庭戴尔（John Tyndall）
1851 年	《约翰・斯特林传》出版。秋季，在罗伯特和伊丽莎白・勃朗宁的陪伴下游历法国。开始考虑将腓德烈大帝作为传记写作的对象

续　表

1852 年	晚夏，首次前往德国。游历与路德（Martin Luther）、歌德和腓德烈大帝等相关的地点
1853 年	12 月，母亲去世。关于黑人问题发表即席讲话
1854 年	开始写作《腓德烈大帝》。收到《艰难时世》，由狄更斯题献给卡莱尔
1855 年	简·卡莱尔开始写日记，所及内容多为抑郁之情。后被焚毁，只留有一册。卡莱尔读后颇负内疚
1856 年	《腓德烈大帝》前两卷完成
1857—1858 年	16 卷统一版《选集》（*Collected Works*，the Uniform Edition）出版
1858 年	《腓德烈大帝》前两卷出版。晚夏，再次前往德国。游历与腓德烈大帝相关的地点
1860 年	弗劳德接任《弗雷泽杂志》的主编，常来拜访卡莱尔，作长谈
1862 年	卡莱尔右手颤抖，影响写作
1863 年	简·卡莱尔的健康情况开始恶化。《腓德烈大帝》第三卷出版
1864 年	《腓德烈大帝》第四卷出版
1865 年	《腓德烈大帝》彻底完成，第五、六卷出版。11 月当选为爱丁堡大学荣誉校长
1866 年	4 月 2 日，在爱丁堡发表《就职演说》。4 月 21 日，简·卡莱尔突然去世。26 日，葬于哈丁顿。卡莱尔有关简·卡莱尔和爱德华·欧文分别写出一份传记性和自传性的回忆录，后纳入《回忆录》之中。秋季，参加总督艾尔辩护委员会，为艾尔在牙买加奴隶叛乱中的镇压行为辩护
1867 年	有关骚塞、华兹华斯和威廉·汉密尔顿（William Hamilton）写作简短的回忆录。8 月，发表《大冒险与其余波》（“Shooting Niagara：and After?”）作为对 1867 年改革法案的讽刺性攻击，同时对环境污染进行攻击。同月，就职演说文稿《论书的选择》（“On the Choice of Books”）发表于《麦克米伦杂志》。罗斯金疏离卡莱尔

续 表

1868—1869 年	准备整理简·卡莱尔的书信出版，最后决定推迟。1868 年秋，外甥女（Mary Aitken）前来照顾卡莱尔
1869 年	30 卷图书馆版《选集》（*the Library Edition*）第二版出版。3 月，与维多利亚女王会晤
1870 年	在《泰晤士报》发表公开信，支持普法战争中的德国一方
1871 年	将一些私人文件和手稿，特别是简·卡莱尔的书信交给詹姆士·安东尼·弗劳德，指定他为自己的传记作者和简书信的编纂人。右手瘫痪，写作困难
1872 年	口述《挪威早期帝王史》。认为口述并非理想的写作模式。晚年留言，友人勃朗宁、达尔文、福斯特、艾略特、丁尼生、庭戴尔、斯蒂芬兄弟等签署
1873 年	肖像由惠斯勒（Whistler）完成。请福斯特代笔记录遗嘱，交代身后各项事宜。大部分剩余文件被转交弗劳德
1874—1875 年	卷入约翰·诺克斯（John Knox）肖像真伪的辩论。口述《约翰·诺克斯的肖像》。1874 年 2 月，接受普鲁士的勋章
1875 年	12 月，80 岁寿辰成为国际性的庆祝活动。收到礼物、荣誉学位、推荐信和金质奖章等。拒绝迪斯累利（Disraeli）的封爵请求
1875—1876 年	在《泰晤士报》发表两封公开信，反对迪斯累利支持土耳其而反对俄国的政策
1877 年	5 月，致函《泰晤士报》主编，对当前危机发表看法
1878 年	《回忆录》、夫人信函等被交给弗劳德，请他酌情处理
1879 年	游访苏格兰。最喜爱的弟弟约翰去世。大多数家人以及私人和社会朋友先卡莱尔而去
1880 年	照例坐马车外出散心，但已无心观览车外风景
1881 年	2 月 5 日，卡莱尔于切宁街去世。2 月 10 日葬于埃克尔费亨墓地，《回忆录》出版

参考文献

此处所列为本书的引用文献。所有参考文献不予列出。如需参考，请参阅相应章节以及注释。

一　原始文献

（一）卡莱尔的作品

本书所有卡莱尔的文献直接在正文之中引用，给出作品名称简写（参见作品名称后方括号）、卷数和页码。

Carlyle，Thomas. *Correspondence between Goethe and Carlyle* [C. – G.]，ed. Charles Eliot Norton. London：Macmillan，1887.

—. *Correspondence of Emerson and Carlyle* [C. – E.]，ed. Joseph Slater. New York & London：Columbia Univ. Pr.，1964.

—. *Correspondence of Thomas Carlyle and John Ruskin* [C. – R.]，ed. George Allan Cate. Stanford，Calif.：Stanford Univ. Pr.，1982.

—. *Early Letters* [Let.[1]]，ed. Charles Eliot Norton，2 Vol. London：Macmillan，1886.

—. "Faustus：from the German of Goethe" ["Fst."]. *New Edinburgh Review*，Vol. Ⅱ (1822).

—. *The French Revolution：A History* [Rev.]，ed. John D. Rosenberg. New York：The Modern Library，2002.

—. *Historical Sketches of Notable Persons and Events in the Reigns of James* Ⅰ. *and Charles* Ⅰ. [Skh.], ed. Alexander Carlyle. London: Chapman and Hall, 1902.

—. *The Last Words of Thomas Carlyle* [Wds.]. New York: D. Appleton and Company, 1892.

—. *Lectures on the History of Literature* [Lec.], ed. J. Reay Greene. New York: Charles Scribner's Sons, 1892.

—. *Letters* [Let.[2]], ed. Charles Norton, 2 Vol. London: Macmillan, 1888.

—. *Letters to his Brother Alexander with Related Family Letters* [L. – B.], ed. Edwin W. Marrs, Jr. Cambridge, Mass.: The Belknap Pr. of Harvard Univ. Pr., 1968.

—. *Letters to his Wife* [L. – W.], ed. Trudy Bliss. Cambridge, Mass.: Harvard Univ. Pr., 1953.

—. *Letters to his Youngest Sister* [L. – S.], ed. Charles Townsend Copeland. Boston & New York: Houghton, Mifflin and Company, 1899.

—. *Letters to John Stuart Mill, John Sterling, and Robert Browning* [L. – M.], ed. Alexander Carlyle. London: T. Fisher Unwin, 1923. Reissue, New York: Haskell House Publisher, 1970.

—. *Letters to William Graham* [L. – G.], ed. Jr. John Graham. Princeton: Princeton Univ. Pr., 1950.

—. *Love Letters* [L. – J.], ed. Alexander Carlyle, 2 Vol. London & New York: John Lane, 1909.

—. *New Letters* [Let.[3]], ed. Alexander Carlyle, 2 Vol. London & New York: John Lane, 1904.

—. *On Heores, Hero – Worship and the Heroic in History* [H. & H.], ed. Carl Niemeyer. Lincoln & London: Univ. of Nebraska Pr., 1966.

—. *Past and Present* [P. & P.], Riverside Edition, ed. R. D. Altick. Boston: Houghton Mifflin Company, 1965.

—. *Reminiscences* [Rem.[1]], ed. Charles Eliot Norton, 2 Vol. London:

Macmillan, 1887.

—. *Reminiscences of my Irish Journey in* 1849 [Rem.[2]] . London: Sampson Low, Marston, Searle, & Rivington, 1882.

—. *Sartor Resartus* [Sar.], The Odyssey Series in Literature, ed. Charles Frederick Harrold. New York: The Odyssey Pr., 1937.

—. *Two Note Books* [Nt. B.], ed. Charles Eliot Norton. New York: The Grolier Club, 1898.

—. *Two Reminiscences* [Rem.[3]], ed. John Clubbe. Durham, N. C.: Duke Univ. Pr., 1974.

—. *Unfinished History of German Literature* [Ger.], ed. Shine Hill. Lexington: Univ. of Kentucky Pr., 1951.

—. *Works* [Wks.], Centenary Edition, ed. H. D. Trail, 30 vol. London: Chapman and Hall, 1896 – 1899.

Vol. 1: *Sartor Resartus.*

Vol. 2 – 4: *The French Revolution.*

Vol. 5: *Heroes and Hero – Worship.*

Vol. 6 – 9: *Oliver Cromwell's Letters and Speeches.*

Vol. 10: *Past and Present.*

Vol. 11: *The Life of Sterling.*

Vol. 12 – 19: *History of Frederick* Ⅱ. *the Great.*

Vol. 20: *Latter – Day Pamphlets.*

Vol. 21 – 22: *German Romance.*

Vol. 23 – 24: *Wilhelm Meister's Apprenticeship and Travels.*

Vol. 25: *Life of Friedrich Schiller.*

Vol. 26 – 30: *Critical and Miscellaneous Essays.*

（二）其他与卡莱尔相关的文献

Adrian, Arthur A. "Dean Stanley's Report of Conversation with Carlyle." *Victorian Studies* 1. 1 (1957).

Allingham, William. *A Diary*, ed. H. Allingham & D. Radford. London: Macmillan, 1907.

Carré, Jean – Marie, ed. "Quelques Lettres Inédites de William Taylor, Coleridge et Carlyle à Henry Crabb Robinson sur la Littérature Allemagne." *Revue Germanique* 8 (1912).

Carlyle, Jane Welsh. *Early Letters*, ed. David G. Ritchie. London: Swan Sonnenschein & Co., 1889.

—. *Letters and Memorials*, ed. James Anthony Froude, 2 vol. New York: Charles Scribner's Sons, 1894.

—. *New Letters and Memorials*, ed. Alexander Carlyle, 2 vol. London & New York: John Lane, 1903.

Espinasse, Francis. *Literary Recollections and Sketches*. London: Hodder and Stoughton, 1893.

Faulkner, Peter. "Carlyle's Letters to Charles Redwood." *The Yearbook of English Studies* 2 (1972).

Flügel, Evald. "Carlyle und Eckermann." *Goethe – Jahrbuch* 24 (1904).

Pitollet, Camille, ed. "Lettres Inédites de Thomas Carlyle, John Murray et J. – D. Aitken à N. – H. Julius." *Revue Germanique* 4 (1908).

（三）其他作家的作品

本书所有亚里士多德、边沁、柏拉图和维特根斯坦的作品在正文中直接引用，或给出章节号，或给出初版边码。

Aristotle. *The Basic Works*, ed. Richard McKeon. New York: Random House, 1941.

Arnold, Matthew. *Culture and Anarchy*, Oxford World's Classics, ed. Jane Garnett. Oxford: Oxford Univ. Pr., 2006. Reissue, 2009.

—. *Discourses in America*. London: Macmillan, 1885.

Austen, Jane. *Pride and Prejudice*, Norton Critical Edition, ed. Donald Gray. New York: W. W. Norton, 2001.

Bentham, Jeremy. *An Introduction to the Principles of Moral and Legislation*, Dover Philosophical Classics. Mineola, N. Y. : Dover Publications, 2007.

—. *The Rationale of Reward.* London: Robert Heward, 1830.

Brontë, Charlotte. *Letters*, ed. Margaret Smith, 2 Vol. Oxford: Clarendon Pr. , 2000.

Cassirer, Ernst. *The Myth of the State*, trans. William H. Woglom & Charles Handel. New Haven: Yale Univ. Pr. , 1950.

Coleridge, Samuel Taylor. *Complete Works*, ed. W. G. T. Shedd, 7 Vol. New York: Happer & Brothers, 1884.

Dickens, Charles. *Bleak House*, Norton Critical Edition. New York: W. W. Norton, 1977.

Dickens, Charles. *Selected Letters.* Oxford: Oxford Univ. Pr. , 2012.

Gissing, George. *Charles Dickens: A Critical Study*, The Victorian Era Studies. London: Blackie and Sons. , 1898.

Hume, David. *A Treatise of Human Nature*, Penguin Classics, ed. Ernest C. Mossner. London: Penguin Books, 1985.

Jenkins, Keith. *Re – thinking History*, Routledge Classics. London & New York: Routledge, 2010.

Kavanagh, Julia. *Rachel Gray: A Tale Founded on Fact*, Copy Right Edition. Leipzig: Bernhard Tauchnitz, 1856.

Kenny, Anthony. *A New History of Western Philosophy.* Oxford: Clarendon Press, 2010.

Locke, John. *An Essay Concerning Human Understanding*, Penguin Classics, ed. Rodger Woolhouse. London: Penguin Books, 2004.

Macaulay, Thomas Babington. *Critical, Historical, and Miscellaneous Essays and Poems*, 3 Vol. Philadelphia: Porter & Coates, 1879.

Mill, John Stuart. *Autobiography*, Penguin Classics, ed. John M. Robson. London: Penguin Books, 1989.

—. *Early Essays*, Bohn's Standard Library, ed. J. W. M. Gibbs. London:

George Bell and Sons, 1897.

—. *The Spirit of the Age*, *On Liberty*, *The Subjection of Women*, Norton Critical Edition, ed. Alan Ryan. New York: W. W. Norton, 1997.

— & Jeremy Bentham. *Utilitarianism and Other Essays*, Penguin Classics, ed. Alan Ryan. London: Penguin Books, 2004.

Nietzsche, Friedrich. *Twilight of the Idols*, *with The Antichrist and Ecce Homo*, trans. Antony M. Ludovici. London: Wordsworth Classics of World Literature, 2007.

Oliphant, Margaret. "The Literature of the Last Fifty Years." *Prose by Victorian Women: An Anthology*, Garland Reference Library of the Humanities Vol. 1893, ed. Andrea Broomfield & Sally Mitchell. New York & London: Garland Publishing, 1996.

Orwell, George. *Essays*, Everyman's Library No. 242, ed. John Carey. London: Random House, 2002.

Plato. *Euthyphro*, *Apology*, *Crito*, *Phaedo*, Loeb Classical Library 36, ed. & trans. Chris Emlyn – Jones & William Preddy. Cambridge, Mass. & London: Harvard Univ. Pr. , 2017.

Popper, Karl. *After the Open Scoiety*, Routledge Classics. London & New York: Routledge, 2012

—. *Conjectures and Refutations*, Routledge Classics. London & New York: Routledge, 2002.

—. *The Open Society and its Enemies*, Routledge Classics, 2 vol. London & New York: Routledge, 2003.

Vol. 1: *The Spell of Plato.*

Vol. 2: *Hegel and Marx.*

—. *The Poverty of Historicism*, Routledge Classics. London & New York: 2002.

Russell, Bertrand. *History of Western Philosophy*, Routledge Classics. London & New York: Routledge, 2008.

—. "On History." *The Basic Writings*, Routledge Classics, ed. Robert E. Egner & Lester E. Denonn. London & New York: Routledge, 2009.

—. "Psychological and Physical Causal Laws." *The Basic Writings*, Routledge Classics, ed. Robert E. Egner & Lester E. Denonn. London & New York: Routledge, 2009.

—. "The Validity of Inference," *The Basic Writings*, Routledge Classics, ed. Robert E. Egner & Lester E. Denonn. London & New York: Routledge, 2009.

Schlegel, Friedrich. *Kritische und theoretische Schriften.* Stuttgart: Reclam, 1978.

Spencer, Herbert. *An Autobiography*, 2 vol. London: Williams and Norgate, 1904.

Wittgenstein, Ludwig. *Tractatus Logico – Philosophicus*, Routledge Classics, ed. D. F. Pears & B. F. McGuinness. London & New York: Routledge, 2001.

二　研究文献

（一）英文

除弗劳德（Froude）的作品（分别为 *First Forty Years* 和 *Life in London*）和萨福德（Richard Herne Shepherd）的作品（*Memoirs*）以简写形式标记外，其余作品均以作品全称标记。

Adrian, Arthur A. & Vonna H. "Frederick the Great: That Unutterable Horror of a Prussian Book." *Carlyle Past and Present: A Collection of New Essays, A Vision Critical Study*, ed. K. J. Fielding & Rodger L. Tarr. London: Vision Pr., 1976.

Altick, Richard D. "*Past and Present*: Topicality as Technique." *Carlyle and his Contemporaries: Essays in Honor of Charles Richard Sanders*, ed. John Clubbe. Durham, N. C.: Duke Univ. Pr., 1976.

—. *Victorian People and Ideas: A Companion for the Modern Reader of Victori-*

an Literature. New York & London: W. W. Norton, 1973.

Anger, Suzy. "Carlyle: Between Biblical Exegesis and Romantic Hermeneutics." *Texas Studies in Literature and Language* 40. 1 (1998) .

Arac, Jonathan. "Narrative Form and Social Sense in *Bleak House* and *The French Revolution.*" *Nineteenth – Century Fiction* 32. 1 (1977) .

Ashton, Rosemary D. "Carlyle's Apprenticeship: His Early German Criticism and his Relationship with Goethe (1822 – 1832) ." *The Modern Language Review* 100, Supplement (2005) .

Baker, Lee C. R. "The Diamond Necklace and the Golden Ring: Historical Imagination in Carlyle and Browning." *Victorian Poetry* 21. 1 (1986) .

Ben – Israel, Hedva. "Carlyle and French Revolution." *English Historians on the French Revolution.* Cambridge: Cambridge Univ. Pr. , 1968.

Bossche, Chris R. Vanden. *Carlyle and the Search for Authority.* Columbus: Ohio State University Press, 1991.

Bouton, Clark W. "John Stuart Mill: On Liberty and History." *The Western Political Quarterly* 18. 3 (1965) .

Bruns, Gerald L. "The Formal Nature of Victorian Thinking." *PMLA* 90. 5 (1975) .

Burtt, Edwin A. , ed. *The English Philosophers: From Bacon to Mill.* New York: The Modern Library, 1994.

Campbell, Ian. *Thomas Carlyle.* London: Hamish Hamilton, 1974.

Carlyle, Thomas. *Sartor Resartus*, Oxford World's Classics, ed. Kerry McSweeney & Peter Sabor. Oxford: Oxford Univ. Pr. , 1987. Reissue, 2008.

Chapman, Raymond. "Thomas Carlyle." *The Victorian Debate: English Literature and Society*, 1832 – 1901. New York: Basic Books, 1968.

Chiclers, Joseph W. "Carlyle's *Past and Present*, History, and a Question of Hermeneutics," *CLIO*, 13. 3 (1984).

Christian, Mildred G. "Carlyle's Influence upon the Social Theory of Dickens (Part One: Their Personal Relationship) ." *The Trollopian* 1. 4 (1947) .

—. "Carlyle's Influence upon the Social Theory of Dickens (Part Two: Their Literary Relationship)." *The Trollopian* 2. 1 (1947).

Cole, G. D. H. *Socialists Thought: The Forerunners*, 1798 – 1850. London: Macmillan & Co., 1953.

Collins, Phillip. *Charles Dickens: The Critical Heritage.* London & New York: Routledge, 1986.

Conway, Moncure D. *Thomas Carlyle.* New York: Harper & Brothers, 1881.

Crimmins, James E. "Bentham and Utilitarianism in the Early Nineteenth Century." *The Cambridge Companion to Utilitarianism*, ed. Ben Eggleston & Dale E. Miller. Cambridge: Cambridge Univ. Pr., 2014.

Cronin, Richard. *Romantic Victorians: English Literature*, 1824 – 1840. New York: Palgrave, 2002.

Culler, A. Dwight. "Mill, Carlyle, and the Spirit of the Age." *The Victorian Mirror of History.* New Haven: Yale Univ. Pr., 1985.

Cumming, Mark. *A Disimprisoned Epic: Form and Vision in Carlyle's French Revolution.* Philadelphia: Univ. of Pennsylvania Pr., 1988.

Davey, Samuel. *Darwin, Carlyle, Dickens: The Fools, Jesters, and Comic Characters in Shakespeare.* London: E. Bumpus, 1879.

Deaton, Mary B. "Thomas Carlyle's Use of Metaphor." *College English* 5. 6 (1944).

Desaulniers, Mary. *Carlyle and the Economics of Terror: A Study of Revisionary Gothicism in* The French Revolution. Montreal & Kingston: McGill – Queen's Univ. Pr., 1995.

Dibble, Jerry A. *The Pythia's Drunken Song: Thomas Carlyle's and the Style Problem in German Idealist Philosophy*, International Archives of the History of Ideas, Series Minor 19. The Hague: Martinus Nijhoff, 1978.

Dibeliu, Wilhelm. *England*, trans. Mary Agnes Hamilton. London: Jonathan Cape, 1930.

Engel, Monroe. *The Maturity of Dickens.* Cambridge, Mass.: Harvard

Univ. Pr. , 1959.

Farrell, John P. "Matthew Arnold and the Middle Ages: The Uses of the Past." *Victorian Studies* 13. 3 (1970).

Fermanis, Porscha. "A 'Poor Crotchety Picture of Several Things': Antiquarianism, Subjectivity, and the Novel in Thomas Carlyle's *Letters and Speeches of Oliver Cromwell.*" *Rethinking British Romantic History*, 1770 – 1845, ed. Porscha Fermanis & John Regan. Oxford: Oxford Univ. Pr. , 2014.

Ford, George H. *Dickens and his Readers: Aspect of Novel – Criticism since* 1836. Princeton: Princeton Univ. Pr. , 1955.

Forster, John. *The Life of Charles Dickens*, 2 vol. London: Chapman and Hall, 1876.

Forster, Joseph. *Four Great Teachers: John Ruskin, Thomas Carlyle, Ralph Waldo Emerson, and Robert Browning.* London: George Allen, 1890.

Froude, James Anthony. *Thomas Carlyle: A History of the First Forty Years of his Life*, 2 vol. New York: Charles Scribner's Sons, 1882.

—. *Thomas Carlyle: A History of his Life in London*, 2 vol. New York: Charles Scribner's Sons, 1884.

Frye, Lowell T. "History as Biography, Biography as History." *Thomas Carlyle Resartus: Reappraising Carlyle's Contribution to the Philosophy of History, Political Theory, and Cultural Criticism*, ed. Paul E. Kerry & Marylu Hill. Madison & Teaneck: Fairleigh Dickinson Univ. Pr. , 2010.

Garnett, Richard. *Life of Thomas Carlyle.* London: Walter Scott, 1895.

Goldberg, Michael. "From Bentham to Carlyle: Dickens' Political Development." *Journal of the History of Ideas* 33. 1 (1972).

Gooch, G. P. "Carlyle and Froude." *History and Historians in the Nineteenth Century.* London: Longmans, Green, and Co. , 1918.

Grant, A. J. *English Historians.* London: Blackie & Son, 1906. Reissue, Port Washington, N. Y. & London: Kennikat Pr. , 1971.

Greg, William Rathbone. "Kingsley and Carlyle." *Literary and Social Judge-*

ment, Vol. Ⅰ. Bosten: James R. Osgood and Co., 1873.

Grierson, H. J. C. *Carlyle and Hitler.* Cambridge: Cambridge Univ. Pr., 1933.

Gross, John. *The Rise and Fall of the Man of Letters: A Study of the Idiosyncratic and the Humane in Modern Literature.* London: Macmillan, 1969.

Hanson, Lawrence & Elisabeth. *Necessary Evil: The Life of Jane Welsh Carlyle.* London: Constable, 1952. Reissue, New York: Octagon Books, 1975.

Harley, Bruce. "Obeying the Laws of Life: Carlyle and Spencer." *The Healthy Body and Victorian Culture.* Cambridge, Mass. & London: Harvard Univ. Pr., 1978.

Harrold, Charles Frederick. *Carlyle and German Thought*: 1819 – 1834, Yale Studies in English 82. New Haven: Yale Univ. Pr., 1934. Reissue, Hamden & London: Archon Books, 1963.

—. "Carlyle and Novalis." *Studies in Philology* 27. 1 (1930).

—. "Carlyle's General Method in The French Revolution." *PMLA* 43. 4 (1928).

—. "Carlyle's Interpretation of Kant." *Philological Quarterly* 7 (1928).

—. "The Nature of Carlyle's Calvinism." *Studies in Philology* 33. 3 (1936).

Heffer, Simon. *Moral Desperado: A Life of Thomas Carlyle.* London: Weidenfeld and Nicolson, 1995.

Helmling, Steven. *The Esoteric Comedies of Carlyle, Newman, and Yeats.* Cambridge: Cambridge Univ. Pr., 1988.

Heydt, Colin. "Utilitarianism before Bentham." *The Cambridge Companion to Utilitarianism*, ed. Ben Eggleston & Dale E. Miller. Cambridge: Cambridge Univ. Pr., 2014.

Houghton, Walter E. *The Victorian Frame of Mind*: 1830 – 1870. New Haven & London: Yale Univ. Pr., 1957.

Hunt, Tristram. "Carlyle and Coketown." *Building Jerusalem: The Rise and Fall of the Victorian City.* New York: Metropolitan Books, 2005.

Ikeler, A. Abbott. *Puritan Temper and Transcendental Faith: Carlyle's Literary Vision.* Columbus: Ohio Univ. Pr., 1972.

Jaeck, Emma Gertrude. *Madame de Staël and the Spread of German Literature.* New York: Oxford Univ. Pr., 1915.

Jann, Rosemary. "Thomas Carlyle: History as Secular Prophecy," *The Art and Science of Victorian History.* Columbus: Ohio State Univ. Pr., 1985.

Jessop, Ralph. *Carlyle and Scottish Thought.* London: Macmillan & New York: St. Martin's Pr., 1997.

Johnson, Edgar. *Charles Dickens: His Tragedy & Triumph.* New York: The Viking Pr., 1977.

Johnson, William Savage. *Thomas Carlyle: A Study of his Literary Apprenticeship*, 1814 – 1831. New Haven: Yale Univ. Pr. & London: Henry Frowde, 1911.

Jones, Jason B. "Chaos and Carlyle." *Lost Causes: Historical Consciousness in Victorian Literature.* Columbus: The Ohio Univ. Pr., 2006.

Kaplan, Fred. *Dickens: A Biography.* London: Hodder & Stoughton, 1988.

—. *Thomas Carlyle: A Biography.* Ithaca, N. Y.: Cornell Univ. Pr., 1983.

Keating, Peter, ed. *The Victorian Prophets: A Reader from Carlyle to Wells.* London: Fontana, 1981.

Lamb, John B. "A 'Chaos of Being': Carlyle and the Shandean Web of History," *CLIO* 20. 1 (1990).

Lehman, B. H. *Carlyle's Theory of the Hero: Its Sources, Development, History, and Influence on Carlyle's Works.* Durham, N. C.: Duke Univ. Pr., 1928.

Levin, Michael. *The Condition of England Question: Carlyle, Mill, Engels.* London: Palgrave Macmillan, 1998.

Levine, Caroline. "Victorian Realism." *The Cambridge Companion to the Victorian Novel*, 2nd Edition, ed. Deirdre David. Cambridge: Cambridge Univ. Pr., 2012.

Levine, George. *Realism, Ethics and Secularism: Essays on Victorian Literature and Science.* Cambridge: Cambridge Univ. Pr., 2008.

MacKenzie, Norman & Jeanne. *Dickens: A Life.* New York & Oxford: Oxford Univ. Pr., 1979.

Marcus, David D. "The Carlylean Vision of *A Tale of Two Cities.*" *Studies in the Novel* 8.1 (1976).

Masson, David. *Carlyle Personally and in his Writings: Two Edinburgh Lectures.* London: MacMillan, 1885.

—. *Edinburgh Sketches & Memories.* London & Edinburgh: Adam and Charles Black, 1892.

—. *Recent British Philosophy: A Review, with Criticism.* London & Cambridge: Macmillan, 1865.

Matz, Aaron. *Satire in an Age of Realism.* Cambridge: Cambridge Univ. Pr., 2010.

Moore, Carlisle. "*Sartor Resartus* and the Problem of Carlyle's 'Conversion'." *PMLA* 70.4 (1955).

Moran, Maureen. *Victorian Literature and Culture.* New York: Continuum, 2006.

Morley, John. "Carlyle." *Critical Miscellanies*, Vol. Ⅰ. London: Macmillan, 1886.

Muirhead, John H. *The Platonic Tradition in Anglo – Saxon Philosophy: Studies in the History of Idealism in England and America*, Muirhead Library of Philosophy. London: George Allen & Unwin, 1931. Reissue, 1965.

Natanson, Maurice. "History, Historicity, and the Alchemistry of Time." *Chicago Review* 15.1 (1961).

Neff, Eremy. *Carlyle.* London: George Allen & Unwin, 1932.

—. *Carlyle and Mill: An Introduction to Victorian Thought*, 2nd Revised ed. New York: Columbia Univ. Pr., 1926. Reprint, New York: Octagon Books, 1964.

Oddie, William. *Carlyle and Dickens: The Question of Influence.* London: The Century Pr., 1972.

Peckham, C. Morse. "Frederick the Great." *Carlyle Past and Present: A Col-*

lection of New Essays, *A Vision Critical Study*, ed. K. J. Fielding & Rodger L. Tarr. London: Vision Pr., 1976.

Pyke, N. O. P. "History as Literature." *The Australian Quarterly* 19.3 (1947).

Le Quesne, A. L. *Carlyle*, Past Masters. Oxford: Oxford Univ. Pr., 1982.

Ralli, August. *Guide to Carlyle*, 2 Vol. Boston: Small Maynard and Co., 1922.

Reed, Walter L. "The Pattern of Conversion in *Sartor Resartus*." *ELH* 38.3 (1971).

Roe, Frederick William. *The Social Philosophy of Carlyle and Ruskin*. New York: Harcourt, Brace and Co., 1921. Reissue, Port Washington, N. Y. & London: Kennikat Pr., 1969.

—. *Thomas Carlyle as a Critic of Literature*. New York: The Columbia Univ. Pr., 1910.

Rosenberg, John D. *Carlyle and the Burden of History*. Cambridge, Mass.: Harvard Univ. Pr., 1985.

Rosenberg, Philip. *The Seventh Hero: Thomas Carlyle and the Theory of Radical Activism*. Cambridge, Mass.: Harvard Univ. Pr., 1974.

Ryals, Clyde de L. "Carlyle's *The French Revolution*: A 'True Fiction'." *A World of Possibilities: Romantic Irony in Victorian Literature*. Columbus: Ohio State Univ. Pr., 1990.

Salmon, Richard. "Thomas Carlyle and Luminous Author." *The Formation of the Victorian Literary Profession*, Cambridge Studies in Nineteenth – Century Literature and Culture. Cambridge: Cambridge Univ. Pr., 2013.

Sanders, Charles Richard. "Thomas Carlyle." *Coleridge and the Broad Church Movement: Studies in S. T. Coleridge, Dr. Arnold of Rugby, J. C. Hare, Thomas Carlyle, and F. D. Maurice*. Durham, N. C.: Duke Univ. Pr., 1942. Reissue, New York: Octagon Books, 1972.

Schapiro, J. Salwyn. "Thomas Carlyle, Prophet of Fascism." *The Journal of*

Modern History 17. 2 (1945).

Seigel, Jules Paul, ed. *Thomas Carlyle*: *The Critical Heritage.* London & New York: Routledge, 1971.

Shelston, Alan, ed. *Thomas Carlyle*: *Selected Writings*, Penguin Classics. London: Penguin, 1980. Reprint, 2015.

Shepherd, Richard Herne. *Memoirs of the Life and Writings of Thomas Carlyle*, 2 vol. London: W. H. Allen & Co., 1881.

Shine, Hill. "Carlyle and the German Philosophy Problem during the year 1826 – 1827." *PMLA* 50. 3 (1935).

—. *Carlyle and the Saint – Simonians*: *The Concept of Historical Periodicity.* Baltimore: The Johns Hopkins Press, 1941.

—. "Carlyle's Early Writings and Herder's *Ideen*: The Concept of History." *Booker Memorial Studies*: *Eight Essays on Victorian Literature in Memory of John Manning Booker*, ed. Hill Shine. Chapel Hill: Univ. of North Carolina Pr., 1950. Reissue, New York: Russell & Russell, 1969.

—. *Carlyle's Fusion of Poetry*, *History*, *and Religion by* 1834. Chapel Hill: The Univ. of North Carolina Pr., 1938. Reissue, Port Washington, N. Y.: Kennikat Pr., 1967.

Smeed, J. W. "Thomas Carlyle and Jean Paul Richter." *Comparative Literature* 16. 3 (1964).

Spivey, Edward. "Carlyle and the Logic – Choppers: J. S. Mill and Diderot." *Carlyle and his Contemporaries*: *Essays in Honor of Charles Richard Sanders*, ed. John Clubbe. Durham, N. C.: Duke Univ. Pr., 1976.

Stange, G. Robert. "Refractions of *Past and Present.*" *Carlyle Past and Present*: *A Collection of New Essays*, *A Vision Critical Study*, ed. K. J. Fielding & Rodger L. Tarr. London: Vision Pr., 1976.

Stawell, F. Melian. "Goethe's Influence on Carlyle. I." *International Journal of Ethics* 21. 2 (1911).

—. "Goethe's Influence on Carlyle. Ⅱ." *International Journal of Ethics* 21. 3

(1911), pp.

Stewart, Herbert L. "Carlyle's Conception of History." *Political Science Quarterly* 32.4 (1917).

Storey, Graham. *Dickens*: Bleak House. New York: Cambridge Univ. Pr., 1987.

Sussman, Herbert L. "The Condition of Manliness Question: Thomas Carlyle and Industrial Manhood." *Victorian Masculinities: Manhood and Masculine Poetics in Early Victorian Literature and Art*, Cambridge Studies in Nineteenth – Century Literature and Culture. Cambridge: Cambridge Univ. Pr., 1995.

—. "Transcendentalism and the Machine: Thomas Carlyle," *Victorians and the Machine: The Literary Response to Technology.* Cambridge, Mass.: Harvard Univ. Pr., 1968.

Swift, Roger. "Thomas Carlyle, 'Chartism', and the Irish in Early Victorian England." *Victorian Literature and Culture* 29.1 (2001).

Symons, Julian. *Thomas Carlyle: The Life and Ideas of a Prophet.* New York: Oxford Univ. Pr., 1952. Reissue, Cornwell: House of Stratus, 2001.

Tarr, Rodger L. "The 'Foreign Philanthropy Question' in *Bleak House*: An Carlylean Influence." *Studies in the Novel* 3.3 (1971).

Tennyson, G. B., ed. *A Carlyle Reader: Selections from the Writings of Thomas Carlyle.* New York: Random House, 1969. Reissue, New York: Cambridge Univ. Pr., 1984.

—. *Sartor Called Resartus: The Genesis, Structure, and Style of Thomas Carlyle's First Major Work.* Princeton: Princeton Univ. Pr., 1965.

Tillotson, Geoffrey. "Carlyle." *A View of Victorian Literature.* Oxford: Clarendon Pr., 1978.

Trevelyan, G. M., ed. *Carlyle: An Anthology.* London: Longmans, Green & Co., 1953.

—. *Illustrated English Social History*, 4 vol. London: Longmans, Green & Co.

Tuman, Myron C. " 'Irritant Poison' : Idealism and Scientific History in Late – Victorian England. " *Studies in Romanticism* 22. 3 (1983) .

LaValley, Albert J. *Carlyle and the Idea of the Modern: Studies in Carlyle's Prophetic Literature and its Relation to Blake, Nietzsche, Marx, and Others.* New Haven: Yale Univ. Pr. , 1968.

Vaughan, C. E. "Carlyle and his German Masters. " *Essays and Studies by Members of the English Association*, ed. A. C. Bradley. Oxford: The Clarendon Pr. , 1910.

Vida, Elisabeth M. *Romantic Affinities: German Authors and Carlyle: A Study in the History of Ideas.* Toronto: Univ. of Toronto Pr. , 1993.

Vijn, J. P. *Carlyle and Jean Paul: Their Spiritual Optic.* Amsterdam & Philadelphia: John Benjamins Publishing Co. , 1982.

Wallace, Elisabeth. "Goldwin Smith on History. " *The Journal of Modern History* 26. 3 (1954) .

Welch, Patrick J. "Thomas Carlyle on Utilitarianism. " *History of Political Economy* 38. 2 (2006) .

Wellek, René. "Carlyle and German Romanticism. " *Confrontations: Studies in the Intellectual and Literary Relations between Germany, England, and the United States during the Nineteenth Century.* Princeton: Princeton Univ. Pr. , 1965.

—. "Carlyle and the Philosophy of History. " *Confrontations: Studies in the Intellectual and Literary Relations between Germany, England, and the United States during the Nineteenth Century.* Princeton: Princeton Univ. Pr. , 1965.

—. *Immanuel Kant in England*: 1793 – 1838. Princeton: Princeton Univ. Pr. , 1931.

—. "Thomas Carlyle. " *A History of Modern Criticism*: 1750 – 1950, Vol. 3, The Age of Transition. New Haven & London: Yale Univ. Pr. , 1965.

Willey, Basil. *More Nineteenth Century Studies: A Group of Honest Doubters.* London: Chatto & Windus, 1956.

—. "Thomas Carlyle," *Nineteenth Century Studies: Coleridge to Matthew Ar-*

nold. London: Chatto & Windus, 1950.

Wilson, A. N. *The Victorians.* New York & London: W. W. Norton, 2004.

Wilson, David Alec. *Carlyle*, 6 vol. London: Kegan Paul, Trench, Trübner, 1923 – 1934.

Vol. 1: *Carlyle till Marriage* (1795 – 1826).

Vol. 2: *Carlyle to "The French Revolution"* (1826 – 1837).

Vol. 3: *Carlyle on Cromwell and Others* (1837 – 1848).

Vol. 4: *Carlyle at his Zenith* (1848 – 1853).

Vol. 5: *Carlyle to Threescore – and – Ten* (1853 – 1863).

Vol. 6: *Carlyle in Old Age* (1863 – 1881).

Windelband, Wilhelm. *A History of Philosophy*, trans. J. H. Tufts. New York: Macmillan, 1898.

Wingfield – Stratford, Esmé. *The Victorian Tragedy.* London: George Routledge and Sons, 1931.

Woody, Thomas. "Of History and its Method." *The Journal of Experimental Education* 15. 3 (1947).

Young, Louise Merwin. *Thomas Carlyle and the Art of History.* Philadelphia: The Univ. of Pennsylvania Pr., 1939.

(二) 法文

Aulard, A. "Carlyle: Historien de la Révolution Française." *La Révolution Française* 62 (1912).

Aymes, Marc. "Historicités." *Labyrinthe* 17. 1 (2004).

Barthèlemy, Edmond. *Thomas Carlyle: Essai Biographique et Critique.* Paris, Mercure, 1900.

Basch, Victor. *Carlyle: L'Homme et l'Œuvre.* Paris: Gallimard, 1938.

Bos, Camille. "Le Kantisme de Carlyle." *Archiv für Geschichte der Philosophie* 8 (1902).

Brée, Germaine. "Rencontre avec Carlyle." *Revue d'Histoire littéraire de la*

France 70. 2 (1970) .

Carlyle, Thomas. *Les Héros, le culte des héros, et l'héroïque dans l'histoire*, trans. J. B. J. Izoulet – Loubatières. Paris: Armand Colin, 1888.

—. *Histoire de la Révolution Française*, trans. Élias Regnault, Odysse Barot & Jules Roches, 3 vol. Paris: Baillière, 1865 – 1867.

—. *Pages Choisies*, trans. Émile Masson. Paris: Armand Colin, 1905.

—. *Sartor Resartus: Vie et Opinions de Herr Teufelsdröckh*, Édition Définitive, ed. Edmond Barthèlemy. Paris: Mercure, 1904.

Carré, Jean – Marie. *Gœthe en Angleterre* . Paris: Plon, 1920.

—. "Un Inédit de Fichte. " *Revue de Métaphysique et de Morale* 22. 1 (1914) .

Cazamian, Louis. *L'Angleterre Moderne: Son Évolution*, Bibliothèque de Philosophie Scientifique. Paris: Flammarion, 1914.

—. *Carlyle*, Les Grands Écrivains Étrangers. Paris: Didier, 1913.

—. *Le Roman Social en Angleterre* (1830 – 1850): *Dickens, Disraeli, Mrs. Gaskell, Kingsley.* Paris: Société Nouvelle de Librairie et d' Édition, 1903.

— & Legouis, E. " L'Idéalisme Philosophique: Carlyle. " *Histoire de la Littérature Anglaise*, 2nd ed. Paris: Hachette, 1925.

Croce, Benedetto. "La Naissance de l'Histoirisme. " *Revue de Métaphysique et de Morale* 44. 3 (1937) .

Gazeau, Jacques. *L'Impérialisme Anglais, son Évolution: Carlyle, Seeley, Chamberlain.* Paris: Arthur Rousseau, 1903.

Halévy, Élie. *La Formation du Radicalisme Philosophique*, 3 vol. Paris: Baillière, 1901.

Vol. 1: *La Jeunesse de Bentham.*

Vol. 2: *L'Évolution de la Doctrine Utilitaire de* 1789 *à* 1815.

Vol. 3: *Le Radicalisme Philosophique.*

—. *Histoire du Peuple Anglais au XiXe Siècle*, 3 vol. Paris: Hachette, 1923.

Mackenzie, J. S. "La Philosohie Contemporaine en Grande – Bretagne. " *Revue de Métaphysique et de Morale* 16. 5 (1908) .

Martinoia, Rozenn. "L' 'Ère Marshallienne': Équilibre, Bien – être et Question Sociale dans l'Angleterre Victorienne." *Romantisme* 133. 3 (2006).

Montégut, Émile. "Thomas Carlyle et John Sterling." *Revue des Deux Mondes* 15 (1852).

—. "Thomas Carlyle: Sa vie et ses écrits." *Revue des deux mondes* 2 (1849).

Scherer, Edmond Henri Adolphe. "Thomas Carlyle." *Études sur la Littérature Contemporaine*, Vol. Ⅶ. Paris: Calmann Lévy, 1882.

Taine, Hippolyte. *L'Idéalisme anglaise: Étude sur Carlyle.* Paris: Baillière, 1864.

Troeltsch, Ernst. "Le Dix – Neuvième Siècle." *Philosophie* 94 (2007).

Vitoux, Pierre. "Carlyle et le Culte du Héros." *Romantisme* 100 (1998).

Yandell, F. F. *Thomas Carlyle: Sa Métaphysique, sa Moral, sa Conception Religieuse.* Lille: Camille Robbe, 1908.

（三）德文

Baumgarten, Otto. *Carlyle und Goethe.* Tübingen: J. C. B. Mohr (Paul Siebeck), 1906.

Carlyle, Thomas. *Sartor Resartus: Oder Leben und Meinungen der Herrn Teufelsdröckh*, trans. Thomas A. Fischer. Leipig: Otto Wigand, 1882.

Dilthey, Wilhelm. "Thomas Carlyle." *Archiv für Geschichte der Philosophie* 4 (1891).

Fehr, Bernhard. "Der Deutsche Idealismus in Carlyles *Sartor Resartus.*" *Germanisch – Romanische Monatsschrift* 5 (1913).

Fischer, Thomas A. *Thomas Carlyle: Eine Geschichte seines Lebens.* Leipig: Otto Wigand, 1882.

Flügel, Ewald. *Thomas Carlyles religiöse und sittlche Entwicklung und Weltanschauung.* Leipzig: Fr. W. Grunow. 1887.

—. "Carlyle and Eckermann." *Goethe – Jahrbuch* 24. 1 (1903).

Hensel, Paul. *Thomas Carlyle.* Stuttgart: Fr. Frommanns Verlag (E. Hauff),

1901.

Kraeger, Heinrich. "Carlyles Stellung zur Deutschen Sprache und Literatur." *Anglia* 22 (1899).

Küchler, Frohwalt. "Carlyle und Schiller." *Anglia* 26 (1903).

Schulze – Gaevernitz, Gerhart von. *Thomas Carlyles Welt – und Gesellschaftsanschauung*. Dresden: L. Ehlermann, 1893.

Smeed, J. W. "Carlyles Jean – Paul – Übersetzen." *Deutsche Vierteljahrsschrift für Literaturwissenschaft und Geistesgeschichte* 35 (1961).

Streuli, Wilhelm. *Thomas Carlyle als Vermittler deutscher Litteratur und deutschen Geistes*. Zürich: Friedrich Schulthess, 1895.

（四）意大利文

Fermi, Laura. *Thomas Carlyle*. Messina & Milano: Casa Editrice Giuseppe Principato, 1939.

Mazzini, Giuseppe. "Genio e Tendenze di Tomaso Carlyle." *Scritti Editi e Inediti*, Vol. Ⅳ. Letteratura. Milano: G. Daelli, 1862.

Roberto, Diego de. *Tommaso Carlyle*. Bari: Gius. Laterza & Figli, 1904.

（五）中文

方志强：《炼狱与新生——卡莱尔的病（1814—1823）与雷丝路事件》，《新史学》2006 年第 17 卷第 3 期。

—.《平民的先知——卡莱尔与英国维多利亚社会》，台湾大学出版中心 2011 年版。

［英］威廉斯：《文化与社会》，吴松江等译，北京大学出版社 1991 年版。

薛鸿时：《浪漫的现实主义——狄更斯评传》，社会科学文献出版社 1996 年版。

三　参考译文

［英］阿诺德：《文化与无政府状态》，第 2 版，韩敏中译，生活·读书·新知三联书店 2008 年版。

［英］边沁：《道德与立法原理导论》，时殷弘译，商务印书馆 2000 年版。

［英］波普尔：《猜想与反驳》，傅季重、纪树立、周昌忠、蒋弋为等译，上海译文出版社 1986 年版。

［英］狄更斯：《荒凉山庄》，黄邦杰等译，上海译文出版社 1998 年版。

［英］卡莱尔：《卡莱尔、爱默生通信集》，李静滢、季云霞、王福祥译，广西师范大学出版社 2008 年版。

—.《法国大革命——一部历史》，刘毅译，吉林出版集团股份有限公司 2017 年版。

—.《论历史》，刘鑫译，《历史理论与史学理论——近现代西方史学论著选》，何兆武编，商务印书馆 1999 年版。

—.《论历史上的英雄、英雄崇拜和英雄业绩》，周祖达译，商务印书馆 2010 年版。

—.《时代征兆（外一篇）》，乔修峰译，《世界文学》2018 年第 4 期。

—.《文学史演讲集》，姜智芹译，广西师范大学出版社 2005 年版。

［英］古奇：《十九世纪历史学与历史学家》，耿淡如译，商务印书馆 1989 年版。

［英］勒·凯内：《卡莱尔》，段忠桥译，中国社会科学出版社 1987 年版。

［英］麦考莱：《论历史》，刘鑫译，《历史理论与史学理论——近现代西方史学论著选》，何兆武编，商务印书馆 1999 年版。

［英］穆勒：《功利主义》，徐大建译，商务印书馆 2014 年版。

［德］尼采：《偶像的黄昏》，卫茂平译，华东师范大学出版社 2007 年版。

［英］罗素：《西方哲学史》第 2 卷，何兆武、李约瑟、马元德译，商务印书馆 1963 年版。

［英］维特根斯坦：《逻辑哲学论》，贺绍甲译，商务印书馆 1996 年版。

［美］韦勒克：《近代文学批评史》卷 3，《过渡时代》，杨自伍译，上海译文出版社 1997 年版。

［古希腊］亚里士多德：《诗学》，陈中梅译，商务印书馆 1996 年版。

人名索引

外汉部分

（以英文字母顺序排列）

A

B

C

D

G

H

I

J

K

L

M

N

O

P

Q

R

S

T

V

W

X

Y

汉外部分

（以汉语拼音顺序排列）

A

B

C

D

E

F

G

H

J

K

L

M

P

Q

R

S

T

W

X

Y

Z